EXPLORAMA

EXPLORE EVERY COUNTRY

IN THE WORLD

2021

Disclaimer :
This book aims to present all the countries and regions of the world, in a succinct way, through their « tourist attractions ». This does not mean in any way that all these places are accessible to all travelers and that they can be visited freely. Indeed, this book does not take into account the social, health, economic, or political problems of the countries of the world. It is only a theoretical presentation, for information and entertainment purposes, and all topics discussed are subject to change without notice, independent of the author's will. The authors, publishers, and distributors of this book cannot be held responsible for any inaccuracies in the information contained in this book. It is up to each person to use discernment, caution and common sense and to inquire with the competent authorities before undertaking a trip, whatever the destination.

Explorama - Explore every country in the world - 2021 ebook edition

All maps @shutterstock.com - All Rights Reserved

EXPLORAMA

2021 Ebook Edition

Index of countries & territories

Within the book, the countries and territories are detailed by continent. For a quicker search, here is a list in alphabetical order.

Afghanistan - 115	Belize - 64
Albania - 165	Benin - 15
Algeria - 14	Bermuda - 64
American Samoa - 242	Bhutan - 118
American Virgin Islands - 95	Bolivia - 65
Andorra - 165	Bosnia and Herzegovina - 168
Angola - 15	Botswana - 16
Anguilla - 58	Brazil - 66
Antarctica - 58	British Virgin Islands - 95
Antigua and Barbuda - 59	Brunei - 119
Argentina - 60	Bulgaria - 168
Armenia - 166	Burkina Faso - 16
Aruba - 61	Burundi - 17
Australia - 229	Cambodia - 119
Austria - 166	Cameroon - 17
Azerbaijan - 116	Canada - 69
Bahamas - 62	Canary Islands - 214
Bahrain - 117	Cape Verde - 18
Balearic Islands - 213	Cayman Islands - 93
Bangladesh - 117	Central African Republic - 19
Barbados - 63	Chad - 19
Belarus - 167	Channel Islands - 224
Belgium - 167	Chile - 71

China - 120	Faroe Islands - 172
Colombia - 73	Fiji Islands - 231
Comoros (islands of the Union of) - 20	Finland - 174
Congo (Brazzaville - Republic of) - 20	France - 174
Congo (Kinshasa - Democratic Republic of the) - 42	French Guiana - 90
Cook Islands - 231	French Polynesia - 232
Costa Rica - 74	Gabon - 25
Croatia - 169	Georgia - 179
Cuba - 75	Germany - 180
Curaçao - 60	Ghana - 26
Cyprus - 170	Gibraltar - 180
Czech Republic - 171	Granada - 87
Denmark - 171	Greece - 181
Djibouti - 22	Greenland - 172
Dominica - 76	Guadeloupe - 88
Dominican Republic - 103	Guam - 235
East Timor - 125	Guatemala - 89
Ecuador - 77	Guinea - 27
Egypt - 22	Guinea-Bissau - 27
El Salvador - 107	Guyana - 90
England - 220	Haiti - 91
Equatorial Guinea - 28	Honduras - 92
Eritrea - 23	Hong Kong - 122
Estonia - 173	Hungary - 189
Ethiopia - 24	Iceland - 190

India - 125	Luxembourg - 199
Indonesia - 129	Macau - 123
Iran - 132	Macedonia - 199
Iraq - 133	Madagascar - 31
Ireland - 190	Madeira - 206
Israel - 134	Malawi - 33
Italy - 191	Malaysia - 142
Ivory Coast - 21	Maldives - 143
Jamaica - 96	Mali - 33
Japan - 135	Malta - 200
Jordan - 136	Marshall Islands - 236
Kazakhstan - 137	Martinique - 96
Kenya - 28	Mauritania - 37
Kiribati Islands - 235	Mauritius (island) - 36
Kosovo - 196	Mayotte - 38
Kuwait - 138	Mexico - 97
Kyrgyzstan - 139	Micronesia - 236
Laos - 140	Moldova - 201
Latvia - 197	Monaco - 202
Lebanon - 141	Mongolia - 144
Lesotho - 29	Montenegro - 202
Liberia - 30	Montserrat - 99
Libya - 30	Morocco - 34
Liechtenstein - 198	Mozambique - 39
Lithuania - 198	Myanmar (Burma) - 145

Namibia - 39	Qatar - 151
Nauru Island - 237	Reunion Island - 43
Nepal - 146	Romania - 206
Netherlands Antilles - 59	Russia - 207
New Caledonia - 237	Rwanda - 43
New Zealand - 238	Saint Kitts & Nevis - 105
Nicaragua - 99	Saint Lucia - 106
Niger - 40	Saint Vincent and the Grenadines - 106
Nigeria - 41	Saint-Barthélemy - 104
Niue (island) - 240	Samoa - 241
North Korea - 147	San Marino - 195
Northern Marianas - 235	São Tomé and Principe - 45
Norway - 203	Saudi Arabia - 151
Oman (Sultanate of) - 147	Senegal - 46
Pakistan - 148	Serbia - 208
Palau - 240	Seychelles - 46
Panama - 100	Sierra Leone - 47
Papua New Guinea - 240	Singapore - 152
Paraguay - 100	Sint Maarten (Saint-Martin) - 105
Peru - 101	Slovakia - 209
Philippines - 150	Slovenia - 210
Pitcairn - 241	Solomon (islands) - 242
Poland - 204	Somalia - 48
Portugal - 204	South Africa - 48
Puerto Rico - 102	South Korea - 153

South Sudan - 49	Tuvalu - 243
Spain - 210	Uganda - 41
Sri Lanka - 153	Ukraine - 219
St. Helena - 44	United Arab Emirates - 157
Sudan (North) - 49	United Kingdom - 220
Suriname - 108	United States - 78
Swaziland - 50	Uruguay - 109
Sweden - 216	Uzbekistan - 158
Switzerland - 217	Vanuatu - 243
Syria - 154	Vatican - 196
Taiwan - 155	Venezuela - 110
Tajikistan - 155	Vietnam - 159
Tanzania - 50	Wallis and Futuna - 245
Thailand - 156	Yemen - 160
The Gambia - 26	Zambia - 53
The Netherlands - 218	Zimbabwe (eSwatini) - 54
Tibet - 124	
Togo - 51	
Tokelau Islands - 239	
Tonga - 243	
Trinidad and Tobago - 108	
Tunisia - 52	
Turkey - 219	
Turkmenistan - 157	
Turks and Caicos Islands - 94	

ARCTIC OCEAN
QUEEN ELIZABETH ISLANDS
Knud Rasmussen Land
Greenland
(Denmark)
King Christian X Land
King Christian IX Land
Denmark Strait
ICELAND
U.S.
NUNNAVUT TERRITORY
CANADA
ROCKY MOUNTAINS
Québec
NORTH PACIFIC OCEAN
NORTH ATLANTIC OCEAN
UNITED STATES
MEXICO
BAHAMAS
CUBA
JAMAICA
HAITI
DOMINICAN REPUBLIC
MAURITANIA
MALI
PORTUGAL
SPAIN
MOROCCO
VENEZUELA
COLOMBIA
GUYANA
SURINAME
ECUADOR
PERU
BRAZIL
AMAZON BASIN
BOLIVIA
PARAGUAY
CHILE
ARGENTINA
URUGUAY
PAMPAS
French Polynesia (Fr.)
SOUTH PACIFIC OCEAN
SOUTH ATLANTIC OCEAN
Antarctic Peninsula
Marie Byrd

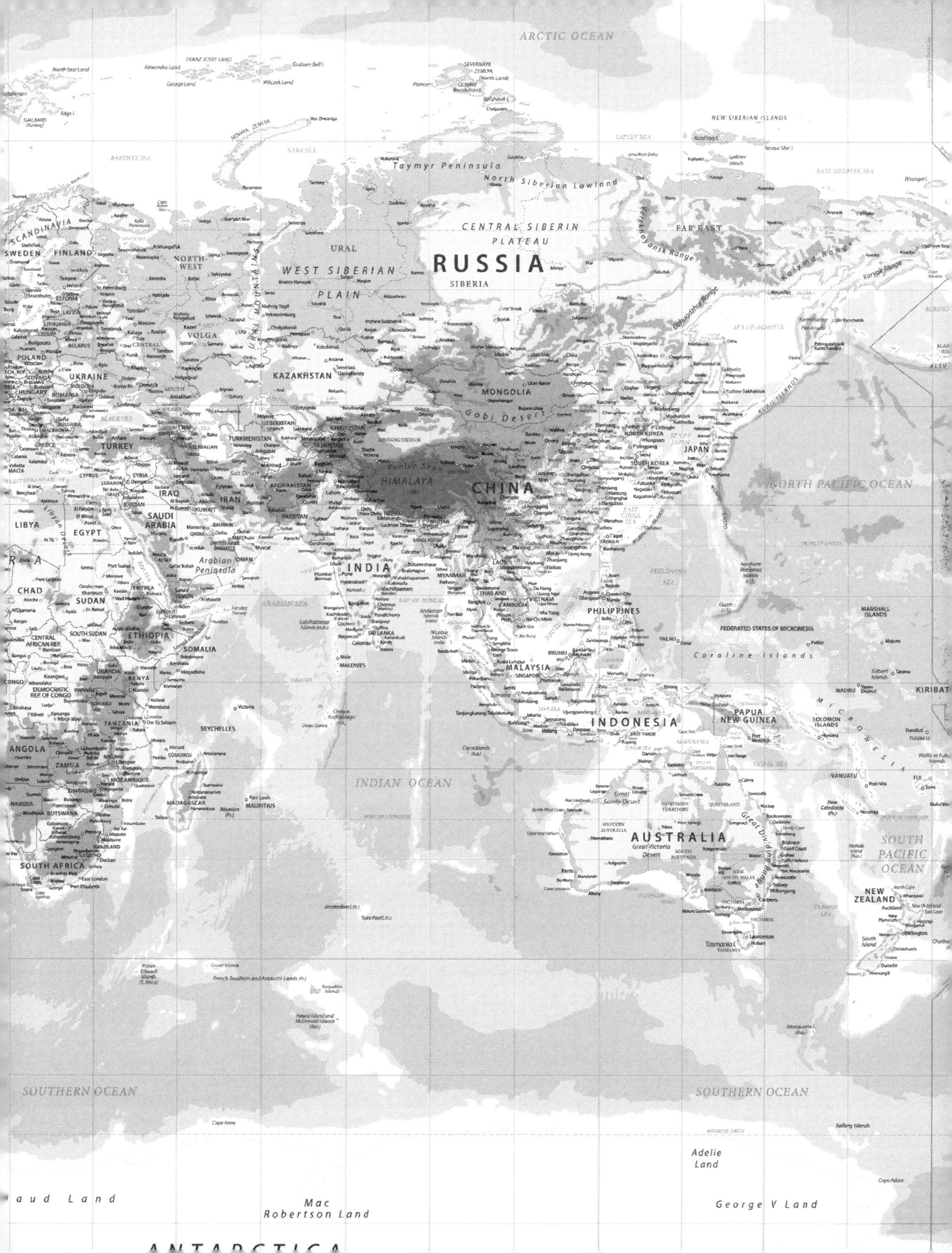

ARCTIC OCEAN
Taymyr Peninsula
North Siberian Lowland
CENTRAL SIBERIN PLATEAU
FAR EAST
RUSSIA
SIBERIA
WEST SIBERIAN PLAIN
URAL
SCANDINAVIA
SWEDEN
FINLAND
NORTH WEST
VOLGA
UKRAINE
POLAND
KAZAKHSTAN
MONGOLIA
Gobi Desert
TURKEY
TURKMENISTAN
UZBEKISTAN
AFGHANISTAN
IRAQ
IRAN
SAUDI ARABIA
LIBYA
EGYPT
CHAD
SUDAN
ETHIOPIA
SOMALIA
KENYA
TANZANIA
ANGOLA
ZAMBIA
NAMIBIA
SOUTH AFRICA
MADAGASCAR
SEYCHELLES
Arabian Peninsula
HIMALAYA
CHINA
INDIA
JAPAN
NORTH KOREA
SOUTH KOREA
PHILIPPINES
MALAYSIA
INDONESIA
PAPUA NEW GUINEA
NORTH PACIFIC OCEAN
Caroline Islands
INDIAN OCEAN
AUSTRALIA
Great Victoria Desert
Great Sandy Desert
Great Dividing Range
SOUTH PACIFIC OCEAN
NEW ZEALAND
SOUTHERN OCEAN
SOUTHERN OCEAN
Adelie Land
aud Land
Mac Robertson Land
George V Land
ANTARCTICA

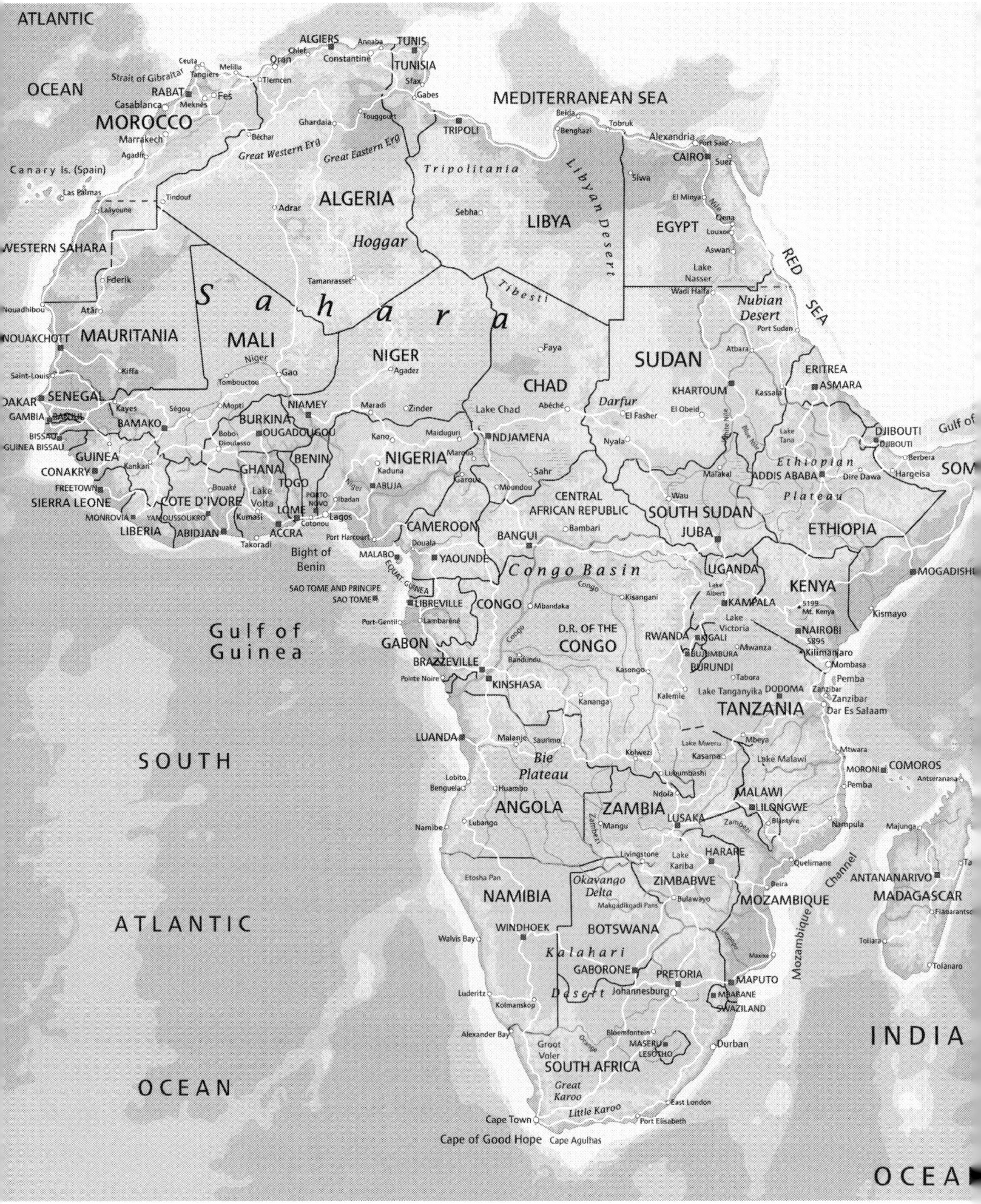

ATLANTIC
OCEAN
ALGIERS
Annaba
TUNIS
Chlef
Oran
Constantine
TUNISIA
Ceuta
Strait of Gibraltar
Tangiers
Melilla
Tlemcen
Sfax
RABAT
Fes
Gabes
Casablanca
Meknès
MEDITERRANEAN SEA
MOROCCO
Ghardaia
Touggourt
TRIPOLI
Beida
Benghazi
Tobruk
Marrakech
Béchar
Alexandria
Port Said
Agadir
Great Western Erg
Great Eastern Erg
CAIRO
Suez
Canary Is. (Spain)
Tripolitania
Siwa
Las Palmas
Libyan Desert
El Minya
Tindouf
Laayoune
Adrar
ALGERIA
Sebha
LIBYA
Qena
Louxor
EGYPT
WESTERN SAHARA
Hoggar
Aswan
RED SEA
Lake Nasser
Fderik
Tamanrasset
Tibesti
Wadi Halfa
Nubian Desert
Nouadhibou
Atâr
Sahara
Port Sudan
NOUAKCHOTT
MAURITANIA
MALI
Faya
Atbara
NIGER
SUDAN
Niger
Saint-Louis
Kiffa
Gao
Agadez
ERITREA
Tombouctou
CHAD
ASMARA
KHARTOUM
Kassala
DAKAR
SENEGAL
NIAMEY
Darfur
GAMBIA
Kayes
Ségou
Mopti
Maradi
Zinder
Lake Chad
Abéché
El Fasher
El Obeid
DJIBOUTI
Gulf of
BAMAKO
BURKINA
OUAGADOUGOU
BISSAU
Bobo Dioulasso
Kano
Maiduguri
NDJAMENA
Nyala
White Nile
Blue Nile
Lake Tana
GUINEA BISSAU
GUINEA
BENIN
NIGERIA
Maroua
Ethiopian
Berbera
Kankan
Kaduna
Malakal
ADDIS ABABA
Dire Dawa
Hargeisa
CONAKRY
GHANA
TOGO
Garoua
Sahr
SOM
FREETOWN
Bouaké
ABUJA
Moundou
Plateau
SIERRA LEONE
COTE D'IVORE
Lake Volta
PORTO-NOVO
Olbadan
CENTRAL AFRICAN REPUBLIC
Wau
SOUTH SUDAN
MONROVIA
YAMOUSSOUKRO
Kumasi
LOME
Lagos
Cotonou
CAMEROON
Bambari
ETHIOPIA
LIBERIA
ABIDJAN
ACCRA
Takoradi
Port Harcourt
Douala
BANGUI
JUBA
Bight of Benin
MALABO
YAOUNDE
Congo Basin
UGANDA
MOGADISHU
EQUAT. GUINEA
SAO TOME AND PRINCIPE
SAO TOME
Congo
Kisangani
Lake Albert
KENYA
LIBREVILLE
CONGO
Mbandaka
KAMPALA
5199 Mt. Kenya
Kismayo
Port-Gentil
Lambaréné
Lake Victoria
NAIROBI
Gulf of Guinea
D.R. OF THE CONGO
RWANDA
KIGALI
5895
GABON
Mwanza
Kilimanjaro
BRAZZEVILLE
Bandundu
BUJUMBURA
BURUNDI
Mombasa
Pointe Noire
KINSHASA
Kasongo
Tabora
Pemba
Lake Tanganyika
DODOMA
Zanzibar
Kananga
Kalemie
TANZANIA
Dar Es Salaam
LUANDA
Malanje
Saurimo
Mbeya
Lake Mweru
Kolwezi
Kasama
Mtwara
SOUTH
Bie Plateau
Lake Malawi
MORONI
COMOROS
Lubumbashi
Antseranana
Lobito
Benguela
Huambo
Ndola
MALAWI
Pemba
ANGOLA
ZAMBIA
LILONGWE
LUSAKA
Blantyre
Namibe
Lubango
Mangu
Zambezi
Nampula
Majunga
Livingstone
Lake Kariba
HARARE
Quelimane
Etosha Pan
Okavango Delta
ZIMBABWE
Beira
ANTANANARIVO
Mozambique Channel
NAMIBIA
Makgadikgadi Pans
Bulawayo
MOZAMBIQUE
MADAGASCAR
ATLANTIC
WINDHOEK
BOTSWANA
Walvis Bay
Kalahari Desert
Limpopo
Maxixe
Toliara
GABORONE
PRETORIA
MAPUTO
Tolanaro
Luderitz
Johannesburg
MBABANE
Kolmanskop
SWAZILAND
Alexander Bay
Bloemfontein
Orange
MASERU
INDIA
LESOTHO
Groot Voler
Durban
SOUTH AFRICA
OCEAN
Great Karoo
East London
Little Karoo
Cape Town
Port Elisabeth
Cape of Good Hope
Cape Agulhas
OCEA

AFRICA

Algeria

The largest country in Africa since the partition of Sudan, Algeria has the enormous advantage of a beautiful duality between a hilly (and preserved) Mediterranean coastline and the vast expanse of the Sahara. On paper it is a first-class destination, both in terms of nature and culture. In practice the country remains little touristic, due to weak infrastructures and a complicated geopolitical situation. The country is perfectly accessible, at least in part, to experienced travelers, but the road is long before it opens up to ordinary tourists.

• The Algerian Sahara is one of the most varied deserts in the world. Trekking, camelback riding or 4x4 vehicles, all means are good to discover the mineral variations of the Hoggar massif and meet the Tuaregs people who live there.

• The Tassili N'Ajjer is the largest prehistoric museum on the planet and it is in the open air. You will be able to admire rock paintings and engravings dating sometimes from more than 4,000 years ago.

• Incredible places of life in the middle of an ocean of dunes, the most striking oases of the country are the red oasis of Timimoun at the gates of the Grand Erg and the palm groves of El Oued and El Kantara.

• The seven fortified cities around Ghardaïa, 600 kms from Algiers, have survived for several centuries in this region where man has fought against desolation. It is a region of an absolute exoticism, as much in terms of geography as of culture (craft industry of carpets).

• Algiers gives the impression to be miraculously taken out of water so much its whiteness shines in the sun, it is nicknamed "the White". With the wire of the lanes, one finds all the history of the past colonizations before getting lost, preferably with a guide, in the Casbah. This old district, punctuated with Ottoman palaces, has been damaged by the years but it is still full of exoticism.

• Oran is a dynamic city that the Algerian youth has appropriated. Cradle of the rai music (Algerian pop music), it is a lively city with many cafes. It also has a remarkable setting, on the mediterranean sea, a classic colonial architecture, and several historic monuments.

• Visiting Tlemcen, the religious heart of the country, will allow you to retrace the history of Muslim art through the different mosques of different eras that adorn the city. However, it should be noted that the majority of the mosques are closed to non-Muslims.

• Like the whole region, the north of Algeria was once under Roman, but also Byzantine and Phoenician domination. There are quite a number of remains, often empty of tourists, the most important of which are in Tipassa, Djemila (triumphal arch of Caracalla), Cherchell, Guelma (theater), or Timgad. The latter houses the ruins of a great city founded by Emperor Trajan. It is one of the most important Roman sites in Africa, but it remains little visited despite its appeal.

• The Mediterranean coast is beautiful in places and offers a parade of creeks or sandy beaches, but the infrastructures are almost non-existent, at least for foreign tourism, and are therefore confidential. This does not mean, however, that they are not visited, Algerians themselves visit them en masse, especially around *Tipassa* and on the *Turquoise Coast*.

Angola

Angola is a mystery that will remain so for a long time to come for a majority of travelers. That said, after a long period of instability and war, the country has, with the exception of a few sensitive regions, become a popular destination for (truly) experienced visitors. It offers a classic Southern Africa, savannah, large fauna, tropics, and more atypical aspects, a rough Atlantic coastline, cool mountains, a mix of African and Portuguese cultural influences. The infrastructure is still very weak, which limits the possibilities and reserves the destination for adventurers, especially outside the capital, Luanda. The rapid development of the country, however, bodes well for significant changes in the near future, although the democratic process seems to have stalled and the tourism sector is not a priority.

* In Luanda, the capital city, you can walk along the promenade along the seafront, which looks like a small cruise ship, and visit the port and the old São Miguel fort built in 1576. In the old colonial city, merchants, especially at the Benfica market, offer a large number of purely Angolan objects: statuettes, ceramics, bronze objects, masks and sculptures made of wood tchokwes or stone (be careful, most items require an official document to be taken out of the country). It is also in the bay of the capital that the beaches of Ilhia are located, the only really practicable ones in the country. Luanda is a strange city, where luxury cars and shantytowns live side by side. Thanks to the oil money the city is developing at a crazy speed and will surprise many visitors by its relative modernity but also by its excessive prices. Today it is one of the most expensive cities in the world.

* The Quiçama National Park, located 70 km south of Luanda, brings together a wide variety of wild animals and is the country's great natural meeting place, even if the infrastructure is still in need of improvements. The pelicans, flamingos, giant turtles, oryx, zebras and springboks of the Cameia and Milando reserves can be observed by a few tourists who are still very rare.

* To the south, the Serra da Chela massif is the most beautiful site in the country. From the desert, suddenly emerges a rocky relief that rises up to 2200 meters creating a series of landscapes more breathtaking one than the other. It is one of the most beautiful postcards of Africa. Continuing south, you will find the Ruacana Falls on the border with Namibia.

* Other waterfalls offer an impressive spectacle: the spectacular Kalandula Falls, near the town of *Malanje*. They are among the highest in Africa (more than 100 meters) and take place in an equatorial jungle setting.

Benin

Benin is accessible and lends itself quite well to tourism, at least for travelers familiar with African destinations. The country stands out above all for its strong cultural aspect (especially voodoo practices, which originated in the country) and its important historical heritage. The setting is typical of East Africa, and the beaches are noteworthy, although the seaside argument is not on the agenda because of the dangerous sea. On the tourist market, Benin is still unknown, but nothing prevents to discover it.

* In the far north, the Pendjari National Park and part of the W National Park offer great photo safari opportunities to meet buffalo, elephants and lions, especially between March and April. To the northwest, overlooking the Pendjari plains, is the Atakora plateau where rivers sometimes cascade. In the parks, don't miss the Tanougou waterfalls at the foot of the Atakora and the Kota Falls, but also the scenic site of Koussou-Kouangou.

* You can discover the country by following the course of the river Ouémé. Each village has its own small market, the ideal opportunity to discover the daily life of the inhabitants. Don't miss the biggest market on the west coast of Africa, that of Dantokpa, in the Jonquet district of Cotonou. On the coast, it is that of Porto Novo which is the most important.

• 18 km north of Cotonou, Ganvié is the largest lake city in Africa. Huts on stilts and floating markets have taken possession of the lagoon and the fishing technique of the inhabitants is one of the main attractions of the surroundings. Another interesting habitat is that of the Somba people, in the Natitingou region, where some houses take the form of small castles.

• Abomey, former capital of the kingdom of the same name, is today the religious capital of the country. From its prestigious past, it has preserved the remains of the ancient palaces of the kings, but it is especially worth the presence of many fetishes, in the city and in the surrounding bush. Benin has seen the birth of voodoo rites that the curious can experience during the Awilé festival where even the uninitiated have the right to participate.

• Open on the Gulf of Guinée, the Beninese coast can boast large sandy beaches shaded by coconut trees such as those of Grand Popo and Ouidah. Unfortunately, swimming opportunities are compromised by currents and the "bar" (a very dangerous wave zone). Instead, you can go up the Slave Route to Ouidah, the former embarkation center for slaves to Brazil and Haïti to discover the so-called "Brazilian" neighborhoods.

Botswana

For the Okavango Delta region, and for the Kalahari Desert, its flora and fauna, Botswana is an incredible nature destination. A stable country with a good standard of living, in the wake of South Africa, it is very accessible and easy to visit, while offering a majestic concentrate of Africa. However, the approach to the great natural sites has to be organized and is often very expensive. More than the spirit of adventure, it is necessary to have deep pockets to travel there, hence the number of visitors rather limited but who invariably come back enchanted.

• The Okavango Delta is a must-see location with an impressive number of tourist attractions. This immense aquatic maze is to be discovered by pirogue (mokoro). In addition to the fabulous landscapes decorated with papyrus and water lilies, this will allow you to meet the thousands of birds that populate it, but also lions and elephants that have made their home on its islands. The spectacle of the arms of the river coming to extinction in the sands of the Kalahari desert is not to be missed and is part of the natural wonders of the world.

• The Kalahari Desert is a hostile set of rocky hills, dry salt marshes and thorny bushes. To discover it, follow the trans-Kalahari road in the company of bushmen guides. You will drive to Deception Valley in the heart of the Kalahari National Park and then continue your red earth journey to South Africa through the fantastic scenery of the Mabuasehube-Gemsbok National Park and Kalahari Gemsbok National Park.

• To the east, between the Limpopo and the Shashe, the private reserve of Mashatu is the most important on the African continent where big cats, antelopes and elephants live. In the northeast, in the parks of Makgadikgadi and Nxai Pan, we can see the migration of zebras, antelopes and wildebeest which, from February to April, cross the unusual landscapes (salt lakes...) of these two parks. Near the Namibian border, more than 30 000 elephants have taken up residence in the Chobe National Park. In the northwest, in the middle of the Okavango Delta, the Moremi Nature Reserve is one of the most beautiful reserves in the country where a very large variety of animals live.

Burkina Faso

Access is easy, but Burkina Faso, the "country of upright men", is not a destination within the reach of all travelers. It is a proud and joyful Africa, but sometimes complicated, which awaits the visitor. A country where culture is part of daily life, music, dances and traditional festivals, Burkina Faso offers both the Africa of large animals and savannah and the Africa of the desert. With preparation, the trip can be undertaken, travel is not complicated, the health situation is low but not alarming. However, it should not be forgotten that this is a very poor country, in the heart of a troubled Sahel region.

• The national parks of Arly and W host a varied fauna of which elephants, hippos and antelopes are the main representatives. The park of Kaboré Tembi, a former Po reserve, also boasted elephants, but poaching has caused significant losses to this population. They can be found in the Deux Balés National Park where many crocodiles also live. Also in the vicinity of Ouagadougou, the sacred crocodile pond of Sabou is worth a visit as well as the sacred catfish pond not far from Bobo-Dioulasso.

• The Sahel, in the north, is dotted with small isolated villages full of authenticity. The Sahara offers large dunes in Gorom Gorom. Going southwest, the green landscape, gum trees, baobab trees, karite, tamarind and mango trees offer their shadows and erosion creates beautiful landscapes such as the cliffs, waterfalls and lakes (Tengrela) around Bafora, the cliffs of Sindou, those of Niansoroni and Negueni and the Takalédougou waterfalls.

• Bobo-Dioulasso has a lively market (Bobo), long shady avenues and a terracotta mosque, to which is added the spectacle of the work of craftsmen from different neighborhoods (dyers and bronze founders in Koko and weavers in Diaradougou). Ouagadougou is also worth for its market and its mosque, but especially for its animation. It is in the small villages of Burkina Faso that you will meet the traditions, music and dances of the country influenced by the Tuaregs, the Fulani and the Sombas.

Burundi

A country with a complicated situation, in a region that is no less complicated. Burundi, a very small country, sees few visitors, and those who do go there are used to traveling without nets. When it comes to nature, the country delivers all the wonders of equatorial Africa, its fauna and flora. It is also the site of the sources of the Nile, a place that makes explorers dream. Security problems, very weak infrastructure, complex access, prevalence of malaria, unstable geopolitics, Burundi is not and is not about to become a mainstream destination. It is therefore above all a trophy for the great adventurers, who will find here nature in its raw state and adventure.

• Burundi offers both the site of the sources of the Nile in the south at an altitude of more than 2000 meters (a monument is dedicated to the explorers Stanley and Livingstone) and that of the shores of Lake Tanganyika, located in the *Rift Valley*, the seventh largest lake in the world. It is home to a wide variety of fish, crocodiles, hippos, and water sports enthusiasts.

• Numerous reserves and national parks protect the country's natural heritage. The Kibira National Park is traversed by families of chimpanzees, baboons, cercopithecus and black colobus. It is reached by crossing the immense tea plantations of Teza and Rwegura which then give way to a forest of great beauty.

• The Rubuvu National Park, framed by high mountain ranges, offers a wide range of landscapes from rocky hills to wooded savannah inhabited by a large number of animal species (hippos, antelopes, baboons, buffaloes, warthogs ...).

• The Rusizi palm grove, on the road to Cibitoke, 10 km from Bujumbura, is also worth seeing for its exceptional flora. The other part of the Rusizi National Park is composed of the swampy area of the Delta where nineteen species of hippopotamus live. The birds of the islets of the managed nature reserve of Lake Rwihinda are also one of the great animal attractions of the country.

Cameroon

At the crossroads of sub-Saharan and equatorial Africa, Cameroon is a nature destination, which is reserved for an informed public but which is not at all inaccessible. The seaside stay is possible, the beaches are beautiful, but they should only be a complement to the trip. The real wealth of the country lies in the nature of the interior and in the traditions of its inhabitants. The sanitary situation is to be watched, as well as everything related to security. The country is under the *threat of regional terrorism, and "African-style" unrest can erupt without warning, especially near the borders and during periods of (undemocratic) elections. The country has good attractions, and is much easier to apprehend than its neighbors such as the Central African Republic or the Congo. To be approached with a spirit of adventure all the same.*

• On the border of Nigéria, at Ruhmsiki, rise the Kapsiki. These hills and rocky peaks are surrounded by volcanic landscapes. Cultivating millet on terraces, the inhabitants live in villages of round huts clinging to the mountainsides, preserving their traditions in a very strongly Islamized area.

• Mount Cameroon is a still active volcano located in the southwest of the country. Its ascent is possible in one or three days, depending on the training. First the forest, then the savannah, before crossing the clouds and reaching the top of the chariot of the Gods.

• The chiefdoms of the north-west like Bamanda or Foumban are obligatory passages to better understand Cameroon. In Foumban, the Royal Palace Museum tells the story of one of the oldest kingdoms of Black Africa, through more than three thousand art objects and pieces.

• Antelopes, buffaloes, warthogs and crocodiles await you in the Benue National Park. Elephants, lions, giraffes and birds live in the Waza National Park. In the north is also the reserve of Boubandjida and Faro, in the south they are called Campo and Dja.

• Kribi is an important seaside resort in Cameroon known for its white sandy beaches and its port. Nearby, you will be able to admire the Lobé waterfalls that flow directly into the sea, a unique phenomenon to say the least.

Cape Verde

Island destination, at the same time clearly African but with South American influences, with the Hawaiian framework (in much more arid), Cape Verde is a small unknown paradise. The country is rather poor but the infrastructures are correct, the access is easy, the trip is quiet. The numerous islands allow to diversify the stay, and the landscapes are everywhere exceptional. A destination for the general public, full of exoticism, but which is far from being overwhelmed by visitors and retains all its cultural particularities.

• The trade winds that sweep the coasts of Cape Verde are the best thing that could happen to riders of all kinds. Funboard, windsurf, kitesurf... all sails are welcome around the coasts of Boa Vista, Praia or São Vicente.

• For those who love diving, it is on the island of Sal that you will have to go to observe the ballet of tunas, manta rays, hammerhead sharks and multicolored tropical fish. Beware of the currents which, at these latitudes, can be dangerous.

• Sinners too may find their happiness. Fishing with big-game or longline, the outskirts of São Nicolau are particularly full of fish.

• For those who prefer the land, the archipelago offers many opportunities for hiking and sometimes biking. The north of Santo Antão, the westernmost of the ten islands, is cut by some beautiful canyons like the ribeiras of Paul and Figueiral. The volcano São Felipe on the island of Fogo and the contrasts of São Vicente are also famous spots.

• In recent years, Cape Verde has emphasized its cultural heritage. The Portuguese colonial architecture of Mindelo on the island of São Vicente or São Filipe in Fogo is part of it, but it is especially the *mornas* sung by Cesaria Evora that will guide the traveler in these cities in the footsteps of the Cape Verdean soul.

• If you are looking for a white sandy beach, you should know that there are few of them, but the seaside argument is attractive all the same. Santa Maria on the island of Sal, which is the most beautiful beach and the first seaside destination of the archipelago, is particularly noteworthy, even if the development is not always graceful.

Central African Republic

A country totally out of the tourist circuits. Many African countries require a certain amount of adventure on a trip, but the Central African Republic (or Central African Republic by its official name) is nothing less than a total adventure. No stability, very poor sanitary conditions, non-existent infrastructure. Equatorial Africa is at its peak, and nature is unbridled, but the journey is very complicated. To be considered, during calm periods, only by hard-core explorers, prepared, aware of the risks and ready to travel in total autonomy.

• 70 km from Bangui, the capital, are the magnificent Boali Falls where the M'bari River flows into the heart of the virgin forest. The lake at its feet is full of crocodiles. The Matakil falls are even higher. The course of the Pipi river is famous for its gorges and the natural sandstone bridge that overhangs it.

• In the surroundings of Bouar, 455 km from the capital, many sites of raised stones built during the 1st millennium BC are worth a visit. In the sandstone landscapes of Ouadda, monoliths (kagas) were used as prehistoric dwellings.

• The Manovo-Gounda Saint Floris National Park, inscribed on the World Heritage List, is home to black rhinos, elephants, cheetahs, leopards, wild dogs, gazelles and buffalos. Other reserves are located in the north of the country such as those of Bamingui-Bangoran and André-Félix. Obviously the tourist framework is almost non-existent there.

• The Lobaye region is covered by a thick forest. Take the road to Mangoumba, south of Bangui, you will cross a veritable maze of greenery, before reaching the village of Mangoumba, located on the banks of the Oubangui River. Following its course, you will meet Bayaka Pygmies whose way of life is organized around gathering and hunting.

Chad

In the heart of a region that is far from calm, Chad is a huge desert country with its feet in equatorial Africa. The country suffers from the evils of this part of Africa, precarious security in many areas (and the abundant presence of mines in the north), various and varied traffic areas out of control, very high terrorist risks, a very poor health network, difficult transportation (no roads in almost all of the country, and the tracks are complicated). A destination that is therefore difficult and largely discouraged. A few tour operators still occupy the Tibesti area, episodically when the situation allows it, but they are for experienced travelers. Experience in complex travel and good preparation, not to mention knowledge of Africa and its traps, are indispensable for all travelers entering Chad.

• The Tibesti Desert promises Saharan trekking in landscapes of unsuspected beauty. Volcanic massifs, deep canyons, "lunar craters" (hole in Natron), desert lakes, rock paintings and prehistoric engravings (Kla Ouenama, Guéhesser) are at the rendezvous. Do not miss the thermal springs, with therapeutic virtues, of Soboroum.

• Other forms of surprising relief, between towers and battlements, dot the Ennedi region, to the north of which lie Chad's most beautiful dunes, those of the Mourdi Depression, and the Ounianga-Kebir lakes. It is also the region of the gueltas, a geographical peculiarity that forms superb landscapes such as the *guelta of Arché* which, nestled at the bottom of a canyon, shelters dromedaries and crocodiles.

• Zakouma National Park is again partially accessible, but it is still strongly discouraged for the moment despite the attraction of a fauna rich in elephants, buffaloes, giraffes, cobs and birds.

• N'Djamena, the capital city, was once considered one of the liveliest cities in Central Africa. If the war has left indelible traces, the historical district remains interesting to discover. Do not miss the main market, exotic, anarchic and sun-crushed.

Comoros

The Comoros Islands are the great forgotten islands of the Indian Ocean. A very poor country, with weak infrastructures, sometimes unstable, the Comoros attracts few visitors, and the latter are invariably experienced travelers. The attractions are the same as in the rest of the region, landscapes, nature, culture. In a rather similar register, the neighboring Malagasy islands are preferred by tourists and are much more mediatized. It is necessary to know how to adapt to this destination, especially to the traditional and religious customs, and to have the taste for exploration in an unmarked framework. A destination that is still far from the spotlight, but which has an undeniable natural beauty coupled with a powerful exoticism and is not really difficult to access.

• Due to the volcanic origin of the archipelago, white sandy beaches are rare, but those that exist are grandiose. On Grande Comore, you will find them mostly on the east (Bouni and Chindini) and south (Chomoni) coasts. In Moheli, they will be on the island of Chissioua Quénéfou and on the west coast (Kavé Hoani, Domoni and Miringoni). They will be less numerous in Anjouan, but those of Moya and Hayoho are worth the detour (on foot or by boat).

• On the ocean side, deep-sea fishing (in November and May) adds to the pleasures of scuba diving. Divers will enjoy an important and very well preserved coral reef where all kinds of multicolored tropical fish species live, as well as swordfish, dugongs, dolphins, sea turtles and manta rays.

• On the land side, you can hike in the jungle that covers the area around the crater of Mount Kartala on Grande Comores. Don't hesitate to go around the island passing by small villages, but also by picturesque sites such as the bay of the Hole of the Prophet, the crater of the salt lake... Moreover if you like walking, it is Anjouan which will offer you the most varied landscapes, dotted with lakes, waterfalls and rivers (Tatinga Falls and the lakes of Dzialaoutsounga and Dzianlandzé) and the most beautiful plantation of Ylangs-Ylangs, a specialty of the country, in the circus of Bambao. Moheli is the wildest island covered with a thick tropical forest that is just waiting to be explored by (very) discerning travelers.

Congo-Brazzaville

As with the entire West Equatorial Africa region, it is difficult to talk about travel without talking about adventure. Congo-Brazzaville, much more accessible and in better "health" than its neighbor the Democratic Republic of Congo, does not however offer the conditions required for classic tourism. Only seasoned travelers who know Africa can afford to explore this Garden of Eden. A pity, because the culture and especially the nature are remarkable.

• Brazzaville has preserved a number of historic buildings, which, combined with the profusion of palm, flamboyant and mango trees, make the capital an interesting dive into equatorial Africa. Do not miss among others the Basilica of Saint Anne of Congo and the popular district of Poto-Poto. Not far from the city, the Pool region has many surprises in store for you such as the Loufoulakari and Béla waterfalls, the Nguela hole, dug by a meteorite, which offers a superb viewpoint on the road to Kinkala or the thousand leaf tree supposed to have all the species of the region.

• 150 km north of the capital is the historic village of M'Bé, capital of Makoko, king of the Teke. The region abounds in unusual panoramas such as the Batékés plateaus and their pink sandstone or the Blue Lake located in a grandiose valley of collapse. Nearby is one of the most important reserves of the country, that of Léfini, where live elephants, buffaloes, hippos, monkeys, antelopes, gazelles, and several kinds of birds.

• If its construction evokes a bloody passage of colonial history, the crossing of the south of the country by the Congo-Ocean railway line will nevertheless allow you to connect Brazzaville to Pointe Noire through sumptuous landscapes. During 10 hours (and 512 km), the railway runs along massifs, over chasms and deep into the virgin forest. To discover the country, it is also possible to take a pirogue or a cruise boat from Brazzaville along the Congo River.

• The loop of the Niari offers surprising landscapes of conical peaks like the mountains of the Moon. In this region there are still a few pygmies who stay away from the common life. A little further towards Gabon, you can visit the caves of Bihoua and the reserve of Mount Mfouari. Then in the region of Bouenza, the waterfalls of the same name, the caves of Nkila-Ntari and Fwalwila and the liana bridge on the Ogoué river on the side of lalékoumou will delight the adventurers.

* Pointe-Noire is located on the Atlantic coast and its port is the economic lung of the country. In addition to the colonial buildings in the downtown area, one can discover its craftsmen's products as well as the beaches of Loango or Pointe-Indienne. In the south of the city, the Diosso cirques or Lake Nanga are also places to visit.

Ivory Coast

A time in the light, carried by a development full of ambitions, Côte d'Ivoire unfortunately took the turn of the millennium by sinking into a crisis with accents of civil war and then again in 2011 with armed clashes against a backdrop of politics. This unstable situation has considerably hampered the tourist attraction of this country with strong potential. In the region it is one of the only ones to be able to offer a convincing seaside argument, as notable as that of North African countries such as Morocco or Tunisia. Abidjan is one of the great cities of Africa. Traditions and culture are interesting, and nature there expresses the whole palette of African colors. From Paris the access to the country is always easy but on the spot the trip remains reserved for experienced or supervised visitors. A slightly bitter observation that remains common to many African countries.

* Going to meet the people and their traditions is one of the aspects that make a trip to Côte d'Ivoire unforgettable. The Senoufo country, in the surroundings of Korogho, is known for its handicrafts such as its chairs and wrought doors or the painted canvases of the city of Fakaha.
 - Man is one of the major cities of western Ivory Coast. It is nicknamed "The city of 18 mountains". It is in this mountainous setting that live the Yacoubas, famous for their stilt dancing.

* In the Malinké country, northwest of Ivory Coast, the savannah is having a field day. The villages are made up of superb huts and the manufacture of shea butter is one of the specialties of the region.

* The liana bridges of Daloa or Danané bear witness to an ancestral way of life. Out of respect for those who built them, one takes one's shoes off (and one takes one's courage in both hands) to cross them.

* To the south, the lakeside village of Tiagba is a curiosity that is worth a visit because of its unique character.

* In the northeast of the country is the largest animal reserve in West Africa: the Comoé National Park. There are elephants, lions, hippos and more than four hundred species of birds. At the end of the dry season, other parks such as Taï, Maraoué and Nimba Mountains are also a pleasure to visit.

* The seaside resorts around Grand-Bassam in the *Bay of Sirens* and wherever the waves allow have been put forward by the government to develop tourism. They are well equipped and mini cruises can be organized as in the Ebrié lagoon. Grand-Bassam, in addition to its beaches, is also worthy of its colonial constructions, whose state of conservation varies greatly.

* The cities are also surprising. Whether facing the modernism pushed to the extreme of Abidjan or the neo-classicism of Yamassoukro, the visitor will be struck by the contrast with the rest of the country.

Djibouti

Very little known, Djibouti is not at all the military counter that one might expect, a small piece of desert sandbagged and hit by a scorching sun. If the sun is indeed relentless (and burning temperatures almost all year round), this country is actually larger and more cosmopolitan than we imagine. It is remarkable for its natural beauty, with some of the most beautiful coral beds in the world, as well as for its desert landscapes and salt lakes. Despite easy access, the weak (and very expensive) tourist infrastructures, the geopolitical context, which is not very reassuring, and a coastline exposed to piracy, are nevertheless major obstacles for tourism, which still borders on adventure.

• The richness of the depths of the Red Sea is the main asset of this destination, especially in the Gulf of Tadjoura (around the islands of Moucha and Maskali), fabulous sites where multicolored fish evolve in corals of exceptional beauty. Further north, the Sept-Frères archipelago, opposite the Ras Syan peninsula, is also one of the most beautiful diving sites in the country. In the south, the beaches of the Serpent Plateau, the village of Dorale and those of Khor Ambato are very pleasant. However we should not forget that the environment is desert, offering superb landscapes but sometimes monotonous, and especially that these various sites are very little exploited and do not have the infrastructures for a traditional tourism.

• Lake Assal is located in the east of the Afar Depression, at an altitude of 153 meters below sea level, making it one of the lowest points on the African continent. It is considered to be the saltiest lake in the world and the salt can be seen bleaching the shores. Under an overwhelming heat, the spectacle of this glittering lake is conducive to mirages. North of it, the Day Forest is one of the only green places in the country. Not far, before Randa, the waterfall of Bankoualé shelters a pleasant palm grove.

• On the border with the Ethiopia, the Lake Abbé with its limestone needles, its hot springs and its pink flamingos (in the rainy season) form a splendid panorama. If you connect the Abbé and Assal lakes by 4x4, you will cross the plain of Gagadé where nomads gather their herds between April and October. You can also go to meet them in the oasis of Dikhil.

• Some cities in the country are also worth visiting. Ali-Sabieh, in the south, is a city of altitude surrounded by the compact sand and cracked clay of the Great Bara Plain. Djibouti-City is worth for its port and its contrasts. Tadjourah, on the north coast of the gulf of the same name, offers the spectacle of its seven mosques facing the sea. Obock, further north, was the first anchorage of the French in the region in 1862, today only about thirty houses and a marine cemetery remain.

Egypt

It is difficult to ignore Egypt in the world of tourism. It is the country of one of the greatest human civilizations of more than five millennia, with an exceptional historical richness and an exotic environment, between desert, Mediterranean and Red Sea, with the backbone of the Nile in its middle. A superb and exciting destination, easy to access, easy to explore (even if some corners are solidly occupied by tour operators, sometimes to the detriment of independent travelers), well established in terms of tourist reception (with adequate infrastructures). The political situation, thwarted lately, invites however to keep abreast of its evolution and to move with precaution in certain regions such as the Sinai and on the desert roads.

• To embark along the Nile is like opening a history book. To begin, here is the necropolis of Giza near Cairo whose three pyramids guarded by the Sphinx are images of Epinal. Then, not far away, follow the site of Memphis (the colossus of Rameses II, the Sphinx), the necropolis of Saqqarah (the pyramid of King Djoser), and the Fayoun Necropolis, also noteworthy. Farther south, you will find the ruins of ancient Thebes, a renowned archaeological treasure, before arriving at the temples of Karnak and Luxor. In the same region are the Colossus of Memnon, one of the wonders of the ancient world. They herald one of the most precious historical sites of mankind, the Valley of the Kings, accompanied by the

Valley of the Queens. There are the tombs of the pharaohs of the New Kingdom, especially the tomb of the most famous of all, Tutankhamun, discovered at the beginning of the twentieth century and which housed both a treasure and a curse. South of Luxor, the Nile is at its most beautiful. The cruise to Aswan is the preferred mode of discovery. Among the countless historical sites, the must-see stops are Edfu (dedicated to Horus, the falcon god) and Kom Ombo (dedicated to Horus and Sobek, the crocodile god). The island of Philae is home to temples dedicated to the mythical goddess and queen Isis. Aswan is also synonymous with a modern monument, subject to controversy, with its immense dam (111 meters high) at the origin of Lake Nasser. Several temples destined to be engulfed by the waters were moved stone by stone to Abu Simbel in the far south of the country. Among these are some treasures of the Nubian Valley, including the rock temples of Rameses II and Nefertari. The unequivocal enumeration of Nile sites, those cited here being only the principal ones, holds the promise of an extraordinary cultural discovery, an encounter with one of the greatest human civilizations of all time.

* Cairo is a fascinating, but tiring, very exotic metropolis. Cairo's museums contain many treasures that have been found in all of the country's historical sites. Among those we can note the future Great Egyptian Museum, immense archaeological appointment at the feet of the pyramids, and the Egyptian Museum which shelters in particular the treasure of Toutankhamon. The city itself abounds with so many old mosques, sometimes thousands of years old, palaces, old Ottoman houses and Coptic monuments that the visit seems never to end. To this we must add the multiple experiences of the city, starting with the Khan el-Khalili, the main souk and certainly the largest market in the world, but also its cafes, its gardens, its urban chaos from which emerges both harshness and poetry. Immersed in exoticism, tossed by history and confronted with its modern vision, the visitor will find in this city a well of explorations and a true great moment of travel. If it wasn't for the constant rush and the bad sides of all megalopolises (pollution, traffic, scams), it would be really hard to leave.

* The fantastic past of Alexandria, Cleopatra's city, is especially imaginable because the great monuments, including the famous lighthouse, were swallowed up. The long seaside promenade offered by the Corniche allows the traveler to do this work of memory with pleasure before plunging into the frenzy of the El-Mansheya district or the darkness of the catacombs of the 1st and 2nd century. The famous Ancient Library, one of the pillars of writing for humanity, is recalled by the futuristic building of the *Bibliotheca Alexandrina*. The city's beaches, stormed by the people of Cairo, are neither the most beautiful nor the cleanest in the country.

* If the Mediterranean coast remains discreet, the spectacular depths of the Red Sea coast give Egyptian seaside tourism an international reputation. The weather is good all year round, the rates are quite affordable and the coral reefs are home to all kinds of fish species that parade before the eyes of even the most amateur diver. - The Libyan Desert, also called the White Desert because of the presence of limestone which provides its reliefs with surprising colors and shapes, stretches west to Libya. Just before the border is the oasis of Siwa where two old earthen fortresses overlook the salt lakes located at the foot of the Great Sea of Sand.

* To the east, beyond the Suez Canal, lies the Sinai Peninsula, an extension of the Arabian Desert, where the supposed Mount of Moses is located and where every sunrise is a reminder of the divine illumination that the prophet would have received. Hikers will also be able to climb Mount St. Catherine, the highest peak in the country, and visit the Orthodox monastery, the oldest in the world, which lies at its feet. Unfortunately, this mythical and mystical region is not safe for the traveller, and it is advisable to make sure you are well informed before going there.

Eritrea

Small but fascinating country, located in the Horn of Africa facing the Red Sea, Eritrea is a purely African nation with French, Turkish and Egyptian influences. Some very few tour operators occasionally take travellers to ancient Abyssinia. A destination far removed from classical tourism, and which is reserved first and foremost for explorers at heart who can discover a part of the Ethiopian Plateau even more remote and out of the world than in the neighboring country. The shores and seabed of the Dahlak archipelago are also true wonders but we are here the complete opposite of the gene-

ral public seaside holiday, the nomadic population knows very little about Western fashions and the heat is really penalizing.

* From Asmara, the capital, to Massaoua are the most beautiful landscapes of the country. A road of a hundred kilometers will take you from the Ethiopian plateau at an altitude of almost 2500 meters to the coastal deserts bordering the Red Sea, through all kinds of panoramas. On the way, don't miss a stop at the Orthodox monastery of Debre Bizen.

* On the border with the E thiopieis the Danakil Depression whose lowest point is about 100 meters below sea level. In spite of the unbelievable heat there (it is the hottest place in the world), wild zebras, gazelles and donkeys live in a scenery of vast salt plains, volcanic lands and other strange mineral formations.

* On the coast, several beaches offer the possibility to sunbathe and discover the Red Sea seabed. Massaoua, an old Turkish port city, was restored after the conflicts of the 90s. The islands of Batsi and Twalet are connected by dikes to the main part of the city. To the north the beach of Gurgussum is a popular seaside resort. From Batsi, one can reach the large island of Dahlak, a natural park populated by gazelles and with hypnotic landscapes.

* The 127 islands and islets of the Dahlak Archipelago as well as the Hanish Archipelago are famous for their immaculate beaches and the richness of their seabed (eagle rays, black coral and hammerhead sharks). The most beautiful spots are located in Shumma, Nora and Isratu but also in Madote and Dissei.

* An old Abyssinian city perched at 2400 m above sea level, Asmara is established in one of the most beautiful urban sites in Africa. The imprint of the Italian colonization is very clearly visible there. Do not miss to visit the Guebbi, the former palace of Negus, now transformed into a museum. Keren is worth for its Fort and its religious sites. Between the two cities, you can stop at the monastery of Debre Sina.

* In the west of the country, on the river Barka, is the city of Agordat where it is the turn of Turkish and Egyptian architecture to take over. If you want to know more about this period, do not hesitate to visit the archaeological sites of Qohaito, Matara, Rora Habab and Adulis.

Ethiopia

Ethiopia is a country well apart, and many travelers do not suspect it. As the cradle of humanity, Ethiopia is one of Africa's unique destinations. A rather cool country (even cold in places because of the altitude), but which proves to be torrid in certain regions, mountainous as a whole but sometimes totally flat and desert, a sacred place of a religion (Rastafarianism) that it does not practice and which is essentially established on an island in the Caribbean (Jamaica), its language is unique (Amharic), and Ethiopia does not even live on the traditional 24-hour day, its days starting at 6am. The cultural identity is very strong in Ethiopia, and the country escapes all the pitfalls of tourism. The traveler will find himself there as if deposited on another planet. It is therefore advisable to be willing to explore and to be ready to go off the beaten track to travel in Ethiopia. The trip is accessible, with simple air connections (and one of the main airlines in Africa), easy domestic transport and adequate tourist infrastructure, but the adventure is almost always there.

* North of Addis Ababa, the 11 rock churches of the monastic city of Lalibela were carved out of the rock in the twelfth century and communicate with each other through narrow tunnels. The Madhane Alem Basilica has five naves making it the most majestic. In January, the Coptic Epiphany (Timkat) festival is a real event. From the end of June to early October, the site is closed due to the rains.

* Aqsum, in the north of the country, was the first capital of the Ethiopian kingdom. Its imposing granite stelae (up to 33.5 m high), the ruins of the Dongur Palace and the Church of St. Mary of Zion (reputed to be the home of the Ark of the Covenant) are not to be missed under any circumstances. Nearby you can visit the monastery of Debre Damo, the oldest in the country.

* 400 km north of Addis Ababa, Gondar is home to 44 ancient churches and royal castles from the 17th and 18th centuries, remnants of its imperial past. Churches and monasteries in the vicinity of Lake Tana are also worth seeing. Harar, in the east of the country, is an ancient fortified town with 99 mosques.

* The great Rift Valley that divides the Ethiopian Plateau in two, has drawn fabulous gorges and offers a spectacular chain of lakes (Ziway, Abiata, Langano, Shalla). In the vicinity of these live many varieties of birds, fishing eagles, flamingos, ibis and marabouts, which can be easily approached.

* The waterfalls offered by the Blue Nile at Tissat, the peaks of the Simen Park, the Sof Omar cave dug by the Ouebi Chebeli, volcanoes like Erta Ale, the Bale Mountain and the lakes of the Danakil depression are all great places not to be missed.

* Omo, Mago and Gambela National Parks in the southwest of the country are home to giraffes, lions, leopards, zebras, buffaloes, cheetahs, elephants, antelopes and many birds. Many photo safari possibilities are available to you. It is also possible to go up the Omo River by boat.

Gabon

An inexistent tourist image, health problems (virulent malaria, especially during the rainy season), a rather marked insecurity in the big cities (no night expeditions), here is the summary of a country which is not, if we can say so, on very good bases. To this situation must be added transports that are complex, with poor road infrastructure and an air circuit that must be avoided at all costs (apart from the major airlines for international connections). Logically, Gabon is not well known, but despite all this, it deserves to be. Its great attraction is the equatorial nature in all its splendor and luxuriance. The Lopé Park in particular is an absolutely exceptional site, especially for its fauna. The beauties of this rather difficult destination are reserved for experienced travelers and connoisseurs of equatorial Africa.

* In addition to the animals, the plant species that grow in the Gabonese forest are part of an exuberant natural spectacle that the government has been seeking to preserve since 2002 and the creation of the thirteen national parks that occupy 10% of the territory. Forests and savannas of the Lopé National Park, mangroves and sandy coasts of the Pongara National Park, or mountains of the Waka Park, there is something for everyone and the enchantment is renewed each time. It is the real jungle kingdom, a living and homogeneous organism where Man is a foreign body that will have to be accepted.

* The pirogue is a good means of locomotion to discover the country's landscapes. Embark on the waves of the Nyanga or the Ogooué. To tame the rapids, you will need a local guide and caution, but the spectacle is worth the candle.

* Mayumba is a small coastal town located in the south of Gabon in the Nyanga province. The bays and lagoons of the region sometimes welcome lute tortus and therefore some tourists.

* Port-Gentil is a port city bordered by magnificent beaches (Cap Lopez and Sogara sector). Swimming is also possible all year round in Ekwata or along the Pointe Denis, opposite Libreville. However, deep-sea fishing is the most popular activity in the region.

* Libreville is so called because it was founded in 1849 to welcome freed slaves. The city has retained the dynamism of the French colonial period. Visit the Mont Bouet market and venture into the Louis district where you will find restaurants and bars.

* Lambaréné is best known for its dispensary created by the famous Doctor Albert Schweitzer. A museum tells the history of the latter.

The Gambia

A country as unknown as it is small (and it is really not big for that matter), Gambia is rarely a stop on the travellers' path. Its attractions are modest but present, especially some beautiful beaches (but all is relative because they cannot compare to the beaches of East Africa) and a luxuriant African nature near the river that gives its name to the country. It is better to be well accustomed to independent stays and not to be apprehensive about entering the trip to fully enjoy the destination. The security situation does not pose a major problem, even if one has to use a lot of common sense, but the infrastructure is rather bad and the health situation is also bad.

* Banjul, the capital, is located on St. Mary's Island at the mouth of the Gambia River. It is extended on the coast by Serrekunda and it is in the very north-west of this one that the white sand beaches (Bakau, Fajara, Kotu and Kololi) extend while benefiting from one of the best climates of West Africa. Nevertheless, be careful, the currents can be dangerous.

* On the border of the S énégaland Gambia are the megalithic circles of Senegambia. More than 1000 volcanic rocks form 93 circles, they have been used at different times by ethnic groups and peoples of different cultures.

* Going up the river inland, you will be able to admire all the landscapes of The Gambia. You will cross different islands such as James Island, which was an important West African trading post for the slave trade, or the islets of Tanji, with a beautiful bird population.

* The Abuko reserve is full of plants, each one more amazing than the other. In addition to birds, you will be able to meet porcupines, monkeys, crocodiles and snakes of all kinds.

Ghana

This country with an average surface area includes a beautiful range of attractions of West Africa. However, it struggles to make a place for itself on the tourist scene. An English-speaking enclave in the middle of a large French-speaking region, Ghana, the former Gold Coast, suffers from an image deficit but this does not prevent it from being a recommended destination. Of appreciable stability for the region, the country possesses the animals, the nature, especially the great tropical forests, and the traditions that are the assets of West Africa. The meeting with the Achanti people, very famous for the talent of its craftsmen, the presence of attractive beaches and the originality of the site of the Volta Lake come to refine a very pretty picture for the travelers. An interesting destination, off the beaten track but accessible without too many complications, Ghana is nevertheless subject to the classic hazards of Africa: malaria and yellow fever, a generally very poor health situation, infrastructures in poor condition, especially roads.

* Kumasi is one of the main cities of the country, located in the south-central part of the country. It was the capital of the Ashantis and they are still the majority there. This population has preserved its customs and you will find its handicrafts (goldsmith's art and Kente fabrics) in the markets of Kumasi and the region. The traditional Ashantis buildings are visible in the northeast of Kumasi.

* Tamale is the capital of Ghana's Northern Region, and is predominantly populated by the Dagomba ethnic group. This city is a conglomeration of villages where the majority of the houses are made of clay. The markets are also famous there.

* On the Ghanaian coast, between Keta and Beyin, the remains of fortified trading posts founded between 1482 and 1786 remain, links in the commercial chains created by the Portuguese. These forts and castles bear witness to the slave trade.

• At 200 km from Accra, the villages of Dixcove and Bosua are the delight of adventurous tourists looking for relaxation and surfing.

• Mole National Park offers viewing of more than 100 species of mammals and reptiles, including the famous elephant. Kakum National Park also offers many safari opportunities.

• Lake Volta is the largest artificial lake in the world. You can take a cruise to discover its picturesque shores. It will take you 2 days by ferry to cross it from north to south.

Guinea

The one also called Guinea-Conakry, to differentiate it from the other Guineas, is a country heavily affected by the great African ills, and especially despite itself by the turmoil of its neighbors Sierra Leone and Liberia. However, the situation is clearly on the way to being cleared up, and the country seems to be able to make the most of its undeniable assets. It is even one of the most interesting countries on the continent, with traditions already widely exported (and with great success) to the West such as the djembe. Nature is also, as often in Africa, a real strong point, especially in the Fouta Djalon massif, a land prized by adventurers, the place of many explorers' tales, and which we see coming back in the offer of tour operators specializing in hiking. Guinea also has the luxury of offering with the islands of Los one of the few truly attractive seaside resorts in the region. That said, the country is still little exploitable by independent travelers, and as in most of Africa, only the connoisseurs, prepared and aware of the difficulties (health, infrastructure, stability) can go there in the immediate future.

• The territory of Guinea is one of the greenest of the whole African continent. From the Fouta Djalon massif, the kingdom of gallery forests (forming an arch over a river or stream), many rivers, including the Niger, flow into the landscape, adorning it with waterfalls during the rainy season. The best known are the Veil of the Bride, near Kindia, Ditinn, Kinkon and Tinkisso.

• Mount Nimba, the highest point in West Africa, is inscribed on the World Heritage List for its great ecological richness and to protect it from new mining operations. Hikes will make you discover the fauna and the particular landscapes of this place.

• Beaches exist on the mainland coast, including some magnificent spots on the Cape Verga peninsula, 200 km from Conakry, but it is the islands of Los that attract the most attention. In Kassa, Roume and Tamara, many water sports are practiced in an idyllic setting. Historical remains and the Fotoba penitentiary offer some pleasant possibilities for visits.

• Poachers and deforestation have caused animals such as elephants to disappear, but the fauna of the Badiar Park (which borders the *Niokolo-Koba* Park in the Sénégal) remains rich enough to amaze visitors. The giant turtles of the islands of Los, also rich in beautiful beaches, and the birds of the island of Alcatraz complete the animal picture of Guinea.

Guinea Bissau

This very small country is, alas, far too affected by an economic (it is a very poor country) and political (stability is very uncertain) slump to be able to appear on the tourist scene on a long-term basis. However, of the three Guineas it is always the one which receives the most visitors. Everything is relative that said, because tourism is low everywhere, and the trend is that Guinea-Conakry will soon assume this role. The Bijagos archipelago is an undeniable asset and the north of the country, if it were better equipped and more accessible, would be a great natural exploration ground. All this is only theoretical because the country can only receive today well-prepared adventurous tourists (and these usually choose other destinations). In addition, political laxity has led to the establishment of large international drug trafficking networks, which have a major impact on security in the country.

⁕ Eighty-eight islands and islets make up the Bijagos Archipelago, inhabited by various animist ethnic groups that have preserved much of their very complex culture. The southern islands are today a UNESCO nature reserve and are home to considerable marine (including sea turtles) and terrestrial fauna and flora, including the famous sea hippopotamus. The islands of Bubaque, Bolama and Caravela are the most populated and most visited while the island of Canhabaque is certainly the most "authentic" and the most secret. The interior of the islands is covered with forests of flamboyant and giant cheese makers where several species of rare monkeys sometimes live. Huge mangroves cover an important part of the spaces between ocean and land.

⁕ The tourism in the interior of the country is organized around the rio Corubal. You will be able to visit traditional villages, admire rapids and waterfalls like those of Cusselinta and observe the fauna of the region (birds and monkeys). The quality of the landscapes makes urban stays in second plan, nevertheless Bissau is an endearing city decorated with some traces of colonial art and a colorful and lively market. The one in Bafatá is also interesting.

Equatorial Guinea

Perfectly unknown on the tourist scene, Equatorial Guinea is well summed up by its name, very humid, warm, covered with a forest most often impenetrable. The lush nature could be a great asset, as much on the mainland of the country as on the island of Bioco, but the infrastructures, or rather their non-existence, prevent the trip. Only the true adventurers, accompanied, used to autonomy (and rain!) and fine connoisseurs of Africa, can envisage it, with the key to the meeting of a totally wild environment and its inhabitants (elephants, gorillas). It is a pity because the security is rather good and it is a relatively stable country. The country does not seem ready to develop in this area, preferring to exploit the economic windfall represented by its oil resources.

⁕ Opposite Cameroon is the island of Bioko, the largest island in the Gulf of Guinée. The coast, 195 kilometers long, is steep and indented in the south, lower and more accessible in the north, with well sheltered ports in Malabo, the capital with discreet colonial charm, and Luba. The latter offers in the surroundings beautiful beaches such as Arena Blanca.

⁕ Bata, a port city located near the Gulf of Guinéein the Rio Muni region, can be used as a base for day trips in the surrounding area. North and south of the city, you can admire some of the most beautiful beaches of Equatorial Africa, stop in small fishing villages or visit the small islands near the coast.

⁕ The equatorial forests cover nearly three-quarters of the country's mainland and are baffling in their humidity and complexity. Those who make the effort to venture there will be rewarded by the surprises that the Monte Alen National Park reserves for them, such as its fauna (elephants, lowland gorillas...), its specific flora and the waterfalls of the rivers Uoro and Lana.

Kenya

The great destination of East Africa, particularly renowned for its wildlife. Animals and safaris are the driving forces of tourism in Kenya, starting with the Masai-Mara Park, symbol of exoticism and synonymous with savannah Africa in the western world. The country also offers a beautiful complementary palette, Mount Kenya, as interesting as Mount Kilimanjaro or on the seaside with the beaches of the Indian Ocean. The access is easy, the travel too, but we must not forget that the country is undergoing social difficulties which invites caution, with some areas where the visit is excluded (in the north and with the border with Somalia), and a real insecurity in the capital Nairobi. No problem to travel there, as long as you have prepared a minimum your trip and do not turn exoticism into blind carelessness.

⁕ The heart of the country is made up of animal reserves that will take care of your camera's memory cards. The "Big

Five" (buffaloes, elephants, leopards, lions and rhinos) are gathered in the Masai-Mara National Reserve in the southwest of the country. Twice a year, one can admire the formidable migration of wildebeest and zebras through the savannah and the ballet of their predators. Other parks are also at your disposal: Tsavo Park, the largest in the country, that of Amboseli, and its panorama on Kilimanjaro, the Samburu Reserve, much less frequented, and the Aberdare National Park on the edge of the mountain.

* Always in the spirit of nature, the park of Nakuru welcomes gigantic colonies of pink flamingos and pelicans on its lake. For bird watching, lakes Baringo and Naivasha are sensational spots, as is Mfangano Island, on Lake Victoria, where nesting eagles, egrets and cormorants, among others, nest. Rock paintings dating back about 18,000 years will also surprise the visitor.

* The shores of the Indian Ocean also reserve you beautiful surprises. Diving and windsurfing are on the program. The Lamu archipelago, in the north, is an incredible place where beaches and exotic fruit plantations follow one another. Besides the tiny (and adorable) villages, the main town, Lamu, is an old city with winding streets that will immediately win your heart.

* In the south, around Mombasa, the Indian Ocean meets the coral reefs to create a favorite place for divers and idyllic beaches. While Diani beach is starting to be known by tourists, Tiwi beach remains quieter and new sites, such as the island of Chale, Shanzu and Galu Kinondo, are starting to make a reputation.

* Malindi, a traditional port town, is famous for its deep-sea fishing opportunities. In the area, you can relax on the long beaches of the village of Watamu and admire the Marafa Gorge, a spectacular depression forming a superb landscape. The forest of Arabuko Sokoke hides many animals, while following the trails, you will find the lost city of Gedi, a Swahili commercial town abandoned to vegetation.

* Mount Kenya, in the center of the country, is of particular importance to the people of the region and the entire country. Eight different trekking routes will take you to its peaks and meet the tribes (Kikuyu, Embu, Masai and Wakamba) who live on its slopes.

* To the north, Lake Turkana shines in the middle of a warm and desert region. The isolation of the region does not attract many tourists, yet great treks to meet the Gabbra, Rendille and Turkana are possible. To the west, it will be the turn of Mount Elgon to delight you with its surprising landscapes.

Lesotho

Far from the clichés of southern Africa, Lesotho is a truly unique destination. Occupying one of the most mountainous territories in South Africa, this small, very poor but welcoming country is nicknamed the Kingdom in the Clouds and it suits it perfectly. It is a country of great natural beauty, with some of the most beautiful African landscapes. Here, there is no savannah or great tropical forest, but a mountainous environment, where one travels more often on horseback than by car. Few travelers go to this country which is not difficult to access but where the infrastructure is of a very low level. Nevertheless, the destination does not present any major difficulties with a minimum of preparation. The discovery of Lesotho can easily be combined with a trip to South Africa. To be explored for those who wish to discover a new Africa.

* To the north is Holtse, a colonial-era tower, once used for archives. Here and in Quting, look for dinosaur footprints. Dinosaurs can also be found in the vicinity of Roma, a university town 34 kilometers southeast of Maseru, the capital, located in a beautiful gorge.

* The road from Holtse to Katse Dam is one of the highest in Africa and winds between magnificent peaks. In Katse Dam is the highest dam in Africa, which forms a lake where various water activities are beginning to develop. Numerous ferries connect the villages on either side of the shores.

* The Sehlabathebe National Park is the best known of the country's reserves, but is still very little visited. Located on more than 6000 hectares in the south-east of the country, it alternates aquatic spaces, high meadows and ghostly rocks and is full of natural surprises (waterfalls and natural pools), animals of all kinds (moose, baboons, jackals, wild cats and otters as well as rare birds).

* Thaba-Bosiu, to the east, is considered an important historical site because it was at the top of this "mountain of the night" that the great Moshoeshoe installed his fortified command post. Remains of the king's tomb and fortress can be seen on the site. Nearby, you will find the rock paintings of Ha Baroana.

* The Maletsunyane Falls in Semonkong fall along a 200-meter high basalt wall. Impressive in summer because of their flow, they are spectacular in winter when the cold transforms them into a long ribbon of ice, unusual for an African landscape. The Ketane Falls are a day's walk or horseback ride away.

* Sani Pass is a mountain pass road that connects the province of KwaZulu-Natal in South Africa and Lesotho. By car or mountain bike, you will admire the sumptuous panoramas of the region.

Liberia

Like its neighbor Sierra Leone, Liberia is a country with a troubled past and a relatively unstable present. The dark hours may be a thing of the past, but the equatorial beauties of this Africa of diamonds and rubber will not be revealed to casual travelers for some time to come. The capital, Monrovia, is an adventure in itself and the country's places of interest are generally not at all equipped for tourism. Lake Piso and Mount Nimba are beautiful areas of discovery, offering the attractions of West Africa, but only the most seasoned travelers will be able to afford to think about them.

* Mount Nimba National Park is an area of great ecological wealth. Its slopes, which dominate the surrounding savannas, are covered with a dense forest that hides a particularly rich flora and fauna.

* The beaches of Buchanan, the second most important port of the country, will be able to make the happiness of the future travellers who will however be careful while bathing, because the ocean can be very dangerous there.

* The swamps of Lake Piso, one of the largest lagoons in Africa, are home to thousands of animal species, including many birds and all kinds of fish. In addition to bird watching and trekking opportunities in the area, fishing and water sports made it a popular destination before the civil war.

* The Kpatawi Falls, Sapo National Park, Providence Island and Monrovia's Waterside Market are some of the other attractions in the country, where nothing is really developed for tourism.

Libya

It is difficult today to conceive of any form of tourism in Libya, a country already fragile that imploded in the civil war. The situation there is anarchic, with several forms of power fighting each other, and security is precarious. In addition, the infrastructure is weak. Even travelers who are perfectly familiar with both complex destinations and deserts no longer venture there for the moment. In times of peace, the attractions of the country are real, starting with its desert character and several archaeological sites with in point of organ the Roman city of Leptis Magna.

* The Fezzan desert is the extension of the tassili N'Ajjer located in Algérie. This part of the Sahara is an undeniable attraction. In addition to the magnificent landscapes of rounded dunes and steep gorges, sites such as Garama or Ghadames attract visitors. The engravings and rock paintings of the first testify to the passage of the *Garamantes* while the ruins and the labyrinth of alleys of the second are characteristic of the oases.

• Built on a piece of rocky territory that juts out into the Mediterranean Sea, Tripoli is the capital and main port of the country. A city of character, it has a number of attractions. The As-saraya al-Hamra, the Red Castle, is a vast labyrinth of courtyards, alleys and buildings that have spanned the centuries and dominate the skyline. The nearby Jamahiriyya Museum is well worth a visit for its mosaics, among other things. The medina, the old fortified city, is in the heart of the current city, and hides within it one of the most authentic souks of the Maghreb. As for the rest of the country, the extent of the destruction linked to the conflicts may have left significant scars in the city.

• On the outskirts of the capital are two sites of renown in terms of archaeology. In Sabratha you will find the largest Roman theater in Africa and in Leptis Magna there are many (and sumptuous) monuments from the same period. The surrounding beaches are havens of tranquility, water sports activities develop south of Tripoli and the diving sites of Leptis Magna are notable.

• Benghazi also has beautiful wild beaches in its surroundings and it is an ideal starting point to visit the Jebel Akhdar mountains with lush vegetation and Roman ruins along the coast. Indeed, the ruins of Tolmeita near Ptolemais, the temples of Zeus and Demeter in Cyrene, and the remains of the Greek city of Appolonia follow one another, interspersed with beautiful beaches. In Appolonia, the submerged ruins offer fascinating diving spots.

Madagascar

Madagascar is not a destination within the reach of all travelers, and requires a good dose of patience and common sense. Even to the most established destinations (Nosy Be, Sainte-Marie Island), the traveler will have to "dive" into the destination. However, even though it is one of the poorest countries in the world, with poor infrastructure, and where it is often very complicated to get around (often difficult network of tracks), the island is still easily accessible and there are no real obstacles to tourism for the discerning traveler. Beyond the problems of the country, the island always fascinates by its exceptional natural characteristics, which make it a real continent in miniature, where everything is unique (fauna, flora, landscapes). A destination so special that no traveler can decently remove it from his list at the risk of missing a magnificent country, but which should not be taken lightly.

• The Amber Mountain National Park at the northern tip of the country is home to a tropical rainforest inhabited by tree and epiphytic ferns and seven species of lemurs. Following forest roads such as the Thousand Tree Path, you will encounter several waterfalls, one of which falls from a height of 80 m and surprising crater lakes.

• The Special Reserve of Ankarana also has a very rich fauna, but it is worth especially for its 25 km long limestone wall formed of rocks of coral origin that erosion has admirably carved. The immense corridors of the Andrafiabe caves offer sumptuous atypical walks. The same Tsingy formations can be found in the Tsingy National Park of Bemaraha.

• The volcanic islands of the Nosy Be archipelago are considered as the pearls of the Indian Ocean. From the village of Ambatoloaka, you will be able to undertake various excursions to discover the flamboyant and ylang-ylangs, and the beaches and lagoons suitable for diving. This paradise knows however two major problems, that of sexual tourism (that the government has difficulty to control in the whole country) and the risks of aggression against the tourists (which multiplied its last years).

• Twenty minutes by pirogue from Nosy Be, Nosy Komba has a much more carefree atmosphere. The tropical forest which covers the island shelters many families of lemurs (makis). The island of Nosy Tanikely, also nearby, has a magnificent coral reserve which will make the happiness of the divers.

• Toliara is a city located south of the west coast of the country and is known for its quiet beaches and rich coral reefs. In the hinterland, an original vegetation grows and several spots are to be visited: the banian of Miary, a royal village of the Masikoro ethnic group, the arboretum of Antsokay and its thousand endemic plants, the sacred cave of Sarodrano and its freshwater basin.

* About sixty kilometers southeast of Toliara are the Seven Sacred Lakes of Ifanato. There are actually about twenty of them on the side of the limestone plateau overlooking the river. Their waters shelter a vegetation that gives them a surreal white color. Even further south is the Mitaho Abyss, a tourist site located near Lake Tsimanampetsotsa relatively easy to access.

* Antananarivo is the economic, cultural, and administrative center of the country. Built on hills, it unrolls its tiled roofs before the eyes of the traveler. This one will not fail to visit the Analekely district, the Palais d'Argent, the zoological park and the Zoma, the big central market.

* Antisrabé is located at an altitude of 1,500 m in a basin surrounded by volcanoes and has the coolest climate in the whole country (and even cold in winter). Many thermal and mineral springs make its reputation. Lake Tritriva, a few kilometers away, is known for its opaque and mysterious green color. It is forbidden to swim there, but the beauty of the site and its legends are worth the detour.

* The landscapes of the Isalo National Park are grandiose. Deep canyons, refreshing rivers and vegetation on rock are offered to the eyes of travelers. From Ranohira, the excursion to the "natural swimming pool" is the most accessible. Treks in the Canyon of the Monkeys (to meet the lemurs) or the Canyon of the Rats (to reach the caves of the Portuguese) will test the bravest. Don't worry, you will also be able to discover the region by taking one of the rivers that cross it, a much easier route.

* The bay of Diego-Suarez is one of the most beautiful bays in the world, in the vein of Rio de Janeiro. It is composed of four smaller coves, the southeastern one being known for its rocky islet called Sugar Loaf, a sacred place where many fijoroana (traditional ceremonies) take place.

* The island of Nosy Boraha (ex Sainte-Marie) is famous for being an ancient pirate's lair in the 18th century. Its humid micro climate gives it a luxuriant vegetation where spices hold the foreground. Lemurs and orchids are part of the island's heritage as much as its coral reefs which make it a first class dive site in the Indian Ocean. The postcard beaches, against a backdrop of tropical forest, attract a good number of visitors, favored by developed tourist structures. Ile aux Nattes, in the south of the island, is one of the most beautiful seaside sites in the Indian Ocean.

* From the capital, you can take the railroad that leads to Taomasina and get a magnificent view of the country. Around this port criss-crossed by rickshaws, you will find many tourist sites such as Foulpointe known for its beaches and historical sites (Fort Manda, tomb of Prince Ramiango).

* The difference in altitude between the Highlands and the intermediate plateau offers the rivers that cross the country the possibility to create beautiful waterfalls like those of the Onive River that runs to the narrow precipices of Ambavaloza and Andremamovoka.

* The city of Fianarantsoa is worth the detour for its exceptional position on the high plateaus. Its long paved street, stairs, small paths and old houses make it a pleasant stopover. In the region, tea plants have harmoniously colonized the reliefs surrounding the valley bottoms occupied by checkerboard rice fields and small lakes.

* The massif of Andringitra, in the southeast of the country, gathers the greatest concentration of known species of lemurs. Lunar landscapes, caves and sacred waterfalls... several circuits make it possible to discover the various richnesses. On the west face of the park, the Tsaranoro cliff is a world famous climbing spot.

* The nature reserve of Berenty, on the south bank of the Mandrare, is known for its lemurs, but it is also home to turtles, giant lizards and butterflies of all kinds. In the same region, around Tôlanaro (Fort-Dauphin), there are many sites not to be missed: the creeks of Lokaro and their islets suitable for underwater exploration, the lake of Vinanibe and its fishing villages, the Pic Saint Louis which dominates the entire region, the beach of Libanona and the Bay of Galleons, and the sacrificial sites of the Antanosy culture.

Malawi

A country to be ranked on the podium in the group of superb and relatively accessible places, but whose name is known to very few travelers. One knows perhaps better the great lake which bears its name and which is one of the major landscapes of the African continent. In addition to the lake, the country also offers the attraction of its tropical mountains, forests that breathe adventure and the fauna of southern Africa that meets the appointment. It is hard to believe that Malawi does not have beautiful tourist days ahead of it, even if the road to recognition is still long and the infrastructure still limited. For travelers who want to discover a welcoming and unspoiled Africa, Malawi is starting to make its way into the brochures of tour operators.

• Lake Malawi is considered one of the most beautiful lakes in Africa. Its shores are one of the main tourist attractions of the country. One can practise a great number of nautical activities there, particularly between the beaches of Nkhata Bay and those of Senga Bay. The fishing villages that dot its coastline and the few rocky escarpments that interrupt its beaches punctuate the landscape.

• Nyika Plateau National Park is located in the north, on the border with Zambia. Leopards, zebras, and antelopes can be found in these vast grasslands. The Kasungu Park in the center of the country and the Lengwe Park in the south also rival their African neighbors in terms of wildlife and exoticism.

• The plateau of Zomba, 70 km north of Blantyre, is one of the prettiest sites in the country. The top of this granite massif is accessible by car and it is also possible to go around it by 4x4. Shady pine forests, small refreshing streams... It is not surprising that the English elected it as a holiday resort in the 19th century. Today, you will meet mostly birds, baboons and maybe leopards.

• In the south-east of the country, in the heart of the city of Mulanje, stands Mount Mulanje, which at 3002 meters is the highest point in Southern Africa. Its plateaus crossed by numerous rivers and streams offer visitors sumptuous landscapes with spectacular waterfalls. Summits such as Chambe or Sapitwa will delight climbing fans and photographers.

Mali

Mali is a great country of adventure, a promised land for travel in Saharan Africa. The desert is majestic, as are the traditions, and the south of the country adds the attraction of greener regions where the African fauna is present. The Dogon country around the mythical cliffs of Bandiagara, the old town of Djénné, a city of pure exoticism, or Mopti, the Malian Venice, are all stages of great interest that mark out the country. The experience of the most famous desert in the world, all at ease in Mali, is also one of the highlights of the trip in the country, whether on the tracks, often difficult, or far from everything during camel trekking. If Mali is unique, it is unfortunately now away from the tourist roads. Already a very complex destination, due to the lack of infrastructure (almost non-existent almost everywhere, few roads, complicated transportation), the harsh climate or the very poor social and health development, Mali has been affected by religious terrorism for the past few years. While the southern region is less exposed, the situation is to be monitored everywhere. Under normal circumstances, the country is already reserved for seasoned or accompanied travelers.

• Gao, capital of the seventh region, is located on the Niger River and was on the route of the caravans carrying out trans-African trade. In the 15th century, the emperor of Songhai, *Askia Mohamed*, had a pyramidal tomb built there, which is now a World Heritage Site. You can also visit the Sahel museum and admire the sunset on the pink dune at the gates of the desert.

• Still following the river comes Timbuktu, much more difficult to reach by car. This city, crossroads between the Sahara and Niger had its heyday in the 16th century and is now threatened by the advancing dunes. Three mosques bear witness to the city's rich past. The mud houses (made of banco, a mixture of clay and straw) adorned with stone, the funnel-shaped crops around the wells and the proximity of the desert make it a fantastical stopover.

• Mopti is a city, located at the confluence of the Niger and its tributary the Bani, nicknamed the "Venice of Mali" because of its numerous pirogues. The frenetic activity of its port, its traditional fish market, its large mosque covered with banco and the many traditional villages in the surrounding area are a fascinating dive into arid Africa.

• Djenne is built on an island between two arms of the Bani river and is at the hinge between the nomadic and sedentary worlds. Its Great Mosque makes the reputation of it, because it is the largest monument in the world built in banco. The typical architecture of the other buildings of the city has made the city inscribed on the World Heritage List.

• Bamako, the capital, is perhaps a little less original than the other big cities of the country, but its position on the river and its markets (the Pink Market and the one in Medina) make it a place full of life at the center of the country's activity. It is also, by far, the best equipped and most modern city in Mali.

• Niger is a fascinating river that runs through the interior of the country. Boats that criss-cross the river from August to November offer an excellent way to discover the interior of the country. The traditions of fishermen and dyers, the fantastic animation and the total change of scenery in the ports, the herds of *Fulani* and *Moors*, and the thousands of birds that populate the reeds will punctuate your trip.

• The Adrar des Ifoghas is a mountainous massif located in the northeast of the country, it is the historic crossing point between the Maghreb and the Sahel. Trekking will lead you to discover these granite landscapes where ruins of ancient cities (Es-Souk), paintings and rock carvings (representation of the chariots of the ancient people of Garamantes), gueltas (water basins) and Tuareg camps will brighten your path.

• The Bandiagara Cliff is a long sandstone range in the southeast of the country that offers extraordinary panoramas to those who come to its feet. In addition to these, the incredible richness of the Dogon culture and imagination is what most tourists come to discover. Hikes will take you from hamlet to hamlet (Kani-Kembolé, Enndé, Dourou, Nombori, Tirelli, Yayé, Banani, Tiogou, the three Youga, Atô and Bongo) to meet the people, their traditions (such as the mask dance) and fascinating customs.

• In the southwest of the country, the Baoulé, a tributary of the S énégalriver, forms a loop. The presence of many permanent water points attracts a diverse fauna, especially during the dry season, from October to May. The Boucle du Baoulé National Park is thus the main wildlife reserve of the country (hyenas, hippos, hipotragues). In addition, this region has an important archaeological heritage with more than 200 listed sites.

• South-east of Kayes, the river S énégalflows into the Talary gorges from a height of 15 to 25 meters with the Manding Mountains in the background. The latter, further south, have caves and spectacular ruiniform rocks such as the Kamandjan Arch near the village of Siby.

Morocco

It's been a long time since Morocco settled in the role of the great tourist destination of the Maghreb. More than Tunisia, which has relied exclusively on beach tourism for the general public, Morocco has managed to impose its mix of culture, tradition and landscapes, while retaining one last ace in its game: its coastline. Carried by a centerpiece, Marrakech, and supported by a profusion of sites (Meknes, Fez, Essaouira), Moroccan tourism is one of the most complete in Africa. Large cosmopolitan city (Casablanca), distinguished capital (Rabat), wild mountains, stretches of desert and oasis, beaches and winter sun (Agadir), you will find a bit of everything in Morocco. The access is very simple, the trip too, while remaining exotic and exotic.

• Of all Moroccan cities, the most touristy is Marrakech which sees every year new riads open their doors to travelers. The *medina is* the historic center of the city, it has a refined and original architecture. To its ramparts, gardens and souks, come to be added jewels like the *minaret of the Koutoubia* or the *medersa Ben-Youssef*. The folklore shows and the animation of the *Jamâa El Fna square* make it a place not to be missed.

- Fez has the largest medina in the world where the deep blue of the ceramics shines since the 12th century. Spiritual and cultural capital of Morocco, it is less easy to approach than Marrakech, but in fact tells its story at every corner of the 2000 streets of the labyrinth that composes it. Mosques, medersas, fondouks, fountains and gardens follow one another until the thirst is quenched.

- Rabat, the country's capital, is located on the country's Atlantic coast and offers a range of socially differentiated neighborhoods, but major architectural projects are transforming the face of the city. The small fortified district of the *Kasbah des Oudaïa* and the architectural quality of its main door are a must see.

- The last of the imperial cities is Meknes and is the least known of the four, as many of its monuments have been destroyed. Today, various restoration operations are in the process of bringing it up to the level of its sisters. The *Bouanania Medersa*, the *Mausoleum of Ismail I*, and the *Bab al-Mansur Gate* are all masterpieces waiting for you there.

- In addition to these four cities, Morocco has many other cities to offer to tourists. Essaouira, for example, is among those that attract the most visitors. The white city lined with red ramparts and set in the blue of the Atlantic Ocean has made more than one lover of its landscapes fall in love with it. The Portuguese fortifications of Safi, the old city of Tangier, its white streets like the Andalusian villages, its promontory on the Mediterranean, the archaeological remains of Moulay-Idriss and the cosmopolitan and urban appeal of Casablanca also make it a pleasant and interesting destination.

- The Atlantic coast of Morocco guarantees sun and white sand all year round. Agadir is the torchbearer with its nine kilometers of beach and its many hotels and vacation clubs. If idleness enthusiasts can sunbathe there even in winter, surfers also meet there to challenge the waves of the Pointe des Ancres. To vary the pleasures, don't forget that south of the city is the wadi surrounded by dunes of the Souss-Massa National Park where thousands of birds live in complete tranquility.

- Continuing southward, the coast that connects Agadir to Dakhla is nicknamed the "White Beach". This region is an exceptional spot for windsurfers and kitesurfers from all over the world. The spot of Foum Labouir is very famous for its perfect wave. The fishermen also find their happiness there, because even from the seaside you can make impressive catches.

- The Rif is the mountainous region in the north of the country. There are many possibilities for hiking in search of hidden treasures, both animal and geological. For example, the Kef Thogobeit is the deepest mountain chasm in Africa that will delight caving enthusiasts.

- The High Atlas peaks at 4000 meters and is the highest massif in North Africa. The plateaus, gorges and canyons of the central High Atlas offer sumptuous landscapes and the Berber populations living there are renowned for their hospitality. The cliffs of Amesfrane, the gorges of the Wadi Dades, but also the palm groves and rose gardens of the region contribute to this reputation.

- On the slopes of the Middle Atlas extend as far as the eye can see cedar forests that sometimes alternate with volcanic plateaus and often with turquoise lakes and waterfalls. Fans of hiking and fishing will find in this region what to spend a wonderful stay. Ifrane National Park is one of the most beautiful places in Morocco.

- The Anti-Atlas also offers sublime mineral panoramas to hikers. If the summits culminate there up to 2000 and 3300 meters, the landscapes already announce the Sahara, lush oases are hidden in this grandiose scenery. From Ouarzazate and its Kasbah of Glaoui, ksours and plantations follow one another to lead to the gates of the desert.

Mauritius

A star among the stars of seaside tourism in the Indian Ocean, Mauritius is a tropical postcard whose image is perfectly in tune with Tahiti, Hawaii and the Seychelles. Having made the choice to focus on high-end tourism, Mauritius has also become one of the must-go destinations for honeymooners. Tropical climate (which however retains in these latitudes a cooler season quite distinct), coconut palms, white sand, turquoise lagoon, and hotels with large stands, the contract is respected but the country also deserves to be discovered for its mixed culture with strong Indian accents, some landscapes that are worth the detour (the Morne, the gorges of the Black River), and a joie de vivre that is not a cliché. Hard to resist in front of this tropical cocktail all in colors and softness. Few of its many visitors are aware of the island's proximity to the French department of Reunion Island (200 kilometers separate them), and the two "sister" islands are an almost perfect combination of nature and beach.

* The northwest coast, sheltered from the wind, is the most frequented coast of the island. Grand Baie, Pointe aux Piments, Pointe aux Canonniers, Trou aux Biches... So many evocative names where you can practice relaxation and water sports. For those who wish to vary the pleasures, the eastern beaches are much wilder, just as spectacular if not more (around Belle Mare), but windier. The Morne Brabant region, in the south-west, offers a crossbreeding of the other regions of the island and offers the natural attraction of the Morne Mountain, a World Heritage Site. In the south, on the Souillac side, swimming is no longer an option, with high volcanic cliffs rising up from the beaches, but the landscapes remain sumptuous (sites of *Gris-Gris* and *La Roche qui Pleure*). In addition, the Souillac marine cemetery is worth a visit.

* Ile aux Cerfs, in the east of the island, is extremely touristy. Accessible in a few minutes of crossing, it is uninhabited and entirely dedicated to water sports. Its beaches are paradisiac and those who move away from the landing stages will find peace and quiet. Further offshore and spread out on the coasts, the other islands, Round Island, Snake Island, Marianne, Periwinkles Island and Amber Island are great spots for birdwatching, but especially for diving. The seabed of the entire lagoon and the coral reef are indeed famous for their clarity and colorful fauna. If you don't go scuba diving, don't worry, between the glass bottom boats, the underwater walk and the water safaris by submarine you will find a way to go and admire the beauties of the sea more closely. In some places the reef is a bit damaged unfortunately.

* From the volcanic origins of the island remain dormant craters, including the Trou aux Cerfs, one of the inland tourist attractions. This crater, where a small lake sleeps, has lush vegetation and offers a panoramic view of the surrounding areas. It is possible to go around the crater by road and descend via trails.

* The flora of Mauritius is particularly remarkable. The garden of Pamplemousses is the most beautiful example. More than five hundred plant species grow there. Talipots, giant water lilies, flamboyant, bougainvillea and palm trees are there. The orchards of La Bourdonnais have a wide variety of tropical fruit trees and exotic flowers that you can discover by bike. The gentle relief of the island, following a long erosion, has allowed, among other things, the cultivation of sugar cane and it is through a few rum tastings that you can appreciate the quality of the rum.

* Many other sites will allow you to vary idleness and adventure. The *Chamarel adventure park* in the heart of the tropical forest, the seven-colored land of Chamarel and the nearby waterfalls, the Black River Gorges National Park and its wild tropical and mountainous landscapes (hiking), the giant turtles and crocodiles of the *Vanilla Park Mascarene Reserve*, the Grands-Bois and Val domains and the Rochester waterfalls are all tourist experiences.

* The cities of Mauritius are always very lively during the day. Port-Louis, the capital, has seen its colonial center transformed under the effect of economic development. Its few buildings dominate an exciting market, bustling streets (during the day) and a waterfront redeveloped into a large shopping center (the Caudan). Its atmosphere close to a small Indian town, less chaotic, makes it a city with a change of scenery. Grand Bay is a seaside resort, which has become a real city, very busy and commercial. It is in Mahébourg, in the south, that you can find the charm of the small Mauritian villages, especially in its market. To go shopping, you will have to overcome traffic jams and cope with the rain, almost daily, in the towns of the central plateau, the true heart of Mauritius, Curepipe, Rose-Hill and Quatre-Bornes, where

most of the shopping centers (and the population of the island) are located. For a more historical approach, the colonial residence Eureka, in the heights of Port Louis, allows you to discover the past of the island.

RODRIGUES :
The smallest of the three islands of the Mascarene archipelago, is located 560 km east of Mauritius and is much less touristic than its big sister.

• Rodrigues is an ideal island to rest. It is a small island, very Creole (where Mauritius is very Indian), where you move around a lot on foot and where everyone says hello. The climate is a little warmer and a little drier than in Mauritius and tourists are much less numerous. The beaches are just as beautiful and the hotels are much more intimate. The hotels Mourouk Ebony, Cotton Bay and Pointe Vénus have a diving center, ideal to discover the gigantic lagoon, twice as big as the island itself!

• To the north is the village of Anse aux Anglais, which is worth seeing for the spectacle of its sunset over its lagoon which dries up completely at low tide during the high tide seasons. Port Mathurin, the small capital of the island, is a quiet and picturesque town. Still to the north, the village of Baie aux Huîtres also sees the tourism industry gradually developing.

• In the south of the island, the owners of the Vanilla Réserve des Mascareignes in Mauritius opened a giant turtle reserve and reintroduced 500 Aldabra turtles and 40 star turtles. More than 100,000 shrubs and trees of 33 indigenous and endemic species have been planted. Two of the 26 limestone caves in the area have been rehabilitated: the Caverne-de-la-Vierge and the Grande Caverne, whose eleven caves are decorated with superb concretions.

Cargados Carajos, Agalega, Chagos Archipelago: *These islands are very sparsely populated and tourism is non-existent because there is no regular transportation to get there.*

• The archipelago of Cargados Carajos is better known under the name of Saint-Brandon, it includes about thirty islets located 390 km north-east of Mauritius. Albatross, Chicken house, Water well, St Brandon, Siren ... About forty islands make up this archipelago which is an important sanctuary for turtles and many bird species.

• Agalega is even more distant from Mauritius, as it is located 1,070 km north of the latter. Of coral origin, it consists of two islets, North Island and South Island, connected by a sandy isthmus. Only 300 people live there, mainly in the villages of Vingt-Cinq and La Fourche on the North Island and Sainte Rita on the South Island.

• The Chagos Archipelago has been part of the British Indian Ocean Territory since 1965, but is claimed by the Republic of Mauritius. About 1'700 military and 1'500 civilians of American, Mauritian, Sri Lankan and Filipino origin, working under contract, live temporarily on the atoll of Diego Garcia. Moreover, part of the rest of the archipelago is a strict natural sanctuary where any human presence is prohibited.

Mauritania

An unfortunate example among so many others in Africa, Mauritania is a true promise of exoticism and beauty, which unfortunately is moving further away every day from its tourist opening. In this troubled region, what was possible only a few years ago is no longer possible, such as stays in the desert to discover the fabulous Adrar plateau and the city of Chinguetti. What a pity! Especially for the Mauritanian people who have an ancestral culture and a kindness reputed among travelers. Adventure in this country is omnipresent. An adventure that has become dangerous because of terrorism and local instability. There are always tour operators present in Mauritania but the trip, whose highlights are the desert around Chinguetti and the Banc d'Arguin on the coast, is far from guaranteed. As a solo traveler, it is better to have a very solid experience and a preparation which is not less solid. Reason dictates to postpone the trip to this astonishing country, the absolute kingdom of the desert.

• The plateau of Adrar is a fabulous desert region where the beauty of the landscapes is equaled only by the kindness of the inhabitants. From Atar to Tidjikja, the tracks will lead you to spectacular sites: the mountain passes of Ebnou and Amodjar, the rock paintings discovered by Theodore Monod, the immense dunes of Erg Maghtir, the salted lakes Sebket Chemchâm or the enigma of Guelb er Richat and the ruins of Fort Saganne. At the end of the journey, often, the city of Chinguetti, ancient holy city of Islam. The formidable libraries where manuscripts dating from the Middle Ages are kept and the entire city are threatened by the inexorable advance of the desert.

* Further south, the Tagant plateau and its cliffs are the last rampart before the Sahel. Apart from a Moorish population and many nomads, it is really not sure that you will meet other travelers there. On your way you will come across some Neolithic villages and if you push to 865 km east of the capital, the ghost town of Tichit and its 16th century remains will dazzle you. On the caravan route, it once had more than 5000 inhabitants, but today only 500 remain. From the splendour of the past emerges a superb mosque surrounded by sand and dried-up vegetation.

* South of Nouadhibou and as far as Nouamghar, on the edge of the ocean, is the Banc d'Arguin National Park where millions of migratory birds are found every year. The waters here are dotted with small sandy islands where, between October and March, herons, flamingos and sandpipers nest. With the help of a guide, a permit from the National Park Authority and a small boat, you can discover their secrets. Small bonus: in the park and its surroundings, dolphins, sharks, killer whales and the last monk seals also live.

* If you are looking for a more classic beach where you can rest with all your emotions, head for the sandy bays of Le Lévrier and Tanit. They are still little known even though the fishing possibilities are attracting more and more people. The port city of Nouadhibou is located just north of the first one and you can even practice water skiing there.

* Nouakchott is a recent capital, yet the desert has already caught up with it. The main attractions of the city are its central market where all the country's handicrafts are spread out and its port where men and women are active around the country's main resource: the sea. Apart from that, the National Museum will give you a better understanding of the nomadic way of life and you can admire the carpets woven by hand by the women of the country at the National Carpet Office.

* Koumbi Saleh is undoubtedly one of the most important medieval sites of the ancient empire of Ghana. Located 1,000 km from Nouakchott, a two-hour drive from the town of Koumbi Saleh, the site reveals its sandy vastness, from which an imposing mosque and a few other buildings made of shale or stone have been excavated. Deposit of salt and gold until the 12th century, it sheltered at its peak more than 30 000 inhabitants. The extent of the site is impressive, but the excavations had to be stopped in the 80s due to lack of means.

Mayotte

Strange territory that Mayotte, a small island in the Comoros, which has become a French overseas department despite the disapproval of the international community. Island of (relative) prosperity in an ocean of great misery, in practice it is a superb site, surrounded by an idyllic lagoon, with fragrant tropical vegetation that has earned it the nickname of the island of perfumes. Despite the possibility of direct flights from Paris, France, visitors are quite rare. The cost of tourist living, limited infrastructure (of questionable quality) and a reputation for social instability mean that tourism remains confidential.

* The northern coast of Grande Terre, from Mamoudzou to Mliha, has some very beautiful beaches. From the tip of Handréma, you can discover on foot the small creeks that cut the peninsula. Then go to the fishing village of M'tsamboro from where you can reach by pirogue the Choizil islets where the beaches are superb. Between July and October, several kinds of whales come to give birth in the protected waters of the lagoon. You can see species that measure up to 30 meters.

* In addition to its forty or so beaches, Mayotte is especially noteworthy for its seabed where corals of all shapes and sizes and a wide variety of tropical fish abound in a huge lagoon with safe waters. The particularity of the latter is to have a double reef barrier. The first one is far from the coast and goes practically all around the island, interrupting itself

for a few passes, including the S-shaped pass, which is world famous in the diving world. The second one, at 200 or 300 m from the shore, accessible without any difficulty with fins, mask and snorkel, is also very beautiful (especially in the south, around the peninsula of Sazilé, south of Bouéni, in the west, off the beaches of Tsohoa, Mliha... and around the islets of Bandrélé and Bambo).

• To discover the inland, take the road to Combani from Mamoudzou. This walk along the ylang-ylang fields will lead you to the village of Vahibé which lives from the distillation of this plant, much used by the great perfumers. You will then arrive at a small forest track that leads to Bouyouni where it is common to meet wild pigs. Then comes the town of Combani near which you can visit the Guerlain plantation where the perfumer cultivates several hectares of ylang-ylang.

• In the center of Petite Terre, the Dziani Dzaha Lake is a testimony to the intense volcanic activity that gave birth to Petite Terre. One can walk around the crater to admire both the green color of the sulfurous water and the nearby lagoon. You can then descend to the beautiful beaches of Moya where you can see turtles.

Mozambique

Facing the Indian Ocean, rich in Portuguese colonial heritage, with the riches of southern Africa (fauna and flora), Mozambique is a destination still confidential but quite exciting. The country is developing little by little, starting with its coastline and particularly the islands. Tourist access is relatively simple, even if the difficulties of Africa apply to it, but the infrastructures remain limited and it is still a journey that is reserved for explorers, at least in spirit. Nevertheless, the country continues to open up and it could be one of the great African destinations of tomorrow.

• Between Maputo and the Tropic of Capricorn, the long coast open to the Mozambique Channel offers sumptuous beaches such as Inhambane, Xai-Xai and Bilene. Palm trees and white sand are there. Numerous diving sites will also delight underwater life enthusiasts in Ponta d'Ouro, Ilha da Inhaca, Barra, Bazaruto and Pemba. Fishing (between Ponta d'Ouro and Inhassoro) and surfing (Ponta d'Ouro and Tofinho) are also possible. The islands also offer beautiful idleness spots, especially the two archipelagos of Bazaruto, in the south, and Quirimbos (much less developed), in the north. Postcard landscapes are on the program, and quite comfortable resorts are starting to appear.

• You can also visit the island of Mozambique near Nacala. In addition to beautiful beaches, there are the Palace of St. Paul, the very interesting Museum of Sacred Art and the Fortress of San Sebastian. The coastal cities have kept some remains of the Portuguese colonization. In Maputo, a certain charm emanates from this fact. Moreover, the capital's colourful markets and nightlife have regained a festive atmosphere resembling the one that led to the country being nicknamed "the Cuba of Africa" in the middle of the last century.

• Many nature reserves were emptied during the civil war, but they are now being repopulated for the happiness of travelers. Most of the elephants, buffaloes, zebras are found in the Niassa reserves in the extreme north of the country and in the Maputo reserve. The most beautiful landscapes of the country are on the shores of Lake Malawi surrounded by peaks that reach nearly 2000 m. It is an unknown site in Africa but is certainly one of the strong points of the continent.

Namibia

Namibia is one of those little-known countries that doesn't even really convey clichés because nobody knows where they stand. The reality is that Namibia is one of the most beautiful countries in Africa, and it is a welcoming destination that is easy to explore, if not cheap. Namibia is similar to its neighbor South Africa in many ways, atmosphere, lifestyle, towns and cities (more modern than you might think, especially the capital Windhoek), without being too much affected by the social problems of the latter (much better security in Namibia than in South Africa). Both emblematic of Africa and rich in particularities (its Atlantic coast, mysterious, the Kalahari Desert) make it a recommended destination for those who already know the continent's best known countries and are looking for unique landscapes.

• Etosha National Park is the great natural reserve of the country. Stretching over 20,000 km, it opens a third of its territory to visitors from mid-March to the end of October. 114 species of mammals, 340 varieties of birds, 16 species of reptiles and amphibians and countless varieties of insects await you on this dry salt lake. You will be able to spend the night in different lodges, especially in the Namutoni camp, a former German fortress. Damaraland, a former Bantustan, and the Waterberg National Park are also two sites famous for their wildlife.

• The country has many other animal surprises in store for you. At Cape Cross, between the Namib and the Atlantic Ocean, is the largest of the 15 colonies of fur seals (more than 6 million individuals). The lagoon of Walvis Bay is home to more than 120,000 birds (including many flamingos and pelicans) which are joined by 200,000 others during the great migrations. As far as flora is concerned, Namibia is rich in rare species such as the welwitschia, a living fossil from the coastal desert, or the kokerboom, a giant aloe that grows on the rocks of the forest of the same name.

• The old Namib Desert along the coast offers several grandiose sites in terms of landscapes. In the southern part of the Kuiseb river is a huge area of mobile dunes which are among the highest dunes in the world like the 375 meter high Sossusvlei dunes. Hiking there is becoming more and more fashionable, as on the routes of the Naukluft massif in the north or further south in the heart of the bare rocks of the Fish River Canyon. A sublime 85 km trail follows the sandy bed of the Fish River to reach the hot springs of Ai-Ais.

• In the northwest of the country, Kaokoland is a completely wild region where the semi-nomadic Himbas live. The coast of this region is continuously plunged in the fog and is nicknamed the "Skeleton Coast", the graveyard of the wrecked ships. Further south, the Brandberg Massif and its rock paintings await you. The painting of the "White Lady" was made by the Bushmen and is one of the oldest in the world. Other petroglyphs can be found in Twyfelfontein, on the Waterberg plateau. If you continue eastward, you will fall on Hoba (near Grootfontein) where is one of the biggest meteorites ever found.

Niger

First there were the internal conflicts, between the government and the Tuaregs, now there is the terrorist threat, very worrying and tangible in many parts of the country. Strongly marked by the footprint of the Sahara, which deploys here the Ténéré, its most arid part, or the Aïr massif and its high blue mountains, Niger would normally be a fabulous destination for desert lovers. In addition to this, there are prehistoric testimonies with many engravings, and a very beautiful national park, the W, which gathers the African fauna in its diversity. The setting aside of the country is all the more regrettable as it has a situation more favorable to tourism than most of its neighbors. If the sanitary aspect remains precarious, the infrastructures are limited but rather correct, especially the roads. A country that could welcome a fairly large panel of travelers attracted by the desert, but which for the moment does not welcome anyone anymore.

• North of Agadez, the Aïr Massif offers visitors sumptuous landscapes that can be discovered by camel, 4x4 or on foot. On this plateau, the surroundings of the Izzeguerit volcano, the Bagzan mountains, oases such as Timia, the monkeys of the Tamgak mountains, the dunes of Temet and the Gréboun massif, the "crab's claw" of Arakao, the rocky amalgams of Adrar Chiriet are all treasures not to be missed. The Neolithic rock engravings (in particular the 5-meter giraffe discovered in Dabous) present in the massif and the Djado plateau are the cherry on this cake of nature.

• At the foot of the Aïr is the Ténéré which spreads its dunes over several hundred kilometers. If you visit it by 4x4, remember that it was one of the most prestigious stages of the Paris-Dakar because of its difficulty. Only the Tuaregs managed to tame it and continue to use the Azalaï track today. Oases such as Bilma or Fachi, crossroads of caravans, hide there.

• Borrowing a pinasse (traditional African pirogue) or a zirdji (river cab) on the Niger, will allow you to meet hippos, observe the birds that live on the many islets and discover the life of the adobe villages. Niamey, the capital, is built on two plateaus overlooking the river. Its markets and its mosque, the largest in the country, are worth the detour.

• In the southwest of the country is the W National Park (common to Béninand Burkina Faso). The reserve is famous for its large mammals: elephants, hippos, leopards, lions, cheetahs, buffaloes, warthogs ... Near the ruins of ancient fortified villages have grown large stands of baobabs. Between February and April, photo safaris are a real pleasure.

Nigeria

A country where the evils of Africa accumulate, overpopulated in places, cut in two by religions, tormented by terrorism, Nigeria is more often taken as an example to illustrate the misery, especially through the absolute urban chaos represented by the city of Lagos, than to present the beauties of the African continent. On paper, the country is not lacking in assets, and brings together the great classics of East Africa, between landscapes and wildlife. It is above all the insecurity, just as real in Lagos as in the remote northern regions, which puts Nigeria on the sidelines of tourism. The difficulty of the trip makes it an unlikely destination, except for the very prepared, cautious and accustomed visitors to the region.

• To the east rise the Mandara Mountains, which offer many opportunities for hiking between volcanic peaks, valleys and hills where monkeys and butterflies live. Hiking is also very popular in the center of the country, where the Jos Plateau hides beautiful waterfalls such as the Kurra Falls in the savannah. 225 km to the east, the Yankari National Park is the best known in the country both for its wildlife and its lake from the Wikki hot springs.

• The vast Niger Delta is occupied by a delirious mangrove swamp where mangrove trees have fun with their feet in the water. Nembe fishermen live there in traditional villages. Don't miss to go to Brass Island where you can stay with the locals and discover an ancestral culture.

• Kano, former capital of the Hausa, is the most interesting city of the country because of its architectural heritage, especially in the Muslim part, and its market. The museum of Ife has a collection of bronze heads of a very high aesthetic level that lovers of black Africa will not be able to miss. Lagos, the former capital of the country, a sprawling and totally chaotic city, does not have a very good reputation even if the only practicable beaches of the Atlantic coast are located in its surroundings such as Palasides, Lekki and Tarkwas. This urban maelstrom is even more difficult for foreigners to navigate than the equatorial jungle.

Uganda

Uganda is a destination at a crossroads. Sometimes the situation seems to be clearing up, and we can see the promise of an interesting tourist development, with the meeting with the famous mountain gorillas in the forefront, excursions well supervised, by very professional guides and in a lost world setting. On the other hand, there are periods when the country regresses, goes back to its ways, and struggles to stabilize in a tormented region. It is difficult to say whether the country will take the path of its eastern neighbors, Kenya, Tanzania, or will be caught in the chaos of its western neighbors, DRC, South Sudan. Uganda has very great assets, but the infrastructure is poor, and the country remains a difficult destination, which should be reserved for frequent travelers or adventurers at heart, accompanied by a professional.

• The "impenetrable forest" of Bwindi and the nearby Mgahinda region hide half of the world's mountain gorilla population. Their encounter in the heart of the exceptional natural environment is a rare and precious moment. Conscious of their immense value, Uganda is trying to protect them like a treasure. Queen Elizabeth Park, Murchinson Falls Park, Lake Mburo Park, Kidepo Valley Park and Kimbale Forest Park have an extraordinarily rich fauna (baboons, elephants, hippos, lions, antelopes, crocodiles, giraffes, zebras, chimpanzees) that can be discovered in a much more adventurous setting than that offered by the parks of neighboring countries. Lake George and the Sese Islands are home to many birds.

• The Ruwenzori peaks in the west are over 5000 meters high and form the most beautiful region of the country between eternal snow and lush vegetation. On the opposite side of the territory, Mount Elgon is one of the highest volcanoes in the world, which is reached after discovering gorges and waterfalls. The latter are also numerous in the Nile Victoria region, especially in Karuma and Murchinson. Lakes Edward, George, Mburo and Victoria are also enchanting places where birds and vegetation offer a wild spectacle of great beauty to admire during a boat ride.

Democratic Republic of Congo

For the traveler, the DRC is a terra incognita. A vast country that occupies the heart of equatorial Africa, the Democratic Republic of Congo, which has little democracy outside of its name, could just as well be on another planet. The relationship to things, the weather, the environment, the nature, the climate, everything there is very different from what the European traveler may know. From a theoretical point of view, it is a country rich in wonders, with the jungle, worthy of the Amazon, the fauna, and the volcanoes as highlights. In practice, the sanitary situation is disastrous, and the country has all the dangers in this matter, security is bad almost everywhere, social tensions are permanent, and to top it all, traveling in the country is always a complicated adventure. This is what you should remember from a trip to the DRC, it is an adventure with a capital A. Only travelers who are prepared and ready to negotiate all possible situations, in complete autonomy and without nets, can envisage this very difficult destination.

• The Orientale province, located in the northeast, has several sites that can be visited from the town of Kinsagani, a modern city on the Congo River where you can admire the work of wagenia fishermen with their nets in the middle of rapids and lokele fishermen living on singular floating villages. There are many waterfalls in the region such as those of the Tshopo. In the forest of Ituri, we will be able to observe the rare okapi which exists only in Congo (observation station of the village of Epulu). At the border with South Sudan is the Garamba park where the last specimens of the Nile white rhino live. The domestication center of Garamba na Bodio offers the possibility of an elephant trek.

• Towards the south extends the mount Hoyo with its caves and waterfalls "Staircase of Venus". In the heart of the vast virgin forest live and hunt the Bambutis, pygmies who, while preserving their ancient customs, know how to welcome travelers. Hiking in the Ruwenzori mountain range (5 119 m) will make you discover the landscapes of these "mountains of the moon" formed by glaciers surrounded by small grey, black and green lakes.

• Lake Kivu is one of the prettiest places in the border region with Rwanda. One can swim there and explore the north shore where there are interesting natural sites: lava fields, Rutshuru falls, hot springs of Mai-ya-Moto... Two resort towns, Goma and Bukavu, the city of the five peninsulas, are built on Lake Kivu and offer bathing possibilities, in the Congolese style!

• To the east, the Virunga National Park and the Kahuzi-Biega National Park are home to some of the most exceptional flora and fauna. Lions, buffaloes, antelopes, warthogs, elephants, hippos and a wide variety of water birds live between the two mountain slopes which are its natural borders, but it is mainly the mountain gorilla families and its spectacular scenery that attract the attention of travelers. Of the 8 volcanoes of the volcanic chain, Nyiragongo and Nyamuragira are still active and can be climbed (particularly impressive at night).

• Kinshasa, once nicknamed *Kin la Belle (Beautiful Kin)*, derives its special charm from the majestic Congo River on whose banks it stretches. Rendezvous at the end of the afternoon on the snowshoe walk to admire the waves laden with water hyacinths. Mount Nglaliema shelters in a magnificent setting the main presidential residence surrounded by the Presidential Park and its zoo which dominate the entire city. It is one of the liveliest cities in Africa, although chaotic is a more appropriate term, to realize it the four big markets are not to be missed.

Reunion Island

It is a French overseas department. A beautiful island, varied, still well unknown. Very healthy climate (risk of cyclone but low), natural wonders, excellent infrastructures, optimal sanitary level, a very gentle welcome. Reunion Island, the "French Hawaii", inevitably suffers from its remoteness, the high cost of living for tourists and a disorganized media coverage. Tourism is developed there, but it is always confidential, very paradoxical for a destination with so many assets in its game. A very easy trip, for everyone, with a natural and sporting argument that takes precedence over the seaside resort. For a complete experience, it combines perfectly with its sister island, neighboring Mauritius, both of which have complementary attractions.

• In the center of the island are three circuses that deserve the expense of a helicopter flight. The Cilaos circus is the best known of the three, notable for its traditions (vineyards, lentils, embroidery) and its thermal springs. Don't miss in the heart of the primary forest the site of the "Marvelous Rock". The cirque of Salazie is famous for its waterfalls, especially those of the Veil of the Bride, and for its picturesque Creole village of Hell-Bourg. The cirque of Mafate is synonymous with isolation, loneliness and inaccessibility. Do not hesitate to go hiking in the heart of this natural sanctuary to meet the inhabitants of the "îlets", villages isolated in nature.

• The cirques are dominated by the Piton des Neiges and the Piton de la Fournaise, one of the most active volcanoes on the planet. The ascent of the latter is relatively easy. You will cross the lunar expanse of the Plaine des Sables and admire the vast crater and the lava flows, which sometimes slide down to the sea. Indeed, between the Tremblet and Piton Sainte Rose, on the east side of the island, the Grand Brûlé is the place where lava flows regularly. The black of the lava once solidified and the bright green of the forest combine to form a sumptuous landscape that you can admire from the road or via hiking trails.

• 800 kms of hiking trails cover the whole island to be discovered on foot. Other sports activities will allow you to enjoy the landscape while filling up with thrills. Paragliding, climbing, mountain biking and rafting are available. Whatever your means of transport, you will be immersed in a natural world with spicy and unforgettable scents. Don't miss the "Spice Road" route up the Mare Longue trail in the Southeast, to the *Perfume and Spice Garden*, one of the most beautiful botanical gardens in the Indian Ocean.

• Reunion Island does not have many beaches. Only 30 kilometers of sand on the west coast will be able to welcome you and your towels. Saint-Gilles-les-Bains is the best known resort. The beach of Boucan Canot, to the north, is pleasant, but the sea is somewhat dangerous, the Hermitage beach bordering the lagoon, which is home to many tropical fish, is the only one to be entirely protected by a coral reef. Further south, another small lagoon is located in Saint Leu, a site also known for the surfing (beware of the current instructions) and diving possibilities it offers. Divers will find on the island an interesting discovery area. A little further, the huge black sand beach of Etang-Salé is often considered as the most beautiful of the island. Finally, in the very south, Grand Anse is a superb bay, very popular for the traditional Reunionese Sunday picnic and whose small swimming pool is a real aquarium.

• Although the "capital" city of Saint-Denis is not often on the visitor's agenda, it is nevertheless interesting. It is here that the majority of the island's historic buildings are concentrated, especially on the rue de Paris where old colonial houses, Creole huts and administrative monuments (prefecture, former town hall) are located. There is also a lively shopping center during the day.

Rwanda

One of the smallest countries in Africa, but also one of the most original. Contrary to what we imagine today, Rwanda has long been one of the big names in African tourism. Of course the terrible civil war, and the genocide that it engendered, resonates today as a sad synonym for the country. Back to stability, logically quite relative (but real) in this complicated region, Rwanda has left in its years of chaos a good part of its infrastructure, which was already not fantastic, and more importantly, much worse, a heavy contingent of its most emblematic population: the mountain gorillas. This is still the great attraction of the country, and the encounter with these giants of the high altitude forests always provides a wonder and the thrill of the adventure intact. However, the journey has become more laborious and above all much more expensive than it used to be. The encounter with the gorillas now comes at a high price. That said, for the gorillas it is no worse, and the accompaniment is undeniably of high quality. The country, mindful of its environment, which is its only wealth, allows prepared (and overwhelmingly supervised) travelers to discover a rather unique Africa, in its primary forests (Nyungwe) and in its mountains, the Virunga. Beware, however, the latter have the reputation of being one of the hardest trekking grounds on the planet, reserving the great explorations for very confirmed sportsmen and adventurous spirits. Beyond the past difficulties, which have left their mark on the country, Rwanda is a destination on a par with equatorial Africa, with a difficult climate (very humid), laborious transportation and a very low level of health care (malaria is very present and basic level of care).

* The Volcanoes National Park is located in the north, on the border with Zaire and Uganda. The Virunga range is made up of seven volcanoes, which in addition to offering magnificent panoramas, are home to the famous Beringei gorillas, which can be approached from two or three meters away to observe their intimacy. The silverback gorillas live in the virgin forest of the volcanoes, close to Ruhenger.

* Parallel to this massif is Lake Kivu which, despite its sad notoriety, has a few tourist resorts. Kibuye is today preferred to the seaside town of Gisenyi which offers a beautiful view of the lake and the Nyiragongo volcano. Do not miss to go and see the Ndaba falls which rush almost one hundred meters high. In the surroundings of Cyangugu, at the extreme south of the lake, tea and cotton are cultivated. It is possible to visit the Rusizi River Falls and the Nyakabuye Hot Springs.

* The Akagera National Park covers 2,500 km, in the east of the country, is dotted with lakes and is rich in wildlife including monkeys, elephants, buffalo, zebras, rhinos, antelopes and lions. In the south, between Butare and Cyangugu, the jungle of Nyungwe Primary Forest is home to ancient trees, about 100 species of wild orchids and several species of primates.

St. Helena

If it were not for Napoleon, deported here by the English, who would know the name of this end of the world lost in the South Atlantic? Completely isolated, somewhere between Brazil and Angola, inhabited by a few thousand Saints (the name of the inhabitants), St. Helena is a strange corner of the former British Empire. Tourists are obviously very rare there. It is not so much the destination that is difficult, since the infrastructures are good, but rather its access, because although there is now an airport, it is very complex to serve because of the particular weather of the island. One thus goes to St. Helena mainly via the St. Helena, a mixed cargo ship that connects the island to Cardiff, the Canary Islands and South Africa. A journey for the sailors, and above all for them, because on arrival there is finally not much to discover, the tomb of Napoleon is empty and the island is not a tropical paradise. Nevertheless, its unusual side and its isolation make it an experience that, for some great travelers, is a potential Grail.

* St. Helena is a British Overseas Territory in the South Atlantic Ocean consisting of eight islands, including St. Helena Island, the main one, Ascension Island and the islands of Tristan da Cunha, Gough, Inaccessible (which with a name like this suggests its isolation), Middle Island, Nightingale and Stoltenhoff which form the Tristan da Cunha Archipelago.

* Only St. Helena Island attracts tourists somewhat around the places reminiscent of Napoleon's imprisonment in the Longwood House and whose ashes were buried, before being repatriated to France 19 years later, near a spring in the Geranium Valley, which has since been called "Valley of the Tomb".

* In addition to Napoleon's exile, St. Helena is also a sought-after destination for explorers at heart. Its total isolation and its access almost exclusively by boat make it one of the last points on the globe where travel evokes as much a journey as a destination. The remoteness, the difficulty and the time of access, the small size of the island, all contribute to make it a very unusual site from a tourist point of view.

Sao Tome and Principe

The small islands of Sao Tome and Principe are so discreet that the overwhelming majority of travelers don't even know them. This small island country, on the equator, a former Portuguese colony, has however master assets in its tourist game. A jungle of great richness, promise of tropical clichés, postcard beaches, very wild, with warm waters and teeming seabed, the roças, old cacao and coffee plantations, a true local institution, a profusion of baobab, a rare and majestic tree. A real little garden of Eden, where you will discover a welcoming population and a very gentle atmosphere. This beautiful destination is very accessible, thanks to direct connections from Lisbon. On the spot, the country is poor but presents few difficulties for the prepared traveler. Walkers will find a superb playground there. To discover absolutely.

* The most beautiful beaches of the island of São Tomé are located south of the capital of the same name, such as Praia Piscina. Divers will choose those of Lagoa Azul, Ilheu das Cabras, Praia Pequena and Praia das Conchas. The beaches of Principe (Praia Banana, Praia Abade or Praia São Joaquim) are even more deserted and are worth the detour for their authenticity and especially for their landscapes.

* In the north of São Tomé, the jungle, sometimes very dense, is full of baobabs, waterfalls and rocky columns that bear witness to the ancient volcanic activity. Some of them can reach 600 m high, such as the Cao Grande, an impressive needle that stands out from the jungle. Close to Trinidade is the São Nicolau waterfall. Adventurers will find in this region a worthy field of exploration, with moderate dangers.

* Also in the north, you will discover the large "roças", plantations of cocoa, copra, coffee and bananas with an architecture of pure Portuguese tradition. Agostinho Neto at 1km from Guadalupe is a perfect example. The roças of Agua Izé, Monte Cafe (the only Arabica producer on the island), Bombaïm (and its waterfalls) or the one of Sundy, on Príncipe, are worth the detour.

* In the south, you will discover the Land of the Angolares, fishermen who lived on the bangs of the Portuguese colonization, visiting the villages of Pantufo and Praia Melão, and the place called *Boca do Inferno*. In the southwest, the Obo Natural Park brings together forests, mangroves and the unique savannah of the country. Don't hesitate to walk along the coastal road to reach the "bamboo cathedral" and then Porto Alegre. From there, you will be able to go to Praia Jalé, one of the protected places for turtle nesting.

* 140 kilometers north of Sao Tome, Principe is a small volcanic island forgotten by the world. Its very preserved landscapes play the full range of equatorial natural beauties, between thick jungle and ocean, where the main activity is hiking especially in the second half of the *Obo natural park* (which has the particularity of being cut between the two islands). With 5000 inhabitants, the island is certainly quiet, and here again the softness of the country is expressed by a welcoming atmosphere where the traveler will not be bothered. A godsend that allows you to explore the trails, paradoxically better maintained than the roads, in complete tranquility. It is a journey within the journey, very exotic.

* In a country dotted with plantations and nicknamed the chocolate island, needless to say that cocoa is the national emblem. Since its introduction in 1822, the culture of Sao Tome and its fetish tree has been merging. The discovery of the country inevitably goes through this path of chocolate, from the pod to the finished product, and through history its exploitation in the roças, between settlers and slaves.

* It is difficult to claim to know Sao Tome and Principe without having attended the Tchiloli. It is the central custom of the local culture. It is a show where the theater mixes with music and dance and whose history takes place during the reign of Charlemagne! A quite amazing cultural peculiarity that is invariably performed at all local festivals.

Senegal

Senegal is a destination that could be described as rather easy. Access is simple, the country is open and does not pose any particular problems for travelers. As for all Africa, apart from exceptions, Senegal remains however far from the European standards of comfort, it should be known, and the inexperienced traveler will therefore prefer an organized trip if he wants to discover the country. The development of tourism has also generated a form of begging that can be quite disturbing for those who have never been confronted with it. The experienced traveler will be at his ease to discover the landscapes of this beautiful country, the streets of Dakar or the colonial testimonies of Saint-Louis.

• Senegal is sometimes nicknamed "African California" because of the fine sandy beaches that stretch along the coast. From Saly to Cap Skirring (with the Gambia cutting the coast in the middle), tourists are welcome. And since recently, an ecotouristic logic is developing there. The seaside argument remains however limited to tour operators, with a mid-range positioning.

• The situation has improved in Casamance. This is the time to go and discover the National Park of Lower Casamance where the tropical climate has chosen vegetation as its queen. Moreover, all along the Casamance River, you will meet men and women living in the respect of traditions.

• If you like birds, two parks will make you happy: the one of Djouj (3rd ornithological reserve in the world) in the mangrove of the Senegal river delta and the one Niokolo Koba where mammals are added to the show.

• 35 kilometers from Dakar is the Lac Rose, known for its original color, but also for being the last stage of the original Paris-Dakar. The spectacle of the salt exploitation is just as fascinating as that of the lake itself.

• At the finish, the excitement of Dakar makes one's head spin. Don't hesitate to soak up this atmosphere by going to the markets. If you're looking for a little peace and quiet, take the boat to Gorée Island whose colonial houses are a reminder of the past. The House of the slaves tells the painful history of slavery.

• Saint-Louis was the first city founded by Europeans in West Africa. The city preserves many typical houses of the colonial period. A heritage that is both a wealth and a scar. Take the Faidherbe bridge to discover the old town built on an island, and don't forget to get lost in the fishermen's quarter.

Seychelles

The tourist image of the Seychelles is clear in the brochures: honeymooners and paradise on earth. Along with Mauritius and the Maldives, it is the great siren of the Indian Ocean, which attracts travelers with its promises of turquoise waters, white sandy beaches, coconut palms and tropical sweetness. The Seychelles combines all of this with the appeal of a welcoming Creole culture, beautiful jungle-covered mountains (one of the archipelago's well-kept secrets) and a palpable sweetness of life. As far as the beaches are concerned, we are really here in the world top and the term "paradise" is not exaggerated, especially for the "stars" like Anse Lazio and especially Anse Source d'Argent. The country is expensive, honeymooners and the luxury obliges, but the independent traveler also has his place there, although the addresses are limited. Travel is very easy, just don't forget that the equatorial climate is more intense than the tropical one, with rains that can be sometimes annoying if you choose the wrong season.

• Mahé is the largest of the Seychelles islands. Victoria, the capital, has been living at the pace of tourism since the airport was established 30 years ago. Here you can discover the islands' heritage by visiting a few museums, immerse yourself in Seychellois daily life by strolling through the Market Street Bazaar, and, of course, relax in the sun. The most famous spot is Beau Vallon in the north of the island. Postcard images are already there. In the center of the island, the Morne Seychellois National Park shelters the highest mountains of the archipelago (almost 1000 meters anyway) and offers a very different atmosphere from the beaches, in a magnificent tropical jungle setting. The possibilities of hiking are interesting.

• La Digue is located 50 kms from Mahé and next to it the capital could pass a metropolis. Time is slowed down at La Digue, and it's not a cliché. Get on a bike and discover the island. 3 miraculous beaches are waiting for you: l'Anse Source Argent, Grand Anse and Anses Cocos. On the way, you will be able to admire an exceptional biodiversity and meet the inhabitants with their ancestral habits.

• Praslin is an hour's boat ride from Mahé and only two small villages are reminiscent of civilization. Early in the morning, discover the Vallée de Mai and its giant coconuts called cocofesses. In the afternoon, relax on the beaches of Côte d'Or and Anse Lazio, the world famous postcard of the Seychelles for its smooth rocks.

While different means (plane, helicopter or boat) are available to move between the main islands, the more isolated islands are harder to reach outside of cruising, but they reach summits of wild beauty that few travelers get to admire.

• Silhouette Island and its virgin forest are 15 minutes by helicopter from Mahé. For hiking enthusiasts, it will be ideal.

• The Bird Islands, half an hour flight from Mahé, are a real dream for professional or amateur ornithologists. Between May and November, black parrots, terns, frigate birds and strawtails jostle each other in the blue sky.

• The atoll of Aladdabra is only accessible by sea (go to Assumption by plane and then charter boat on the spot). There are five times more giant tortoises than in the Galapagos.

• As far as diving is concerned, thousands of fishes are waiting for you below the water in the coral reefs. The seabed is exceptional especially in the small islands such as Curieuse, Bird, Frigate, Silhouette, Cocos or Félicité.

Sierra Leone

In the minds of travelers, Sierra Leone is most associated with two things: the world's lowest life expectancy and the diamond trade. An image largely linked to a terrible civil war that has left the country in a catastrophic and anarchic state, prey to all kinds of trafficking. Years have passed and Sierra Leone is (very) slowly rebuilding. Nothing is really simple in Sierra Leone for the traveler. The health situation is really very bad, security is still relative, and the infrastructure, especially roads, is in very poor condition (when they exist). In a future, which seems quite distant, the country will be able to count on some good assets such as beautiful tropical beaches, the site of the capital Freetown which has potential, and some beautiful portions of nature. In practice, the country is still totally on the fringe and only exploratory travelers venture there.

• Sierra Leone's 402 km of Atlantic coastline includes some of the most beautiful beaches on the West African coast where, for once in the region, there is no danger from rollers. The beaches are mainly concentrated in the Freetown area (Lumley Beach and River N°2 Beach) or in Lakal. The Turtle Islands, 60 km south of Freetown, are also famous, especially for water sports.

• To the north, the forests and hills of the Outamba and Kilimi reserves are teeming with monkeys as well as many mammals, including elephants and buffalo. The Loma Mountains Forest Reserve is a dense forest with monumental trees in the Mount Bintumani area where monkeys, especially chimpanzees, are legion. To the southeast, the Tiwai Island Wildlife Sanctuary is located on an island in the Moa River and is home to crocodiles, hippos, monkeys and 120 species of birds.

• Its English colonial houses and markets such as the Basket Market and the Cotton Tree make Freetown, the capital, an interesting stopover, far, far off the beaten track.

Somalia

Forgotten by all and the world, here is how one could summarize the fate of Somalia. This country, which is no longer really a country of anarchy, where nothing has been going well for decades, has the sad irony of not being of great interest to tourists. As a matter of fact, nobody has been coming to Somalia for a long time, and except for the northwestern region of Somaliland (which has become a de facto independent country, and where the rock paintings of Laas Gaal are located), the country is totally inaccessible (although air links do exist). The infrastructure does not exist, and beyond that the vast majority of the country is actually a field of ruins eaten away by the desert. The coasts of the Indian Ocean are given over to piracy, the tracks are given over to armed gangs, extremists rule terrorism near the borders. The only eyes of travelers who land on the country are those of the passengers of the planes that fly over its territory at an altitude of 10 kilometers.

In better times, the *Ogo Mountains* (2500 meters above sea level) in the north of the country, for their landscapes, the kilometers of white sand beaches on the Indian Ocean (coral reef), or the Neolithic paintings (6000 BC) of *Laas Gaal*, could be a tourist asset, but it is a possibility that seems very distant.

South Africa

A vast country, surfing on an important wave of popularity. That's well justified, because, let's face it, South Africa is one of the most beautiful countries in the world. It has all the landscapes and wildlife typical of the African postcard. To this must be added the exoticism of southern Africa and this extreme south with the accent of California. It is a very varied territory, which knows notable differences according to the regions as much in terms of geography as of climate. There are arid deserts as well as Mediterranean-looking coastlines, modern cities bristling with skyscrapers and villages of traditional tribes punctuated by huts. Everywhere, the light is fantastic. It is one of the heavyweights of African tourism, with the Kruger Park, the superb beaches of the coast and the city of Cape Town at the top of the list. Very easy to access, with excellent infrastructure, South Africa suffers however from high travel costs and its image suffers from the chronic and worrying insecurity of its major cities.

• Cape Town is a spectacular coastal city in an environment that is no less spectacular, often considered the most beautiful on the continent. It can be admired from the top of *Table Mountain*, one of the natural wonders of the world. To visit the peninsula, take *Chapman's Peak Drive*, a road of great beauty. The city is widely regarded as the trendiest city in Africa, with its trendy restaurants, bars and stores. Closer in spirit to New York than Nairobi, Cape Town is a microcosm within the country. *Robben Island*, where Mandela was incarcerated, the *Waterfront*, a modern shopping mall, and the popular and bohemian Bo *Kaap* district with its colorful houses, are must-sees for a visit. Not far from the city, the *Kristenbosch* Botanical Gardens are also worth a detour for amateurs.

• Around the city, the vineyard region and its beautiful villages (*Franschoek* and its white houses), or the Garden Route along the ocean (seaside resorts of *Knysna* and *Plettenberg Bay*; *Wilderness* nature area), are two very popular destinations, and rightly so because it is one of the most beautiful corners of the world for landscapes. The optimal tourist infrastructure, for various budgets, and the ease of exploring the region independently, which is rare in Africa, make it one of the continent's musts.

• As a worthy representative of Southern Africa, the country offers one of the greatest animal diversity on the continent and opportunities to approach wildlife are generally both easier and better organized than in neighbouring countries. Amongst many animals, the famous "Big Five" can be found there in its entirety (buffaloes, elephants, leopards, lions, rhinos). The country has no less than 22 national parks. The most famous and visited is the Kruger, which is also the largest. In the bush and the savannah, typical vegetation of the dry tropical zones, encounters are numerous and the park is perfectly equipped with comfortable lodges. Other parks are classics of the circuits, such as Addo and its elephants and Hluhluwe-Umfolozi (big five). The less frequented parks do not miss attractions either and deploy the very vast palette of the landscapes of the country like Kgalagadi, Mapungubwe or Richtersveld. For a trip purely focused on nature parks and African wildlife, South Africa is an unbeatable destination.

• The great mountainous barrier of the country, the Drakensberg, conceals incredible sites such as the canyon of the Blyde River, superb playground for hiking or simply to admire the landscapes. At the foot of the Drakensberg, the charming and quiet village of Clarens has become one of the most popular destinations in the country with some beautiful addresses and memorable starry skies.

• The coast of the Indian Ocean is the warmest, but it should not be forgotten that the country is almost entirely outside the tropical zone. In winter, swimming is cold everywhere and the water is cold all year round in the Cape region. Durban, the city of Gandhi, with notable Indian influences, is both a popular resort and a large city typical of the country. The Wild Coast has the preferences of nature lovers and hikers. It is inhabited by the Xhosa people who live in traditional huts. Around the Cape we appreciate especially the beauty of the immense ocean beaches on bottom of mountains, we practice the surf (famous spot of *Jeffreys Bay*) and we observe the passage of the whales in winter, in particular in *Hermanus*. Some seaside cities close to the Cape like *Camps Bay* evoke definitely more California than Africa. The coasts of the country also offer the possibility to meet the great white shark, the biggest predator of the planet, or to swim near schools of sardines (*sardine rush*), an unforgettable experience.

- It is now possible to discover the popular black neighborhoods of the big cities, the famous *townships, in the* company of a guide. We can mention Soweto in Johannesburg, Nelson Mandela's district. To enter a *township is* to discover all sorts of African traditions, and in a sense the reality for the majority of the country's population, far from the glittering buildings of the city centers.

• To the north of Johannesburg, the large tourist site of Sun City is a kind of small African Las Vegas, with all that one can imagine of leisure activities, in a cardboard décor which reproduces for example a lost city and composed exclusively of top-of-the-range hotels.

• While all the kitchens are in South Africa, particularly in the three cosmopolitan cities of Johannesburg, Durban and Cape Town, the national specialty is braai, which is widespread throughout the country. It refers to the barbecue, which is done both at home and outside, especially on Sundays. This tradition can be found throughout southern Africa and even throughout the southern Indian Ocean.

North & South Sudan

What was the largest country in Africa, before its partition between Sudan and South Sudan, has never had good press in the tourist world. Listed as an unstoppable ally of global terrorism, mired in violent crises, with Darfur at the top of the list, the country has collapsed even further by splitting in two following nearly 25 years of more or less latent civil war. Whether one is in the north or the south, Sudan remains a country strongly discouraged from visiting. However, in the north the site of Meroe and the pyramids of the black pharaohs constitute an asset of immense value, and in the south the fauna and the environment are in the vein of neighboring Kenya.

• The great assets of Sudan (from the north) are the monuments of the ancient kingdoms, whether Christian (site of Dongola), or pharaohs (called black pharaohs, to distinguish them from the pharaohs of Egypt). Among the various sites, the most remarkable is the necropolis of Meroe with its palaces and pyramids. The landscapes of Sudan are a continuity of southern Egypt, mainly desert, crossed by the backbone of the Nile. On the Red Sea coast, even topo, the seabed there is as exceptional as in the northern neighbor, even more so because the total absence of infrastructures (and even cities outside of *Port Sudan*) has totally preserved them. The only snag is that access is almost impossible. About in the center of the country, Khartoum, the capital, is a huge agglomeration, with a terribly hot and continuously sunny climate, which seems to merge with the desert. Its ochre hue and the majority of its sandy streets confirm it. Apart perhaps from its markets, the city does not present any interest but the change of scenery is total.

• Southern Sudan is a country where the African nature unfolds just as much as in neighboring countries (Kenya, Uganda). Several decades of war have greatly reduced wildlife contingents, but the three national parks (Boma, Nimule and Southern) are still home to a vast array of Africa's menagerie (buffaloes, cheetahs, giraffes, elephants, antelopes). The total lack of equipment is obviously a major brake on tourism, which in any case is an excluded idea in this country considered as the most fragile on the planet.

Swaziland

The kingdom of Swaziland, where the monarchy is absolute, is a small independent region wedged between South Africa and Mozambique. Although it is not totally landlocked within South Africa, like Lesotho, the country is nonetheless totally dependent on its large neighbor. The immediate proximity to the richest and most developed country in Africa makes little difference, Swaziland is an isolated, poor, and sparsely traveled land. Visitors most often come as part of a tour package to South Africa, which usually includes a short excursion to Swaziland. The kingdom, poetically nicknamed the African Switzerland, for the predominance of its mountains, is nevertheless of interest. With very short distances, especially compared to its neighbor, on roads or tracks that are generally of good quality (but where driving is still complicated), the country deploys a good number of national parks where you can discover the nature and animals of southern Africa. Moreover, in the west of the country, the Drakensberg massif, one of the most beautiful mountain landscapes in Africa, is no less attractive than on the South African side. A country of traditions, Swaziland also offers a plunge into a timeless Africa, far from the buildings of Johannesburg and where tribal rites are supervised by the almighty king. The kingdom is much more traditional than its large neighbor, and the traveler should not expect to find the same infrastructure or the same quality of service. Access is fairly simple, but the health situation is very poor (50% of the population is affected by HIV) and the level of equipment is rather precarious, although the main roads are in fairly good condition.

• The country's variety of landscapes is significant: mountains along the borders with Mozambique and South Africa, savannahs in the east and rainforests in the northwest. The highlight is the Drakensberg Massif, which the country shares with South Africa and which has some of the most beautiful landscapes on the continent, especially in the Usutu Valley.

• The discovery of fauna, flora and landscapes are the main tourist interests of the country, especially through numerous parks and reserves, such as Malotja (where the *Ngwenya* mine, the oldest in the world, is located), *Ehlane*, *Mkhaya*, *Phononyane* or *Mlilwane*. The fame of these parks is limited but the discovery of wildlife and natural environment (the bush) is no less remarkable than in South Africa.

Tanzania

With its Kenyan neighbor, Tanzania is the other great tourist country of East Africa, the one of big animals, savannah, exoticism, original nature. If Kenya has a greater reputation, Tanzania is actually the richest of the two countries in terms of tourism, with major sites such as Ngorongoro, Serengueti, Kilimanjaro or the island of Zanzibar. Nevertheless the two countries complement each other well and the continuity of certain large parks (Serengeti and Masai Mara for example) means that they are often the subject of a single stay. Tanzania for its part is a magnificent destination, which requires a minimum of preparation but which is safer (and generally more welcoming) than Kenya and within the reach of all travelers who want to discover Africa in all its splendor, provided, as often on the continent, that they pay the price.

• The Serengeti is one of Africa's major natural parks: more than 14,000 km² where 35 species of large mammals such as elephants, lions, giraffes, impalas and wildebeest live. Every year, the latter, together with zebras and some species of antelopes, cross the great plains towards the Masai-Mara in Kenya. More than 2 million animals make this formidable migration, a spectacle that is simply breathtaking and unique in the world. The migration, in the footsteps of water (rain), is obviously a journey strewn with pitfalls that culminates with the passage of the Grumeti River where the enormous Nile crocodiles are in ambush.

• The Ngorongoro crater, the caldera of an ancient volcano, is most certainly the site that most conveys this cliché of the African Eden where Man is only the observer of the great parade of wildlife. For its landscapes alone, Ngorongoro is worth the trip to Tanzania but it is the wildlife that is the highlight. In total between 20,000 and 40,000 animals (depending on the importance of the wildebeest migration), zebras, elephants, lions, cheetahs, hippos, rhinos (white or black, the latter being very rare) ...

• The parks of Lake Manyara (which closes the classic Tanzanian safari trio), Tarangire (vast park famous for its pythons), Ruaha (many elephants) and the Selous Reserve (savannah and jungle, plain and mountain), are also famous for their countless safari possibilities, the great wildlife and the typical landscapes of savannah Africa.

• The snows of Kilimanjaro at 5892 meters altitude (Uhuru Peak) are not eternal as we thought, they might have completely disappeared within a few years. In the meantime, many people are trying to climb its majestic slopes. From 5 to 10 days of hiking, along more or less difficult routes (Marangu and Machame routes, the most complicated), but always in the unique and varied landscapes from the plains to the roof of Africa. Next to it, Mount Meru at 4566 meters of altitude often acts as an acclimatization but it is an already exciting and arduous ascent. We also pass through the palette of local landscapes, bush, jungle, moorland and alpine desert, and we come across many animals. Of course the ascent is rewarded by the view of the Kili.

• All along the Rift Valley, volcanic activity is out of the ordinary and out of the ordinary. At the foot of the sacred volcano (for the Maasai people) Ol Doinyo Lengai whose white lava is unique in the world is Lake Natron where 2.5 million lesser flamingos live.

• Tanzania shares with DRC and Zambia the shores of Lake Tanganyika where the *Kalambo River* flows. The falls of the same name impress by their height and beauty. Another lake, Malawi, shared with the country of the same name, also offers superb scenery, particularly through the meeting with the Livingstone massif. The two lakes are undoubtedly the secret gems of the country but competition is tough in such a rich environment.

• Like the entire region, Tanzania does not usurp its nickname of the cradle of humanity. The prehistoric site of the Olduvai Gorge where the skeleton of an Australopithecus 2 million years old has been discovered. Located in the Ngorongoro sector, the site is usually stopped during the tours.

• Proof, if proof were needed, that Tanzania offers a wide range of attractions, the country has a seaside facade that is the perfect combination of safaris. The highlight is of course the archipelago of Zanzibar. It is famous for spices, its old town built of black coral, very picturesque and exotic although it is in ruins (Stone Town) and its white sandy beaches. On the islands of Pemba and Mafia, apart from the attraction of tropical beaches lined with coconut palms, the magnificent marine fauna of the coral reef awaits diving enthusiasts.

Togo

Like its neighbor Benin, the small country of Togo is poorly perceived by the traveling community. In West Africa, it is certainly one of the major destinations and it is an open and accessible country, which will not pose any problems for the slightly experienced traveler. It is also a good starting point to discover sub-Saharan Africa, by familiarizing oneself with travel in the region. Be careful however, this does not mean that Togo is a trouble-free destination. The risk of terrorism is present there and one should be vigilant (but it is not a tangible risk as in some neighboring countries), Lomé, the capital, poses some security problems at night, and the country does not have the stability and facilities of a western country, far from it. Health conditions are not very good, but no worse than elsewhere in the region, and transport infrastructure is poor (roads are degraded). Nevertheless, on a regional scale, the country remains a good introduction. From the point of view of attractions, visitors will be able to discover a rich country, between the classic West African fauna *and flora (crocodiles, elephants, hippos), the remarkable landscapes of forests (Kpalimé) and mountains (Agou Peak), and rich and visible traditions, including voodoo. The only downside is that the coastline is not very accessible and in all cases dangerous.*

• Lomé is no longer the tourist capital that it was before the 90s, nevertheless, the atmosphere of its three-storey market, the National Museum dedicated to the country's arts and traditions and its festive nights make it a notable destination. Located along the coast of the Gulf of Guinée, it has some pleasant beaches, but unfortunately, as on the whole Togolese coast, the ocean is very dangerous. You can swim at Robinson-Plage, 9 km east of Lomé. You should pay attention to safety on the beaches, and everywhere in town as soon as night falls. Lome is more dangerous than cities in Ghana or Benin.

• Lake Togo, 25 km from the capital, is a very peaceful lagoon lake which admirably compensates for this seaside handicap. Most water sports (sailing, water skiing, windsurfing, windsurfing) can be practiced in a nice forest setting. On the shores of Lake Togo, in Agbodrafo, you can embark on the fishermen's pirogues to haul up the nets with them and join in a collective pirogue the village of Togoville which remains strongly influenced by animist and voodoo practices.

• In the southwest of the country, the plateau region is a mountainous area whose surroundings of Kpalimé are the flagship in terms of landscape with beautiful tropical forests, waterfalls and plantations of teak, coffee and cocoa. Do not hesitate to climb to the top of Mount Agou (986 m) from where you have a panoramic view of the entire region. In the surroundings of Badou, the Akloa waterfall flows at the end of a valley lined with exotic orchards. For the experience, you can stay at the Benedictine monastery on the Danyi plateau.

• In the north, the Kabyè country has many surprises in store for you. 15 km north-east of Kara, Mount Kabyè is home to several villages where traditional forms of handicrafts and terraced culture are still practiced. The villages of Landa and Kétao have interesting handicraft markets, while Farendé is famous for its metalwork, and Pagouda for its music. Also visit in the surroundings of Kandé, the Tamberma valley whose villages are known for their incredible *farm castles*, tatas.

• Crocodiles and hippos on the shores of Lake Mono, deer and monkeys in the Togodo forest, antelopes, buffaloes and elephants in the Kéran National Park and lions in the Malfakassa hunting reserve make Togo an interesting country in terms of wildlife, and well anchored in the African tourist imagination.

Tunisia

What can be said about Tunisia that has not already been said, except that we must absolutely try to get away from the beaches and hotel clubs to perceive its true nature. Tunisia is still resonating above all with the promise of a very easy, very cheap and exotic seaside trip, which has been badly affected by a turbulent geopolitical situation. A formula on which the country has staked everything, at the risk of finding itself a little overwhelmed by the rise of the tourist market. Tunisia can also rely on a beautiful cultural heritage and a beautiful stretch of desert, rich in traditions and remarkable landscapes. It is here that the Sahara is the most easily accessible, and the most emblematic, for the inexperienced traveler. Easy access, good infrastructure and perfectly marked tourist paths make Tunisia a perfect introduction to North Africa.

• Tourism in Tunisia is mainly based on its coastline and beaches. From Nabeul and Hammamet to the island of Djerba, one finds on the whole coast hotels of all standards, white sand beaches bordered by a clear sea and thalassotherapy complexes. Farniente, hotel clubs and sun are the key words of the region. Only the island of Djerba, nicknamed the sweet, offers an attraction that goes beyond the seaside, with its souks, its mixed atmosphere and its historical testimonies.

• The south of Tunisia, kingdom of the Sahara, is covered with dunes which are just waiting for you to come and discover their secrets. By camel or 4x4, go to Tozeur, one of the most beautiful oases in Africa, cross the salt desert of the El-Djerid chott or visit the troglodytic scenery of Matmata.

* The medina of Tunis and that of Sousse deserve a stroll and curiosity; the mosques of Monastir, Mahdia and Kairouan a contemplative admiration; the museums of Carthage and the remains of El-Djem, Bulla Regia, Sbeïtla and Dougga an attentive visit. Tunisia, a crossroads of civilizations for thousands of years, is a destination of remarkable richness.

Zambia

As with its southern neighbor (Zimbabwe), tourist Zambia relies primarily on the Victoria Falls, one of the wonders of the world. Still like its neighbor, the other regions of the country remain in the shadows, yet there are many attractions, especially in terms of nature, starting with the remarkable Luangwa Park. Access is most often via South Africa (and usually on excursion). Security in the country is quite good, but it is not a destination for carefree travelers. Outside of organized tours, it is best to prepare properly and have some experience in Africa to explore Zambia. If one were to indulge in a few formulas, Zambia could be described as authentic Africa.

* The incredible spectacle of Victoria Falls is the highlight of a trip to Zambia. You can watch the Zambezi River pour 546 million cubic meters of water per minute over a distance of 2 km wide from the Victoria Falls Bridge by taking a microlight, hiking along the cliff in front of the falls or going down to the Boiling Pot. Mosi-oa-Tunya National Park runs along the Zambezi River for 12 km from Victoria Falls. It covers an area of only 66 km², but is home to many species of antelope, zebra, giraffe and more recently white rhino.

* The whole region is becoming the land of adventure in Southern Africa. It offers extreme sports, breathtaking scenery and many other activities for outdoor enthusiasts. Rafting in the Batoka Gorge, bungee jumping from the Victoria Falls Bridge, canoeing on the Zambezi River, horseback riding along the Zambezi River and in the surrounding teak forests, bodyboarding in the Zambezi Rapids, abseiling down the cliffs of the Victoria Falls Gorge, tandem kayaking in the raging Zambezi Rapids, safaris in the outer reaches of the Zambezi, speedboating in the rapids... anything is possible.

* The vastness of Lake Kariba, the largest artificial lake in the world, is the scene of spectacular scenery. Do not hesitate to visit this dam which was so controversial, socially and ecologically, at the time of its construction. A paradise for fishermen, the lake hosts the annual tigerfish fishing competition in May on the way to Sinazongwe. Be sure to take a boat cruise, especially on a full moon evening to see the purple sun set on one side of the lake while the glittering moon rises on the other side. 21 km from Chirundu, on the way to Lusaka, lies the Chirundu Fossil Forest, a fossilized forest containing trees over 150 million years old.

* Zambia has 17 waterfalls in all. Besides Victoria Falls, the most notable are Ngonye Falls towards Sioma village on the Zambezi River, and Kalambo Falls, an incredible waterfall on the Kalambo River on the Zambia-Tanzania border, Kundalila Falls and their natural basin on the Kaombe River near Kanona, Lumangwe Falls near the Chipembe ferry in the Northern Province, Ntumbachushi Falls, Chipoma Falls, Chisimba Falls and Kundabwika Falls. Each of these can be traveled.

* To the east, the Luangwa National Park is the most interesting in the country, and one of the most remarkable in Africa. Lions, buffaloes, zebras, giraffes, elephants, leopards and antelopes share the territory. Along the Luangwa River, hippos and crocodiles can be seen, and its surroundings are particularly suitable for bird watching. For your photo safaris, various means of transportation are available: open roofed vehicles, on foot or on horseback. Kafue National Park, 200 kilometers west of Lusaka, covers an area of 22,000 square kilometers, making it one of the largest nature parks in the world.

Zimbabwe (eSwatini)

If Zimbabwe (now officially called eSwatini) is a rather large country, with a remarkable nature, it is especially known from a tourist point of view for the Victoria Falls. A majority of visitors come there on excursions from South Africa, so much so that the rest of the country is much less frequented. While the destination is certainly for seasoned travelers, it is not a very difficult country. Despite a catastrophic structural and social condition, with a long-lasting dictatorship, great poverty, and much corruption, security is good, health is far from good (especially water), but repatriation routes (especially to South Africa) are well established, and transportation is not a particular problem (provided that one avoids the roads, which are not very busy anyway). Apart from the Falls, the prepared traveler can discover some beautiful attractions such as the Mana Pools and the Hwange Park, rich in wildlife and fulfilling the promises of the Southern African postcard.

* Zimbabwe shares Victoria Falls with Zambia. With a width of almost 2 kilometers and a maximum height of 108 meters, it is one of the great natural sites of Africa. From the air, water or on foot, from above or below, the spectacle of the Zambezi pouring up to five million cubic meters of water per minute is most striking.

* More than 200 species of animals and about 400 species of birds are waiting for you in the large national parks, great shots of southern Africa (Mana Pools, Hwange, Matusadona, de Matobo …).

* One of the rare vestiges of the ancient history of Black Africa is located near *Lake Kyle*. The stone monuments, palaces, towers, ramparts, of Great Zimbabwe form the remains of the ancient capital of a Bantu kingdom. On a land rather marked by its natural footprint, this archaeological site is unique.

Victoria Island
Baffin Island
Davis Strait
King William Island
Foxe Basin
Hudson Bay
Labrador Sea
CANADA
Alaska US
BROOKS RANGE
ALASKA RANGE
ALEUTIAN RANGE
Aleutian Islands
Aleutian Trench
MACKENZIE MOUNTAINS
ROCKY MOUNTAINS
Gulf of Alaska
Queen Charlotte Islands
Vancouver Island
PACIFIC OCEAN
CASCADE RANGE
SIERRA NEVADA
GREAT BASIN
GREAT PLAINS
UNITED STATES
APPALACHIAN MOUNTAINS
NORTH ATLANTIC OCEAN
North American Basin
Gulf of Mexico
MEXICO
SIERRA MADRE OCCIDENTAL
SIERRA MADRE DEL SUR
BAJA CALIFORNIA
YUCATAN
FLORIDA
Nova Scotia
Cape Breton Island
St-Pierre et Miquelon (Fr)
Greater Antilles
Lesser Antilles
THE BAHAMAS
NASSAU
CUBA
LA HABANA
JAMAICA
KINGSTON
HAITI
PORT-AU-PRINCE
DOMINICAN REPUBLIC
SANTO DOMINGO
PUERTO RICO
ANTIGUA AND BARBUDA
ST KITS AND NEVIS
DOMINICA
BELIZE
BELMOPAN
GUATEMALA
HONDURAS
CARIBBEAN SEA
Hawaiian Islands US
Honolulu
Hilo
Guadalupe Mexico
Bermuda UK
Hamilton
OTTAWA
WASHINGTON
MEXICO CITY
Prudhoe Bay
Kotzebue
Unalakleet
Fairbanks
Circle
Anchorage
Seward
Homer
Kodiak
Beaver Creek
Dawson
Mayo
Whitehorse
Ross River
Watson Lake
Dease Lake
Haines
Juneau
Sitka
Prince Rupert
Kitimat
Queen Charlotte
Inuvik
Paulatuk
Fort Good Hope
Coppermine
Echo Bay
Yellowknife
Hay River
Uranium City
Cluff Lake
Repulse Bay
Iqaluit
Inukjuak
Radisson
Schefferville
Goose Bay
Fermont
Moosonee
Sept-Iles
Natashquan
Baie-Comeau
Grande Prairie
Edmonton
Prince George
Jasper
Banff
Calgary
Williams Lake
Bella Coola
Port Hardy
Vancouver
Victoria
Regina
Winnipeg
Thunder Bay
Quebec
Montreal
Toronto
Fredericton
Charlottetown
Halifax
Seattle
Portland
Salem
Boise
Helena
Billings
Bismarck
Fargo
Duluth
Minneapolis
St Paul
Pierre
Cheyenne
Denver
Salt Lake City
Carson City
Sacramento
San Francisco
Las Vegas
Los Angeles
San Diego
Tijuana
Mexicali
Phoenix
Santa Fe
Albuquerque
El Paso
Ciudad Juárez
Omaha
Lincoln
Topeka
Kansas City
Des Moines
Jefferson City
Wichita
Oklahoma City
Milwaukee
Madison
Chicago
Lansing
Detroit
Buffalo
Cleveland
Pittsburgh
Columbus
Indianapolis
St Louis
Charleston
Frankfort
Nashville
Memphis
Little Rock
Dallas
Fort Worth
Austin
San Antonio
Houston
Galveston
Baton Rouge
New Orleans
Jackson
Mobile
Birmingham
Montgomery
Atlanta
Tallahassee
Jacksonville
Orlando
Tampa
Miami
Key West
Charlotte
Columbia
Raleigh
Richmond
Norfolk
Baltimore
Philadelphia
New York
Hartford
Providence
Boston
Albany
Montpelier
Concord
Portland
Augusta
Hermosillo
Chihuahua
Ciudad Obregón
Culiacán
Monterrey
San Luis Potosí
Tampico
Guadalajara
Leon
Morelia
Toluca
Puebla
Veracruz
Orizaba
Acapulco
Mérida
Campeche
Cancún
Pinar del Rio
Matanzas
Camaguey
Bayamo
Santiago de Cuba
Cayman Is UK
San Juan
Virgin Islands UK
Montserrat UK
Guadeloupe France

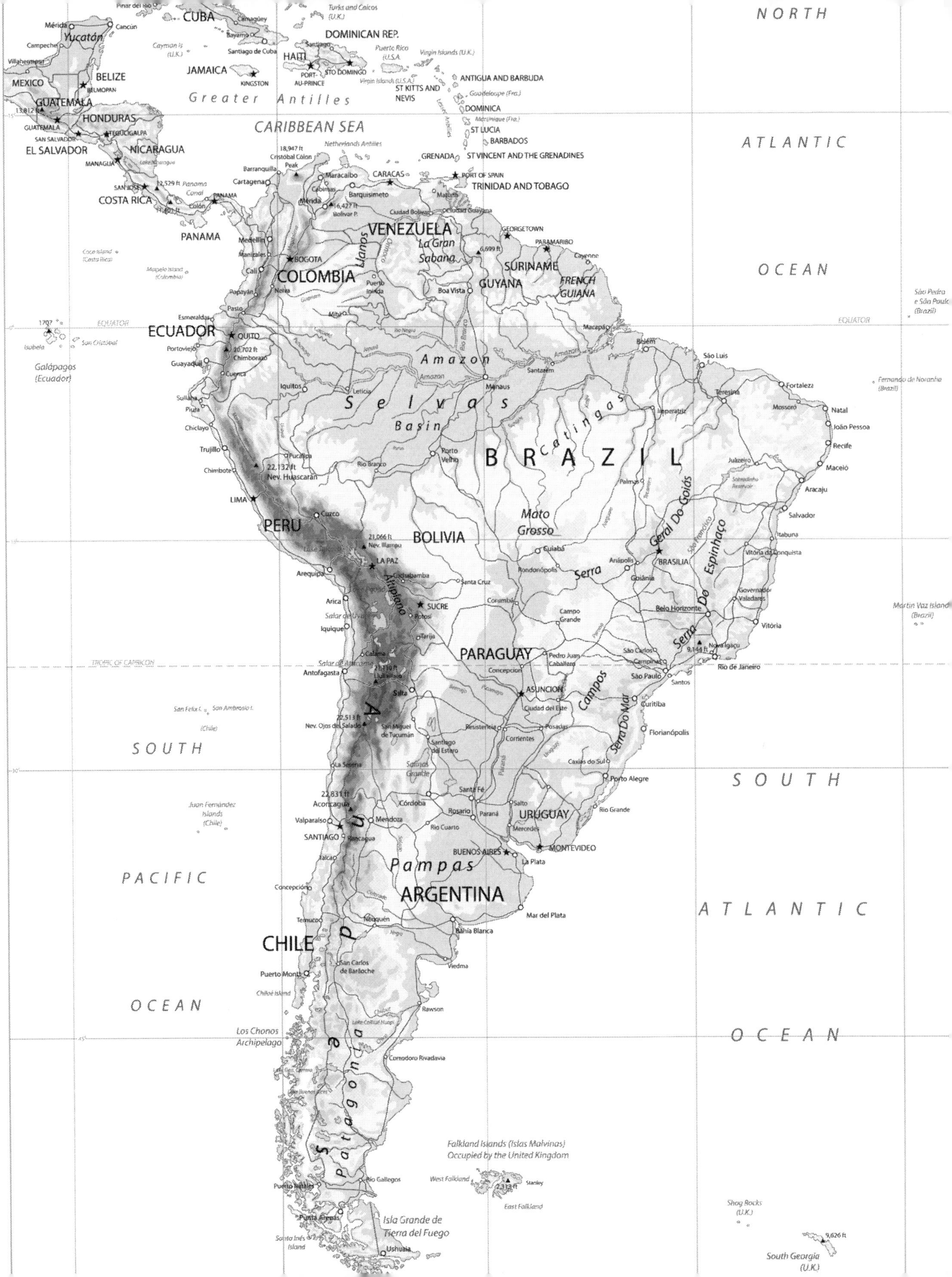

NORTH
ATLANTIC
OCEAN
CUBA
Turks and Caicos (U.K.)
DOMINICAN REP.
HAITI
PORT-AU-PRINCE
STO DOMINGO
Puerto Rico (U.S.A.)
Virgin Islands (U.K.)
Virgin Islands (U.S.A.)
ANTIGUA AND BARBUDA
ST KITTS AND NEVIS
Guadeloupe (Fra.)
DOMINICA
Martinique (Fra.)
ST LUCIA
BARBADOS
GRENADA
ST VINCENT AND THE GRENADINES
PORT OF SPAIN
TRINIDAD AND TOBAGO
Cayman Is (U.K.)
JAMAICA
KINGSTON
Santiago de Cuba
Camagüey
Bayamo
Cancún
Mérida
Campeche
Yucatán
Villahermosa
MEXICO
BELIZE
BELMOPAN
GUATEMALA
13,812 ft
HONDURAS
TEGUCIGALPA
SAN SALVADOR
EL SALVADOR
NICARAGUA
MANAGUA
Lake Nicaragua
SAN JOSE
12,529 ft
COSTA RICA
Panama Canal
Colón
PANAMA
Greater Antilles
CARIBBEAN SEA
Netherlands Antilles
18,947 ft
Cristóbal Colón Peak
Barranquilla
Cartagena
Maracaibo
CARACAS
Cabimas
Barquisimeto
Mérida
16,427 ft
Bolívar P.
Ciudad Bolívar
Ciudad Guayana
Maturín
VENEZUELA
La Gran Sabana
Llanos
Orinoco
GEORGETOWN
PARAMARIBO
Cayenne
6,699 ft
SURINAME
GUYANA
FRENCH GUIANA
Medellín
Manizales
BOGOTA
Cali
COLOMBIA
Cocos Island (Costa Rica)
Malpelo Island (Colombia)
Popayán
Pasto
Boa Vista
Puerto Inírida
Neiva
Mitú
Macapá
EQUATOR
Esmeraldas
ECUADOR
QUITO
20,702 ft
Chimborazo
Portoviejo
Guayaquil
Cuenca
1707
Isabela
San Cristóbal
Galápagos (Ecuador)
Belém
São Luís
Amazon
Santarém
Manaus
Iquitos
Leticia
Selvas
Basin
Fortaleza
Teresina
Mossoró
Natal
João Pessoa
Recife
Maceió
Aracaju
Imperatriz
Juazeiro
Catingas
BRAZIL
Porto Velho
Rio Branco
Pucallpa
Sullana
Piura
Chiclayo
Trujillo
Chimbote
22,132 ft
Nev. Huascarán
LIMA
PERU
Cusco
21,066 ft
Nev. Illampu
LA PAZ
BOLIVIA
Palmas
Mato Grosso
Cuiabá
Serra Geral Do Goiás
Serra Do Espinhaço
São Francisco
Salvador
Itabuna
Vitória da Conquista
BRASILIA
Anápolis
Goiânia
Rondonópolis
Serra
Arequipa
Cochabamba
Santa Cruz
Altiplano
SUCRE
Potosí
Corumbá
Campo Grande
Arica
Salar de Uyuni
Iquique
Tarija
Governador Valadares
Belo Horizonte
Vitória
Martin Vaz Island (Brazil)
São Pedro e São Paulo (Brazil)
Fernando de Noronha (Brazil)
9,144 ft
Nova Iguaçu
Rio de Janeiro
Serra Do Mar
TROPIC OF CAPRICORN
Salar de Atacama
Calama
Antofagasta
22,110 ft
Llullaillaco
PARAGUAY
Pedro Juan Caballero
Concepción
São Carlos
Campinas
São Paulo
Santos
ASUNCION
Ciudad del Este
Campos
Curitiba
Salta
22,513 ft
Nev. Ojos del Salado
San Miguel de Tucumán
Santiago del Estero
Resistencia
Posadas
Corrientes
Serra Do Mar
Florianópolis
San Felix I.
San Ambrosio I.
(Chile)
SOUTH
PACIFIC
OCEAN
La Serena
Salinas Grandes
Caxias do Sul
Porto Alegre
SOUTH
ATLANTIC
OCEAN
22,831 ft
Aconcagua
Juan Fernández Islands (Chile)
Córdoba
Santa Fé
Rosario
Paraná
Salto
URUGUAY
Mercedes
Rio Grande
Valparaíso
SANTIAGO
Mendoza
Rancagua
Río Cuarto
BUENOS AIRES
MONTEVIDEO
La Plata
Talca
Pampas
Concepción
ARGENTINA
Mar del Plata
Temuco
Neuquén
Bahía Blanca
Andes
CHILE
Puerto Montt
San Carlos de Bariloche
Viedma
Chiloé Island
Rawson
Los Chonos Archipelago
Comodoro Rivadavia
Patagonia
Falkland Islands (Islas Malvinas) Occupied by the United Kingdom
West Falkland
2,313 ft
Stanley
East Falkland
Río Gallegos
Puerto Natales
Punta Arenas
Isla Grande de Tierra del Fuego
Santa Inés Island
Ushuaia
Shag Rocks (U.K.)
9,626 ft
South Georgia (U.K.)

AMERICA

Anguilla

Eel-shaped, here is a small island in the northern Caribbean, sunny, calm and does not suffer from the sometimes gloomy social situation of other islands. Its beautiful beaches and upscale hotels, often coupled with good restaurants, have earned it a solid reputation among the tourist clientele, mostly American. Despite all this, the island remains little-known. It is nevertheless a remarkable site for a Caribbean stay in all its seaside splendor. The access can be made relatively easily (via Saint Martin) and the island is perfectly equipped for a stay without any problem. Only small shadow in the picture, outside the seaside, the island does not offer much.

• Its 33 white sandy beaches make Anguilla a small paradise on earth. 19 km of coastline along waters of intense blue and ideal temperature. On the menu: Mounday's Bay at the foot of the Cap Juluca Resort which hosts the stars of the world, Little Bay where from the cliffs pelicans dash in search of food and Shoal Bay, the most famous, whose coral reef protects the most turquoise waters of the island.

• Small deserted islands off the coast of Anguilla await you for even more pleasure and tranquility. Dog Island and Sandy Island are their names. A short day trip on a catamaran will allow you to reach them and also to visit Prickly Pear, another piece of paradise.

• On land, if you feel rested enough by all this idleness, you can go horseback riding, birdwatching (136 recorded species), cycling, and, for a change, taste the alcohols of the Pyrat Rum Distillery. A visit to the caves of Big Spring will allow you to contemplate the Arawak Amerindian inscriptions carved in the stone of the walls. Objects from the same period are preserved in the Heritage Collection Museum.

• Cuisine is one of the important components of the "Anguilla Experience », and the island is referred to as the gastronomic capital of the West Indies. In addition to the luxury restaurants, you can eat anywhere, thanks to the roadside barbecues, beach bars and grills prepared all along the coast. After dinner, everything happens at Sandy ground where all the rhythms are on the go.

Antarctica

An unusual but increasingly fashionable trip, especially among a clientele of travelers attracted by the ends of the world. The cruise from Argentina and Tierra del Fuego remains the only real option for the trip. It is not necessarily neither very complicated nor too uncomfortable but it is still very expensive. On arrival, discovery of fauna and landscapes of another planet, in an extremely harsh environment. Antarctica is a very atypical destination but, apart from its cost, it can be opened to all travelers with a spirit of adventure (and a definite attraction for cold regions, of course).

• Cruises along the Palmer Peninsula, the Lemaire Canal and Graham's Land will allow you to admire the cliffs of icebergs sometimes reaching up to 50 m in height. You can follow in the footsteps of the oceanographer Charcot, visit a few scientific stations and, if you have the means, board an icebreaker to discover the Ross Barrier or the Erebus volcano.

• Aside from the majestic landscapes, the traveler will find himself confronted with the most astonishing fauna on the planet. The most impressive penguin colonies live in these latitudes. Marine mammals such as elephants and leopard seals, humpback whales, seals, killer whales and rorqual whales can be admired from the deck of the boats.

• Away from the icy continent, the Kerguelen archipelago, part of the French Southern and Antarctic Lands (Taaf), is an extraordinary gathering place for mammals and seabirds that come here to breed. Albatrosses, penguins, petrels, skuas, elephant seals... they are the masters of these lands. If the islands are close to the Antarctic environment, they have the particularity of being partly free of ice. Their access is very regulated and is only by boat, via a long trip from Reunion Island.

Antigua and Barbuda

Magnificent beaches (certainly among the most beautiful in the world, including Half Moon Bay), beautiful coves, historic sites and an exotic and lively capital make Antigua a very good destination in the Caribbean. The icing on the cake is the small island of Barbuda, which completes the archipelago, almost entirely devoted to unspoiled nature (which is not so common in the region).

* St. John's, the capital, lies in a deep bay on the northwest coast of Antigua. The Cathedral, the National Museum, housed in the oldest building in the city, and the area's weekend farmers' market can be visited. To enjoy an exceptional view of the island and its surroundings (Guadeloupe can be seen there), take a tour to the site of Shirley Heights.

* The Indian Town Reserve on the east side of the island, as well as the famous Devil's Bridge cliff, are home to various species of birds. The megaliths of Greencastle Hill, probably erected in honor of a local sun goddess, stand on the west coast and are the occasion of a pleasant excursion.

* The coast of the Caribbean Sea has the most beautiful beaches, such as Half Moon Bay, Runaway Bay and Dickenson Bay, for example, as well as the most beautiful luxury hotels. At the southernmost tip of the island, English Harbour Bay attracts the international Jet Set because of its privileged location, which protects it from hurricanes, its idyllic scenery and its marina. It is also home to the historic site of Nelson's Dockyard, a colonial construction that is the most visited site on the islands.

* Voluntarily preserved from mass tourism, Barbuda has been able to preserve a flora and fauna of great richness that leaves an indelible impression on all those who are lucky enough to be able to contemplate this corner of nature. On the other hand, the seaside appeal is less than in Antigua.

Netherlands Antilles

Those still wrongly called the Netherlands Antilles, now dissociated and with autonomy, form a very different group of islands. The islands in the northern Caribbean and those in the south are completely opposite. In the north of the Caribbean arc, two pebbles (Saba and St. Eustatius also called Statia), with confidential tourism, a kind of end of the world, with undeniable exoticism, to which we must add the southern half of the island of St. Martin, highly urbanized and Americanized (large hotels and casinos). In the south, near Venezuela, three islands, Curaçao, Bonaire and Aruba, which have become autonomous regions of the Netherlands, combine the advantages. Located outside the hurricane zone, their climate is very sunny and so dry that it hosts cactus deserts, a landscape that is unheard of in the Caribbean. The colonial legacy has left a remarkable architecture, especially on Curaçao. The beaches are superb, as are the seabed, and the infrastructure is excellent. The clientele is largely American. The island of Aruba, the most touristic and independent island, has its own chapter.

BONAIRE :

* Located on the west coast of the island, the capital of Bonaire, Kralendijk, is a quiet and relaxed town. The colorful streets, lively markets, bars and restaurants guarantee a friendly atmosphere at any time of the year. Don't miss Fort Orange, built to defend the island in the past.

* Pink Beach, which stretches south of Kralendijk, is famous for its pink sand. Indeed, pulverized corals give it this very particular coloration. Ideal to contemplate the sunset, this beach is very busy on weekends.

* For more tranquility, visit Washington-Slagbaai National Park. Arriving at the black sand bay of Boca Cocolishi, dive into the warm and fishy waters of the protected coral reef where sponges bloom.

* For even more wilderness, make an appointment to visit the private Rooi Lamoenchi Reserve, east of Kralendijk. Cactus and aloe fields, here is one of those plantations that evoke the past. The poor huts of the slave house, located in the south of the island, are the counterpart.

CURAÇAO:

* Willemstad is the territorial capital of the Netherlands Antilles. The center of the city, with its peculiar colorful architecture (a governor having banned white houses), its beautiful natural harbour entrance and the Koningin Emmaburg floating bridge, has been inscribed on the UNESCO World Heritage List. In the evening, it is the turn of the casinos to illuminate the city with their colors.

* Curaçao benefits from the same climatic conditions as Bonaire, but has the advantage of having a much larger coastline than its neighbor, thus offering a greater variety of underwater sites accessible to divers. Sites such as Oswaldo's Dropoff, Car Pile or Jan Thiel will make them happy.

* For those who like to laze around, there are many beaches. From the most popular among the locals (Caracas Bay and Maria Panpoen) to the most discreet (Playa Kalki) and the best equipped (Jan Thielbay) there is something for everyone.

* You can round off your stay by visiting the Curaçao distillery, where the famous Curaçao liqueur is produced in Willemstad.

THE LEEWARD ISLANDS :

They are a thousand kilometers northeast of the previous ones, but are still part of the same whole, even though since 2007 the Netherlands Antilles has been gradually dissolving and the territories have become either regions or autonomous municipalities within the Netherlands.

* Saba and Saint Eustatius (Statia) are confettis, very isolated, and do not have beaches capable of competing with their southern sisters (only one beach, black sand, in Saba), but attract divers and hikers for the quality and preservation of their natural environment. The latter will be able to climb Mount Scenery in Saba and Mount Quill in St. Eustatius, which is drowned in the jungle. In the small villages, the atmosphere is timeless. Two superb destinations and two excellent surprises in prospect for curious travelers who will take the trouble to discover them.

* In a completely different register, here is Sint Maarten (Saint Martin). This island, shared by the Dutch and the French, has been experiencing a tourist boom for many years. Relaxation, water sports, diving, casinos and duty-free shopping... the program is the same as in the big international seaside resorts. Tourists are numerous, brought in particular by the huge cruise ships. The Dutch part is the most urbanized and Americanized, and thus the most touristic. Faced with the development the island has lost its identity and if it has everything of paradise for some, others find no interest except the color of its waters.

Argentina

This large South American country has a mixture of the exotic and the familiar. Undermined by an unprecedented crisis, which has led to insecurity and a degradation of infrastructure, Argentina remains a fairly easy destination without any particular problems. From the tropical jungle in the north, to the almost polar expanses of the south, the palette of landscapes is fabulous. Everything is spectacular in Argentina, the mountains, the immensity of the Pampa, the vastness of Patagonia. There is a little bit of everything, but it is better to venture there with time and preferably a certain budget to enjoy it fully.

The Andes Cordillera, which covers the whole length of the country, scrolls through the panoramas.

* The Quebrada de Humahuaca is a deep canyon where giant cacti grow. The beautiful landscapes are interspersed with small villages like Purmamarca, Maimará, Tilcara or Humahuaca where many pre-Columbian and colonial remains are preserved.

* Further south, the Moon Valley offers mineral landscapes with strange shapes. Paleontology enthusiasts will be able to look for vertebrate remains and saurian footprints.

* Then comes the "Roof of the Americas". The Aconcagua culminates at 6962 m and awaits hikers on foot (no pun intended). The light and wind are stronger here than elsewhere, and the vegetation is scarcer. It is up to you to exceed your limits in this exceptional adventure.

* The Lake District, around San Carlos de Bariloche, combines the natural beauty of the great American open spaces with the attraction of its villages that look like the Switzerland of the antipodes.

* The National Glacier Park opens the door to Patagonia. After the moving glaciers of Lago Argentino (including the famous Perito Moreno), you can admire the Fitz Roy massif, and then head straight to the southernmost city in the world: Ushuaia.

* To the north, on the border with Br, are ésilthe d falls, 'Iguazúwhich are among the most beautiful in the world. In the middle of the tropical forest, 275 waterfalls make up a thunderous landscape which you can approach within a few meters.

* Buenos Aires is one of the most populated cities in South America. It is divided into 48 neighborhoods, the *barrios*, and each one has its own particular atmosphere. Numerous museums and churches are scattered throughout this modern city and will allow you to take a break in the midst of the city's lively pace.

* A little further south is the p éninsule Valdèswhich is home to a very important marine fauna. Penguins, sea lions, sea lions and elephant seals, penguins, southern right whales and flamingos make up the Nuevo Gulf population.

* Occupying the southern third of the country, the famous Patagonia is a sparsely populated area, wild, made of immense plains. At its extremity, here is Tierra del Fuego, shared by Argentina and Chile. This archipelago is composed of several hundred islands and conceals landscapes of infinite beauty. Do not hesitate to embark from Ushuaia to go around the bay or discover the Beagle Channel.

Aruba

Now almost an independent country, Aruba remains nevertheless largely attached to the image of the South Netherlands Antilles. I.e. idyllic climate (no hurricanes, ideal year-round temperatures, maximum sunshine), dream beaches, multicolored marine life and American clientele. Americans are big fans of the small island and the infrastructure is entirely dedicated to them, starting with the often imposing hotels, in a style close to Florida. Aruba retains its appeal, especially for those who know how to look behind the hotel complexes, especially towards the Arikok Park and its astonishing expanses of cactus. For the rest, the beaches and the seabed are a sensation, and rightly so, carried by a never-ending summer.

* Many water sports are available on the island. Sailing, kitesurfing, windsurfing, deep-sea fishing, diving... there is something for everyone. Wrecks, coral and tropical fish populate the underwater landscape.

* Palm Peach, Eagle Beach, Rodgers Beach, Baby Beach, Hadikurari Beach... the beaches are not lacking and are faithful to the image of Epinal of the beautiful Caribbean. If you want to vary the pleasures, go diving in the natural pool or "conchi", called "Cura di Tortuga". This secret place is only accessible by 4x4, on horseback or on foot for the bravest.

* Arikok Park, which occupies almost 20% of the island, welcomes hikers. Numerous animals, rare and exotic plants, and drawings of the Arawak tribe will enliven your walk in this rather unique natural space.

* On the first Sunday of every month the roof and onion-shaped red copper towers of the Rococo Plaza Antique Museum host a flea market frequented by locals.

Bahamas

The name of this island country alone is enough to make people's minds wander. The Bahamas, supported by a strong tourism policy, are certainly among the great names in seaside tourism worldwide. Exoticism to be resold, the breath of the trade winds, the comfort of a high level and varied hotel infrastructure, easy access (Miami, an international city, if there is one, is only a hundred kilometers away), and of course, fine sand to be made of. This is the irresistible cocktail of the country. If the destination is adored by Americans, who come as neighbors and find all the comfort they are looking for while being kindly disorientated, Europeans are much less numerous. It must be said that it is not, far from it, a cheap destination, that the cold spells sometimes occur in winter although high season (most of the archipelago is north of the Tropic of Cancer, contrary to popular belief it is not a tropical destination) and that the image of the big resorts, with the Atlantis of Paradise Island at the head of the bow, chills some travelers. However, it should not be forgotten that the archipelago is vast and varied and offers hundreds of possibilities to isolate oneself in magnificent nooks and crannies. A superb destination on the whole, competing with its neighbors in the eternal Caribbean register, namely sun / price / activities.

* Of course, who says Bahamas, says beaches! They are magnificent, of fine white sand, sometimes pinkish, invariably bordered by a turquoise or emerald sea. A paradise which, although not in the tropics, has all the enchantments. In addition to relaxation, which is the primary activity, the beaches of the archipelago are also choice destinations for water sports, including sailing, deep-sea fishing and especially diving. The coral seabed is among the most beautiful in the world and offers a profusion of colors and marine life, with some stars like dolphins and reef sharks.

* The main island in terms of population is New Providence. It is notably home to Nassau, a small, lively capital city with Florida faux-air and British influences, where the historic center offers beautiful colonial architecture. There are also some museums such as the Pirates Museum. Every end of the year, the Junkanoo, the carnival, gathers the crowd in disguise in the streets to the rhythms of the calypso.

* The beautiful islands of Bimini, with moderate development, are above all prized by diving enthusiasts. In a superb setting one can discover the famous Bimini Road, an alignment of underwater stones which would be according to the legend the buried remains of the famous city of Atlantis. For most travelers the search for the lost city is however limited to the discovery of Paradise Island, located at the gates of the capital Nassau and connected by a bridge. This island entirely dedicated to tourism is home to Atlantis, one of the most extravagant hotel complexes on the planet. Giant aquariums with glass tunnels, reconstructions of monuments, this is the craziest thing east of Las Vegas.

* The island of Grand Bahama is the country's second largest tourist destination after New Providence and Paradise Island. American-style hotel infrastructures, superb beaches, numerous golf courses, sea excursions, the interests are concentrated around the second city of the country, Freeport and especially its seaside resort Port Lucaya.

* The archipelagos of the so-called "outer" islands, Abacos, Exuma and Andros, have similar and unstoppable assets. Postcard landscapes and Technicolor seabed. In Andros you can also discover the mangrove. Tourism is relatively limited and contrary to popular belief, the Bahamas is not a destination of great luxury but rather of simplicity.

* Great Inagua is little known, yet it is a paradise for nature lovers. It is inhabited among others by turtles and flamingos. Some guest rooms welcome travelers who come here.

• Harbour Island or Cat Island, in the Eleuthera archipelago, offer an idyllic version of the exotic islands where nature is queen, heavenly beaches, some of them pink sand, and divine sunsets. It didn't take much to make the Eleuthera the most exclusive archipelago in the country, with chic hotels and magazine-style guest houses. Far from the big hotel complexes, some islands offer small structures, with their feet in the sand, and in a colorful style of the most beautiful effect.

Barbados

Do you wonder what the English countryside would look like in the tropics? Look no further, Barbados is a piece of England in the Caribbean, a somewhat surreal but beautiful combination especially when tropical vegetation meets Victorian architecture. Independent, the island is still strongly marked by its former colony, with all the specificities of the region in terms of climate and landscapes, including postcard beaches. Propelled on the marketing plan by its international star, Rihanna, Barbados now officiates in the course of the great Caribbean tourism. It is a beautiful, well-equipped and easy to discover destination with a standard of living that is notoriously higher than on the surrounding islands and a social climate that is more welcoming.

• The west coast of the island is bathed by the Caribbean Sea. It extends its white sandy beaches punctuated with coconut and palm trees along these transparent waters, a little piece of paradise dedicated to idleness. In terms of activities, a wide choice is available to you: snorkeling and scuba diving in Paynes Bay, water sports in Holetown, picnic at Mullins beach, swimming in Speightstown and golf in Sandy Lane and Westmoreland.

• The south coast is the tourist epicenter, famous for its animation. Just after Bridgetown, restaurants and bars follow one another as in Accra Beach. If we add the lagoon of Sandy Beach, the windsurfing possibilities offered by the southern cape as in Silver sands and the fish market of Oistins, near Saint Lawrence Gap, this region is among the favorites of the tourists.

• If you're looking for a little more tranquility, you'll find it on the southeast coast at Full bay, Crane beach and Bottom bay. The east coast faces the Atlantic making it a much wilder area where the ocean has carved out the rock to create beautiful beaches that surfers will enjoy. Bathsheba, Cattlewash and Soup Bowl are the main spots. However, swimming there is dangerous.

• With its neo-Gothic parliament and its 18th century cathedral with its crenellated bell tower, Bridgetown has a London flair, all things considered. Elegant colonial homes, including Dacota's Mail on Broad Street, have been restored near the old port. The island was indeed under British rule for more than three centuries and the tradition of tea time and cricket are still alive and well.

• Inland is dotted with "chattel houses", colonial wooden houses that look like pavilions. From Wildey House to Sunbury Plantation House to the Morgan Lewis Sugar Mill, the Barbados National Trust organizes tours to discover the old plantations and properties of Barbados. The Francia Plantation in the center of the island, the Villa Nova to the east coast and St. Nicholas Abbey are also to be seen.

• In the vicinity of Mount Hillaby is the site of Harrison's cave, gateway to a network of caves connected by underground rivers. You can enter via an electric tramway to discover stalactites, stalagmites and natural waterfalls.

• In the vicinity of Bathsheba are the Andromeda Botanic Gardens where the most prestigious collection of tropical flowers and plants in the Caribbean is located. The Flower Forest is another park where fruit trees such as mango are in the spotlight. On the wildlife side, the Barbados Wildwife Reserve is home to green monkeys, flamingos, pelicans, turtles and caimans.

• The Caribbean is famous for its rums. In Barbados, its production dates back to the 17th century. A visit to the Mount

Gay Rum Visitors Centre or the West India Rum Refinery will give you a better understanding of the manufacturing process and allow you to taste it over a delicious Bajan lunch.

Belize

At the height of exoticism, in the heart of the Mayan Country, Belize is a small corner of Central America, little known and very different from its neighbors. Its population is different, its language as well, but the landscapes have nothing to envy to the jungles of Guatemala or the coast of the Mexican Yucatan. In reality, Belize could be a very big destination, as it has multiple attractions, between its tropical islands bordered by the second largest coral reef in the world, its jungles and Mayan ruins. On paper, everything is fine, but in practice the country is spoiling its own chances because of disastrous social management, which has led to significant insecurity in the main city of Belize City. Overwhelmed by internal conflicts, Belize does not sell itself well to the rest of the world, and tourism remains underdeveloped. Outside the islands, the tourism infrastructure is in its infancy, if not non-existent, and travel to Belize is therefore reserved for an experienced public.

- While northern Belize is made up of lowlands and swamps, these are gradually being replaced by pine trees and sugar cane fields before giving way to tropical forest in all its splendor. The rainforest hides a large community of howler monkeys that can be observed in the Community Baboon Sanctuary or in the wild in Bermudian Landing Village, near Belize city.

- In the center and west of the country is a more mountainous region where wildlife is protected in the Mountain Pine Ridge Forest Reserve. Caves, natural pools and waterfalls are to be discovered such as the Five Sisters Falls or the Hidden Valley Falls. The Guanacaste National Park, 4 km east of the capital, is full of mango trees, orchids, giant ferns... Going down south, the surroundings of the Mayan Mountains have a magnificent virgin forest that opens slowly to hiking even if the rains sometimes make the trails difficult to walk.

- The temples, pyramids, tombs and rich burial furnishings of the Mayan site of Altun Ha, 55 km north of Belize City, are among the great attractions of the interior. Lamanai, 58 km south of Orange Walk, Xunantunich 9 km west of San Ignacio, Nim Li, Punit and Lubaantum are other interesting sites where ruins of Mayan cities mingle with lush nature.

- To the north, the islets of the coast, the cays, are at the edge of a very long coral reef which makes them exceptional dive sites. Indeed, Caye Caulker for example, 1 hour by boat from Belize City, offers sumptuous coral gardens where all kinds of multicolored fishes live. The incredible visibility allows to dive up to 60 meters deep. A maze of underwater caves awaits the most experienced divers off the west coast.

- North of these, Ambergris Caye is the largest of the islands in the lagoon. Fishing villages and beautiful beaches make it a nice spot to radiate in the surroundings. You can organize a dive at the Blue Hole, a large sea hole that you can explore with a flashlight up to 40 m deep.

- For those who would not appreciate diving, the cayes also reserve some animal surprises on land and in the skies. Half Moon Caye is a bird reserve where 98 species of birds live. From June to August, turtles also come to lay their eggs on the beaches of the island.

Bermuda

Amazing small archipelago, in reality a single group of islands, the largest of which are connected to each other. If the name is famous, for the triangle and the tax haven it evokes, its location is unknown to the general public. Only confirmed geographers know how to locate Bermuda, which is willingly placed in the Caribbean while it is in the middle of the Atlantic, off the coast of South Carolina. We are therefore here largely outside the tropical zone. Nevertheless, the islands have the peculiarity of having a coral reef (exceptional at this latitude) and white sand beaches worthy of the

South Seas. Prized by a very wealthy American clientele, this British overseas territory plays the luxury card. Isolation and high prices make the archipelago a confidential destination.

• The most beautiful beaches of the South Coast, such as Horseshoe Bay and Warwick Long Bay are located in South Shore Park, between Southampton and Warwick. Many hotel complexes have been built there. The coral reef, in addition to providing quiet swimming areas, offers pink sand beaches and interesting marine life. In addition to this, there are numerous shipwrecks due to this famous triangle.

• While the more rocky north coast is not very conducive to swimming, apart from the beaches of Tobacco Bay, on the island of St. George, and Shelly Bay, in the municipality of Hamilton, it offers several sites that are worth a visit. You can visit the caves and underground lakes of Leamington Cave and Crystal Cave. The cities of Hamilton and St. George's have several historic monuments to see. In the west of the archipelago, Fort Scaur, near Somerset, will offer you a magnificent view of Great Sound Bay and its surroundings. On the western tip, don't miss the Royal Naval Dockyard in Sandys, an imposing fortress where the history of Bermuda is told.

Bolivia

Bolivia is often reduced to a few clichés. The traditional outfits of the Quechuas, the sickness of the mountains in La Paz, the cold of the Andean peaks, the dazzling salt desert. Yet Bolivia is much richer than that. From the top of the Andean mountains to the confines of the Amazon jungle, the country offers an incredible diversity for the visitor to explore. Not everything is easy, starting with transportation, but Bolivia does not present great difficulties for the traveler with a little experience. It should be kept in mind, however, that the country is still subject to episodic social crises and that poverty is more pronounced here than in neighboring countries. The infrastructure is not very well developed, and it is not an easy destination in terms of health (lack of means and multiple risks, whether related to altitude or tropical diseases in the Amazon region). A beautiful destination but one that is being prepared.

• The entire southwestern part of the country is crossed by the Andes which, at more than 4000 meters above sea level, unfurl their landscapes. Among them, exceptional sites such as the Uyuni Salt Flat, the largest salt desert in the world, or the Laguna Verde dominated by the famous Licancab volcanoúr.

• In perfect contrast, the east and southeast of the country are the domain of Amazonia, jungles and savannahs. The populations, the atmosphere and the climate are radically different there. In addition to the Mercado National Park, one discovers there a part of the Pantanal, an immense swamp where the fauna is abundant (annacondas, capibaras).

• Lake Titicaca that Bolivia shares with the P is érouone of those lakes that haunt our imagination. It is the largest in South America and the highest navigable lake in the world. L 'île du Soleiland its archeological sites like the palace of Pilkokaina, as well as the îles flottantes des Urosdecorations of the legend of the *children of the Sun*, the founders of the Inca empire.

• La Paz is the melting pot of the country where many Amerindian cultures mingle. This capital, the highest in the world (3660 meters), is surrounded by high Andean peaks that are both protective and frightening. To plunge in the tumult of the city is to discover festive traditions, its craft industry and some beautiful monuments (baroque church San Francisco) but also the reality of a country with many inequalities. Near the city, the landscapes of the Moon Valley and its fairy chimneys is a popular excursion.

• The Spanish colonization left its mark in many villages and cities like in Potosi whose Silver Mountain, the *Cerro Rico*, made the immense wealth in the sixteenth century or in Sucre and its white architecture.

• Pre-Columbian sites are also worth a visit. The ceremonial center of Tiahuanaco and its half underground temple, the Inkallatja Inca city and that of Samaipata tell a history buried for a long time, but which only asks to be recognized and developed.

Brazil

An immense country that could be described as the United States of the South, Brazil is an enchanted land. The land of embers remains dominated in the imagination of travelers by the wonderful city of Rio de Janeiro. Its carnival is the ultimate Latin fiesta experience and its bay is a Holy Grail for tourists. But beyond Rio, Brazil unfolds a natural and urban panorama that has almost no equal in the world. Largely located in the tropics, it blends exuberance, colonial flavor and lush. Salvador, Olinda, Floripa, Sao Luis, Ouro Preto, here are some urban stops not to be missed, among many others. The natural heritage is of infinite richness, with the Amazon and its mysteries as a highlight. To the south, the immense Pantanal marshland is home to a unique fauna. Of course, Brazil is also a coastline that unrolls thousands of kilometers of paradisiacal beaches with turquoise waters. Of course, there is the back of the postcard, in a country that is gnawed by inequality, where misery is still the daily life for many Brazilians, where violence in the favelas poses a serious social problem. Environmental problems are also of growing concern. This should not hinder a trip to the country, which remains easily accessible, well-equipped, with high sanitary standards. The traveler, even a beginner, is welcome here, but he will show common sense and a little caution if he wants to make the most of the Brazilian experience, one of the most beautiful in terms of tourism.

STATES OF RIO AND SÃO PAULO :

• Rio is "the only big city in the universe where the simple fact of existing is a true happiness" said *Blaise Cendars* in front of this urban jungle at the edge of the tropical forest with the ocean as a horizon. Undoubtedly, the social climate was not so degraded in his time and many cariocas may not see the existence of such a happy eye in their city. Several sites are unavoidable in the Wonderful City: the Sugar Loaf and the Corcovado from where you will have a breathtaking view of the bay, the Jardim Botanico, one of the most lush parks in the city, the Lapa and Santa Teresa neighborhoods, the small *Montmartre carioca*, the churches of the Centro and Lapa and, of course, the mythical beaches of Copacabana and Ipanema. You will be able to visit samba schools and even enter the favelas if you are accompanied by a local agency. Finally, if you come in February, you will not escape the festive madness of the carnival.

• In the Rio region, it can be interesting to venture into the mountains, less than 100 kilometers from the city. *Petropolis*, *Teresopolis* or *Nova Friburgo* are temperate and very European stages, in the heart of a beautiful alpine nature.

• Paraty, the Mecca of Brazilian tourism, 280 km from Rio, is a small colonial town of the 18th century almost intact and very well restored.

• Ilha Grande, between Rio and São Paulo, is a preserved island, surrounded by turquoise waters. There, everything is order and beauty, luxury, calm and adventure! Tourism is regulated there for the protection of the site. You will be able to discover the jungle there in complete safety, and take advantage of the beaches to practice all kinds of nautical activities.

• São Paulo, a gigantic megalopolis and the economic capital of the country, will immerse you in the raw Brazilian life. Carried away by the crowd, you will come across far fewer tourists than elsewhere. Visit the gigantic city center, with its forest of buildings but also its historical constructions, especially the Patio do Colégio. The MASP and Pinacoteca museums are also worth a visit. Finally, for shopping and restaurants, the city is unparalleled on the continent. It's a world city that you have to know how to tame, however, and which will not be to everyone's taste, with its glaring inequalities and its sometimes intimidating side.

• Florianopolis, nicknamed *Floripa*, is one of the most popular tourist spots in the south. The city is located on the island (and state) of Santa Catarina, in a region of gentle mountains with subtropical forests. You will be charmed by the endless beaches, the authentic fishing villages and the surrounding nature: the ideal setting for a romantic or family vacation.

MINAS GERAIS AND CENTRAL WEST :

• Ouro Preto is a baroque pearl not to be missed which was one of the largest gold deposits in Brazil. Churches not knowing what to do with it are scattered all over the streets, some were built and decorated by the famous Aleijadinho who lived here. The whole city is classified as a World Heritage Site. Not far, you can visit the gold mines of Passagem by going down there in a wagon worthy of Indiana Jones.

• Diamantina is a site of important diamond mines also classified as a World Heritage Site for its preserved colonial character. In spite of its undeniable charm, tourists are less numerous there, which gives the opportunity to dream a little.

• Brasília, the capital, a former architectural masterpiece inspired by Le Corbusier, has aged a little but is still interesting. The originality of its situation lost at the borders of the country, perched on a plateau in the middle of a luxuriant jungle, nevertheless gives it a certain interest. Do not hesitate to follow a guided tour of the modern city, to go up to admire the panorama from the television tower, and to be surprised by the numerous monuments and buildings with a delirious architecture...

• In Foz do Iguazu, 200 waterfalls, reputed to be among the most beautiful in the world, spill their waves from the top of their 75 m, on a 2.5 km long front. That is how many liters per 100?

• Campo Grande, capital of Mato Grosso do Sul, can be a starting point to radiate in the Pantanal, the most beautiful natural reserve of animals in Brazil.

• Bonito, southwest of Campo Grande, is a very pleasant stop for its varied flora and fauna, waterfalls, crystalline lakes and numerous white water and caving activities.

THE NORTHEAST :

• Sao Luis do Maranhao, which was nicknamed in its time "Brazilian Athens", especially for its artistic lights, is a beautiful colonial city that the remoteness and restoration programs have preserved from the aggressions of time. Today, it is the Brazilian capital of reggae! This island is classified as a World Heritage Site. Stroll through its beautiful historic center and, if possible, take a boat trip to the magical village of Alcantara.

• From Sao Luis, you can easily get to the National Park dos Lençois Maranhenses, one of the most unmissable sites in the country. Imagine giant white dunes which undulate on hundreds of thousands of hectares, interspersed with thousands of small freshwater lakes in shades of green and blue... The departure is precisely from Barreirinhas, a nice little provincial town.

• Salvador da Bahia, the most African city of the continent will fascinate you with its tropical and festive character. Don't miss the Pelourinho district and its baroque churches (especially the Bonfim church), the Convent of São Francisco and the capoeira *rodas* at Fort Santo Antônio, Terreiro de Jesus or the Fundação Mestre Bimba. If you add to this the Bahian gastronomy of the region and the sumptuous beaches (Itapuã, Estella Maris, Barra, do Flamengo and Jardim de Alá), it is likely that you will never be able to leave.

• Recife is nicknamed the Brazilian Venice, which is a bit presumptuous let's be honest. The old city offers some attractions (churches, small squares and market), but the whole is rather dilapidated, which contributes to give the city a special (and not always very welcoming) atmosphere. The beaches, famous for sharks, are to be avoided outside the seaside district of Boa Viagem, a Miami Beach with a Brazilian sauce, protected by a rocky barrier.

• Olinda, bordering Recife, has kept its authenticity. Like Ouro Preto, it is considered a historical jewel. It is a small colonial town full of colors, very touristic, adored by young bohemians and classified as a World Heritage Site. One could deplore its Disneyland side, but a little enchantment can sometimes do some good. Its carnival, as well as that of Recife, is one of the most particular and popular in Brazil.

* A little further inland, Fazenda Nova (the New Jerusalem), is a city copy of the Jerusalem of Palestine at the time of Christ. During Holy Week, hundreds of inhabitants participate in the theatrical and grandiose re-enactment of the Passion of Christ throughout the city.

* Natal, a large city and state capital, is known for its beaches and sunny climate. The city will be especially your starting point for excursions in buggy to the beaches and lagoons of the surroundings, like in Genipabu where your driver will give you strong sensations while hurtling down the sand dunes. Don't hesitate to go snorkeling in Pirangi and Maracajau or to spend a few days in Pipa, a cosmopolitan and trendy surf spot with beautiful cliff landscapes.

* Fortaleza is a large city with a square shape and a large waterfront lined with buildings and palm trees, a sort of Miami in the Brazilian style. Goodbye history lovers and welcome to the party people! The nightclub "O Pirata" is the largest in the world. It is also an excellent starting point to explore Ceara and its fabulous beaches.

* To the north of Fortaleza, discover the fishing village of Canoa Quebrada, where you will find the most famous beach in the region with its red rock landscapes and waterfalls rushing into the sea. Specially developed for tourists, it is a good place to live during the week, because on weekends and holidays the place is crowded. You will be able to make in the surroundings nice excursions in buggy.

* The old fishing village of Jericoacoara mixes coconut palms, dunes, cliffs, lakes, white sand and sweetness of life for the happiness of the tourists who are more and more numerous to succumb to its charm. One reaches it only in 4x4, because even if the place is connected, the streets are still made of sand and the electricity weakens. The detour by this paradise certainly takes a little time, but is really worth it.

* The archipelago of Fernando de Noronha, 400 m from the coast, is a national natural park classified you know where. These exceptional atolls abound with varieties of birds, fish and marine mammals, including dolphins. Hiking, boat trips, snorkeling, diving, surfing, contemplation will be on your menu.

THE AMAZON :

* Manaus is the gateway to the Amazon, which experienced a major boom at the beginning of the 20th century with the exploitation of rubber. Remains today the vestiges of this opulence that you will discover with astonishment while visiting the old town and the opera house.

* It is from Manaus that you will be able to organize day trips by boat or canoe. A must is to go to the meeting of the waters: the unique spectacle of two rivers that meet in the same bed and continue to flow side by side without mixing.

* Of course, the main activity of the region is the discovery of the jungle, wild and teeming at will. From 3 days to 3 weeks and more, many types of expeditions are possible. It's up to you to organize according to your time, your money and your desire for adventure, 3 types of excursions will be proposed to you: in a lodge in the surroundings of Manaus, roaming by sleeping in hammocks in camp, or a river excursion by sleeping on the boat, in hammocks or in a cabin.

* Belém is an excellent base to shine in the great mouth of the Amazon. On the spot, discover the port, the old town and the Ver-o-Peso Amazonian market, parks and museums. In the surroundings, the excursion to the parrot island is a must for a sunrise with a cloud of colorful birds.

* At 170 km from Belem, the island of Algodoal is for lovers of virgin nature and simplicity. On the program: walks and horseback riding along the beaches, ornithological excursions, boat and bicycle trips to the surrounding villages, kayak trips with camp on the beach, all in the heart of the largest jungle in the world.

Canada

Canada shines especially in the eyes of travelers with its gentle alchemy between large metropolises and infinite natural spaces. Far from being overshadowed by its imposing neighbor to the south, Canada imposes its calm, the quality of its welcome, and its varied tourist offer. Toronto, Montreal and Vancouver, the country's three major cities, are just as deserving of discovery as New York, Chicago and Los Angeles. Other notable urban stops complete the picture, including the capital Ottawa, the oceanic city of Victoria, and historic Quebec City, the only fortified city in North America. Exploring nature is just as easy, but sometimes access takes time, and remote areas require good organization to be explored. The only real danger in the country would be to go on an adventure without a minimum of preparation. For the rest, the traveler will find Canada a very easy destination, where the infrastructures are of excellent quality. Winters, which are very harsh outside the extreme southwest of the country, will put off the most timid but it is important to know that the country is perfectly adapted to these conditions. The summer is much hotter than one might imagine (swimming is not excluded on some coasts and lakes), even if it does not last long. A major destination.

THE WEST :

- BRITISH COLUMBIA, ALBERTA, YUKON, NORTHWEST TERRITORIES -

* The Rocky Mountains dominate all of western Canada. Banff and Jasper, two major national parks in the southwest, are connected by the "Glacier Highway" and can be explored on foot in the summer or on skis in the winter. The most spectacular of the two is Banff because of the beauty of its lakes where you can see grizzly bears, brown bears and wolves.

* The archipelagos and fjords of the Pacific coast offer superb and sometimes inaccessible stone architecture. On Vancouver Island is the great forest of Cathedral Grove where the firs rise to breathtaking heights. It is also on this island that the capital of British Columbia is located: Victoria, a nice maritime city, with Victorian architecture (obviously).

* The Northwest Territories is the largest and coldest region in Canada. Have the courage to brave the conditions to meet the Inuit, the icebergs and the tumultuous rivers that flow through it. The canyons born of the South Nahanni are to be discovered by kayak. This river finally joins the Mackensie River which ends spectacularly in the Far North.

* Vancouver is a cosmopolitan city with a relaxed atmosphere and temperate climate. The parks, the seaside, the backdrop of mountains, the rugged coastline make it a panorama city. Within 30 minutes from downtown, if the bridges are not too congested, a mountainous region offers its slopes to skiers in the resorts of Grouse Mountain, Mount Seymour and Cypress Mountain. About 100 kilometers north, the famous resort of Whistler-Blackcom lives up to its international reputation.

THE CENTER :

- SASKATCHEWAN, MANITOBA, NUVANUT -

* The economy of this region is mainly based on the cultivation of wheat and this can be seen in terms of the landscape. Huge meadows crossed by the wind stretch as far as the eye can see, beavers and moose have made their home here. Cold in winter, very hot in summer, it is not a very touristic territory except for example on the shores of Lake Winnipeg for fishing and canoeing fans.

* To the north of the region, the Churchill River waters many rivers and waterfalls before reaching Hudson Bay. It is here that in the fall, you will be able to admire the polar bears gathering before reaching the ice pack.

* Even further north is Nunavut. Lovers of tundra and other icy lands, welcome! This is a territory in its own right where 25,000 Inuit live between tradition and modernity. Snowmobiles, dog sleds and cross-country skiing will be perfect means of locomotion to meet them.

THE EAST :

- ONTARIO -

Canada's most Americanized province is an almost logical continuation of the neighboring United States, with the added benefit of Canadian tranquility. Main engine of the country's economy, the most populated province, Ontario is, with Quebec, the Canadian region that is the most complete in terms of tourism.

• One of the world's most popular tourist attractions is in Ontario: Niagara Falls. They are not so high (only 48 metres) but they are exceptionally wide and have the most powerful flow in North America. On the Canadian side, floodlights illuminate both sides of the falls until midnight so you can enjoy the spectacle day and night.

• Algonquin Park and Quetico Park as well as the Great Lakes region will delight travelers with the beauty of their landscapes and the lively Indian traditions of its inhabitants. On Lake Huron, for example, Manitoulin Island is the home of the Ojibwa Indians.

• Toronto is Canada's largest city and the country's main economic metropolis. In this, it competes with *Montreal*, but also because of its cosmopolitanism and its cultural life, unequalled in the country. Its buildings are impressive, such as the CN Tower which reaches 553 meters in height, and its museums are numerous. The Canadian counterpart of New York is a city full of energy, the pulsating heart of the country.

• The federal capital, Ottawa, is often overlooked by tourists, who generally travel from Montreal to Toronto (and vice versa) without stopping there. Too bad, because it is a surprising city, literally straddling the two sides of the country, French and English. The lively Byward district, the superb Canadian Parliament, the Rideau Canal Parkway in the heart of downtown, numerous museums, and great energy make the city a recommended stop for a few days.

- QUEBEC -

Quebec, in the east of Canada, is the most touristic province in the country among francophones, and for good reason, French is spoken there! This "America in French version" is an exciting and very rich destination. From the Eastern Townships, a region reminiscent of New England, to the expanses of the Far North with its perpetual winters, through the metropolis of Montreal and the historic city of Quebec, the Belle Province is definitely worth a visit.

• The St. Lawrence River is the backbone of the region. Its 1,800 kilometers are dotted with ancient coastal villages, islands, bird and marine mammal sanctuaries, lighthouses, and rural or steep coastlines. In the estuary of the river, it is the turn of whales and their relatives to take part in shows, especially in Tadoussac Bay between April and October.

• At the gateway to Quebec City, the Charlevoix region and, further south, the Mont-Tremblant National Park, you will be amazed by their flora, fauna and typical villages. Cross-country skiing, snowshoeing, hiking, canoeing, mountain biking, wilderness camping and swimming are on the program to get you moving while admiring the scenery.

• The Gaspé Peninsula is the peninsula in central Quebec where the continental part of the Appalachians ends. Taking Route 132 allows you to take a complete tour of this vast region and access all its tourist attractions. Hikers will choose Forillon National Park, northern wildlife enthusiasts (deer, caribou and moose) will choose Gaspésie, and paleontologists will choose Miguasha. Ornithologists will head to Bonaparte Island, where thousands of gannets gather between April and November, and those who are also tempted by salmon fishing will head to Anticosti Island. Further on, the Magdalen Islands offer the change of scenery of small colorful villages and superb landscapes.

• 36,000 km of marked trails await travelers on snowmobiles, dog sleds and snowshoes. The Mont Sainte-Anne, Outaouais, Lac Beauport and Laurentian region resorts welcome skiers of all kinds every winter.

• Montreal, the metropolis, and Quebec City, the historic capital, separated by about 3 hours of driving, combine European culture and North American modernity and charm visitors with their vibrant atmosphere, energy and human character. A visit to both cities is both complementary and a must during a trip to the Belle Province. In *Montreal, the* wide avenues, the buildings, the trendy neighborhoods, the shopping, the many restaurants, the red brick architecture, so typical of North America, but also the Old Montreal, very cinematographic. In *Quebec City, the* small streets, the cafés, the Château Frontenac overlooking the St. Lawrence River and the historic squares of the historic district of Petit Champlain. Montreal is also considered to be the most festive and lively city in the country, a Latin spirit obliges, as for Quebec City, it is by far the most proudly francophone.

THE ATLANTIC REGION :

- NEW BRUNSWICK, NOVA SCOTIA, PRINCE EDWARD ISLAND, NEWFOUNDLAND -

* The national parks in this region will delight all hikers, to name just two: Kouchibouguac Park and its barrier islands, dunes, forests, lagoons and salt marshes and Fundy Park where you can walk on the ocean floor at low tide.

* All along the Atlantic coast, autumn is a season when the red color of the maples makes every patch of the landscape shine. Prince Edward Island and Cape Breton Island are destinations in their own right, invigorating and restful.

* In northern Labrador, you can go and watch the icebergs pass by during the months of May, June and July. As for the whales, they arrive with the capelin in June and you can see them all summer long. The aurora borealis lights up the sky of the region, especially in autumn and winter.

Chile

The immense South American serpentine that is Chile is a relative mystery to the traveler. Its remoteness and an unknown tourist offer leaves it in the shadow of its neighbors, especially Peru and Argentina. Nevertheless, Chile is one of the most varied destinations in South America. It is a richer and safer country than most countries on the continent. Only Uruguay resembles it in these respects, but it cannot claim to rival Chile's immense variety. Although it is undeniably South American, the country has a rather marked European side in its atmosphere. Its landscapes are truly splendid and very varied, from glaciers and tundra to arid deserts and Mediterranean-type valleys in the center of the country. Transportation is not a problem, except in Patagonia where the 4x4 is necessary and the tracks are sometimes bad. Only the wilderness (especially in the deserts and cold regions), requires preparation to explore it. Chile is a beautiful destination for all kinds of people.

THE NORTH :

* At the border with Bolivia is the Lago Chungará. At 4500 meters above sea level, flamingos live there in the shade of volcanoes like Parinacota. All around is the Lauca National Park where vicuñas, viscaches and guanacos live in landscapes of a staggering beauty.

* To the north, Chile is separated from the P érouby the Atacama Desert, the driest desert in the world. From San Pedro de Atacama, go on an expedition to the salt lakes (such as the Atacama Salt Lake or the Surire Salt Lake), the lagoons (Miscanti) et Miniquesand the d. geysers. 'El Tatiolf you go as far as the north of Calama, you will find the open-pit copper mine of Chuquicamata. 13 km west of San Pedro de Atacama, lies the valley ée de la Luneand its fantastic landscapes.

* A little further south, here is the "Little North" going from Chanaral to the Aconcagua River. Land of contrasts, this region is home to one of the prettiest cities in Chile, La Serena. A unique phenomenon occurs there, the heavy rains and the presence of the el niño current give rise to the *desierto florido* (where the arid desert is covered with a thousand flowers).

THE CENTER :

• The Chilean coasts are not particularly exploited for tourism. It is in the region of Valparaiso that you will find the ideal places to relax. Valparaiso is criss-crossed by funiculars that will allow you to visit the cerros where a joyful (and colorful) architectural anarchy reigns. Nearby, Viña del Mar is the tourist capital of Chile because of the beauty of its beaches and its proximity to the capital.

• Santiago de Chile is located in the center of the country. Different from the other capitals of South America, much more European, it will be able to occupy you the time of a stop by visiting its various museums and the cohabitation of its various architectural styles, between modern buildings and old historical center. In addition, it presents a mosaic of interesting neighborhoods.

• The owners of the haciendas of the Colchagua Valley have organized themselves to give tourists the opportunity to discover the country's vineyards along the "wine route". Visits to the wineries and wine tastings are available.

• Chiloé is an island off the coast of Puerto Montt known for its multicolored habitat on stilts. On the archipelago, the Chiloé mythology, more than 500 years old, is still alive and has penetrated into the beautiful wooden churches of the island, more than 16 of which are classified by UNESCO as World Heritage.

THE SOUTH :

• In the Northern Ice Field of Patagonia lies the Laguna San Rafael, the most equatorial marine glacier in the world. Electrically blue, it throws itself and breaks into the ocean in whole sections.

• Torres del Paine National Park is located between the Andes Mountains and the Patagonian Steppe. Mountains, glaciers, valleys and large blue-green lakes make up the landscape. Numerous hiking trails, punctuated by refuges, make it a must for all trekking fans.

• Tierra del Fuego and the fjords of Southern Patagonia offer, as in Argentina, an incredible spectacle. Separated from its neighbor by the Andes mountain range, nature expresses itself in the same disproportion. The black rock of Cape Horn at the tip of the continent abounds in legends that are as high as the landscapes. With the North Cape and the Cape of Good Hope it is part of these mythical places, true ends of the world.

- Easter Island -

Halfway between Chile and Tahiti, Easter Island is an isolated island in the southeastern Pacific Ocean, particularly known for its monumental statues. Although it is a Chilean territory, the Rpanui community jealously watches over the traces of its history with the help of UNESCO, which inscribed it on the World Heritage List in 1995.

• This island is famous for its megalithic remains of the Rapanui. The archaeological heritage includes about 900 basalt statues, the moais, 4 m high on average, and nearly 300 terraces piled at the foot of these statues, the ahû. Elaborated between the year 800 and 1680, these statues are almost all erected on the periphery of the island and turning their backs to the ocean.

• The majority of the statues come from a huge quarry extending on the slopes and in the crater of the volcano Rano Raraku. We can see a very large number of moais, some of them finished and erected at the foot of the slope, others still in different states, from the draft to the near completion.

• The Pu-Kao are the hats of the Moai intended to be added on top of the statues, they recall the traditional hairstyle of the islanders. They are made of a reddish lava stone, while the one of the moais is grey. They come from the crater of another small volcano, the Puna Pau. The largest can reach up to 3 meters in diameter. They are sometimes found lined up on the ground.

* In some sites, we find the trace of old houses, probably very rudimentary in the shape of an overturned boat. One can also observe some better preserved constructions such as hen houses.

* At the place called the "navel of the world" there is a huge pebble of volcanic stone around which are arranged four rocks representing the four cardinal points. If you approach a compass to check its orientation, you will see the needle panic.

* The Rano is the southernmost volcano of the island, on which the civilization that succeeded the Moais at the end of the seventeenth century built the ceremonial site of Orongo on the south face. The "Bird Man" ceremony took place there where the champions of each tribe had to descend 300 meters down the cliff and swim almost two kilometers to the Moto Nui islet to wait for the female Manutara bird to lay her eggs. Spectators waited for them in circular houses made of flat stones piled up with a roof covered with grass.

* Most of the surface of the island is a national park and is not inhabited. It is criss-crossed by hordes of wild horses brought by Westerners. Formerly, almost the whole coast was inhabited by different clans. Today, there is only one village left, that of Hanga Roa, where there are small shops, houses separated by low lava stone walls and a small cemetery.

Colombia

Magnificent Colombia, splendid and large country that combines the beauty of the tropical Andes with those of the Caribbean coast. It shares with its neighbor Venezuela some of the most beautiful landscapes in the world. It is a highly exotic country but still trapped in a faded image. It is therefore time to visit Colombia. Its colonial cities, some of which have become real metropolises, are beautiful stopovers, Cartagena in the lead, but also Medelin, whose name was linked to the drug cartels and which is now a lively student city where an eternal spring reigns. Nature has been generous with Colombia, offering it the splendid natural park of Tayrona, embellished by the Ciudad Perdida, source of the legends of Eldorado, and its beaches among the most beautiful in the world, or a corner of Amazonia. Tourism is now a reality in Colombia, but the destination is still reserved for experienced travelers. Transportation remains problematic, and the plane is recommended compared to the road which can be dangerous, especially at night and especially in isolated sites. Some internal conflicts still exist and the border region of Panama is still really not recommended. However, it is useless to postpone a trip in the country, as long as one prepares a minimum. Much more than security, it is more classical sanitary problems that could slow down the visitors today. The country has many areas of yellow fever and malaria is found everywhere at low altitude.

* The San Agustin Archaeological Park is located in the heart of the Andes in the region of El Huila. 300 monumental sculptures, both realistic and abstract, bear witness to the art of a civilization that reached its peak during the first eight centuries of our era, all immersed in a sumptuous forest dotted with waterfalls.

* 50 km northeast of Bogota is the colonial city of Guatavita and the famous Laguna de Guatavita, sacred lake of the Muiscas Indians and cradle of the Eldorado myth. This lake, at the bottom of a harmonious funnel probably due to the impact of a meteorite, is perched at 3000 meters above sea level and offers splendid panoramas.

* The fall of the Tequendama jump, 32 km from Bogota, is also worth the detour. One comes there as much for its mysterious ghost hotel as for the landscape. The Rio Bogota plunges perpendicularly before crashing 132 meters below. Legend has it that Bochica, a demigod descending from the sun, opened the rocky bar of his scepter to save his people from the accumulation of water due to the flood.

* Located on the Caribbean Sea, Cartagena, former stronghold of the Kingdom of Spain, is a city in the Andalusian style. Its flowered patios, churches, fortress, cobbled streets and brightly colored houses, all perched on the turquoise Caribbean Sea, make it the country's premier tourist site. The beaches of Boccachia (next to the fortress of San Fernan-

do) or Marbella are superb. Two hours by boat to the south, you will find the islands of the Rosary, a true paradise for divers, fishermen or simple bathers. Much further away, the islands of San Andrés and Providencia are two small pearls of the Caribbean, still not very touristy and notable for their lagoons.

• The big cities in Colombia have long had a bad reputation, built by pickpockets in *Bogotá* and drug dealers in *Medellín*, among others. Yet, here again, things have changed. Bogota's old town, its mus, ée de l'Orconvents and churches make it an interesting stopover. Climb up to the sanctuary of *Montserrate* to see the sprawling city as a whole. Medell, ín- meanwhile, is the country's main cultural center located in a beautiful site at the foot of the Andes mountain range.

• Tayrona National Park, in the northwest of the country, is gradually becoming one of its major tourist attractions. Between luxuriant jungle and turquoise sea, the park unfolds exceptional landscapes, a rich fauna, and superb beaches.

• It is impossible to talk about Colombia without talking about coffee. The plantations of the Coffee Triangle, in the center of the country near *Manizales*, offer both the charm of landscapes and haciendas.

Costa Rica

A real textbook case of tourism success, Costa Rica is the heavyweight of tourism in Central America (excluding Mexico) and certainly its most accessible destination. Not so long ago, this small country was, like its neighbors, the field of exploration for the only adventurers. Here, the jungle is queen and nature is a symphony. Where some countries in the region have remained mired in social crises that penalize them greatly, Costa Rica has taken the path of eco-tourism, wisely and successfully. Stable, safe, with infrastructures that can still be improved but quite correct, it offers nature lovers the unique opportunity to dive into the wonders of the volcanoes and the tropical forest, with the greatest possible ease. Beware, this does not mean that the environment has been tamed or even that it is an "easy" adventure, the jungle remains the jungle, but it is certainly one of the most favorable places for its discovery. The coasts are the other great asset of the country, even if the Pacific waves are merciless. An exploration within the reach of the majority of travelers, who will nevertheless prepare their trip and will not go totally unexpectedly. To approach the country well one should not idealize it either. If it is doing significantly better than most of its neighbors, it is still tossed in the old ways of Central America, with a delinquency all the same problematic (although the tourist circuit is not more concerned than elsewhere), quite dangerous roads (winding and chaotic driving), and a level of health far from Western standards (public infrastructure is weak, tropical diseases are very present even if it should be noted that malaria is almost eradicated). All in all, a remarkable destination for its nature, its rather unique eco-touristic approach, and its exoticism without major difficulties.

• Let's start with the most touristy place in the country: the Pacific coast. South of the exceptional site of Puntarenas and around the Nicoya Peninsula, tourists enjoy the beaches despite the waves which can be very strong. For the divers, the paradise is called the Cocos Islands a few dozen kilometers from the coast.

• For those who would rather choose the Atlantic coast, know that you will not be disappointed either. Palm trees and coral reefs are reminiscent of the most beautiful beaches of the West Indies. In summer, you can observe the laying of green turtles in the Tortuguero area (which can only be reached by boat or plane). Howler monkeys, crocodiles and poisonous frogs also inhabit the park of the same name.

• For the budding Indiana Joneses, the country holds many other surprises in terms of fauna and flora. The lute tortuses lay their eggs on the Pacific coast in the Santa Rosa National Park, the quetzals nest in the Monte Verde region and birds, alligators, reptiles, jaguars and anacondas hide in the Corcovado National Park.

• Taking the railroad that goes from Puerto Limon to Puntarenas will allow you to cross the whole country from the Atlantic to the Pacific through the jungle and the Central Cordillera. For the brave who want to observe more closely the treasures of the center of the country. Hiking on foot or horseback is quite feasible.

- Several active volcanoes are located on this axis that divides the country from north to south: the Arenal, the Poas and the Irazu. The ascent of the latter presents no difficulty and will give you a rare opportunity to admire the Atlantic and the Pacific from the same summit.

Cuba

It's always complicated to present a destination whose good sides are also the bad sides, you don't know on which foot to dance. The socialist regime, dictatorial and repressive, has left Cubans in a misery that is sometimes quite shocking (the grocery store shelves are usually empty, famine is a reality) and a notable isolation (there is a double circuit of infrastructures, one for locals, the other for tourists). However, by voluntarily moving away from globalization, the country has kept intact a good part of its cultural specificities. One immediately thinks of the rhythms of salsa, a Cuban trademark, the scent of cigars, the old cars of Havana, and in general the incredible Technicolor aspect of this country which seems to be trapped in the 50s. Cuba is one of those destinations that is unlike any other, and that can be immediately identified, even without knowing it. Then, between this real misery and this real (cultural) richness, the traveler will always be able to cling to some very beautiful corners of nature. The beaches are magnificent, although the separation between Cubans and tourists is bitterly regrettable. Inland, the largest island in the Caribbean shows a beautiful diversity, even if the plains are sometimes monotonous, with the highlight being the magnificent Viñales Valley, which alone deserves the trip. And then, on the city side, there is Havana, a symbol of exoticism, a powerfully euphoric city when one discovers it, at once colonial, Latin and African, in the languor of the tropical climate. Cuba is still the prerogative of the tour operators, which is a good indication of a cautious tourist opening towards the unsupervised traveler. Beaches are often the domain of large hotels for groups, transportation is sometimes laborious (roads are generally bad), infrastructures are deficient and the sanitary level is low (although insularity limits certain risks, and fortunately). On the other hand, the country offers excellent safety conditions, which is not so common on the American continent.

- According to the magic formula of the Caribbean, strong sunshine, mild temperatures and beaches go hand in hand. With more than 4,000 kilometers of coastline, Cuba has one of the region's greatest potential for beach tourism. The beaches are therefore superb as in the rest of the Caribbean, but have a "ghetto chic" aspect that can be disturbing, although the days when no Cuban could visit the seaside areas are over. It is in the north that the spots are the most numerous, from Varadero to Guadalavaca, beaches and islets (cayos) have an undeniable attraction. Many sports activities are also available and divers will find their happiness in Maria la Gorda, on the Isla de la Juventud (rather complicated to access and which has no other real interest) and in the Bay of Pigs (Playa Larga, Playa Girón).

- The country's three major mountainous areas are welcoming more and more hikers. To the east, you will find the large natural park of the Sierra Maestra where the guerrillas took shelter during the revolution. Volcanic rocks, conifers, cedars, mahogany, wild orchids and ferns dot the path to the highest peak of the island, Pico Turquino. In the center of the country, a beautiful road leaves Trinidad to cross the Sierra del Escambray, its lakes and coffee trees, until Santa Clara. To the west, in the Sierra de los Organos, unique karstic rock formations await you in the Viñales Valley, the most beautiful of the country and certainly its major landscape. This valley leads to the island's most famous tobacco plantations, where the famous Cuban cigars are made.

- Havana is that capital that your imagination populates with old American cars, salsa and cigars, and it lives up to it. The old neighborhood, the Habana Vieja, is classified as a World Heritage Site. Palaces, houses, museums, churches have benefited from a vast renovation project. The waterfront and its slightly more dilapidated baroque habitat can be visited via the Malecón. A third Havana, the modern Vedado, has impressive avenues and above all a (Revolutionary) Square.

- Trinidad, in the south, is also part of the World Heritage of Humanity. Its cobblestone streets and pastel-colored houses will give you the impression that time stopped somewhere during the colonial era. Cienfuegos, in the same region, was also marked by the Spanish, but also by the French and Italians. Its historical center and botanical garden have made it "the pearl of the south".

» For those who let the myths guide their steps, you will find Hemingway at La Finca de la Vigia, a few kilometers east of Havana and you can read *The Old Man and the Sea*, sitting at a terrace in the small port of Cojimar. As for Che, it is in Santa Clara that he rests with his guerrilla companions.

» In the east of the country, two other cities are worth a visit for their colonial heritage. Baracoa, the first Spanish city in the New World, and Santiago, the former capital, have several walks to offer. As in the rest of the country, this is an opportunity to meet a welcoming people whose joie de vivre and humor are the weapons to survive today.

Dominica

Situated between the two large islands of the French West Indies, Guadeloupe to the north and Martinique to the south, Dominica is obviously very much in the forefront of the French tourist market. Volcanic, of great tropical beauty (the forest is one of the wildest and most beautiful in the Caribbean), Dominica also has a strong cultural identity, with a great carnival in February. The island has a few beaches, but its seaside appeal is limited, especially in a highly competitive region at this level. It is above all an island of nature, all in relief, which have moreover allowed the Caribbean Indians to find their last refuge there. The destination is far from presenting the same facilities as the neighboring French islands, both in terms of equipment, health and road infrastructure. Travel there is a little complicated, but Dominica can still be explored quite simply. Those for whom the Caribbean rhymes with mass tourism and crowded beaches are likely to be strongly disorientated, in the right direction. A beautiful trip, for sure.

» The beaches of Dominica are made of black sand, you will find them mainly in the north of the island like in Toucary Bay. The east coast is windier and therefore less crowded if it is not the divers who choose Calibishie Bay or Batibou Bay. The most beautiful site to discover the seabed is located at the southwestern end of the island in Scotts Head Bay. Portsmouth also offers some pleasant dive sites. Off the southern tip, one can potentially observe sperm whales and dolphins.

» Dominica has one of the most mountainous configurations in the Caribbean. These reliefs are covered with a large tropical forest, almost unexploited. They are irrigated by numerous streams forming a vast network of rivers and natural pools (including the astonishing Boiling lake as its name suggests), embellished by numerous waterfalls (Victoria and Sari-Dari in the southeast). This nature is the refuge of many rare species including parrots, hummingbirds and frogs of impressive size.

» In the south-central part of the island lies the Three Peaks National Park, an ideal playground for nature lovers. Starting from Roseau, many hikes are possible to discover the lush vegetation, the superb Trafalgar Falls and Middleham Falls. The latter cascades into a basin in which one can swim. You will also find the Fresh Water Lake, installed in an ancient crater at 1000 meters of altitude and supplied by sulphurous water springs, then the Boeri Lake, with cooler waters.

» The "Valley of Desolation" is a valley of very sulphurous volcanic origin, fed by hot springs that prevent the development of any plant life, thus contrasting with the surrounding tropical forests. On the borders of the Three Peaks National Park, this fantastical landscape with its pools of grey mud and water will also lead you to the Boiling lake.

» On the west coast of the island, the village of Pointe-Michel alone evokes the character of Dominica: a superb but cramped haven in an environment of high mountains and cliffs. Roseau, the small capital, has the old-fashioned charm of old colonial towns, with its wooden houses, its jalousie windows and its hanging balconies. Portsmouth has to offer two exceptional sites: Fort Shirley reconquered by the nature of the Cabrits National Park and the waters of the Indian River. In southwest Dominica, the small village of Soufrière is renowned for its proximity to the hot springs, the Soufrière Sulphur Springs.

Ecuador

Situated on the most famous latitude in the world, little Ecuador is a country that is really unknown in Europe. Much less mediatized than its neighbors, it does not have large sites that cannot be ignored but a variety that makes it an excellent summary of South America. Colonial cities, coolness of the plateaus and volcanoes of the Andes, favorable to beautiful hikes, warmth and exuberance of the Amazonian forest, Amerindian culture, Ecuador offers a beautiful range of attractions, which are easily combined because the distances are reasonable. In the heart of the Pacific, more difficult to access, the Galapagos Islands form a region apart in the country. A refuge for nature, these mythical islands are always the promise of a great adventure, meeting one of the world's biodiversity hotspots. Everything would be almost perfect if the country were not affected by the classic trouble of the continent, the important (and unfortunately penalizing, with some regions out of bounds) delinquency. Nothing prevents you from visiting Ecuador, but it is still advisable to be very careful and the neophyte traveler will be advised not to disembark without being prepared. The sanitary facilities are very good (at least in the big cities, but not in the Galapagos, it is important to know that) and the road network is surprisingly good compared to the complexity of the terrain. Nevertheless, transportation is a small adventure, due to geography on the one hand, but mostly due to the chaotic local driving habits.

• From north to south, the Avenue of Volcanoes is a paradise for the hiker who, as soon as he arrives in Quito, the capital perched at 2850 m, gets used to the altitude quite quickly. You will have the choice between many peaks. Reaching the 6310 m of Chimborazo will allow you to be as close as possible to the sun from planet earth. The ascent of the Cotopaxi cone will make you overcome the highest active volcano in the world.

• For those who want to live an Andean adventure without paying the price of breath, the tracks of the Andean paramó will make you go from surprise to surprise. Llamas and vicuñas, small villages cut off from the world, volcanic lakes (such as the sumptuous Laguna Quilotoa)... encounters that will give you memorable sensations. You will be able to embark on the roof of the small Andean train, a railway prodigy, which winds along the mountainside making spectacular swings.

• For those who prefer the tropical climate, the Amazon awaits you in the east of the country where it represents half of the surface area. In the heart of the Oriente, you will embark on a dugout canoe to discover the primary forests and the thousand-year-old traditions of this region. Don't hesitate to spend the night in the middle of the jungle and "taste" the vegetarian specialties of the region.

• If the Indian culture manifests itself in every village, especially in the markets, you will discover the colonial heritage of the country in Quito and Cuenca. Cuenca is a small provincial town where life is good and really worth a little detour.

- GALAPAGOS -

Approximately 1000 km from the coast of the Equateur, the Galapagos Islands and their volcanic relief contain treasures of nature, including many protected species. Listed as a World Heritage Site, they served as a testing ground for Darwin and are now visited by thousands of tourists every year. In spite of the great influx, they are extremely protected and only about fifty sites that change regularly are accessible.

One of the most effective ways to discover this archipelago is to take a cruise èrethat will take you from island to island. You will then be accompanied by a guide, which is mandatory to enter most of the authorized zones. At the same time, you will have to pay an entry fee to enter the Galapagos territory, in the order of a hundred dollars. The expedition is expensive and can sometimes be stressful, but it is obviously advisable for all lovers of nature and long journeys.

• In Santa Cruz is Puerto Ayora, the most important city in the Galapagos and the obligatory stopover for those who have just landed in Baltra (island airport nearby) and embark on a cruise. Don't hesitate to plan a day on the spot to be able to visit the Charles-Darwin Research Station where different kinds of turtles of all ages live. To see them in freedom, go to the El Chat and Rancho Permiso Reserve.

* Near Santa Cruz there are several small islands. On Isla Seymour, in front of Baltra lives one of the largest bird communities in the archipelago. The spectacle of the madmen à pattes bleuswhich takes place there continuously is not to be missed. Isla Mosquera is a tiny piece of land where sea lions are queens. You can have the pleasure of swimming with them. Then come the Islas Plazas where a hike through a cactus forest will allow you to meet land iguanas before arriving at the edge of cliffs where all kinds of birds come and go. Access to the Daphne Islas is more difficult and more limited. Thousands of blue-footed boobies and their cousins, the masked boobies, can be found there. Southeast of Santa Cruz, Isla de Santa Fé has the largest opandia cactus in the archipelago.

* Isla San Cristobal also has an airport and the port city of Baquerizo Moreno is the administrative center of the archipelago. From there, many excursions are possible, but it is the surfing which is famous there as well as the possibilities of diving which are in the surroundings in particular around Leon Dormido (Kicker Rock), in the cave of Roca Ballena or around the wreck of the cargo ship Caragua. The marine fauna of the Galapagos is just as impressive as that living on land, more than 300 species have already been recorded including sharks, rays and sea turtles.

* In the south, the southernmost islands are Isla Santa Maria and Isla Espanola. On the first one you can leave a postcard at the surprising Post Office Bay, but above all you can snorkel in one of the most interesting and beautiful places of the region: the Corona del diablo. As for Isla Espanola, it is home to colonies of Galapagos albatrosses along the most beautiful cliffs of the archipelago.

* Northwest of Santa Cruz, Isla San Salvador fascinates visitors with the thousands of red lava crabs and marine iguanas that have taken possession of Puerto Egas, a long strip of black lava where the water has dug basins. Sea lions à fourrurealso bask in the sun in the islets of the bay. Don't hesitate to follow the trail that leads inland to the Sugarloaf volcano and its sublime panoramas. Facing the east coast is Isla Bartolomé where you can swim with the penguins that live there.

* Isla Isabela is the largest of all the islands and consists of five intermittently active volcanoes. The Alcedo volcano is famous for its large caldera, its fumaroles and the giant turtles that live there. Above these beautiful volcanic landscapes, frigate birds live on the top of the volcano, while on the coast cormorants, penguins and sea lions live peacefully. To the west, Isla Fernandina is the youngest of all the islands of the archipelago. The site of Punta Espinoza is incredible; hundreds of marine iguanas can be observed moving slowly on the lava formations.

* In the north of the Galapagos, there are other islands like Genovesa, nicknamed "the island of the madmen" because of the number of birds or Marchena, famous for the famous diving sites that surround it.

United States of America

Here it is, this great country that crystallizes more than any other country in the world the clichés, superlatives, passions and resentments. Let's be honest from the outset, there is no country more varied, more accessible, more fascinating (and sometimes more depressing too) than the USA. A life as a traveler is not complete without having set foot on American soil at least once. As its name suggests, the country is a collection of small countries united into a big one, and each state brings its diversity to America's tourist panel. This one is immense, and its wonders are numerous. No word in any guide can ever replace the first vision of Manhattan's skyline, the vastness of the Grand Canyon, the splendor of Hawaii's Na Pali cliffs, the natural majesty of Yosemite, or the grandeur of Yellowstone. And these are just a few crumbs of the cake, to which one could add the excitement of walking down Hollywood Boulevard, strolling along the Golden Gate, diving into the art deco atmosphere of Miami, exploring the mysteries of the bayous and plantations of Louisiana, admiring the splendor of the southwestern deserts, or the hallucinations of Las Vegas. We could go on and on for pages and pages. In a country that is believed to be overly urban, we actually discover an even larger nature, often very wild, a refuge for biodiversity. Let's not even talk about Alaska, this immense territory, almost entirely virgin and where nature is unbridled. Travel in the country is very easy, the infrastructures are excellent, travel comfort is almost unequalled, in short it is a destination for all travelers, from the most novice to the most experienced. The key is to know how to explore beyond clichés, to accept the country as a whole, a country that one thinks one knows but is generally confusing, like its inhabitants.

- THE EAST -

The Eastern United States is populated by cities with a glorious historical past. The beaches of the coast and lakes attract as many vacationers eager for sports and culture as the mountains, forests and inland waterways delight nature lovers. Apart from New York City, the region's main tourist destination, this part of the United States has many beautiful surprises in store for you.

New England

Maine - New Hampshire - Vermont - Massachusetts - Rhode Island - Connecticut

• New England includes the states of Maine, New Hampshire, Vermont, Massachusetts, Rhode Island and Connecticut. Those who love the great outdoors will appreciate the former for its thousands of lakes, its impressive coastline, and the sumptuous colors of the vegetation in the fall. The different regions of New Hampshire also each have their own attractions and have managed to preserve a wild landscape. Vermont is not to be outdone, even though it is the only one without a coastline. As in all of New England, skiing is at the forefront, fall is the best season and the maple syrup is delicious.

• Massachusetts is famous for its Indian summer and the color of its maple trees in this season. The Berkshires Range, once the domain of the Mohicans, is crossed by many hiking trails including the Apalachian Trail and welcomes skiers and snowboarders every winter in its resorts. In Boston, the alleys of Beacon Hill have a scent of England. Don't hesitate to take the Freedom Trail route to go back in time and discover the history of the city. The colonial village of Salem, but also the beaches of Cape Cod and the islands of Martha's Vineyard and Nantucket are other sites not to be missed.

• In Rhode Island, the smallest of all the states, 640 km of coastline awaits you and the billionaire homes of Newport rival the colonial homes of the Mile of History in Providence. In Connecticut, the luxury resorts of Litchfield and Essex are popular, the visit to the Yale University campus in New Haven is impressive, and the Long Island Strait is a real gateway to the region.

The Eastern Seaboard

New York - New Jersey - Pennsylvanie - Delaware - Maryland - District de Columbia - Virginie - West Virginie - North Carolina

• New York is impossible to describe in a few lines as it is so full of things to do. In addition to the most famous sites such as the Statue of Liberty, the Empire State Building or Times Square, "the city that never sleeps" will have something to delight and exhaust you whatever your desires. New York is not a city, it is a universe, a symphony of the urban world, harassing but fascinating. The rest of New York State is equally exciting, adding to the landscapes of the Hudson Valley, the gorges and valleys of the Finger Lakes region before ending up in apotheosis with Niagara Falls on the Canadian border.

• New Jersey's 200 miles of Atlantic beaches are the largest expanse of fine sand in the United States, only an hour from New York City. If you like casinos and gambling halls, Atlantic City is the place to be. In the northwestern part of the state are the lakes and forests of the Kittatinny Mountains, which offer great walking opportunities.

• Pennsylvania has much to offer as a testament to its glorious past. Philadelphia's historic neighborhood, Independence National History Park, the elegant colonial homes of the Society Hill neighborhood and the city's museums make it an ideal gateway to a better understanding of the United States. Ninety miles to the west is Lancaster, in the "Dutch country" where the Amish and Mennonite sects have maintained a way of life that has not changed since the 17th century. Visit the Amish Farm and House and Lancaster Central Market for a glimpse of this community.

• Delaware was the first state to adopt the Constitution of the United States on December 7, 1787 in Dover, the capital. TheDover Heritage Trail will take you through the city to discover some 20 historic sites. The Delaware coastline is very popular with tourists, especially at Rehoboth Beach where lazing around, surfing, fishing and seafood tasting are a must.

• While Maryland has been the scene of many battles in the past, today it is recreation that has the upper hand in the region. Skiing in the winter at Wisp or Wintergreen, hiking in the western mountains in the fall and lounging in the summer near Deep Creek or Smith Mountain Lakes, the diversity of the state is interesting if not spectacular. The Chesapeake Bay, which divides the state in two, is the largest estuary in the world, rich in seafood specialties, and its cliffs are well known for the many fossils found there.

• The District of Columbia, bordering the Potomac River, is home to the U.S. capital Washington, DC. The White House, the Lincoln Memorial, the Capitol, as well as the numerous museums of the city make it a historically and culturally very rich stopover. You can also visit the Arlington National Cemetery where the Kennedy graves are located.

• The first state in the history of the country, Virginia is considered the cradle of the United States. In Williamsburg, capital of the state from 1699 to 1780, you can visit the largest open-air living museum in the country where the daily life of the pre-Revolutionary settlers is staged by actors. At the Confederate Museum in Richmond, the current capital, you can discover the southern perspective of the Civil War. One can also go to Jefferson's house in Monticello or George Washington's house in Mount Vernon. In terms of scenery, all you have to do is take the 170 km Skyline Drive that crosses the Shenandoah National Park, to have the opportunity to admire some of the most spectacular panoramas of the Atlantic coast. On the other side, the Blue Ridge Parkway will take you from Shenandoah National Park to the ridges of the Blue Ridge Mountains.

• West Virginia's mountainous terrain is ideal for outdoor activities, with the Monongahela Forest with over 300 kilometers of marked trails and the Highland Scenic Highway winding through the mountains. The rivers (Gauley, Cheat and Tygart, for example) that intersect the state make it an exciting rafting spot. Throughout the year there are many festivals and fairs that will give you a better understanding of the region's culture.

• North Carolina is also one of the thirteen colonies that founded the United States of America. From the Great Smoky Mountains National Park in the west to the string of islands of the Outer Banks and the low rounded hills of the Piedmont, the landscapes are pleasant and varied. The main cities are Raleigh, known for its Capitol and its many oaks, and Charlotte, the main center of textile production in the United States.

The Great Lakes

Ohio - Michigan - Indiana - Illinois - Wisconsin

• Ohio offers a pleasant mix of rural and urban attractions. Some of the country's most popular amusement parks (Cedar Point Amusement Park, Paramount King's Island, Sea World of Ohio, Lake Geauga) are located here. Lovers of the great outdoors will be delighted by the 72 state parks. The two cities of Cleveland and Cincinnati add a touch of culture and Lake Erie allows the practice of many water sports.

• Michigan, contoured by four of the five Great Lakes, is divided by Lake Michigan into two vast peninsulas that meet almost at the Strait of Mackinac. While the lower peninsula is the domain of industry, to the north the forested hills that cover the area are dotted with resorts. Don't miss the city of Detroit, famous for being the automotive capital of the world, but with many other attractions.

• In northern Indiana, the sand dunes on the shores of Lake Michigan, forests and lakes offer an enchanting setting for all kinds of sporting activities. Indianapolis is known for its racetrack, which brings together thousands of enthusiasts every year. In the southern part of the state, in Park County, more than thirty covered wooden bridges punctuate the region's hilly landscape.

* Mostly visited for Chicago, the third largest city in the United States, a mecca for modern architecture, blues and culture in the center of the country, Illinois is also home to the Amish communities of Arcola and Arthur, the largest American Indian cemetery (Cahokia Mounds), and many charming towns on the banks of the Mississippi River. Illinois is criss-crossed by waterways and has about 30 beaches along Lake Michigan in Lake and Cook counties.

* Apostle Islands National Lakeshore, in northern Wisconsin, Lake Superior, is a beautiful archipelago of 22 islands off the shores of Bayfield, ideal for canoeing, sailing and fishing. The Door Peninsula is dotted with resorts, beaches, small fishing harbors and recreational facilities. The diversity of Milwaukee's ethnic heritage, with its German, Italian, Irish, Polish and African-American colonies, is reflected in the festivals and regional gastronomy.

- THE SOUTH -

The South has a heritage and culture quite distinct from other parts of the country. It is up to you to choose between the beaches and the dynamism of Florida, the charm of the Old South's old plantations or the adventure in the footsteps of the cowboys and Indians of the Old West.

Florida

* Florida's subtropical climate, its palm trees and long beaches of brilliant white sand, licked by the turquoise and warm waters of the Atlantic Ocean and the Gulf of Mexico, make it one of the most popular vacation destinations in the United States. You can explore the state by taking your pick of the countless bike paths or hiking trails that crisscross the state. In terms of culture, but also in terms of festive atmosphere, the Latin city of Miami will meet your expectations. Don't miss the resorts of Fort Lauderdale (the Venice of Florida), Palm Beach (very luxurious) and West Palm Beach, Naples (chic), St-Petersburg (on Tampa Bay, white sandy beaches), the alligators of Everglades National Park, the coral reef of Key Largo, the Caribbean atmosphere of Key West and of course the amusement parks around Orlando (Disneyworld, Universal).

The Old South

South Carolina - Georgia - Alabama - Mississippi - Louisiana

* South Carolina is probably the most "southern" of the Old South states, with its magnolias, mint julep, plantations and hospitality. The most famous city is Charleston for the beauty of its gardens and the refinement of its architecture. The former homes of Boone Hall and Middleton Gardens are the best example of this. The coast is very popular with vacationers looking for relaxation and recreation. Myrtle Beach, to name but one, is more than 100 kilometers long.

* Cotton fields as far as the eye can see, this is what we imagine of Georgia, especially if we have read and seen *Gone with the Wind*. Savannah, on the Atlantic Ocean, is one of those Old South cities with an old-fashioned charm, with its old houses, its 24 public gardens and its local gastronomy. Next to Charleston, it is certainly the most beautiful American city. Atlanta, with an equally heavy past, stands out from the rest of the region as a truly international and modern metropolis, home to some American icons such as CNN or Coca-Cola (which each have their own museum).

* Alabama was the scene of the Civil War. Visiting the Country Plantation will allow you to admire majestic estates of the Old South, such as the Sturdivant Hall, even though many of them were destroyed during the war. Birmingham is home to many mansions and remains of the aristocratic Old South, such as the Arlington Ante Bellum Home and its gardens. At Gulf Shores, Fort Morgan was one of the last Confederate forts to surrender.

* Mississippi represents the heart of the Old South, with its houses with white porticoes, the sweet fragrance of its magnolias, its cotton fields and the blues accents that come from the Delta. The town of Natchez preserves more than five hundred houses from before the Civil War, including imposing mansions that have often been converted into hotels or bed-and-breakfast. For sunbathing, go to the sandy beaches of the Gulf of Mexico (at Bay St.Louis, Gulfport or Pass Christian). To listen to the blues, take Highway 61 or 49, there are plenty of blues clubs.

• Louisiana has been able to blend French, Hispanic, African-American, Creole and Indian cultures to create a charming mix. Plantations and dawn boats (in the vicinity of Baton Rouge), bayous and alligators (in the vicinity of Lafayette), but especially Jazz are the key words that characterize this destination. New Orleans is one of the most amazing and exciting cities in the United States, Flanez on Bourbon Street in the footsteps of the greatest American jazzmen, in a Belle-Epoque setting. To get a nice view of the state, don't hesitate to take the Creole Nature Trail from Lake Charles to Sulphur through the famous bayous, very atmospheric, along the Gulf of Mexico.

- THE CENTER -

Kentucky - Tennessee - Arkansas

• Kentucky is renowned for its hospitality, horses (the thoroughbreds around Lexington) and bourbon (the distilleries in Frankfurt). There are also beautiful expanses of forest and the largest concentration of caves in the world. In the heart of the state, the underground chambers of the Mammoth Cave National Park are so vast that they can be explored by boat.

• Bordered to the east by the Great Smoky Mountains and to the west by the Mississippi River, Tennessee is the cradle of country music. Bristol, at the eastern tip of the state, but especially Nashville and Memphis are its leading figures. Today, more than half of the musical recordings in the United States are made in this state. Graceland, in Memphis, was owned by Elvis Presley and has become a place of pilgrimage visited by thousands of fans from all over the world.

• In northern Arkansas, the picturesque Ozark Mountains hide historic villages where crafts and lifestyles of the past are preserved. Ninety miles southwest of Little Rock, Hot Springs National Park has 47 mineral springs that are exploited in numerous spa facilities. Eureka Springs is one of the state's most charming towns, renowned for its springs and mountain architecture.

- THE OLD WEST -

Oklahoma - Texas - New Mexico

• Oklahoma is perhaps the most authentic state in the United States, the only one to have been designated as an Indian Territory. Thirty-seven Indian nations still live on this land and punctuate its daily life (especially in the summer) with various assemblies and demonstrations. The "Red Earth", the largest pow-wow in the country, is held annually in Oklahoma City. The traditions of the Old West have also been preserved, and visitors can participate in livestock gatherings, horseback riding, or excursions in wagon convoys. In Pawnee, 56 km northwest of Tulsa, buffalo and longhorns roam freely in a city park. Note that Oklahoma is crossed by the historic Route 66.

• The second largest state after Alaska, Texas combines the Wild West, including the canyons and deserts of Big Bend National Park, with historic sites such as Fort Alamo and the great metropolises of Houston and Dallas. It's an ideal region for a wide range of activities: lazing on the beaches of the Gulf Coast, fishing at Aulac Caddo Lake, hiking in the Guadalupe Mountains, canoeing in the Big Thicket and birding in the Rio Grande Valley. You can also enjoy the Old West by spending a day at one of the "Dude ranches" that offer a wide range of western-style activities (horseback riding and working with cowboys, barbecue around a wagon and square dancing at nightfall).

• New Mexico is one of the states with the largest amount of virgin land. The remarkable heritage of the Indians is beautifully preserved in many sites throughout the state, such as the Chaco Culture National Historical Park or the Petroglyph National Monument and the Aztec Ruins National Monument. Santa Fe has been deeply influenced by its Indian, Spanish and Mexican heritage, and has a special charm, emanating from its narrow streets, patios and Hispano-colonial architecture. Lincoln County is home to the famous Billy the Kid, don't miss the museum dedicated to him at Fort Sumner.

- THE NORTH -

From the Great Lakes to the Rocky Mountains, the northern and central United States offer spaces so imposing that they make you dizzy. Nature reigns supreme and the contrasts imposed by climate change and vast distances give the traveller the impression of changing countries several times.

• Utah, a land of Mormon predilection (the headquarters of the Church of Jesus Christ of Latter-day Saints is in Salt Lake City), is home to a very large number of parks amidst a variety of landscapes ranging from deserts to mountains, from arid highlands to immense fir forests. The most visited parks are Canyonlands National Park, Arches National Park, Zion National Park and Capitol Reef National Park. Two gigantic lakes are ideal for water sports, Lake Powell in the south and the Great Salt Lake in the north. The ski resorts in the north of the state are famous for the winter sports that can be practiced there.

• From the Rocky Mountains to the canyons, via the Arkansas River or Colorado River, each site in Colorado is an invitation to relive the great era of the Wild West. With its ranches, its national parks and monuments (Mesa Verde, Great Sand Dunes, Rocky Mountain...) or its ghost towns (Cripple Creek and Victor), Colorado is a true land of adventure. Hiking, horseback riding, climbing, rafting, canoeing and fishing in the summer, thrill seekers will be delighted. In winter, it is the turn of skiing to take over in the resorts of Aspen, Vail, Breckenridge or Telluride. Take the Pikes Peak Cog Railway, the world's highest cog railway, to reach the Pikes Peak, which overlooks Colorado Springs from a height of 4,298 meters.

• In Wyoming, the great plains meet the Rocky Mountains and form the sumptuous landscapes of the Wild West. In Cheyenne, the capital city, the world's largest outdoor rodeo show is held every year in July. In Cody is the Buffalo Bill Historic Center. In the northeastern part of the state, the Devil's Tower served as a landmark for those trying to get further west. Today, however, it is Yellowstone National Park and its 10,000 geysers and hot springs that attract the most visitors.

• Much of Idaho is still wilderness. This paradise for sports enthusiasts who can practice all kinds of activities in a natural setting is still unknown to the general public. Explore the Seven Devils and Hell's Canyon area by boat up the Snake River. See the highest sand dunes in North America in the Bruneau Dunes Desert state park south of Boise or the lunar landscapes of the Craters of the Moon National Monument. The most famous spot in the area is Sun Valley, a world famous ski resort.

• Montana is one of the least populated and most rural states in the country, which in the past attracted thousands of gold seekers, as evidenced by the hundred or so ghost towns scattered throughout its territory. The "Ravine of Last Chance" in Helena and the Anaconda Copper Mine near Butte will definitely plunge you into the past. On the nature side, 1,600 km of excursion trails await you to discover the fifty glaciers and 200 lakes of Glacier National Park in the northwestern part of the state. In the center of the park, take a boat to admire the mountain passes of the Montagne Sauvage.

• North Dakota also has memories of the pioneers, trappers, cowboys, farmers and cavalry soldiers who did it in the past. Today, the Badlands of the Theodore Roosevelt National Memorial Park are populated by elk, bighorn sheep, coyotes and prairie dogs, while the rest of the state is dotted with large grain farms, ranches and small rural communities dominated by grain elevators. While western South Dakota is made up of forest (Black Hills), Indian reserves and cattle ranches, on the other side of Missouri, to the east there are more cities. Do not miss, in the Black Hills, 40 km southwest of Rapid City, the giant heads of four presidents of the United States from Mount Rushmore.

• Nebraska is an agricultural state where wheat growing and cattle raising are the two main activities. Crossed like its neighbors by the Oregon Trail with the Scotts Bluff National Monument as a landmark, the region has preserved the memory of the West in a thousand places. The pioneer village of Minden, the Buffalo Bill Ranch a few miles north of the North Plate and the Homestead National Monument of America near Beatrice are the most telling examples. In the center of the United States, Kansas remains the heart of the nation where cowboys and herds continue to make their way.

• At the western gate, Missouri brought the first country and rock hits to the rest of the country. While Chuck Berry and

Johnnie "B. Goode" were born in St. Louis, it is today in the dozens of concert halls in Branson, near Springfield, that the musicians take flight. In the south of the state, lush forests, steep cliffs and deep caves shape the landscape, while in the north the plains are crisscrossed by numerous rivers. Indeed, with over 1,800 km of waterways including the Mississippi, Missouri is Mark Twain's home, the scenery of the river city of Hannibal inspired him to create the settings for Tom Sawyer's Adventures.

• Iowa invites you to discover its folklore, traditions and festivities with its grid pattern of neat farms and corn plantations. Several farms are also open to the public and offer an atypical way of staying. The Living History Farm, near Des Moines, also invites you to discover this agricultural heritage. On the other side of the state, don't miss Sioux City, a true cultural center, and the covered bridges of Madison County.

• From the shores of Lake Superior to the headwaters of the Mississippi River, Minnesota is intertwined with 40,000 km of rivers and streams and is known as the land of 10,000 lakes. To discover its beauty, follow the north shore of Lake Superior towards Port Arthur, Ontario, or walk the 43 km Skyline Parkway that overlooks the lake. On either side of the Mississippi River, the Twin Cities of Minneapolis and St. Paul are nationally significant artistic centers.

- THE WEST -

The American West is a particularly tourist destination. Spread over several states, the diversity of the landscapes will not leave you indifferent and everyone will find what they are looking for. It goes from the Californian coasts to the deserts, from the canyons to the Native American villages, without forgetting the incredible national parks and the craziest cities of the United States.

• California is an immense territory where the diversity of activities is such that everyone can everyone could find what he's looking for. Let's start with the southern part of California. Los Angeles is the largest and most dynamic city in the region with its collections of highways, beaches, arid hills, uptown neighborhoods, internationally renowned museums and the Hollywood myth. On the coast, Santa Barbara is the ideal place to observe whales, dolphins and seals. It is also a beautiful, chic city with a Mediterranean atmosphere, nicknamed the American Riviera. 44 km south of Los Angeles, in Anaheim, the 80 hectares of fairy-tale Disneyland await you. San Diego, fits perfectly with the image of idyllic California with its huge beaches, surfers and historic districts, including the beautiful Gaslamp District. 144 km east of San Diego, Palm Springs is a recreation resort in the desert. 290 km northeast of San Diego is the Mojave Desert crossed by Route 66. Further north, it is the turn of Death Valley to stretch its dry landscapes and welcome tourists from all over the world.

• In the northern part of California, San Francisco gives the answer to Los Angeles by choosing a completely different and much more "peaceful" route and rolls out its hills covered with wooden houses to the ocean. Its beauty and elegance is matched only by the feeling of freedom that permeates every street in the city. Monterey, 120 km to the south, was the setting for many of John Steinbeck's novels. From Carmel, a few kilometers south, to Big Sur you will discover a coast with a fascinating cut-out before going north-east up to Merced, to enterYosemite National Park and admire the most magnificent landscapes of the region. Another 320 km northward and you will arrive at the blue waters of Lake Tahoe. Returning to San Francisco by the road to Sacramento (capital of the state, and sunniest city in the world between June and September) you will cross the ghost towns of the gold rush and the country of sequoias.

• Oregon also offers a very wide and spectacular variety of landscapes. The 500 km of the Pacific coast is dotted with immense beaches (including Cannon Beach), seaside resorts (such as Florence or Newport), cliffs and superb dunes. The east of the state offers its mountains and gorges (Mount Hood & Columbia River Gorge in the north, and Mount Bachelor in the center) and allows you to discover the great spaces of the "Far West", much drier and desert. The south of the state is particularly popular with sports enthusiasts who throughout the summer practice fishing, rafting, kayaking, but also mountain biking, hiking and caving. The region also has one of the most beautiful American parks, the Crater Lake National Park with its ancient volcano and lake district. The capital of the state, Portland, the "City of Roses", is a relaxed city, on a human scale, in the heart of a superb nature that its inhabitants have at heart to protect. An artistic and literary city (it has the largest bookstore in the country), filled with parks (including a veritable forest), cafés and brasseries, there's no need to say that it's one of the most pleasant cities in the country.

- The major cities of Washington State are clustered around "Puget Sound", a huge inlet that creates a temperate but humid climate. Seattle is the largest city in the region, the largest port on the West Coast and the cradle of Grunge music. It is also one of the most progressive cities in the country and among the most pleasant to live in. Less than three hours drive away, the tropical rainforest of Hoh is one of the highlights of the Olympic National Park. South of the Pacific coast of this same peninsula, resorts and vast beaches offer all kinds of attractions. Mount Rainier National Park, 2 hours and a half southeast of Seattle, is crossed by hundreds of kilometers of scenic roads.

- At the time, Nevada was known for its gold and silver miners who searched the land relentlessly. Today, Las Vegas and Reno attract more visitors than ever who dream of making a fortune in a card trick. Las Vegas is a huge attraction where casinos and hotels, such as the Venetian, Caesar's Palace, Luxor and Treasure Island, compete with each other in terms of size and decorum. Reno, to the north, offers a more modest version of the same theme. Virginia City, in the north of the state, epicenter of the mining era in the Wild West, has retained its charm of yesteryear with its boardwalks, saloons, mines that can still be visited and its authentic steam train.

- Arizona will seduce you with the beauty of its landscapes. Apart from the Grand Canyon, which offers one of the most grandiose spectacles in the world, the state can boast of the famous Monument Valley where Navajo Indians live in the heart of strange shapes carved by erosion, the Petrified Tree Forest which contains fossil bones, plants and petrified trees dating back 190 million years and the Sunset Crater, a volcano surrounded by lava flows near the Wupatki National Monument which contains many Indian ruins. The western landscapes of the Red Rock State Park, the vegetation of the Coconino National Forest, the colors of the Painted Desert and the troglodytic dwellings of the Navajo National Monument are some of the other great surprises this state has in store for you.

- ALASKA -

With its glaciers that produce icebergs, its volcanoes that carve lunar valleys, its mountains that continue to rise towards the sky, Alaska, with its ever-changing landscapes, is the opposite of terra firma. The change of scenery and climate gives travelers the opportunity to experience an extraordinary adventure.

- Embarking on a cruise in the southeast of the state (Inner Passage) will allow you to best admire the formidable glaciers that make Alaska a fascinating land. This is the classic Alaska tour, via the capital Juneau, and the small historical and tourist towns of Ketchikan, Sitka and Skagway. It will also be a good opportunity to get to know the locals: whales, sea lions and seals. If in September, the colors of the autumn magnify the landscapes, they reveal hundreds of lakes in the spring (beware of mosquitoes) and in summer the sun sets very late. Only winter makes tourism more difficult, although the climate in the southeastern region of the state is ultimately less snowy (and often less cold) than that of New York at the same time.

- Wrangell-St. Elias National Park, to the south, is accessible by road from Anchorage (the state's main city, a classic American metropolis). Two rugged roads will take you through the park to discover the hundreds of glaciers it contains, such as the spectacular Malaspina Glacier. Glacier lakes and mountain landscapes form the landscapes of this immense natural park, very wild.

- Denali National Park and Reserve, in the center of the state, is the state's tourist mecca, and has the highest peak in North America, Mount McKinley (6194 meters), one of the most difficult peaks to climb in the world. Five large glaciers, some of which are 70 to 80 kilometers long, descend the slopes of the mountain. A large population of grizzly bears and black bears is present on the territory of the park. One can also observe caribou, mouflons, elk, wolves and a very large variety of birds. It is here that Christopher McCandless, whose adventure is recounted in *Into the Wild*, died.

- Katmai National Park and Reserve, on the Alaska Peninsula, remarkable for its Ten Thousand Smokes Valley formed following the volcanic eruption of Novarupta in 1912, its 14 volcanoes still active and for its brown bears, estimated to number more than two thousand. The latter gather in large numbers at Brooks Falls to catch migrating salmon.

- Kenai Fjords National Park, with its 40 glaciers, in the south, offers sumptuous landscapes of bays, fjords and rocky islets where penguins, puffins, cormorants, seals, Steller sea lions, gray and humpback whales, killer whales, Dall's porpoises and sea otters can be seen. Kayaking, hot springs and fishing enthusiasts will find plenty to do here. The Yukon and Tanana Rivers as well as the Lynn Canal can be discovered on a cruise.

• The high sand dunes of Kobuk Valley National Park, the vastness of the Gates of the Arctic National Park, and the active tundra, forest and volcano landscapes of Lake Clark National Park are small jewels of adventure. For those who would like to follow in the footsteps of the gold rush, the best known route is located in the southeast of the state. You can take the short railway line from Skagway to Whitehorse, Canada.

- HAWAII -

Hawaii is a U.S. state located in the heart of the Pacific Ocean. 122 islands make up this tropical archipelago, with an idyllic reputation, of which the seven main ones are Oahu, Kauai, Maui, the big island of Hawaii, Molokai, Lanai and Niihau. As you can imagine, dream beaches, flowered shirts, surfers and exotic dances are on the program, but we should not forget the hiking possibilities offered by the volcanic landscapes of the archipelago, and the Hawaiian culture, the famous Aloha, which makes the islands very different from the rest of the country. Hawaii is often a favorite destination, and rightly so.

• Oah'u is the most populated island of the archipelago and proves to be a clever mix between the exoticism of Polynesia and the atmosphere of America. The capital of the state, Honolulu, is located here. Its world renown is built around the beach of Waikiki and the volcanic crater of Diamond Head. Surfing, windsurfing, bodyboarding and snorkeling are the order of the day on the famous beach. In the evening, Waikiki comes alive. Constantly flooded with tourists (mostly American and Japanese), Waikiki is a kind of Tropical Disneyland, rich in shopping, restaurants, ukulele concerts, hula demonstrations and cocktails at sunset. Its idyllic but overrated appearance will leave you either enchanted or doubtful, depending on what you are looking for. Another major attraction on Oahu, don't hesitate to go to Pearl Harbor to visit the USS Arizona memorial site, but also the USS Missouri or the submarine USS Bowfin. The rest of the island is much wilder, especially the North Shore, famous for its beautiful sandy beaches where the biggest waves of the planet come to hit every winter. It is the epicenter of world surfing. On the windward coast of the island, Kailua is one of the most beautiful beaches of the archipelago, a real postcard of the tropics.

• Kauai, the oldest of the main islands, is one of the favorite locations for many big American productions. Its extremely lush vegetation has earned it the nickname "Garden Island". To discover it, you can kayak on the Na Pali coast against the majestic volcanic walls, cross the national parks on horseback, or admire the dazzling landscapes from a helicopter. To relax, 69 pristine beaches including Tunnels Beach, Lumahai Beach, Poipu Beach and Hanalei Bay Beach await you. The most beautiful diving spots are located on the east coast. The bubbling geyser of Spouting Horn, the depths of Waimea Canyon, the humidity of the Waialeale Crater and the animals of the Alakai Wilderness Reserve are all places of interest not to be missed.

• Maui is also called "The Valley Isle" after the very fertile isthmus that separates its two volcanoes, Haleakala and Mauna Kahalawai. Those who dream of luxury hotels will find their happiness on the west coast, while those in search of authenticity will choose to spend their stay on the east coast. All will have to visit Haleakala Crater, the largest dormant volcano in the world. For a glimpse of the island's beauty, don't hesitate to take the Hana Highway that runs through it from one side to the other. In addition to its immense beach, Kaanapali is known to be the best place for whale watching from December to April. You will also be able to see them on Molokini Island where the underwater life is extremely diverse.

• The island of Hawaii (or Big Island) is larger than all the other islands combined. It continues to grow with the constant lava flows from Kilauea volcano, the largest active volcano in the world. On the nature side, you can discover the Volcanoes Park (home to the world's most active volcano, Kilauea), the black, green, white or pepper and salt sandy beaches, the tropical plants of the city of Hilo, the sumptuous landscapes of the Waipio Valley and the Akaka Falls. On the luxury side, about twenty golf courses await you as well as the visit of the largest private ranches in the country.

• The largest coral reef in the United States and the highest cliffs in the world are in Molokai where they reach 1,005 meters above the Pacific Ocean. The small island of Lanai is almost entirely covered with pineapple plantations, it is especially known for its diving spots around its coral reefs and the wrecks that can be seen from Shipwreck Beach. Niihau, finally, is a private island of 180 km2 whose access is controlled in order to protect the Hawaiian culture.

Granada

Like the other islands of the southern Caribbean, the small archipelago of Grenada has many assets, beautiful beaches, mountains covered with tropical forests, a nice animation and a perfume of sweet exoticism. Here is a relaxed country, where nature is omnipresent, the evenings are sweet and the trip is quite simple. The three small islands do not compete with the heavyweights of tourism in the region but it is above all a question of marketing and nothing prevents travellers attracted by the Caribbean from going there. The tourist mix is really pleasant, waterfalls, forests, relief, tropical beaches tempered by trade winds and a rum cocktail to crown the days, Grenada delivers all the classics of the islands, in beauty.

* Saint George's, the capital, is a small city of 20,000 people that has retained a colonial character, a legacy of the British and French. The pretty horseshoe-shaped harbour (called the Carénage) is pleasant for a stroll and the market is a place not to be missed while shopping and watching life go by. Fort Frederick and Fort George offer beautiful views of the city.

* The closest beach to the capital is Grand Mal, but the most popular is Grand Anse, which is only a few minutes away by cab. To the south, at Morne Rouge, are more intimate beaches as to the east at Anse des Epines.

* Rum is part of the traditions on the island of Grenada. Visit the oldest rum distillery on Mount Rose. The River Antoine rum distillery has been in existence since 1785 and production is still done manually. As for spices, you can visit the Gouyave Nutmeg Processing Station, the largest nutmeg producer on the island.

* Granada is characterized by a number of explosion craters of volcanic origin. The most remarkable are those of Grand Etang and Lake Antoine. In the park where the former is located, hikers can hike the Seven Sisters Trail in search of the 7 waterfalls that cross the route.

* Other waterfalls are worth the detour, those of Concorde. You have to crawl to be able to admire the spectacle of these three waterfalls, but the reward is great, especially since you can swim in the fresh water of the natural pools.

* In the north of the island is another paradise for hikers, the Levera National Park, which has many natural riches: mangroves, lake, bird sanctuary. This national park is also known for its beautiful white sandy beaches and coral reefs that are a delight for divers.

* Carriacou, known as "the island surrounded by reefs", is the largest island in the Grenadines and is reputed to be one of the most beautiful in the West Indies. It offers long white sandy beaches, fairly deep bays, relief and anchorage sites. The main town is Hillsborough known for its small colorful wooden stores. Divers will be able to discover Bianca C, the largest wreck in the Caribbean.

* The island of Petite Martinique is located about 1.5 km from the island of Carriacou. Of volcanic origin, it does not have as beautiful beaches as its neighbors, but allows for pleasant walks along the coastline.

* The Three Islands emerge from the Caribbean Sea. Sugar Low is private, the other two remain uninhabited. It is possible to go by boat to Sandy Island, from the town of Sauteurs, to enjoy deserted beaches with transparent waters.

Guadeloupe

The former Karukera, the butterfly island, is the largest of the Lesser Antilles between Puerto Rico and Trinidad. If Guadeloupe refers mainly to the two almost glued islands of Basse-Terre and Grande-Terre, there is actually a whole small archipelago. A French department in its own right, Guadeloupe is not a tourist mecca in the Caribbean region, especially when compared to the big tourism machines that are Barbados or Aruba, to name only these two. It is however a very beautiful destination, with a fantastic potential and to which one reaches very easily. The carpet of Caribbean attractions is unrolled there, the Creole culture (colorful markets), the white sand beaches, the countryside planted with sugar cane (from which a very famous rum is made), the tropical forest and volcanism (piton de la Soufrière). Each wing of the butterfly has its own type of tourism, the seaside for the Grande-Terre, nature for the Basse-Terre. The other islands of the archipelago make excellent destinations for excursions and add an undeniable attraction to the destination. The infrastructures are excellent, even if the hotel industry is often modest, the sanitary level is up to European standards, the only drawback comes from a welcome that is not always cordial and which strongly penalizes the tourist image.

BASSE TERRE :

• Zigzagging between the mountains, the Route de la Traversée, or Route des Deux Mamelles, is the only road to link the Lower Mainland from east to west through the interior. During these 50 km, many sites will attract your attention such as the Zoological and Botanical Park, the Maison de la Forêt or the Cascade aux Écrevisses.

• The National Park of Guadeloupe is crossed by many hiking trails that will lead you to the discovery of a dense and humid forest and its inhabitants. You can climb the volcano Soufrièreau in the middle of a rocky and chaotic landscape of beauty. In one hour, via the Chemin des Dames, you will reach the summit where the spectacle of fumaroles, sulphurous vapours and hot springs rivals the panorama. The Carbet Falls, at the foot of the volcano, are also a quality tourist attraction.

• Near Deshaies, a small village of Creole huts, is Grande-Anse, one of the most beautiful beaches of the island. For 1 km, its caramel-colored golden sand of volcanic origin blends perfectly with the deep green of the vegetation and the blue of the surrounding sea. It is a touristic place, but much less frequented than the beaches of Grande-Terre. The rest of the beaches of the island veiled with black sand are much less known and even more peaceful.

• The tiny village of Bouillante owes its name to the hot springs of its region. Fountains of boiling water gush out everywhere, including in the sea. The beach of Malendure is one of the most frequented of the island. The beauty and richness of the "Cousteau Reserve" attracts divers and visitors aboard glass-bottomed boats.

• The bay of Grand Cul-de-Sac Marin is bounded by the widest mangrove belt and the longest coral reef in the Lesser Antilles. The mangrove is a swampy area composed of trees and shrubs, mostly impenetrable. Corals, gorgonians and sponges form the coral reef which is home to about 250 species of fish. From Baie-Mahault, take to the sea to visit the bay's islets.

GRANDE TERRE :

• Main city and economic center of Guadeloupe, Pointe-à-Pitre is located at the crossroads of these two butterfly-shaped islands. Several times ravaged by cyclones and fires, the historical center presents a heterogeneous architecture between colonial facades and modern fronts. The two places that will best allow you to immerse yourself in the atmosphere of the city are the Place de la Victoire at the exit of the masses of the Basilica of Saint-Pierre-et-Saint-Paul or the quays at sunrise when the fishermen finish unloading their merchandise and the market is getting ready.

• Le Gosier, the most important seaside resort in Guadeloupe, occupies part of the south coast, with the resorts of Sainte-Anne and Saint-François. White sandy beaches, turquoise water and coconut palms are the dream setting. In Sainte-Anne, the Caravelle beach is very popular with water sports enthusiasts.

- Continuing up the coast, you will leave the coconut trees behind you to reach the cliffs torn by the waves of the Pointe des Châteaux. If you can't swim there, the detour is still worth it, the sea spray will invigorate you and the panoramas will delight you. Take the coastal discovery trail to reach the Pointe des Colibris where an orientation table will allow you to enjoy a breathtaking view of the sea, the islands of Désirade, Petite-Terre and Marie-Galante.

THE REST OF THE ARCHIPELAGO:

- In Marie Galante, you will taste the rum reputed to be the best of all the West Indies. To vary with the idleness (beaches of Anse Canot and Anse du Vieux-Fort), do not hesitate to visit the ruins of the Murat house which was in the 19th century the biggest sugar cane plantation of Guadeloupe or to make a stroll to the Gueule Grand Gouffre, a stone arch above the waves.

- Les Saintes is composed of two very mountainous islands: Terre-de-Haut and Terre-de-Bas and seven other uninhabited islets. The Bay of Les Saintes is one of the most beautiful bays in the world, just like those of Rio de Janeiro or Halong. Rent a scooter, the only motorized vehicle authorized in Terre-de-Haut to discover small beaches such as those of Pain de Sucre and Pompierre. Don't forget to visit Fort Napoleon, which from its 140 m high offers an exceptional panoramic view. Terre-de-Bas is much less frequented by tourists and is less interesting. Only 2 roads criss-cross this small part of the world.

- The very small Désirade, 11 km by 2, lives at the rhythm of its fishermen. Its beautiful white sand beaches and the clarity of its lagoons are on a par with the rest of the archipelago. Nearby, the islands of Petite Terre are mainly inhabited by iguanas and attract many divers, seduced by its natural aquarium and wild landscapes.

Guatemala

An essential partner of southern Mexico to form what tour operators call the Mayan Country, Guatemala is the first destination in Central America, alongside Costa Rica. However, if the country welcomes many visitors in organized trips, it is not a very easy destination for the independent traveler. Guatemala is poor, the infrastructures are bad, the climate is sometimes difficult (fairly heavy rainy seasons in recent years), but the biggest black spot remains violence. Drug trafficking and gangs (maras) are the source of delinquency which should lead to real caution, especially in the capital where public transportation is now formally discouraged. Experienced and knowledgeable travelers in the region will be able to survey the roads, preparing themselves, but it is better to discover the country in a group setting. Paradoxically, beyond its social problems, Guatemala offers a great wealth of tourism. At the top of the list is the Mayan site of Tikal, one of the most famous of all, the Mayan culture, still alive, Antigua, one of the most beautiful cities in the Americas, the lakes including the Atitlàn, the lush jungle of the Petén, a real adventure in its raw state, or the volcanoes (including the majestic Agua and the mysterious Chicabal). It is a very interesting destination, but a little complicated.

- The formidable pre-Columbian ruins of Tikal are plunged in the heart of the tropical forest in a luxuriant vegetation.

- Antigua, the former capital of Guatemala, is a colonial jewel with colorful streets and baroque monuments surrounded by still active volcanoes.

- Lake Atitlan is one of the most beautiful in the world, surrounded by volcanoes, lush vegetation and villages like Panajachel where the hippies who came in the 70s are still present.

- Twice a week (Sunday and Thursday) the famous market of Chichicastenango takes place. In the heart of the city, the church of Santo Tomás is a shamanic place of worship that is still active.

- On the outskirts of Guatemala's second largest city, Quetzaltenango, is San Francisco El Alto, where the largest market in Central America is held, although it is much less touristy than the one in Chichicastenango.

• Livingston has two peculiarities: you can only get there by boat along the Rio Dulce, where you can meet the Garifunas, those "Black Caribbean" descendants of African slaves and Caribbean Indians whose culture is totally different from the rest of the population.

Guyana

To begin with, Guyana is not another name for Suriname and even less for French Guiana. It is an independent country, poor, totally unknown and left to nature in its most total exuberance. Like the Congo in Africa, Guyana is not what one might call the last frontier, it is far beyond. Tourism there is non-existent, or almost non-existent, and diplomatic representations are scarce. A far west, in all its splendor. The capital and only real city, Georgetown, is the urban jungle and all around it is the jungle, the real one, with a very big J. Minimal road network (and in bad condition), complete panoply of tropical diseases (malaria zone 3), piracy on the coasts, important insecurity in the capital, natural risks of all kinds just as important outside the cities. The traveler who is not experienced and who has not traveled around the world has no place here. Adventurers will find here what they came for, adventure, and one of the true white zones of the planet. In the heart of the Amazon and on the tepuy, it is a lost world, where some places have never seen a human presence before.

• The Kaieteur Falls, the most impressive site in the country, are hidden deep in the Amazon. At the edge of the Pakaraima and Roraima mountains, the Potaro River plunges more than 220 meters high and swirls through the lush vegetation to offer the brave visitor a most grandiose spectacle. The Canister Falls on the Essequibo River, Itabru on the Berbia River, and Frederic Willem IV on the Coeroeni River are other impressive sites. The rapids formed by the rivers offer the possibility of going up some of them in dugout canoes. Swimming, on the other hand, is often prohibited because of the many caimans that live there.

• The Iwokrama forest in the northeast is a protected area where you can spend a few days in camp to better discover its natural wonders. It indeed holds several records in terms of animal life. Jaguars, black caimans, anaconda, bats... are waiting for you. On the other hand, the Rupununi savannah, in the south, is an area where only dry grass grows. Nevertheless, parakeets, falcons and storks offer a permanent spectacle.

• The coasts of Guyana are not the most ideal to rest in the sun. Indeed, in the northwest, Shell Beach is mainly composed of mangroves. However, it is worth the detour in April when sea turtles come to lay their eggs in the rare beaches that punctuate this region. However, access is tricky, and piracy is just as endemic as turtles.

French Guiana

French Guiana is a French department, yet in South America and in the heart of the Amazon, French Guiana is very little known. Of all the French overseas territories, it is by far the most exotic, and even if the prefecture of Cayenne looks like a modest provincial town, the nature at its gates is the kingdom of the largest jungle in the world. For those who want to measure themselves against it, it is certainly the best possible destination. The lack of mountains gives it a certain monotony but an expedition to the Green Hell remains a beautiful adventure. It is not really within the reach of all travelers, the uninitiated may find themselves submerged there, but the well-established tourist circuit and the general infrastructures much more efficient than in the neighboring countries make it possible to envisage an excursion rather serenely. One should not deprive oneself of it, because it is a fantastic experience, between river descents in dugout canoes (the only means of travel outside the coast), the meeting with the Amerindians, and of course the discovery of the forest with its impressive flora and fauna (the jaguar king and the giant anaconda, among others). All this is greatly facilitated by the French language. Another attraction of the department, the human sites, whether historical, the terrible prison of the Salvation Islands, or modern, the space center of Kourou. French Guiana offers a trip unlike any other (between the Amazon and rocket launches, it is a region that is difficult to compare). There are few drawbacks for visitors, provided they are willing to sacrifice a little comfort (you sleep in hammocks in the jungle and bugs are part of the scenery...), apart from an often difficult climate, very rare beaches and a not always pleasant atmosphere in the cities (especially in Cayenne). A destination with a very high potential, still very little traveled.

• The country's rivers are the basis of Guyanese tourism. The rapids of these rivers welcome canoes and pirogues for an emotional descent. Whether on the Maroni (four days of pirogues between Maripasoula and Saint-Laurent-du-Maroni), the Oyapock, the Mana or the Inini, you will be able to discover the landscapes in a sporty way, hang your hammock in the carbets and meet the Amerindian peoples. The Approuague is also famous for the Grand Kanori Falls and the site of the Saut-Athanase famous for swimming, fishing, canoeing and gold panning.

• The Creole village of Saül, in the center of the country, is a great starting point to discover the primary forest via hiking trails dotted with orchids and 5000 other plant species. Don't hesitate to take a guide to help you spot jaguars, agoutis, anacondas and black caimans, but also sloths, parrots, urubus, jacanas, red ibis and toucans. For those who are somewhat repelled by the jungle, the zoo of French Guiana covers 65 hectares in Macouria. A 1 hour and a half marked out walk will allow you to meet several of the 450 animals counted.

• The swamps, the coastal plain and the mangrove swamp contain many other surprises. Don't miss to visit (only by river), the Kaw-Roura marshes, east of Roura and south-east of Cayenne, to witness the spectacle of the red ibis. You can also visit the Amana nature reserve in the north-west, which welcomes every year the laying of sea turtles. To relax, there are superb beaches in Rémire-Montjoly, near Cayenne and Kourou (Roches beach).

• The Creole houses of Cayenne, the palm trees of the Place des Palmistes, the mixed population, the fish market and the vegetable market make the capital of French Guyana an attractive port city. Go to Fort Cépérou to admire the view of the bay. If you wish to better understand the History of French Guiana, the Franconi Departmental Museum is for you.

• Kourou is known for its space center, at the forefront of European technology. It is possible to attend an Ariane space rocket launch there (on request) or more simply to go to the Carapa site from where one has a good visibility. The visit of the center itself and the Space Museum is exciting.

• 15 km off the coast of Kourou are the Salvation Islands, where the Cayenne penal colony housed 90,000 prisoners. On Île Royale, you can visit the former prison district, the hospital and the chapel, but it is on Île du Diable, its neighbor whose currents forbid access, that the most famous political prisoners such as Alfred Dreyfus were detained.

• Originally built by and for the Penitentiary Administration, many of the official buildings in Saint-Laurent du Maroni are of a unique style of architecture, a mix of colonial and penitentiary styles all dressed in red. A visit to the Transportation Camp is very striking. If you need to digest all this on your way out, go to the last rum distillery in operation 2 km south of the city: the Saint-Maurice rum distillery.

Haiti

The poorest country in America, Haiti occupies the same island as the Dominican Republic, but does not have the same success with tourists. The two countries are very different and it is useless to compare them. Haiti is a truly fascinating country, with exceptional potential, but seriously (and regularly) affected by a multitude of crises, social or natural, which inexorably hinder its opening. It is a unique destination, with a lot of peculiarities, and with a very beautiful nature. White sandy beaches, untouched coral reefs, tropical mountain massifs, landscapes of rice fields, the country's natural palette is large and can be easily measured against the rest of the region. The traditions are just as remarkable, between the mysterious voodoo rites, the merengue (a very playful dance and musical style shared with the Dominican Republic) or the naive, very interesting, colorful art. To crown it all, the cities (each with a carnival) have an architecture with the allure of tropical Louisiana. A journey apart therefore, full of surprises, which in today's globalized world would allow the country to stand out easily, and rightly so. Alas, a thousand times alas, Haiti is struggling in a great depres-

sion, tortured by repeated natural disasters (devastating hurricanes, earthquakes), and unable to get its head above water. Infrastructures are extremely bad, the sanitary situation is deplorable and transportation is anarchic. Travel is not impossible but on the spot it is complicated. While waiting for days that we wish much better, Haiti is therefore reserved for experienced travelers and aware of the realities of the field.

- The beaches of Haiti have nothing to envy to those of the rest of the West Indies. To those of Port-au-Prince often invaded by crowds, you will find the alternative of the black sand of the beaches of Congo and Raymond les Bains near Jacmel. The beaches of Cormier and Rival, in the vicinity of Cap-Haïtien, are also very well equipped in terms of tourist infrastructure and therefore very popular. Everywhere you will be able to discover the beauty of the seabed, knowing that the most magnificent of them are on the outskirts of the island of La Gonave.

● If the north coast of Turtle Island is only cliffs whipped by the swell to the point of being nicknamed the "iron coast", its south coast offers excellent sheltered refuges, including the Basse-Terre harbour and magnificent beaches. One of them, "La Pointe-Ouest", has been named one of the ten most beautiful beaches in the Caribbean. In addition to these natural sites, it has played a role in the history of the Piracy, making it a dream destination in two ways.

● The inland is just as sumptuous. The lush forests around the Pic de la Selle, the lakes, caves and waterfalls of the Bassin Bleu and the landscapes of the southern peninsula between Les Cayes and Jérémie hold many natural surprises in store for you. Go and discover them: on your way you will also meet the Haitian cultures whether it is the handicrafts of the village Kenscoff or the voodoo celebrations of the waterfall Saut d'Eau, near Mirebalais.

● Port-au-Prince, the capital, is known for its animation, but also for its relative anarchy. The Iron Market, an impressive place to live, is nevertheless worth a visit, in the company of a guide for example. The frescoes of the Holy Trinity Cathedral will allow you to see how Catholicism and local beliefs are intertwined, while the Haitian Art Museum at St. Peter's College will make you an expert in naive art, and the National Pantheon Museum will give you a better understanding of the country's history.

● During this period, Haiti experienced a more prosperous period during which the superb Palais de Sans-Souci, in Milot in the north, now in ruins, and the largest fortress in the Caribbean, the Citadelle La Ferrière, 15 km south of Cap-Haïtien, were built. Both buildings are worth a visit. In Pétionville, Forts Jacques and Alexandre also bear witness to this past.

Honduras

Like its neighbor Guatemala, Honduras is a country that offers a great wealth of tourism, but where travel conditions are particularly poor. On the good side, we can mention the Mayan site of Copan, a must in the jungle, the omnipresence of mountains that give the country very beautiful landscapes, and the islands of the Bay, a typical Caribbean seaside resort, with a long coral reef. The site of Copan (often combined with a neighboring country) and the island of Roatan are the only two destinations advertised by tour operators, and in fact the other regions are only accessible to informed and prepared travelers. In the list of things less good, Honduras is unfortunately not outdone. Apart from the generally poor infrastructure, it is security that is particularly problematic. The statistics are unflattering because Honduras is the most insecure country on the planet, outside the war zone. Gangs are well established and it is important to be really careful, without pretending that danger is around every corner. The atmosphere in the capital, Tegucigalpa, is not very pleasant. This is enough to chill travelers who have long since left the country. Too bad because in a better situation Honduras would have beautiful tourist days ahead of it.

● The Mayan site of Copán is located in the middle of the jungle only 12 km from the Guatemalan border. Together with Tikal (Guatemala) and Chichén Itzá (Mexico), it is one of the most beautiful and interesting sites from this civilization. The Great Square is known for the stelae and altars that cover it and the size and state of conservation of the ball field make it a remarkable construction. Nearby, one can visit the beautiful colonial churches of Copán Ruinas and Santa Rita de Copán, as well as enjoy the hot springs present in the area.

• The Islas de la Bahia (Guanaja, Roatan and Utila) and the entire Caribbean coast, especially around Tela, offer beaches on a par with the rest of the Caribbean. The clarity of the seabed and the richness of the aquatic flora and fauna allow the divers to enjoy themselves there. The black coral reefs of the Cayos Cochinos reefs, 17 km off La Ceiba, are not to be missed. The only drawback of this paradise on earth is the strong presence of mosquitoes, especially during the rainy season. The Pacific coast is more restricted, but has gems such as the small volcanic island of El Tigre in the Gulf of Fonseca where the landscapes are superb and the beaches deserted.

• Tegucigalpa, the capital, is located in altitude and enjoys a pleasant climate. If the Cathedral of St. Michael the Archangel is worth a visit, you should not miss the Basílica de Suyapa, a huge Gothic church that stands 7 km southeast of the city center. The Cathedral of Saint Mary of Comayagua, 80 km northwest of the capital, is also an architectural jewel.

• The mountains (Sierra de Opalaca, Sierra de Espiritu Santo, Sierra de Agalta) cover 4/5 of the country and the landscapes evoke in turn the Andes Cordillera, the jungles of the Amazon, and the arid mountains of Mexico or the United States. It's up to you to create your own itinerary according to your desires. In the northeast of the country, you can discover the Mosquitia region and live with the Mosquito, Payas and Sumo Indians. From Palacios, you will be able to go down the Rio Negro to the Rio Platano Biosphere Reserve to meet the exceptional fauna found there (monkeys, manatees, alligators, jaguars, armadillos...).

Cayman Islands

The three Cayman Islands are best known for their tax haven status. There is wealth on the islands, which are certainly a top-of-the-range destination. Not much to say about this confidential destination, a British Overseas Territory with the typical Caribbean landscape of small islands. Some beaches are paradisiacal, white sand, turquoise water, and the underwater show is to the endorsement. Seven Mile Beach is certainly one of the most beautiful beaches in the world and those who are not here for the banks come first and foremost for it. Perfectly touristic site, but unknown in France, with very good infrastructures, the islands can be interesting for those who are already familiar with the Caribbean classics, and who can afford it.

• Seven Mile Beach on Grand Cayman is considered one of the most beautiful beaches in the Caribbean. Luxury hotels, restaurants and stores have chosen it as their favorite place. On the other side of the North Sound Bay, Rum Point is just as luxurious, but quieter. You will have to go to the nearby islands to spend a real quiet vacation. The deserted beaches of Preston Bay and Sandy Point on Little Cayman and those of Stake Bay, Halway Ground and Spot Bay on Cayman Brac await you.

• The archipelago has identified more than a hundred diving sites near its coasts, such as Parrot Reserve. The translucent seabed populated with corals and wrecks offers a wonderful spectacle to anyone wishing to put their head underwater. Although, even without it, you will be able to admire the numerous stingrays of the City of Rays at the extreme north of the west coast of Grand Cayman and swim and play with them. If you prefer turtles, they are waiting for you on the same island in the turtle farm.

• Inland there are a few possibilities for hiking. On Grand Cayman, you will go to the discovery of a dry tropical forest. Cayman Brac has a set of nice caves to explore. Little Cayman will give you the opportunity to get passionate about the red-legged boobies and frigate birds that live in the Bloody Point Reserve.

Falklands

The Falkland Islands (from the name of their first explorers, the sailors of Saint-Malo) or Falkland Islands, form a part of the world where there is not much, nor a big world. Tourism there is almost non-existent in itself, but expeditions to Antarctica sometimes stop there. It should be noted that in all cases the individual trip is not easy, the roads are tracks, the accommodation must be prepared months in advance (and through an agency), and the prices are exorbitant. Like all very isolated places, the access is very expensive. On the spot, one discovers a cold, mineral universe, where there are no more trees, with wild and rough landscapes. The great attraction remains the fauna, lions and elephant seals, penguins, numerous birds, which will attract above all the true enthusiasts. For the experienced traveller the Falklands also represent a very unusual destination, far off the beaten track. For the others it is almost as if we were talking about another planet. It should be noted that Argentina and England are fighting over the islands, and even if the situation is very calm on the spot it is always advisable to find out what is happening before embarking on this very long journey.

• The archipelago is composed of two main islands, West Falkland and East Falkland, separated by a wide channel, the Falkland Strait, and more than 750 islands and islets.

• The small Falklands archipelago offers the daring traveller its dry scenery swept by an icy wind where large colonies of animals live.

• Albatrosses, gorfus, penguins, penguins, sea lions, elephant seals, cormorants and giant petrels share this territory and will delight the wildlife photographers who have ventured so far. In the southeast of the archipelago, the small island of Sea Lion and its colonies of elephant seals attract the curious during the austral summer. For birdwatching, New Island, in the West Falkland Islands, is ideal, while Carcass will welcome you with a large number of Patagonian ducks and dolphins.

Turks & Caicos Islands

Very little known, the Turks & Caicos Islands are nevertheless one of the Caribbean paradises par excellence. The seaside aspect is of course predominant there, small size of the islands obliges, and the amateurs of white sand and turquoise water will have for their expenses. The landscapes are not to be outdone and the infrastructures are very good. Obviously the destination is developing, in the wake of the Bahamas, and the busiest island, Providenciales, already has a false air of an American resort. Nevertheless, it is especially the wild character which still dominates, especially on the other islands, and the archipelago offers a sizable bonus, whale watching in season. It goes without saying that if the trip is simple, it is not cheap.

• Numerous natural lakes dot the flat relief of the Turks and Caicos Islands, but the surrounding aridity will naturally push you to take advantage of the 370 km of beaches bathed by translucent waters whose purity is the main asset.

• On Providence (Provo), the most developed island (but neither the largest nor the capital) you will find the lively beach of Grace Bay and its large hotels. Elsewhere on the archipelago, the atmosphere is much calmer and more traditional. West Caicos will delight divers as much as South Caicos. Budding Robinsons will choose the beautiful deserted beaches of North Caicos while lovers of postcard landscapes can explore Middle Caicos where limestone caves and cliffs crowned with pine trees alternate with sandy bays. The waters of Salt Cay, very rich in plankton, are the best place in the Caribbean for whale watching between January and March.

British Virgin Islands

As one might decently expect, the British side of the Virgin Islands is wilder and far less touristy than its American counterpart. The last islands north of the Lesser Antilles arc are nevertheless a very beautiful destination, where the equipment is optimal and the trip is easy (but expensive). On the program, the classics of the region, beautiful beaches (and the original bathing site of the Baths), diving (wrecks in Anegada), and a superb setting especially in Tortola where the vegetation is particularly lush. Little frequented by French-speaking travelers, the British Virgin Islands have great assets to offer to Caribbean lovers.

• The coasts of Tortola oscillate between large beaches shaded by coconut palms and small quiet coves. To the north on the Atlantic coast, those of Apple Bay and Brewers Bay are the favorites of the beach-goers who practice sailing, diving and surfing. Don't hesitate to make an excursion to the island of Sandy Bay, a confetti fallen from paradise. On Virgin Gorda, in addition to the long strips of fine sand, you will find "the Baths", a natural pool made of huge rocks and salt ponds. To the north, Saba Rock has plenty of room for a bar and a diving club. What more could you ask for?

• Diving is really one of the most appreciated activities in the area. Peter Island, south of Tortola, is the starting point of the most famous scuba diving in the Caribbean, where you will discover the gigantic wreck of the postal boat "Rhone". Around Anegada Island, and especially off Salt Island, there are also hundreds of wrecks. In winter, humpback whales come to reproduce in the Drake Strait.

• Dense subtropical forests cover the vast majority of the archipelago's flat relief. The vegetation of Mount Sage National Park on Tortola will delight the senses of walkers apprentice botanists. The most beautiful panorama offered on these green islands is at the top of Gorda Peak on Virgin Gorda.

U.S. Virgin Islands

American part of the archipelago of the Virgin Islands, the three "saints" are superb nooks and crannies of the Caribbean, but are strongly influenced by the typical development of Uncle Sam. That said, the historical (the islands were Swedish in the past) and geographical (at the gates of the Greater Antilles) peculiarities make the American Virgin Islands an interesting destination. The landscapes are superb, both near the coasts and inland (especially on St. Croix, the wildest island), and the towns and villages, including Charlotte Amalie, the small capital, have a nice tropical look. Of course the infrastructure is up to American standards, and so are the prices of the trip. The destination, a must for American cruise passengers, is very touristy in high season, and rightly so, but this makes the appeal of a combination with the British Isles all the more appreciable.

• These islands are a paradise for lovers of idleness and sailing. On St. Thomas, the most beautiful beaches are located on the north coast, such as Magens Bay (the most popular), Saphire Beach and Coki Beach. For more tranquility, take a boat to Hassel Island and Great St. James. Fans of diving and snorkeling will have more than 3,000 hectares of protected seabed to explore in the St. John National Park. The main spots are Trunk Bay (underwater course), Reef Bay and Honeymoon Bay. The island of St. Croix is surrounded by a coral reef and conceals some isolated beaches such as Coaklay, Great Pond and Caneel Bay. Feel free to visit the uninhabited Buck Island where the beach and seabed are even more incredible.

• The natural parks of the archipelago have lush vegetation and invite travelers to hike. Saint John won the prize for the most unspoiled island with some 20 trails available for walkers. The most interesting are those leading to Bordeaux Mountain, the highest point on the island, and the one leading to the former Annaberg sugar plantation. The most beautiful panoramas of St. Thomas can be found on the heights of Drake's Seat and at Botany Bay on the west coast. The drier landscapes of St. Thomas are dotted with former plantation owners' homes.

Jamaica

Within the range of countries with a strong identity, Jamaica obviously has its place. Its first trademark is first of all music, ska and all its more or less modern derivatives, passing of course through reggae. The idol, Bob Marley, attracts the crowds, and still lives in the Jamaican popular consciousness. Then comes a culture of its own, including a particular religion, Rastafarianism, which if it is not followed by the majority of the inhabitants (contrary to a tenacious cliché), permeates the life of the island. That said, Jamaica is not limited to that, it is also a historic island, the ancient land of wood and water of the Arawak Indians and marked by piracy (Port Royal was one of the strongholds of all pirates in the Caribbean). It is finally, and above all, an island with the typical attractions of the Greater Antilles, beautiful beaches, tropical mountains and lush forests. So much for the good side of the picture, but the other side is much less pleasing. Jamaica is a socially complicated country, where insecurity is unfortunately very present, and where tourist sites tend to be landlocked. The island remains quite poor and its exploration off the beaten track is reserved for travelers who are nevertheless prepared. A trip to a seaside hotel in Negril is simple, but the discovery of the country is more complex. This does not change the attractions of the island, but it is better to know it and be aware of it. Infrastructures, apart from seaside areas with all comforts fitted out for the American clientele, are sometimes deficient, especially in the interior of the country.

• Jamaican shores are one of the main reasons to spend some time on the island. The most famous are on the north coast and often belong to hotels. Negril has 14 km of white sand and dive sites around South Negril Point. Ochos Rios benefits from a hinterland where the waterfalls sing (you can go up by boat to Dunn's River Falls) between plantations and houses of the colonial period. Montego Bay and Port Antonio also have some beautiful beaches. The eastern beaches around Port Antonio have been made famous by the attendance of many Hollywood stars and the shooting of many movies. The southern beaches, such as Savanna la Mar, are less numerous, but generally quieter.

• Inland there are great opportunities for excursions. In the mid-west, go to Cockpit Country, an original limestone ensemble. To the east is the peak of the Blues Mountains, which is home to an abundant flora animated by numerous parrots. In the south of the country, north of Black River, you will find a large swampy area where the last large crocodiles of the island live. South of San Antonio, you can visit the Nonsuch Caves and raft down the Rio Grande.

• Spanish Town, the former capital, has some jewels of colonial architecture, but security in the city is not good. Colonial era also witnessed by Port Royal, former pirate stronghold. Kingston, the capital, is a bustling city, with intense activity where you can visit the museum of Bob Marley, child of the island (Nine Miles).

Martinique

As complete as Guadeloupe in terms of tourism, but often reputed more welcoming, and with more developed tourist facilities, Martinique is a major site in the Caribbean. It remains however very confidential outside the French market (the island is an overseas department of France). The island, larger than one can imagine, has a beautiful diversity, and well marked regions. The south is seaside, with superb beaches, and the north is wilder, especially around Mount Pelee. Pleasure of beaches and hiking, nature, mountains, diving, cultural discovery, the offer is varied. It is a very interesting destination, whose access from France is very simple (many daily flights from Paris and competitive rates). Travel comfort is optimal, with excellent infrastructure. The only real drawback is its capital, Fort de France, which is charmless and sometimes not very pleasant.

• At the northern tip of the island, Le Prêcheur has a sumptuous black sand beach: Anse Couleuvre. It will take you about ten minutes of walking in the tropical forest to reach it and enjoy its absolute calm.

• The Caribbean coast is a true paradise for those who love to relax. From Trois-Ilets to the Anses d'Arlets, everything is only enchantment. In addition to sunbathing, you can practice sailing, water skiing, kayaking, jet skis and quad biking.

• Accessible by boat, the site of the Diamond Rock attracts divers by the transparency of its bottom which allows to see an abundant underwater fauna. The islet also shelters the best preserved beach of the island.

• Four kilometers from Sainte-Anne, Grande-Anse des Salines is extremely popular with locals and tourists who often call it "the most beautiful beach in the West Indies". At the southern end, one can admire the Table-au-Diable and Cabrits islet.

• On the Atlantic side, at the end of the Caravelle peninsula is the Caravelle Nature Reserve, which is crossed by numerous hiking trails from the mangrove edges to the foot of the ruins of the Dubuc castle. The beach of Tartane is appreciated by the amateurs of waves.

• The same is true on the entire east coast, which is more suitable for surfing and kitesurfing than for swimming. The bay of François is a remarkable body of water for its sandy shallows, its islands and the color of "white bottom" waters such as that of the Baignoire de Joséphine.

• Located 40 kilometers northwest of Fort-de-France, Mount Pelée is a dormant volcano that rises to an altitude of 1,397 metres, and can be climbed to its fullest potential. The Volcanological Museum of Saint Pierre nevertheless reminds us that from this superb crater was born the fiery cloud of 1902 which completely destroyed the town of Saint Pierre.

• About thirty marked trails run through this northern region to discover forests and waterfalls, but also gardens and plantations of great beauty. Near the village of Ajoupa-Bouillon, the Falaise gorges offer a spectacular landscape with its natural swimming pool dug into the rock. The opportunity to discover the sensations of canyoning.

• At the northern end of the island, the road stops at Grand'Rivière, a fishing village, wedged between the ocean and Pelee Mountain, which surprises by the diversity of its landscapes. The river flowing down from the volcano is a popular swimming spot throughout the island. The town is also the starting point for many hikes.

Mexico

A large country, with an immense heritage and generous nature, Mexico ranks among the most beautiful destinations on the planet. The legacy of pre-Colombian civilizations, led by the Mayans, gives the country a superb appeal, as well as the many colonial cities and the multiple landscapes from deserts to jungles to mountains. Thousands of kilometers of coastline, from the turquoise lagoons of the Caribbean to the wild beaches of the Pacific, complete this fantastic panorama. The infrastructures are good, even if the countryside is still far from western standards. On the other hand, the bat hurts on the level of security, which is problematic throughout the country, including in sites that are very famous like Acapulco. Gang warfare, drug trafficking, and deep-rooted corruption mean that discovering the country in its broad expanses is reserved for seasoned travelers (mastering the Spanish language is already a good start). However, neophytes should not rule out Mexico from their list, because organized travel is very well established there and even independently it remains relatively simple to make a tour, being prepared. The tourist image of the country is a little tarnished, but we should not stop there, Mexico is an absolutely major destination.

• The archaeological sites of Mexico and their pyramids are like images of Epinal in our imagination. However, do not doubt that, in front of them, you will find yourself amazed before you even understand that the civilizations that built them had not invented the wheel. The first site you visit is often the one near the capital: Teotihuacán, the largest city in pre-Columbian America in the classical era. Here rise the pyramids of the Moon and the Sun which you will have to climb to admire the whole site and its road of the dead lined with temples and palaces.

• The other most important Mayan ceremonial centers in the country are the following: Palenque whose ornaments are only equalled by the vegetation surrounding them, Uxmal and its surprising state of preservation, Chichén Itzá which was the main religious center of *Yucatán* and Tulum, a white city overlooking the Caribbean Sea, to form one of the most famous postcards of the country. Also, don't miss the one that the Zapotec civilization erected on the mountain range of Monte Albánafter having flattened its summit.

• The Spanish civilization then landed and eliminated these civilizations. Mexico City was built on the Aztec site of Tenochtitlan. Religious and urban art blended together in a sumptuous baroque style that makes every street a work of art. This overpopulated and polluted capital has indeed many treasures in addition to its lively atmosphere. To set the tone, the Metropolitan Cathedral, which dominates the immense Zócalo Square, is the largest cathedral in America; just like the Basilica of Our Lady of Guadalupe, on the outskirts of the city, can accommodate 20 million pilgrims each year (it is the most visited Catholic monument after the Vatican City). In the midst of this excesses, don't forget to visit, in addition to the National Museum of Anthropology, Trotsky's house, Frida Kahlo's Blue House and the Museo Estudio Diego Rivera.

• Many other colonial cities are also worth a visit. The mountainous site of Taxco (famous for its goldsmiths), the baroque churches of Puebla (where the chocolate-based mole poblano was born), the architecture of Santiago de Querétaro and Mérida, the white city, are just a few examples. Oaxaca la Verde is a very pleasant cultural city where the baroque also takes pleasure in slipping into the smallest details. It is the same in San Miguel de Allende or Morelia. Finally, Chiapas hides many villages with an Indian character in its heart, the easiest example being San Cristobal de la Casas and its marketé. Nearby, in San, Juan de Chamulaa Catholic church welcomes the Tzotziles and their pagan religion, a rare syncretism not to be missed.

• Mexico's beaches attract as many tourists, if not more, as the archaeological sites each year. It is the shores of Yucatán, on the edge of a turquoise sea, which are the most popular. From Cancún to Tulum, on 120 km long, the "Mayan Riviera" spreads its white beaches under the Caribbean sun. The sites of *Cancún* and Playa del Carmen are at the top of the list, but the one of Cozumel is the most sought-after in terms of scuba diving. Do not hesitate to go to Isla Mujeres, a little more affordable, a little less crowded and with a more harmonious development.

• On the other side of the country, the Pacific projects its waves against the beaches of Acapulco, Ixtapa and Puerto Valarta. The three bays are famous, especially Acapulco, but they are big tourist machines that are primarily oriented towards the American clientele. It is the surfers who will be the most satisfied with spots like Puerto Escondido. If you do not like the architecture of the Seventies, nor the tourist atmosphere, go a little further east towards Puerto Angel, Zipolite, et San Augustinillo. The sea is sometimes dangerous there, but you will be alone on paradisiacal beaches to taste a ceviche accompanied by a very fresh beer. On the way, don't miss the Centro mexicano de la tortuga in Mazunte to admire the turtles.

• Still on the beach side, those along the Baja California are even more atypical. A superb coastline stretches along the peninsula and you will find quiet places like San José del Cabo or more lively places like Cabo San Lucas. This last spot is very appreciated by bodyboarders and skimboardeurs for its very powerful shorebreak, just as Todos Santos is another paradise for surfers. But the particularity of this coast is especially for the grey whales which pass there between February and March. Thus, the site of the hare-eye lagoon in Guerrero Negro is famous for seeing whales mating and calves being born. Other animals await you in the Sea of Cortes, such as rorqual whales, dolphins, sea lions, seals and sea lions around Espiritu Santo Island and elephant seals on Cedros Island.

• In this same region, the inland will also hold many surprises for you. The candelabra cactus forests of the Vizcaino Desert, one of the driest deserts on the planet, rival those of the Los Cirios Valley, where cardoons can sometimes be over 700 years old.

• The western Sierra Madre can be discovered by taking the Chepe, the train that connects Los Mochis to Chihuahua. Between the pines, canyons, each one more majestic than the other, carve out the landscape and the train's route allows you to appreciate all the beauty of the Parque Natural Barranca del Cobre. To the north of this is the Parque Nacional Cascada de Basaseachi where one of the highest waterfalls in the world can be found.

• Between Guadalajara and Veracruz, volcanoes have sculpted some of the most beautiful landscapes in Mexico. To be seen from west to east: the basilica of San Juan Parangaricutiro buried by the Paricutín lava, the lake of Pátzcuaro and the island of Janitzio where the famous statue of Morelos is located and the 16th century monasteries built on the slopes of the Popocatépelt volcano.

Montserrat

Despite its very small size, this small pearl-shaped island is a rather surprising destination. Far from the classic clichés of the Caribbean, this emerald stone sometimes takes on a false Irish air. One comes there above all for the mountainous landscapes of the center, the hike on the volcanoes (destructive, as shown by the great eruption of the 90s), and as a bonus for some beaches where there are generally not many people. It is a very original destination, whose access is not very easy because the island is isolated but where the infrastructures are of good level, although few.

* The climbs of Galway's Soufrière and Chance's Peak are the two most famous on the island. The beaches are mainly located on the north coast, where the inhabitants who chose to stay after the eruption of the Soufrière in 1997, which led to the destruction of the southern part of the island and in particular of Plymouth, the capital, now a ghost town, took refuge.

* The island is also good for diving and snorkeling, for example at Woodlands Bay and Lime Kiln Bay.

Nicaragua

Nicaragua, like Honduras, like Guatemala, is a very interesting country but suffers from chronic instability and a fairly high level of violence. As a result, this automatically distances it from mainstream destinations. That said, the situation is improving and among travelers the country is now acting as an understudy to Costa Rica, too mainstream for some. Seasoned and prepared travelers will be able to discover some very beautiful sites, mountains, volcanoes, the great Lake Nicaragua and two very different coasts, on the Caribbean and Pacific sides. A rich and diversified panel, on a small area, which could easily ensure beautiful tourist days in the country. The best way to discover Nicaragua remains to rely on tour operators, especially specialists in adventure travel and trekking, who have succeeded in establishing well-established tourist circuits, thanks to a political and social enlightenment that we hope will be sustainable. For independent travel, it is better not to go blind and to be prepared.

* Nicaragua is crossed by a volcanic axis that offers a ribbon of peaks suitable for ascents. Depending on the eruptive conditions of the moment, you will be able to choose between the Cerro Negro and the superb desert of volcanic ash that stretches out at its feet, the Telica and the sulphurous earth of San Jacinto, or the Masaya and its intense volcanic activity. All of them will offer you breathtaking shows. For more tranquility, the Monbacho has two craters covered with thick tropical vegetation where many mammals and birds live.

* The most beautiful landscapes of Nicaragua are undoubtedly in the Isabella, Dariense and Yolaina mountain ranges, and in the region of Lake Nicaragua, especially on its main island: Ometepe. This one is formed by two volcanoes: the still active Concepción and the extinct Madera. The ecosystem is very rich, with many species of birds and howler monkeys. At the top of the Madera there is a lagoon that can be accessed by taking one of the three possible routes for the ascent.

* The beaches of the Caribbean coast, especially those south of Bluefields, are already well known to North American tourists. The Spanish culture coming from the west of the country mixed with the Creole culture of the region, English-speaking (the Mosquito coast was for two centuries under the protectorate of England). This ancient pirate's den has beautiful beaches like the one in the bay of San Juan del Norte. It is easier to reach it by plane or boat than by road.

• However, the country's best known seaside resorts are located on the Pacific coast. One hour's drive from Managua, the country's capital, the Montelimar Beach resort and San Juan del Sur are among the best known spots. The beaches of Pochomil and Masachapa, among others, are paradises for surfing and fishing.

• Returning to the interior, you will discover villages where live a welcoming people that you can easily meet by going to the markets for example. On the cultural side, the old town of Granada is known for its well-preserved colonial architecture and Moorish Andalusian style buildings. León has long been the cultural center of the country and is famous for its churches, including the great Cathedral of San Pedro.

Panama

Panama, its famous canal, its no less famous hat, its contradictory images. We don't really know where to classify Panama, which looks like the United States, sometimes like Asia, and always with a Latin soul and an exacerbated tropical nature. Link between the north and the south of the American continent, the country is most often disappointing for the traveler worn by these images. This is another of its contradictions, as much as Panama is not overly interested in its "pile" side (Panama City, the canal), as much as its "face" side is a call for adventure. The Darién region, bordering Colombia, is a fantastic jungle, primary and intact, almost unexplored. It must be said that for many years it was the hideout of the FARC army, not to mention trafficking of all kinds, a lawless zone where kidnappings were commonplace. It remains an almost inaccessible and dangerous area. If the situation improves, it could become a major asset in the country's tourist offer. For the moment, Panama is behind its neighbors and remains a confidential destination.

• The Panama Canal, a true masterpiece of human engineering whose creation was initiated by the same architect as the Suez Canal, remains one of the major attractions of the country. The various lakes artificially created at the bend of the numerous locks have developed an original aquatic environment.

• Panama's 3000 km of coastline, Caribbean and Pacific, offers many postcard beaches, as well as more than 1500 islands. The archipelago of Bocas del Toro is a quality scuba diving spot, as well as those of Las Mulatas and Las Perlas. The San Blas Islands are an archipelago of 365 coral islands populated by Kuna Indians who live from hunting and fishing. An hour's boat ride from Balboa, the island of Taboga combines white sand, multicolored flowers, small tropical jungle and black pelicans to offer an exotic paradise to the traveler. The Pacific coast, in Coronado for example, is more sheltered than the Caribbean coast. The proximity of the capital Panama City also gives it better infrastructure.

• Inland, you will be able to cross the Darién National Park and its immense and wild tropical rainforest to meet the eagles, tapirs, jaguars, iguanas and golden frogs that populate it. South-east of Panama City, the Anton Valley is ideal for eco-tourism with its hills, waterfalls and the interest of its fauna and flora.

• In the province of Chiriquí there are many museums where the remains of civilizations dating from 800 to 1500 AD are kept. The village of Portobelo, opposite Panamá city, also has traces of the colonial period and archaeological remains.

Paraguay

Neighbor of Bolivia, with whom it shares little apart from great poverty, Paraguay is without a doubt the least known of the Latin American countries. It is not a great destination like Brazil or neighboring Argentina, but it is not an uninteresting country for all that. Its first asset is precisely the fact that it is not very touristy and everything is off the beaten track, which attracts its share of adventurers. Another attraction is the duality of the landscapes between the east, where the jungle and swamps dominate, and the west, where a huge steppe, the Chaco, is unique. For the interested traveler, it will be necessary to be organized and prepared, because the infrastructures are quite bad and the decades of dictatorship have left a palpable tension in the cities. Nature, wild and self-sufficient, is intense but must be approached with caution.

• The territory of Paraguay, divided in two by the Paraguay River, offers a strong contrast between the green east with the forests of Alto Paraná and the often arid west of the Chaco steppes. Do not hesitate to go up the river by boat to Conceptión.

• In the National Park of "Defensores del Chaco", pumas, tapirs, crocodiles, toucans and parrots have taken up residence. The Ybicuy National Park, south of Asunción, offers many possibilities of ideal hikes to enjoy the same animal spectacle and the waterfalls that dot the territory.

• Jesuits who came to meet the Guaraní Indians in the 17th century are still many remains of missions and sanctuaries in Trinidad, Damian, Yaguaron and San Cosmé. The museum of San Ignacio also bears witness to this passage, while in Asunción, the capital, there is the old military college, built by their company in Independence Square.

• Asunción is worth for its avenues, its market (mercato quatro) and its zoo. Nearby is the pleasant seaside resort of San Bernardino on Lake Yacaparai. From Ciudad del Este, whose numerous duty-free stores delight the Brazilian neighbors, one can visit the site of the Iguaçu Falls at Brésil.

Peru

Great destination, carried by the incredible inheritance of the Inca civilization, Machu Picchu in head, and proposing at the same time the mountains of the Andes, the Amazonian jungle, the colonial cities and the modern South American metropolises (with their qualities and their defects), Peru is one of the most beautiful countries of the planet, rich in discoveries. In South America only Brazil can decently compete. The two countries also share some similarities, starting with a well-developed network of tourist infrastructure, but also social instability and insecurity sometimes embarrassing, especially in the cities. In Peru, the traveler is invited to be cautious. In terms of general development, however, Peru is clearly below Brazil. With preparation and common sense the trip is rather simple but the less experienced visitors have all interest to start there in company of a tour operator.

• Machu Picchu is the most majestic of the testimonies left by the Inca civilization. Perched on a rocky promontory at more than 2400 meters of altitude, the 172 constructions of the site dominated by the sugar loaf of Huayna Picchu will satisfy even the most demanding in terms of panorama, especially at sunrise. It is reached via the "Inca Trail" after four days of intense walking or by taking the Andean train from Cuzco. Nearby, do not hesitate to linger in the "Sacred Valley", the arch site and éologique de Pisacthe fortress of Ollantaybambo are really worth the detour.

• The Incas were preceded by other civilizations which left important traces. In the valley of La Leche on the northern coast of Peru, one should not miss the sites of Túcume and Sipan inherited from the Lambayeque civilization as well as the Archaeological Museum of the city of the same name where there is a unique royal tomb. Still on the coast, the nine enclosures of the site of Chanchan are the remains of the ancient capital of the Chimu kingdom. In the heart of the White Cordillera, the ceremonial center of Chavin and its stone sculptures have given their name to another pre-Columbian civilization. South of Lima, the ruins of Pachacamac evoke the past splendor of an ancient sacred and ceremonial place of the Ica-Nazca.

• Between 200 B.C. and 600 A.D., the inhabitants of the valley ée de Nazcadrew geoglyphs, huge lines representing animals and plants, on the ground of the pampas. Several theories, from the most scientific to the most mystical, try to understand their meaning and purpose. On the coast, a little further north, is the Candlestick of Paracas engraved in the same way on the desert side without being able to date it and assimilate it to the productions of the Nazcas. It can be admired during the boat trips organized to go to the islandsles Ballestas.

• Cuzco, which was the capital of the empire of the Sun, mixes at 3400 meters of altitude, the Inca vestiges and the colonial constructions. The convent of Santo Domingo had even covered the rests of the temple of the Sun which were revealed at the great day at the time of an earthquake in 1950. The city, sublime and alive, is dominated by the imposing fortress of Saqsaywaman with walls made of enormous stones assembled together without any mortar. Nearby, do not miss the site of Raqchi, one of the rare two-story Inca remains still standing.

• To complete the picture, don't miss the Larco Museum in Lima which offers an exceptional panorama of the 3000 years of development of the history of ancient pre-Columbian Peru. Lima is also worth a visit for its historical center where the colonial architecture of the houses, the baroque cathedral and the church of San Francisco shine, and its places to stroll (Paseo Colon, Exhibition Park, Park of the Reserva...). In the surroundings, the olive garden of San Isidro, the sea front of Miraflores and the center of Barranco are also very pleasant during a walk.

• The Altiplano offers the spectacle of snowy valleys and peaks with the highlight of Lake Titicaca that Peru shares with Bolivia. Legendary cradle of the Sons of the Sun, it can be discovered by boat and docked on different islands such as Amantani and Taquile where Quechuas and Aymaras live. D'autres îles plus surprenantes, made of floating reeds, dot the lake, you will meet the descendants of the Uros Indians.

• Northeast of Lima, the White Cordillera is the highest tropical mountain range in the world. Thirty-five of its peaks are higher than 6,000 meters, while more than 250 high altitude lakes illuminate the glaciers with the color of their bottoms. There are countless possibilities for hiking. As an example, let's mention the four-day hike that starts from Huaraz and takes you to the snowy mountains of Quitaraju and Alpamayo, the Jatuncocha Lake and beautiful lagoons.

• To the south, in the r égion d'Arequipa(a city with a very interesting religious heritage), volcanoes like the Misti with its perfect cone, canyons like the Colca canyon and its 3400 meters deep, and natural viewpoints from where you can admire the flight of the condors are all attractions for the hiker. The stone forest of Huaron, in the south, also offers a magnificent spectacle, as well as the peaks of the Vilcanota mountain range to the east of Cuzco and the salt marshes of Maras near the "Sacred Valley".

• To discover the Amazon, the expedition begins in Iquitos, a city established between the Amazon, Nanay and Itaya rivers or from Puerto Maldonado at the confluence of the Madre de Dios and Tambopata rivers. In both cases, you will be able to embark on peque-peque, long pirogues, to discover the forest (the largest biodiversity in the world), its inhabitants and their practices. In order to preserve this region, the government has created large natural parks such as the Manu Park and the Tambopata-Candamo Reserve.

• The islands les Ballestasoff the coast of Pisco, located 300 kilometers south of Lima, are accessible in 2 hours by boat from Paracas. Their black color comes from the guano which covers them, it is indeed a true ornithological reserve where multiple colonies of sea birds cohabit, including penguins. In addition to these, there are several thousand sea lions and an ocean populated by more than 180 species of fish and 10 varieties of dolphins.

• The beaches of Paracas have the peculiarity of presenting one of the richest ecosystems of the coastline, lovers of diving and fishing will find their happiness. For surfing, go to Costa Verde in the Lima region. Beaches such as Herradura and Pico Alto and especially those of Punta Rocas are famous for the size of their waves. For swimming, you will choose Cerro Azul, but be careful, as on the whole Peruvian coast, the water is quite cold. The beaches of Arequipa in the south have a slightly warmer climate.

Puerto Rico

Puerto Rico, or Puerto Rico, is the heart of the Caribbean region. The last of the "great" Antilles to the east, the island is an American territory, where Spanish is spoken. It is not a state of the USA, but apart from the language, the tropical scenery and the Spanish colonial cities, it is just like it is. It is one of the most touristic islands of the Caribbean. The capital, San Juan, is also the largest city in the region, the richest and the local air hub. The big American-style hotels line up on the beaches there, especially in Condado, the local Waikiki (or Miami Beach). However, behind the big chain hotels, the island has a strong character and it is one of the best Caribbean destinations. Very complete, the island offers lagoon or surf beaches, colonial cities (including the old San Juan, a jewel) and plantation villages, lush jungles (the superb El Yunque park) and urban jungles where even shopping lovers will find their account. Real strong point, the infrastructures are very good, almost at the level of the continental United States, and the journey is very easy. The only black point is the not always pleasant atmosphere with a social situation which, as everywhere in the USA, is not at its best. However, with a little caution and preparation the traveler will have no problem exploring this small piece of overseas America.

• Its proximity to San Juan, but especially the beauty of its coastline, make the east one of the most touristic regions of Puerto Rico. The beaches of Vacia Talega, Luquillo, Fajardo, Punta Quebrada Honda, Punta Tuna, but also La Cordillera will make the happiness of all, even if the surfers will prefer the rollers of the beaches of Aviones, Tocones (near Loiza) and La Pared (on Luquillo Boulevard) or those of the beaches of the North-West. In the southwest, scuba diving enthusiasts will enjoy the sites of Playa Ballena (Guanica), Bahia Fosforescente (Lajas), the island of Mona (in the Cabo Rojo area) and off the coast of Parguera. The island of Vieques will offer visitors some of the most beautiful beaches in the Caribbean, including a bio luminescent beach, and those on the island of Culebra are bordered by sumptuous coral reefs.

• By occupying the center of the island, the Central Cordillera adds to the pleasure of a seaside stay that of hiking in landscapes where the flora is extremely rich such as those of the tropical rainforest of El Yunque, in the east, known for its varieties of orchids. Do not miss the Camuy cave, one of the natural curiosities of the region. Nearby, the Bosque Estatal de Pinones is 60% covered by mangroves and 40% by dunes, beaches and lagoons. The National Forest of Carite in the south and the National Forest of Guanica in the southwest also offer many hiking opportunities.

• San Juan, the capital, is well worth a visit for its stores, restaurants, bars and cultural heritage. During the day, you can discover the colonial past of the city through its old quarter and its fortresses El Morro and Fortaleza. Once the evening comes, the Puerto Rican culture will offer itself to you between pina coladas and merengue. To the south, the city of Ponce is also worth visiting for its thousand historical buildings and its artistic and cultural potential, while San German boasts one of the oldest churches in America.

Dominican Republic

Having long since chosen, and with immense success, the path of cheap beach tourism, the Dominican Republic has made the exoticism of the Caribbean affordable to many Europeans. The Dominican Republic is now seen as a vast array of club hotels, where good taste is not always in the picture. Some sectors are indeed entirely devoted to organized tourism (Punta Cana in the first place), and the trio tong sunscreen rum is the common thread of the vacations, but the Rep Dom is also much more than that. First of all, whether one likes or dislikes the atmosphere, there is no denying that the beaches, even the busiest, are magnificent. They are certainly among the most beautiful in the world, with bright white sand, coconut palms flirting with the trade winds, clear water and multicolored fauna. The postcard of the Caribbean is here (among others). Beyond the beaches, the country is much less visited and can reserve a good surprise, especially in the mountains and jungles of the center. With an easy access and a very affordable cost, the Dominican Republic is a complete tropical destination, where the traveler does not have to stop at clichés.

• The Coconut Coast in the southeast is crowded with resort hotels. Boca Chica, Punta Cana, La Romana... These names evoke a week of well-deserved idleness between turquoise waters, sandy beaches and coconut palms. Some bays frequented by the inhabitants have kept their charm even if fishing villages like Bayhibe have been transformed into a seaside resort and diving.

• The atmosphere of the southwest coast, from Barahona to Oviedo, is the opposite. The wild coast with its rough waters dotted with fishing villages is much less invaded by tourists. Impressive, the beaches offer a panorama of the mountains of Bahoruco.

- To the northwest, in the province of Puerto Plata, lies the Amber Coast (so named for its huge amber deposits). Small beaches with turbulent waters, coves and coral reefs offer tourists the possibility of diving, but also surfing and other water sports. The beach of Kitebeach in Cabarete is famous for this type of activities.

- To the east of the Amber Coast is the Costa Verde which, on the Samana peninsula, offers the most tranquil and authentic sites. On the coastline of the El Seibo region, kilometers of beautiful and deserted beaches await you. As a bonus, humpback whales stay here from January to March to give birth.

- Santo Domingo, the capital, was the first seat of Spanish power in the New World. The Faro Museum is dedicated to Christopher Columbus and the Santa Maria La Menor Cathedral, opposite Columbus Park, is the first cathedral built in America. Pleasant to live in, magnified by the colonial remains, one finds there a concentrate of the joyful and musical atmosphere of the country. The Malecon, 12 kilometers long seafront, is lined with restaurants and nightclubs.

- In the province of San Juan, the Cordillera Central exceeds 3000 meters in places. You will be able to make the ascent of the pico Duarte, the highest peak of the Caribbean: 18 km of walk for 2000 meters of unevenness from La Ciénaga. At the top, the panorama is superb. At the foot of the massif, the tropical forests unfold their luxuriant vegetation.

- To the southwest, in the Jaragua National Park and to the northwest in the region of Monte Cristi, the landscape is almost totally desert. The salt lake of Enriquillo, at 44 m below sea level, as well as the Cabritos Island that it hosts, contains an interesting fauna (crocodiles, flamingos, iguanas) like the lagoon of Oviedo.

- The bay of Samana also lends itself to hikes to discover the northern hills, but it will be by boat that travelers will set off to explore the mangrove of the park of los Haïtises, south of the bay, and its particular fauna. Cave paintings of animals were left in caves in the region by the first inhabitants of the island, the Tainos.

Saint-Barthélemy

A very small island in the north of the West Indies, a small pebble attached to France, which was once Swedish, and populated by descendants of Breton and Norman sailors. Far from the standard tropical image, Saint-Barthélemy evokes more Provence than Amazonia. Its scrubland landscapes and blond sandy creeks give it a natural appeal reinforced by a very high level of sunshine. But above all, Saint-Barth' is the island of luxury in the Caribbean. There are few hotels there that do not have at least 4 stars and the prices are consequently very high. Gourmet restaurants, select bars, everything is in tune. Villas are more expensive than on the French Riviera and the small capital, Gustavia, has luxury boutiques in its streets and huge yachts in its marina. Of course the Caribbean invites you to relax and the atmosphere is much less overrated than one might think, especially since luxury has had the merit of preserving the island from the excesses of tourism. We will have to accept that there is no other form of authenticity and that we must be prepared to spend a lot of money for the traveller who wishes to stay there. In most cases, the island can be visited during an excursion from the neighboring island of Sint Maarten.

- The Bay of Saint John, the most urbanized bay on the island, offers a colorful spectacle between the green of the gardens, the red of the houses and the emerald of the waves. The beach is one of the longest on the island, where you can stroll, rest and practice various water sports. It is also the case in Grand Cul de Sac. In Anse de Public is the sailing school.

- The most beautiful beach on the island is the Governor's beach. Flamands is also a very beautiful and long beach of blond sand at the foot of a hill. L'Anse de Marigot is wilder and has its grey sand and coconut grove. It is one of the rare beaches to have one, with that of Le Maréchal, just as discreet.

- L'Anse de Lorient is an ideal place to discover turtles and multicolored fish. It is also the meeting place for surfers. Petit Cul de Sac, one of the favorites of the inhabitants, Colombier, more remote, and Petite Anse are also great places for snorkeling. Surfers also find themselves on the beach of Toiny, at Grand Fond and Anse des Cayes where the current, too strong for swimmers, is ideal for them.

• Grande Saline is the beach of choice for naturists, Corrosol is the beach of choice for fishermen and Shell Beach is the beach of choice for shell collectors. The latter, near Gustavia, also offers a beautiful panorama of the Gros Ilets located a short distance from the coast.

• By taking the coastal road, you will discover beautiful landscapes. Between Lorient and Grand Cul-de-Sac, admire the Pointe Lorient and the islets Frégate and Toc-Vers. The Eastern road, between Petit Cul-de-Sac and Anse du Grand Fond, is dominated by the Morne Vitet, the highest point of the island, at the top of which you will have a superb view of the sea as well as the arid land covered with candle cactus and frangipani trees.

• Gustavia, the capital of the island, is a charming town with a lively port and luxury boutiques. It owes its name to the time when the island was Swedish. Do not hesitate to go up to the ruins of Fort Gustav to admire the magnificent view of the port. In Corossol, the International Shell Museum gathers a collection of more than 9000 pieces from different countries. On the north coast, the small village of Lorient also deserves a small stop.

Saint Kitts and Nevis

Two islands that form a small and friendly Caribbean country. It is not a great Caribbean destination but it is certainly one of the most authentic. Far from mass tourism or the boisterous tourism of some neighboring islands, the country highlights its limited but attractive human and natural heritage. A few beautiful beaches make up the tourist showcase of the islands, which for the rest is focused on cruises. Nevis is a small piece of Anglo-Saxon countryside, with tropical accents, which is an ideal place for those who wish to discover an unspoiled Caribbean region. The access is simple (direct flight from London) and so is the trip. The atmosphere on the islands is calmer and more pleasant than on many others.

• St. Kitts can boast of its fort on the hill of Brimstone, built at the tip of the strait separating the island of Nevis and nicknamed the "Gibraltar of the West Indies". For the exotic touch, note that the island has thousands of monkeys in the wild. A few beaches, in the southwest, gives it a seaside attraction (but nevertheless weaker than its neighbors).

• Nevis, smaller, has as its main city, Charlestown, a typical Anglo-Saxon city with its Georgian architecture that unfolds around the Memorial Square. The Botanical Gardens of Nevis and the sulfur baths are the two main attractions of the island. The landscapes of the interior of the island offer a beautiful countryside around the volcano of Nevis Peak and the possibilities of accommodation are growing.

Sint Maarten (Saint-Martin)

An island that we know especially for its geopolitical peculiarity because it is shared between France (northern part) and the Netherlands (Sint Marteen, southern part) and sometimes also for its airport, on the beach which gives rise to an impressive aerial ballet. One passes from one to the other of the parts without border but that gives to the island an originality which continues to attract the travelers. Whatever the side of the island, tourism is very developed, even massive. This is particularly true of the southern part, with strong American accents, where the big hotels are lined up. The French part is a little wilder but is still very well marked out. Nature is no less beautiful than on the other islands but it is above all the seaside resort that dominates the tourist landscape. The island is more affordable than its neighbor, Saint-Barthélémy, but the high end of the market dominates all the same. A gap with the social situation, rather bad, which sometimes creates an unattractive atmosphere.

● Marigot, the French capital of the island, has beautiful traditional houses dating from the 19th century. Nearby, don't hesitate to visit the Loterie Farm, a former sugar cane plantation that has become a magnificent private nature reserve. Several kilometers of trails allow you to discover this tropical forest and to follow the ancient routes used by slaves between the slopes of the sugar plantation and the sugar factory itself, located at the top of Pic Paradis.

● Located in the north, with its small wooden houses behind flowery gardens, the small French village of Grand Case has kept all its charm. There are the best restaurants and the most beautiful houses on the island. In the early morning, you will be able to admire the spectacle of seine fishing and the coming and going of the boats of fishermen bringing back their catches from the traps dived off the Creole Rock, before going to rest on the fine sand beach of the bay of Grand Case or to explore by yourself the seabed especially those of the Creole Rock.

● In the northeast of the island, the small hamlet of Cul de Sac is the starting point for a getaway to Pinet or Tintamarre islet. The former, in the heart of the nature reserve of Saint-Martin, has a long tongue of fine sand that forms a very beautiful break in the sea and a famous snorkeling spot. The second is deserted and its main beach, Baie Blanche, is one of the most beautiful on the island.

● The two kilometers of white sandy beach in the eastern bay are the most frequented of the island, a paradise for relaxation and water sports (parasailing, jet skis, windsurfing, surfing and flysurfing). After the oriental bay, just before the Orleans neighborhood, is the butterfly farm which shelters magnificent specimens. All along the east coast and the nearby islets, sea turtles are found during their egg-laying season, as well as humpback whales during their breeding period (January to May).

Saint Vincent and the Grenadines

The Grenadine Islands, here is a name that certainly makes you dream and instinctively evokes the tropical paradise. We have to admit that we are not far from it, as long as we don't want to look further than the tip of our coconut tree. The beaches there are heavenly, attracting a wealthy clientele that has transformed some islands into chic ghettos. For those who can afford it, a trip to the Caribbean Maldives is worth the candle. St. Vincent, the main island of this small country, is quite different from the idyllic pebbles that surround it. It is no less beautiful, but in a different register, volcanic. The black sand beaches contrast with the jungle. Superb destination on the natural plan, the majority of the travelers discover it during a cruise. Small, isolated and off the main roads, access to the islands requires time, and above all means, but for the traveller who has both, you should not deprive yourself of them.

● The tiny islands of the Grenadines are very popular for the transparency of their waters and the whiteness of their sandy beaches. A favorite destination for sailing and jet set enthusiasts from all over the world, they offer luxury vacations among coconut palms and superb coral reefs. The islands of Bequia, Canouan and Mosquito (the most select) are the best known.

● Much less touristic than its neighbors because of its black sand beaches, Saint-Vincent and the tropical forest with lush vegetation that spreads around its volcanic relief are worth the detour. La Soufrière and the Falls of Baleine are the two most famous spots in terms of hiking and tourism.

Saint Lucia

Martinique's southern neighbor is to the American market what the latter is to the French market. The two islands are similar, even if St. Lucia wins the prize for wilderness. Volcanic, rich in lush vegetation, with beautiful beaches, St. Lucia also has the attraction of its Creole culture and features such as wooden houses. It is a beautiful island with good tourist infrastructures and adapts to all travel desires. Very often, the French-speaking traveller goes there during an excursion from Martinique precisely, the time to appreciate the beauty of the Pitons of Saint Lucia, its most beautiful landscapes.

• The coasts of St. Lucia are jagged and formed of small bays hidden at the mouths of rivers, steep cliffs and long sandy beaches. Rodney Bay is the island's largest marina and busiest seaside resort. Cape Estate and Marigot Bay are also popular with boaters. The coasts of Vieux-Fort are popular with windsurfers, and the best anchorages are around Soufrière and Anse des Deux-Pitons.

• The reliefs of the island are marked and covered by lush tropical vegetation. We will admire the twin beauty of the two peaks, we will go to bathe in the Sulphur Springs, sulphureous springs in the hollow of a lunar crater or in the natural pools of Diamond Falls, cascades of sulphureous water with medicinal virtues and we will admire the panorama from the top of Fort Rodney in the Pigeon Island National Park.

• The wooden houses in the villages of the island form attractive sites such as Soufrière, the former capital, or Gros-Ilet. The main street of the latter is transformed into a vast popular festival every Friday evening, a local peculiarity famous throughout the Caribbean. It is better to enjoy it at the beginning rather than at the end of the evening.

El Salvador

Complicated is a weak word to describe the trip to El Salvador. This small Central American country is gnawed by a violence that can hardly be ignored. The gangs of the maras ravage the image of the country and ruin the efforts undertaken at the end of the terrible civil war. Crushed by competition from Costa Rica, Guatemala and even Nicaragua, El Salvador is left with only a few crumbs of the tourist cake, which only adventurous and well-prepared spirits come to pick up. Volcanoes and virgin forests, to which one must add the Mayan remains and coffee plantation villages, are serious assets for discovery but everywhere caution is required. Some sites are secured, for others, an escort can be considered. Nevertheless, this creates a tension that reserves the destination for experienced travelers and if possible already connoisseurs of Central America. Infrastructure is adequate, roads are good, but transportation is often dangerous. Escapades in nature, especially in the Monte Cristo forest, superb and very wild, must be prepared with the greatest care.

• The coastal plain, wedged between the slopes of the volcanoes and the Pacific Ocean, is a maximum of 22 kilometers wide. The ocean, constantly agitated, attracts mainly surfers. If on the Costa del Sol, the black sand beaches are home to some tourist establishments, the other side of the peninsula is submerged by the large mangrove of Estero de Jaltepeque while the coast of Bálsamo has some deserted beaches at the foot of the cliffs that cut it.

• In the west of the country is the Volcanoes National Park. From the flanks of the extinct Cerro Verde volcano, one enjoys a breathtaking view of the Izalco volcano, the youngest in the country. There are many possibilities for hiking, especially the one that will take you to the Coatepeque lake, a huge crater filled with blue, at the foot of the Santa Ana volcano.

• 76 km northwest of San Salvador, the village of Chalchuapa has many archaeological sites in its surroundings : Las Victorias, Peme, El Trapiche, Casablanca, and especially Tazumal, whose Mayan ruins of the ceremonial center are the most important in the country.

• The winding mountain road that connects Sonsonate to Ahuachapán has been nicknamed the Route of Flowers. During 36 kilometers, you will cross the heart of the country where coffee plantations and charming small villages intertwine. It is in May that this itinerary is at its most sumptuous when the white flowers of the coffee trees cover the surrounding landscapes.

• Suchitoto, 47 km north of San Salvador, is a small town with colonial buildings and paved streets overlooking the Suchitlan lake, a migration area for more than 200 species of birds. Every weekend, the town comes alive with various cultural events.

• In the northeast of the country, the rainforest of the Monte Cristo National Park (2,400 m) has remained untouched except for the hiking trails that run through it. From the village of Metapan, you will be able to discover a rare fauna (quetzals, ocelots, otters, spider monkeys, pumas and toucans) in the heart of a varied nature interspersed with waterfalls and superb panoramas.

Suriname

Neighbouring French Guiana, Suriname is a former Dutch colony, now an independent country. To say that it is the land of the forest is an understatement because the Amazon jungle is a real entity in its own right. It emerges at each exit of the city and seems ready to regain its rights at the slightest opportunity. A destination totally off the tourist maps, Suriname is an adventure for explorers. Once left the few cities of the coast, which do not have a good reputation, the traveler is there in total autonomy, in a very complicated forest. The only possible ways of progression are the rivers which one goes down in pirogues. At the far end of the country, near borders that do not really exist, live the Amerindian peoples, some of whom have probably never had any contact with the outside world. The possibilities of discovering the jungle are therefore limited, and necessarily supervised by one or more guides, but they are already unforgettable adventures. Of course, the country is far from being a model of stability, the sanitary level is very low and the infrastructures are poor (when they exist).

• The rivers that run through the country make it possible to discover the country by pirogue. The descent of the Tapanahoni, a tributary of the Maroni, makes it possible to cross several rapids and reach the region of the Wajana Amerindian people. Other waterfalls are to be admired such as those of Anora and Wonotobo on the Courantyne, or the Raleigh Falls on the Coppename. To make more encounters, you can go to the region of Asidonhopo where live the descendants of slaves called "maroons".

• The Central Suriname Nature Reserve includes the Voltz Berg Park, the Tafelberg and the Eilerts de Haan Reserve in the heart of the country. This tropical forest remains difficult to access, but the vegetation creates extraordinary shows reserved for true adventurers.

• On the coasts, the Wia Wia Reserve gathers an important colony of five species of sea turtles that come to lay their eggs there between April and June. The one of Galibi is also known for its leatherback turtles. The rest of the Atlantic coast, little exploited, is studded with small villages such as Totness, between expanses of coconut trees and mangrove areas.

Trinidad and Tobago

Two islands, complementary, a short distance north of Venezuela. Trinidad (or Trinidad), the big one, and Tobago, the small one. The latter presents the classic image of the Caribbean island, beautiful beaches and exuberant seabed. It is a little frequented destination, where tourists are not taken by the hand but which reserves a good reception to those who go there. Trinidad, much more imposing, is a small island country. Its capital, Port of Spain, is a large city, a kind of Creole metropolis enveloped by equatorial humidity. The rest of the island offers superb natural escapes, between mountains and lush jungles. Nevertheless, you will have to be prepared and expect a destination that is a bit rough on the edges (the infrastructures are in half-tones and you have to be able to be autonomous and use common sense). Experienced travelers without looking for adventure and exploration will find a beautiful trip, off the beaten track and original, especially if it coincides with the carnival, the craziest north of Rio.

TOBAGO :

- Tobago is sought after above all for the beauty of its beaches, which Defoe would have taken as a backdrop in writing Robinson Crusoe. Pigeon Point, Store Bay and Castara Bay are the two most beautiful sites on the island. For diving, Bucco Reef has the coral reef that will make you dream.

- Boat excursions are offered from Tobago to Little Tobago, an islet where many tropical birds live, including the rare bird of paradise.

- The falls of King's Bay, beyond Roxborough, with their 33 meters high, are the most impressive of the archipelago.

TRINIDAD :

- Less coastal than Tobago, Trinidad has nevertheless a beautiful beach on the north coast, the Maracas Beach. Swimming there is much less dangerous than on the east coast beaches such as Mayaro Bay, Cocos Bay and Manzanilla Bay, which are nevertheless not lacking in charm.

- The most beautiful walks to do are in the north of the island, discovering the superb green landscapes of the Diego Martin Valley (one will not fail to bathe under the waterfall of Bassin Bleu), the ornithological reserves of Spring Hill Centre and Caroni and the mud volcanoes of Devil's Woodyard.

- The forest and hills of the Northern Range whose slopes descend beautifully to the beautiful beaches of the north coast of the island and the even more breathtakingly dense Southern Range will intoxicate you. A thousand flowers, each one more fragrant and brilliant than the next, have taken up residence here.

- To the south, Pitch Lake is the largest pure asphalt lake in the world. A unique geological feature.

Uruguay

This country is called the Switzerland of America and this sums up quite well what can be expected from Uruguay. Very quiet, generally pleasant, with good infrastructures and remarkable social peace in South America (only Chile can boast of being so safe and stable). Uruguay is undoubtedly the most European of the countries of the great South America, with a capital, Montevideo, with a false air of southern Madrid. In addition to offering a very simple trip, accessible to all (except financially, due to its remoteness) including travelers who are discovering the continent, Uruguay has many strings to its bow that deserve to be interested in it. In addition to its capital, the country has a very pleasant coastline, where oceanic and subtropical influences mingle. Punta del Este, the country's great seaside resort, is considered the South American Saint Tropez. There are also colonial cities and especially a large, peaceful countryside, where the gauchos, the cowboys of South America reign. In the lands of the immense estancias (farms), where rural tourism is well developed, one will cross as many horses as bulls, and one will be able to taste good products. A beautiful destination, which deserves to be more in the light.

- On the banks of the Río de la Plata, Montevideo is a peaceful and airy city. Its very picturesque architecture mixes Spanish, Italian and Art Deco influences. A stroll will make you discover the old-fashioned charm of the old streets of the Plaza de la Constitución. Do not hesitate to climb to the fortress El Cerro to enjoy a superb view of the city. At the port, the wooden tables of the 19th century market are the ideal place to enjoy a huge steak.

- To the east of Montevideo, the coast is superb, very wooded, small bays and deserted beaches follow one another. Punta del Este and its translucent waters, 139 km from the capital, is the most exclusive resort in the country. Many walks are possible in the surroundings of Piriápolis between wooded hills and white beaches as well as in the dunes of Cabo Polonio.

● The discovery and crossing of the Río de la Plata will allow you to discover the impressive landscapes due to the size of this estuary that separates Uruguay from Argentina. Sailboat, catamaran or yacht will take you on the ochre-colored waters and it will be up to you to decide on your stops. For example, you can make a stop in Colon, ía del Sacramento opposite Buenos Aires, which, with its fortifications, narrow streets and old central square, is one of the most beautiful cities in the country.

● Inland there is a landscape of rivers, mountains and estancias. Carnivores and riders will find their happiness in encounters with the gauchos. From the south of the Br ésilto the Argentinean humid pampas, passing through Uruguay, an eco-tourism project has been set up with 50 ecomuseums, mainly estancias, with the aim of providing a joint effort between small and medium producers, cultural agents and artists to promote friendly tourism and spread the gaucho culture, which remains the most lively equestrian culture in the world.

Venezuela

Seen from home, Venezuela and Colombia are a little confused. One never knows which is which, nor what to think about it. To put it simply, both countries are among the most beautiful in the world, but their stories intersect. While Colombia is emerging from a long dark period and opening up more and more to tourism, Venezuela, once open, is closing in and plunging into an era of uncertainty. From now on, a trip to Venezuela is a real adventure, which should only be considered by very experienced or perfectly supervised travelers (in the case, for example, of the ascents of the tepuyes). The major problem is the social situation, which is very tense, and the very high level of insecurity that reigns in a large part of the country and in most cities. Caracas is generally cited as the most violent city in the world. However, Venezuela is a truly sensational country, where you can find among other things the highest waterfalls in the world (Salto Angel), a fantastic Caribbean shoreline (Los Roques) and above all a huge region of jungles, rivers, mountains and tepuyes, unique tabular reliefs that are all lost worlds. Many sites have never been explored before and adventurers will find the Amazon in all its splendor. Tour operators have not left the field and visitors continue to visit, but one can only observe a certain waste in a country with such great potential. It is necessary to be aware that travel conditions are very deteriorated there, with infrastructures that are sometimes abandoned (especially in terms of health) because of the total social instability. Even the supply of basic commodities is hazardous. Lastly, insecurity is real and the traveler will undoubtedly have to face several situations of tension (sometimes, even often, due to the control of the authorities). We can only hope that Venezuela will one day find its way back to tranquility and that we can rush towards what is undoubtedly the most beautiful promise of adventure on the planet.

The Guyana massif is one of the most beautiful reliefs in South America and the world.

● Within the Great Savannah (Gran Sabana) we find the famous tepuyes (or tepuis), high sandstone plateaus whose feet are drowned by the tropical forest and the summits present ecosystems isolated from the rest of the world. The Indians worship them, the (rare) tourists climb them. Conan Doyle located his novel The Lost World there. Mount Roraima, one of the wonders of the world, is the most famous of the tepuyes. Its ascent and the discovery of its mysterious summit is the subject of treks that are among the highlights of the country.

● The Rio Carrao is dispersed in the massif in several waterfalls called saltos. The Salto del Angel is the highest in the world (970 m) but remains difficult to access. In the footsteps of the conquistadores looking for the Eldorado, you will nevertheless be able to admire many others.

● The Orinoco River surrounds Venezuelan Guiana, you can navigate there by taking the curiaras, canoes of the Waraos Indians. Between rapids, crocodiles, anacondas, freshwater dolphins, toucans and other natural wonders, the journey will live up to the legend of the river. The region of the Upper Orinoco, inland following the course of the river, is a land of mystery, many places of which have never been explored, such as the immense Humbolt Abyss, an enigma for science.

• In the west of the country, the Merida mountain range culminates at Mount Bolivar (5007 meters). It is the extension of the Andes Cordillera. Between high altitude lakes, fields of flowers and immense panoramas, this region is one of the most beautiful tropical mountainous areas. Some very beautiful villages punctuate the valleys, adding an additional attraction to nature. As in all mountain regions, the Cordillera is a beautiful hiking area, but like the rest of the country, excellent preparation is required and the terrain is known to be difficult.

• Between the mountains to the west and the Great Savannah to the east, the plains of Los Llanos stretch endlessly. Populated by the llaneros, the Venezuelan cowboys, these plains, flooded for part of the year, are, along with the Brazilian Pantanal, one of the great sites of world biodiversity. The exoticism is total and the fauna is omnipresent. The encounter with a giant anaconda never leaves anyone indifferent.

The Caribbean shores of Venezuela, with its undeniable beauty, make it a top seaside destination.

• Margarita Island has 75 beaches where one could say, if one wanted to push the cliché, that hammocks, rum and cigars are the order of the day. It is an affordable destination, where the seaside appeal is complemented by mountain scenery.

• The archipelago of los Roques, more advanced in the Caribbean Sea is much more tropical. On the forty or so islands, you will find postcard landscapes, exotic beaches and abundant seabeds on the program. Los Roques remains one of the few sites in the country to remain slightly away from social tensions.

• On the mainland, the Paria Peninsula is a very attractive area, where the fine sandy beaches often take the tropical forest as a backdrop.

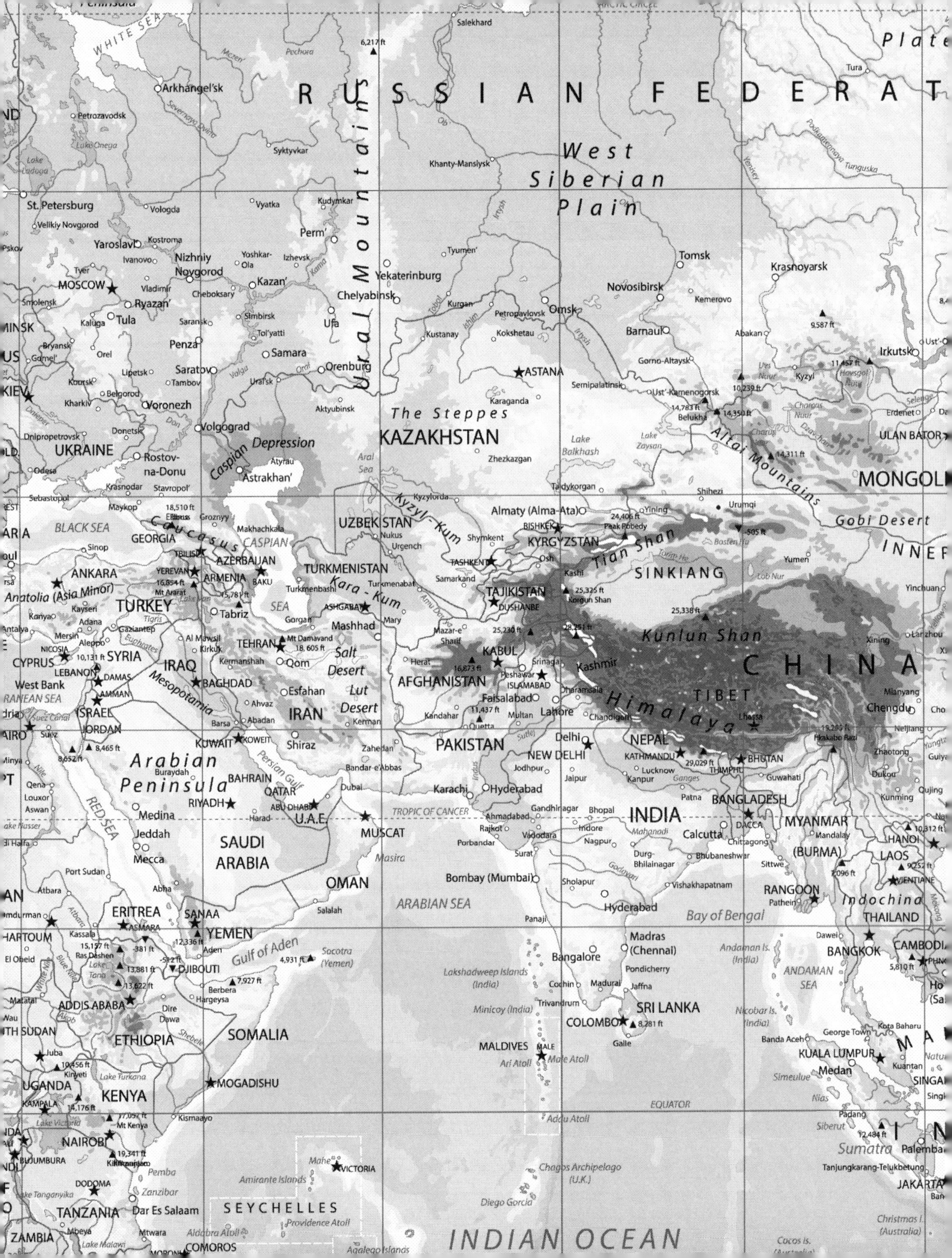

RUSSIAN FEDERAT
West Siberian Plain
Ural Mountains
WHITE SEA
Salekhard
Pechora
6,217 ft
Arkhangel'sk
Petrozavodsk
Lake Onega
Lake Ladoga
Syktyvkar
Khanty-Mansiysk
Tura
Podkamennaya Tunguska
Yenisey
Ob'
St. Petersburg
Velikiy Novgorod
Vologda
Vyatka
Kudymkar
Perm'
Irtysh
Pskov
Yaroslavl
Kostroma
Ivanovo
Nizhniy Novgorod
Yoshkar-Ola
Izhevsk
Kama
Tyumen'
Tomsk
Krasnoyarsk
Tver
MOSCOW
Vladimir
Kazan'
Yekaterinburg
Chelyabinsk
Novosibirsk
Kemerovo
Smolensk
Ryazan'
Cheboksary
Kurgan
Tobol
Ishim
Petropavlovsk
Omsk
MINSK
Tula
Kaluga
Simbirsk
Saransk
Tol'yatti
Ufa
Kustanay
Kokshetau
Barnaul
Abakan
9,587 ft
Bryansk
Orel
Penza
Samara
Irkutsk
Ust'-
Gomel'
Saratov
Volga
Orenburg
Ural
Gorno-Altaysk
Kyzyl
11,457 ft
KIEV
Kursk
Lipetsk
Tambov
Ural'sk
ASTANA
Semipalatinsk
Ust'-Kamenogorsk
10,239 ft
Belgorod
Kharkiv
Voronezh
Aktyubinsk
Karaganda
14,783 ft
Belukha
14,350 ft
Erdenet
Dnieper
Don
The Steppes
Volgograd
Donetsk
Dnipropetrovsk
Caspian Depression
KAZAKHSTAN
Lake Balkhash
Lake Zaysan
Altai Mountains
ULAN BATOR
UKRAINE
Rostov-na-Donu
Atyrau
Astrakhan'
Aral Sea
Zhezkazgan
14,311 ft
MONGOLI
Odesa
Krasnodar
Stavropol'
Taldykorgan
Shihezi
Urumqi
Sebastopol
Maykop
18,510 ft
Elbrus
Groznyy
Makhachkala
Kyzylorda
Kyzyl-Kum
Almaty (Alma-Ata)
Yining
24,406 ft
Peak Pobedy
BISHKEK
Gobi Desert
BLACK SEA
Caucasus
CASPIAN
UZBEKISTAN
Nukus
Urgench
Shymkent
KYRGYZSTAN
-505 ft
Bosten Hu
INNER
GEORGIA
TBILISI
AZERBAIJAN
TASHKENT
Osh
Tian Shan
Tarim He
Sinop
YEREVAN
BAKU
TURKMENISTAN
Kashi
SINKIANG
Yumen
ANKARA
16,854 ft
Mt Ararat
ARMENIA
Turkmenbashi
Kara-Kum
Turkmenabat
Samarkand
Lob Nur
Anatolia (Asia Minor)
15,781 ft
Lake Van
Tabriz
SEA
TAJIKISTAN
DUSHANBE
25,325 ft
Kongur Shan
Yinchuan
TURKEY
Tigris
ASHGABAT
Amu Darya
Konya
Gorgan
Mary
25,338 ft
Antalya
Kayseri
Adana
Gaziantep
Mashhad
Mazar-e Sharif
25,230 ft
28,251 ft
Kunlun Shan
Lanzhou
Mersin
Aleppo
Euphrates
Al Mawsil
Mt Damavand
18,605 ft
Xining
NICOSIA
CYPRUS
10,131 ft
SYRIA
Kirkuk
TEHRAN
Qom
Salt Desert
Herat
KABUL
16,873 ft
Peshawar
ISLAMABAD
Srinagar
Kashmir
CHINA
LEBANON
DAMASCUS
IRAQ
Kermanshah
Mesopotamia
BAGHDAD
AFGHANISTAN
West Bank
AMMAN
Esfahan
Lut Desert
Faisalabad
Dharamsala
Himalaya
TIBET
Mianyang
RANEAN SEA
ISRAEL
Ahvaz
Kandahar
11,437 ft
Quetta
Multan
Lahore
Chandigarh
Chengdu
Suez Canal
JORDAN
Barsa
Abadan
IRAN
Kerman
Lhasa
19,295 ft
Hkakabo Razi
AIRO
Suez
KUWAIT
KOWEIT
Shiraz
Zahedan
PAKISTAN
Sutlej
Delhi
NEPAL
Neijiang
8,652 ft
8,465 ft
Arabian Peninsula
Persian Gulf
Bandar-e'Abbas
Indus
NEW DELHI
KATHMANDU
29,029 ft
THIMPHU
BHUTAN
Zhaotong
Minya
Nile
Buraydah
BAHRAIN
QATAR
Dubai
Karachi
Hyderabad
Jodhpur
Jaipur
Lucknow
Kanpur
Ganges
Guwahati
Dukou
Qena
Luxor
Aswan
RED SEA
RIYADH
ABU DHABI
U.A.E.
Ahmadabad
Gandhinagar
Bhopal
Patna
BANGLADESH
Qujing
Kunming
Lake Nasser
Medina
Harad
TROPIC OF CANCER
INDIA
DACCA
MYANMAR
10,312 ft
HANOI
Wadi Halfa
Jeddah
SAUDI ARABIA
MUSCAT
Rajkot
Porbandar
Vadodara
Indore
Nagpur
Mahanadi
Calcutta
Chittagong
Mandalay
(BURMA)
LAOS
Mecca
Masira
Surat
Durg-Bhilainagar
Bhubaneshwar
Sittwe
7,096 ft
9,252 ft
VIENTIANE
Port Sudan
OMAN
Bombay (Mumbai)
Godavari
Sholapur
Vishakhapatnam
Abha
Atbara
ARABIAN SEA
RANGOON
Pathein
Indochina
Mekong
Omdurman
ERITREA
SANAA
Salalah
Panaji
Hyderabad
Bay of Bengal
THAILAND
KHARTOUM
ASMARA
YEMEN
Kassala
15,157 ft
Ras Dashen
-381 ft
12,336 ft
Aden
Gulf of Aden
4,931 ft
Socotra (Yemen)
Madras (Chennai)
Andaman Is. (India)
Dawei
BANGKOK
CAMBODIA
El Obeid
Lake Tana
Blue Nile
13,881 ft
-512 ft
DJIBOUTI
Bangalore
Pondicherry
ANDAMAN SEA
5,810 ft
PHNOM
13,622 ft
Berbera
Hargeysa
7,927 ft
Lakshadweep Islands (India)
Cochin
Madurai
Jaffna
Ho Chi (Sai
Malakal
ADDIS ABABA
Trivandrum
Minicoy (India)
SRI LANKA
COLOMBO
8,281 ft
Nicobar Is. (India)
Wau
Akobo
Dire Dawa
SOMALIA
Kota Baharu
George Town
TH SUDAN
ETHIOPIA
Shebele
MALDIVES
MALE
Male Atoll
Ari Atoll
Galle
Banda Aceh
KUALA LUMPUR
Juba
Kuantan
10,456 ft
Kinyeti
Lake Turkana
Medan
Simeulue
SINGA
UGANDA
MOGADISHU
KENYA
KAMPALA
14,176 ft
17,057 ft
Mt Kenya
EQUATOR
Nias
Padang
Lake Victoria
Kismaayo
Addu Atoll
Siberut
NAIROBI
12,484 ft
BUJUMBURA
19,341 ft
Kilimanjaro
Mahe
VICTORIA
Chagos Archipelago (U.K.)
Sumatra
Palemba
Pemba
Amirante Islands
Tanjungkarang-Telukbetung
DODOMA
Lake Tanganyika
Zanzibar
JAKARTA
SEYCHELLES
Diego Garcia
TANZANIA
Dar Es Salaam
Providence Atoll
Christmas I. (Australia)
ZAMBIA
Mbeya
Mtwara
Aldabra Atoll
INDIAN OCEAN
Cocos Is.
Lake Malawi
MORONI
COMOROS
Agalega Islands

Aykhal
Mirnyy
Lensk
Yakutsk
Lena
Vilyuy
Aldan
Ust'-Nera
9,852 ft
Pobeda
Indigirka
Kolyma
Kolyma Range
Koryak Range
8,405 ft
Anadyr
Gulf of Anadyr
St Lawrence I.
St Matthew
Magadan
Palana
Dzhugdzhur Range
SEA OF OKHOTSK
BERING SEA
Kamtchatka
10,771 ft
15,584 ft
Kronotskaya Sopka
11,880 ft
11,389 ft
Petropavlovsk-Kamchatskiy
Commander Is.
Iles Near
Rat Islands
Andreanof Islands
Aleutian Islands
Olekma
Vitim
8,094 ft
Tynda
Skovorodino
Amur
Shantar Is.
Sakhaline
5,279 ft
Chita
Aginskoye
Blagoveshchensk
Komsomol'sk-na-Amure
Manzhouli
Hulun Nur
Choibalsan
Birobidzhan
6,857 ft
Fuyuan
Khabarovsk
Qiqihar
Daqing
Yuzno-Sakhalinsk
Harbin
Mudanjiang
Lake Khanka
Wakkanai
Kuril Islands
Changchun
Jilin
7,513 ft
Asahi Dake
Sapporo
MONGOLIA
Yanji
Vladivostok
Nakhodka
Fuxin
Shenyang
Chongjin
NORTH
Hakodate
Hokkaido
Zhangjiakou
Datong
NORTH KOREA
Aomori
PYONGYANG
Hamhung
SEA OF JAPAN
Honshu
Akita
BEIJING (PEKING)
Dalian
Tientsin
Baoding
Niigata
Sendai
Dongying
Yantai
Inchon
SEOUL
JAPAN
Kanazawa
Zibo
Qingdao
SOUTH KOREA
Taegu
Kyoto
TOKYO
Jinan
Pusan
Kobe
12,388 ft
Yokohama
Hiroshima
Nagoya
Zhengzhou
Xuzhou
YELLOW SEA
Kitakyushu
Osaka
Kochi
Huaiyuan
Cheju I.
Fukuoka
Shikoku
Nagasaki
Hefei
Nanjing
Kagoshima
Kyushu
PACIFIC
Shanghai
Hangzhou
Wuhan
Ningbo
EAST CHINA SEA
Jingdezhen
Dongting Hu
Nanchang
Wenzhou
Bonin Is. (Japan)
Fuzhou
Hengyang
Ryukyu Is.
T'AIPEI
Meizhou
Xiamen
Volcan Is. (Japan)
TROPIC OF CANCER
Marcus I. (Japan)
Shantou
TAIWAN
13,113 ft
Shenzhen
Kaohsiung
Hong Kong
Macao
Hainan
OCEAN
Northern Mariana Islands (U.S.A.)
Wake I. (U.S.A.)
Luzon
SOUTH CHINA SEA
9,610 ft
Quezon City
Saipan
Micronesia
MANILA
Mindoro
PHILIPPINE SEA
Guam (U.S.A.)
MARSHALL ISLANDS
Spratly Islands
PHILIPPINES
Samar
Puerto Princesa
Yap Is.
Ratak Chain
Cebu
Surigao
Palawan
SULU SEA
Cagayan de Oro
Ralik Chain
13,455 ft
Kinabalu
9,692 ft
Davao
KOROR
PALAU
MAJURO
Zamboanga
Mindanao
Chuuk
Pohnpei
PALIKIR
Sandakan
Sulu
General Santos
Kosrae
BRUNEI
Tawau
CELEBES SEA
Caroline Islands
FEDERATED STATES OF MICRONESIA
Sibu
Borneo
Manado
Moluccas
TARAWA
Atoll Tarawa
Kapingamarangi
EQUATOR
Samarinda
Gorontalo
Palu
PAPUA NEW GUINEA
YAREN
NAURU
11,335 ft
Sula
9,905 ft
Jayapura
Tabiteuea
KIRIBATI
INDONESIA
Banjarmasin
Celebes
Buru
Seram
16,499 ft
Peak Jaya
New Guinea
New Ireland
Ujung Pandang
BANDA SEA
14,793 ft
Mt Wilhelm
7,871 ft
7,999 ft
8,809 ft
New Britain
Surabaya
12,060 ft
9,255 ft
Aru
Melanesia
Nikumaroro
Bali
10,308 ft
12,224 ft
Flores
7,051 ft
DILI
Tanimbar
13,363 ft
FUNAFUTI
Atoll Funafuti
EAST TIMOR
9,711 ft
HONIARA
7,644 ft
Sumba
Kupang
Timor
ARAFURA SEA
PORT MORESBY
TUVALU
Tokelau (N.Z.)
30°
15°
0°

ASIA

Afghanistan

A country that thrills great travelers, Afghanistan is a terra incognita whose only images that reach the rest of the world are war and fundamentalism. Yet if there is one country for which travel seems to have been invented, it is Afghanistan. This country is a permanent and total discovery, where the landscapes seem to come out of a science-fiction book and where everything is absolutely exotic. For the neophyte this will be hard to believe but at a time not so long ago, the country was a great destination, widely (and freely) traveled by travelers on the road to India. This was in the 1970s, and the legendary hospitality of the Afghans was praised from London to Delhi. Unfortunately, since then, wars and terrorism have locked the country in, driving visitors away. Over the years, tourism has changed, leaving Afghanistan completely on the sidelines until it has become a country not to be talked about. Needless to say that any idea of travel is now excluded, instability is very high, terrorism is still active, the infrastructure is very bad (Kabul is not in ruins, contrary to popular belief, but power cuts are long and very frequent, among other disadvantages) and above all security is very precarious. Between the foreign armies still on the ground, the regular army and the armed groups, there are far too many weapons for the traveler to escape the tensions. That said, the country is not closed (although it is not possible to obtain a tourist visa), air links exist (especially to Dubai), and a few visitors cross the border each year. They need to be completely self-sufficient and have a very keen traveling instinct. For others, Afghanistan, with its majestic mountains and the lakes of Band-e-Amir, its greatest jewel, remains a distant mirage.

• The capital, Kabul, is an anarchic city, where the climate is harsh (icy in winter, torrid in summer) and where the situation is precarious in every respect (very frequent power cuts). Nevertheless, it is a city that grows very quickly and whose commercial vitality is well evoked by its huge bazaars, highly exotic. The National Museum, however rich in wonders, is only a memory destroyed by wars and looting.

• The giant Buddhas of Bamiyan, dug out of the mountain 1500 years ago, no longer exist. They were once a notable site of the Silk Road. In spite of their absence they continue to materialize Afghanistan as the crossroads of influences from the Middle and Far East. World Heritage, they could be rebuilt in better days.

• The Minaret of Jam, or *Jam*, is located in the middle of a canyon in the middle of the desert. It is probably the least visited World Heritage Site in the world. Fewer than a dozen foreigners arrive there every year. It is the only testimony of a huge palace of the Ghurid dynasty that reigned here in the 13th century.

• In the north of the country, the commercial city of Mazar-e-Sharif is home to the *Great Blue Mosque*, one of the most beautiful in Islam. Its domes and beautifully patterned minarets form the setting for Ali's tomb, which is the site of a major pilgrimage each year.

• Herat, on the borders of Iran, is the most interesting city of the country. It is a different city because it is very influenced by its Persian neighbor. The poverty is also less marked there because of the commercial exchanges. Historic city, Herat is home to the Alexander Citadel, an old medieval city quite unique in the Muslim world and the superb 12th century Friday mosque, a jewel of Islamic art.

• In this vast country of desert, some landscapes are truly grandiose. Among these, one can quote the lakes of Band-e-Amir, literally "the jewels of the Emir", which form the most remarkable site of all Central Asia. These six high mountain lakes are famous for their colors, turquoise, emerald, and their purity.

• Mountains characterize the country, especially in the northeast, between the valleys and peaks of the Hindu Kuch and Pamir. The fantastic landscapes of these regions are much less affected by the conflicts that the country suffers because of their isolation. There are a few peaks at over 7000 meters and a population whose nomadic traditions are worthy of an adventure film (caravans of snow camel drivers, game of *bouzkachi* which consists in catching on a horse a goat's head thrown into the mountains).

• The Great Mosque of Makkah is visited every year by more than a million Muslims from all over the world to perform Hajj, the obligatory pilgrimage in the life of every good Muslim. Non-Muslims will not be able to enter the mosque, nor will they be able to visit the Holy City of Madinah where there are other important mosques such as the two Qibla, Quba, Al-Dirá and the Tomb of Hamza.

Azerbaijan

Small country of the Caspian Sea, out of the USSR since 1991, Azerbaijan is a very unknown country, between Russia and Iran. The country is moreover at the crossroads of these two immense neighbors, both geographically and culturally, and we must add to this a significant Turkish influence. For a long time immersed in a very destructive ethnic conflict with neighboring Armenia, which has left scars, the country has only recently emerged from the depths of the maps, in the light of a rather spectacular development driven by hydrocarbons and gas. Between Soviet and Iranian influence, focused on energy trade, needless to say that the country does not have an image of great openness to tourism. On the spot, the country is proving to be a bearer of unsuspected wealth. Behind the new modern buildings of the capital Baku hides a historic district which is most certainly the jewel of the destination. The attractions of Azerbaijan are also to be found in the mountainous region of the Great Caucasus with its traditional villages and very spectacular landscapes. Finally, one cannot deny that it is a land of particular exoticism where the traveler will be highly disoriented, between the Soviet heritage, the imprint of Islam (much less rigid than in neighboring Iran) and a cultural identity of its own. Nevertheless, it is a journey which, while far from being impossible for the traveler, still has a few drawbacks. The general infrastructure is still poor (the main roads are quite good but the network is generally bad and dangerous; public hospitals are certainly free but of poor quality and private establishments, much more recommendable, are very expensive), but especially although security is rather good in the country, the geopolitical situation is on the other hand very complex and by going to the wrong place the traveler explodes at heavy penalties. A destination off the beaten track, which therefore needs to be prepared, but which has some serious assets.

- Baku, the capital, is located in the far east of the country on the southern shore of the Abheron peninsula. The old fortified city with its narrow and winding streets is a real scenery and is listed as a World Heritage Site with its Maiden Tower (Qiz Qalasi) and the Shirvanshahs Palace. The mild climate in the summer and the beaches of the peninsula make it an original place to stay, to say the least.

- The Gobustan Reserve, about 65 km southwest of Baku, is home to about 600,000 rock paintings depicting fascinating scenes of prehistoric life in this region. Another attraction of the region are the mud volcanoes, visit the Firuz crater, the Gobustan or Salyan, where you can coat yourself with a mud with reputed therapeutic virtues. With the help of a pebble, do not hesitate to touch the large flat stones that populate the region, a tambourine sound will then escape from these monoliths called "gaval dash".

- Gandja, formerly Kirovabad, is located at the foot of the Lesser Caucasus Mountains. The 14th century mausoleum of Imam Zade and the 17th century Grand Mosque are both worth a visit.

- In the north of the country, Shaki was on the Silk Road, as evidenced by the caravanserais in the city. Its fortress and richly decorated palace make it a most interesting stopover.

- The Caucasus Mountains offer an almost unlimited choice of treks, on foot or on horseback, to the fortresses inherited from the Silk Road or the small villages nestled in the valleys. Starting from Tengialti, a small village at the entrance of a narrow and sumptuous gorge, you will be able to discover some of them.

Nagorno-Karabakh

This region is predominantly populated by Armenians and has declared its independence from Azerbaijan. The international community does not recognize the independence of Nagorno-Karabakh and considers it part of Azerbaijan. Its capital, *Stepanakert*, suffered greatly from bombing during the war. In *Shusha*, on the other hand, a fortress town not far from the border with Armenia, the architecture of the past remains present and its beauty is enhanced by the mountainous landscapes that surround it. It should be noted, however, that the traveler is liable to imprisonment in Azerbaijan if he visits this region.

THE NAKHICHEVAN

Nakhichevan is an autonomous republic of Azerbaijan without territorial continuity with the rest of the country. This territory, located between the Arakse River and the Zanguezur Mountains, is an arid, semi-desert and mountainous region. In Naxçivan, there is the Mausoleum of Momine Khatun, a hexagonal tower rising about 35 meters. The rest of the region is not densely populated, but the roads meander through beautiful landscapes that blend into those of Armenia, Turkey and Iran.

Bahrain

As a kingdom of the Persian Gulf, Bahrain has neither the fame of Dubai nor the spending spree of Qatar, nor does it have a major airline that plays the role of promoter among its neighbors. In fact, Bahrain is therefore an unknown on the European tourism scene. It is an oil power, of course, and it is characterized like the whole region by a very desert environment. The financial windfall of oil has allowed the kingdom to develop considerably, especially in terms of infrastructure and offers comfortable and trouble-free travel conditions. However, tourists are rare, except for business travelers. However, although the destination is not exceptional, with a little help from advertising, Bahrain could attract curious people staying with the neighbors. It thus proposes certain attractions, in particular cultural with some monuments in the capital and a traditional souk, but also seaside. Let's not forget that Bahrain is an archipelago of about thirty islands located at the latitude of the Bahamas. The beaches are beautiful, little frequented and well equipped, suitable for diving and other water sports. Finally, the landscapes of the desert are always striking, and there again their access is quite easy. The western traveler will find himself at ease in this Gulf country still quite preserved from the excesses of superficiality that can be found in the region, provided that he has the means to do so.

* If the 33 small islands that surround the main island are still ignored by the general public despite the promising seabed, you will find on the east coast the resort of Al-Bender and, on the west coast, the beach of Al-Jazair with modern infrastructure that offers great opportunities for water sports and idleness.

* In the north, sublime desert landscapes dominate the sea. One finds there mosques hidden in the heart of the fruit trees of the palm groves. In the center, near A'ali, the tombs of the oldest necropolis in the world mix with the oil wells. In the surroundings of Manama, 4x4s and skyscrapers are increasingly taking over the traditional dwellings of the nomads and their camels. Every Friday races are held on the beautiful Sakhir racecourse, won on the desert. Nevertheless, nomadic traditions, such as falcon hunting, are still very present.

* If Manama is the most modern city in the country, we can find the traditions through the souks (Bab Al- Bahrain), near the mosques (Al-Khamis), and in front of the spectacle renewed every afternoon of the wooden boats (dhows) leaving for daily fishing. The National Museum, the House of the Koran and the old quarter of Awadiya are also worth a visit.

Bangladesh

Plunged into abject poverty, this country generally leaves a memory common to all travellers who visit it, like a footprint, that of a mass of humanity that is both stifling and exciting. Don't venture here who wants to, and Bangladesh is a very confidential destination, where the tourist is far from being taken by the hand, and which is only for very prepared travelers who if possible already have a good knowledge of the Indian subcontinent. In addition to the poverty, which is often shocking, it is better to be warned, you will have to go through the encounter with the human crowd, which can be frightening at first contact, but also manage possible disaster situations (which are frequent) such as cyclones or floods, and finally always be on your guard so as not to get caught up in the chronic political instability that agitates the country. In addition to this, there is a very poor infrastructure network and a very low level of health care. This does not make Bangladesh a destination for the general public, far from it. Ironically, the country is not very well off in terms of tourism either, it does not have the size of India, nor the landscapes of Burma. As a highlight, the mangroves of the Sundarbans, *populated by man-eating tigers, illustrate this country which is above all an experience to live, a dive on another planet.*

• Bagerhat, in the west of the Ganges delta, is a real monument city classified as a World Heritage Site. The most beautiful building is the Shait Gumba mosque with its 77 domes. 8 km away, you can also visit the Khodla Math, one of the largest Hindu temples.

• In Paharpur are the remains of a huge Buddhist monastery, the Somapura Mahvira, where decoration and architecture blend together to form a unique artistic achievement. Nearby, the temple of Tara still has votive stupas. Other Buddhist sites in the country are Itakhola, Mainamati and Rajshahi.

• The waters of the Ganges delta and those of the Brahmaputra river can be discovered by boat to discover the green rice fields and the authentic way of life of the inhabitants of the region. In the south, these agricultural landscapes give way to the Sundarbans region, the largest mangrove in the world. Its access is strictly regulated, you will have to get a permit at the Khulna Forestry Division office and be accompanied by a guide to discover its fauna (Bengal tiger, snakes and crocodiles) and flora (sundari trees). It is easier to discover this region on the Indian side. The highlight of this real adventure is of course the tiger, undisputed king, feared by men but more and more threatened. The meeting with a tiger remains a rare and unforgettable but dangerous event.

• The forested hills of Chittagong, the tea plantations of the Sylhet area and the fine sandy beaches around Cox's Bazaar and Inani Beach are the other natural attractions of the country. Lovers of exotism and nature will find an interesting terrain here.

Bhutan

Away from the main tourist routes, Bhutan is a secret corner (isolated for centuries) of the Himalayan range where Dzongkha is spoken and where one pays in ngultrum and that informed travelers know especially for two things: it is the country of happiness, and it is a destination where not everyone can enter. A bit of China, a bit of Nepal, a bit of India, the country is actually quite unique. In order to preserve its traditions, its tranquility and above all its natural heritage, Bhutan has chosen to practice drip tourism, where travelers are limited in number each year by a quota and a visa that requires certain administrative pirouettes before being obtained. The lucky ones can then set off on the roads of this country above the clouds, where the population is reputed to be the happiest in the world. Difficult to verify but no doubt that the spectacular landscapes of Bhutan have enough to make even the most jaded of visitors smile. The Himalayas reveal themselves in all their splendor, even if the highest peaks are elsewhere, and one can also travel through the jungle. This amazing kingdom is also notable for its Buddhist temples, often perched on mountainsides. Mainly coveted by trekking enthusiasts and great travelers, Bhutan is a happy but not necessarily easy country. Money does not make happiness and the country remains very poor, the infrastructures are in their infancy and far from western standards. The international airport is an experience in itself and on the whole we can describe the trip in this country as a small (or even big) adventure. One must be prepared to travel there, especially since the intact culture of the country necessarily implies a rather marked cultural shock, compensated however by the hospitality and the very real kindness of the inhabitants of this country which still remains a mystery.

• The north of the country is occupied by the Himalayan peaks which culminate at more than 7,500 m. Few marked routes cross them, you will almost necessarily have to go through an agency, and the cost of the services remains high. You very quickly find yourself alone in the world, a great advantage that can turn into a disadvantage in case of a problem. You will be able to reach Thimbu (the capital) to Paro in 4 days by the "Druk trail" or to go to meet the yak farms by passing by the base camp of Chomolhari, at 4000 m. The most adventurous and sporty will embark on the Lunana Trek which during 18 days will take them through the most sumptuous landscapes of the country.

• Hiking in the Bumtang valley will allow you to visit many villages with a simple and preserved way of life and especially sumptuous monasteries-fortresses, the dzongs. If they are not all open to the public, the Jampey Lhakhang temple, the site of Kuje and the monastery of Tamshing Gonpa really deserve a visit, especially during the festivities (tsechus) which punctuate the life of the country between February and April.

• In the same vein, do not miss the Paro fortress temple, Rinpung Dzong, and the Dungtse Lhakhangen below it, but also the complex of Kyichu Lhakhang temples still in the Paro Valley, and the Taktsang hermitage that dominates it. Coming from Paro, just before arriving in Thimbu, one discovers the Simtokha dzong then the Thimbu dzong before arriving in a region covered with a tropical jungle dotted with small active towns such as the border posts of Phuntsholing, Geylegphug and Samdrupjonkhar.

Brunei

A small incongruous country, in the middle of East Malaysia on the island of Borneo, the Sultanate of Brunei Darussalam is first famous for its sultan who has the reputation of being the richest man in the world. Thanks to abundant oil resources, the country is not to be outdone and Brunei presents itself as an island of prosperity in the heart of the equatorial jungle. This is at least true for its capital, because beyond the forest takes back its rights. It is a modern country, with efficient infrastructures, but whose interest for the traveller is limited. Only the capital, and the jungle for those who know how to approach it, can justify a trip, most often as an excursion during a trip to Malaysia.

• Half of the capital, Bandar Seri Begawan, is made of wooden bungalows on stilts. Make no mistake, you will find inside all the western comfort you might need. We move around the city along the canals by motorboat. The city's most striking architectural ensembles are the Omar Ali Seifeddine III mosque, its golden dome and Italian marble cladding, and the sultan's palace on the outskirts of the city. Unfortunately, you will only be able to visit the latter on July 15, the Sultan's birthday. The Hassanal Balkiah Aquarium and the Royal Regalia Museum are the other assets of the city.

• Along the coast are the majority of the country's oil wells, however, there are a few beaches if you feel like it in Kuala Belait, Lumut near *Tutong* and Muarat. The inland is covered by a thick equatorial jungle which is absolutely unmarked and is reserved only for adventurers in autonomy. Only the Ulu Temburong National Park allows you to approach this exceptional ecosystem by pirogue and through the mangroves. One can cross there the amazing nasal monkey, among many other species.

Cambodia

Between Vietnam and Thailand, small Cambodia is in the shadow of its large neighbors well established on the tourist scene. But this country, which until recently was only a logical passage on the Southeast Asian circuit, is becoming a destination that counts, carried by its major and unmissable site, the temples of Angkor. Cambodia is developing at high speed, following in the wake of Thailand, with which it shares the smiles of its inhabitants and its Buddhist traditions. A destination that charms travelers as much by its welcome as by its landscapes or its historical sites, the country is easily accessible and the trip is quite simple. However, on the spot it is always a small adventure and the traveler will have to be resourceful and know how to let himself be carried.

• Angkor is the major site that justifies alone the trip to Cambodia. This architectural complex is composed of the ruins of seven hundred temples scattered in the jungle. The grandeur and harmony of Angkor Wat make it the most beautiful testimony of Khmer art with the Bayon, temple of Angkor Thom. The vegetation that surrounds the stones makes it all even more magical.

• Other Khmer sites are also worth the detour such as Banteay Chhmar in the north-west of the country, Sambor Prei Kuk west of the Tonle Sap lake or Prah Vihear in the north (the latter is only accessible from the Thaïlande). To explore the region, it is better to be autonomous, rent a motorcycle or have a driver.

● The Tonle Sap Lake is the largest freshwater lake in Southeast Asia and is of paramount importance to the country. An amazing phenomenon occurs there during the monsoon, at this season the surface of the lake is multiplied by 6. To the east of this lake, bamboo forests, waterfalls and red earth await hikers (follow the marked trails).

● The capital, Phnom Penh was known in the 1920s as the pearl of Asia. Since then it has continued to grow while going through the trials and tribulations, and today it is being reborn and following in the footsteps of other Asian capitals before it. Follow the Mekong River and you will be able to admire its monuments and colonial style facades, before the skyscrapers overshadow them. The National Museum is worth a visit for its collection of Buddhas and Khmer art.

● On the south coast of the country, Sihanoukville is developing at a fast pace but is still a quite enjoyable seaside resort, bathed by very warm waters. From here, one can access islands that are still very wild, with small hotels, without water or electricity, welcoming travelers looking for a disconnection.

China

The Middle Kingdom has fascinated Westerners for centuries, and rightly so, for China is undoubtedly one of the most exotic, interesting and unique countries in the world. Since Marco Polo opened the way, many travelers have gone there to, like him, "live enough adventures that they can't tell more than half of them for fear of not being taken seriously". This very large country is certainly apart, culturally, politically, economically. With more than a sixth of the world's population, China remains relatively unknown. A rather closed world, where tourists are still perceived as extraterrestrials in many places, the country is exceptionally diverse. From the frozen lands of the north, where ephemeral cities are made of ice, to the implacable desert confines of Central Asia, through the lush tropics, the high mountains of the Himalayan foothills, and the gigantic megalopolises, the destination is an inexhaustible source of travel. As a highlight, a few must-sees await the visitor, the Great Wall, the Forbidden City, the Silk Road, among others. Since the 2008 Olympic Games, the country has opened up widely, notably Beijing and Shanghai, its two showcases alongside the former British colony of Hong Kong (treated separately). The downside is that with the progressive opening, and the explosion of its domestic tourist market, the country's interesting sites tend to lose their soul by being overexploited in a very cardboard-paste style. However, China remains a destination for explorers at heart because it is not such a simple trip, especially by going off the beaten track, which are ultimately few in number. At the exit of the few international zones, the traveler will quickly find himself isolated and autonomous, cut off from others by languages and a cultural and social system very opaque to foreigners. The country does not present any particular danger and the infrastructure tends to improve but still remains very far from Western standards, especially in the countryside, which is still very poor. With the aim of becoming the world's leading power, the Chinese economy remains highly contrasted. To fully enjoy your trip to China, you must prepare it, or choose to go with a professional. How many visitors already find themselves confused at the airport when they try to connect to Google or Facebook, which are censored there. And this is only the beginning of the immersion...

NORTH AND NORTHWEST :

- Gansu, Xinjiang -

● The ancient capital Xi'an was the starting point of the Silk Road and the whole region was criss-crossed for centuries by merchants. It is your turn to take this legendary route. Before you set off on this route, you may not forget to visit the Mausoleum of Emperor Qin, famous for its terracotta army of 6,000 warriors and life-size horses. Starting from Xi'an, you will visit the Binglinsi Buddhist caves decorated with clay sculptures and murals. Then, near Dunhuang, it is the 492 caves of Mogao which will deserve your attention. Heading north is the Tourfan Trench, a succession of oases at the foot of the mountains of the Gobi Desert where the ruins of the former imperial capital Gaoshung are worth a visit. Then comes Ürümqi, the capital of Xinjiang, which is one of the bastions of Chinese Islam where 20 mosques compete with each other. In Kashgar, last Chinese stage of the Silk Road, the Id Kak mosque is the largest of the country.

● On the fringe of this route, large desert complexes invite hikers to follow the example of the writer Jacques Lanzmann.

The Taklamakan desert is nicknamed the "Sea of Death", because the temperatures, which vary between -40 ° c. in winter and +50 ° c. in summer, deprive the dunes of all life. This desert is traversed by a 2000 km long river, the Tarim, which ends in the Lop Nor, a huge salt marsh located south of Tourfan. The landscapes of all this region are of a rare beauty that only the bravest and/or the most affluent among us will be able to admire. The Dzoungarie is another desert, located in the northern part of Xinjiang. Between the two, the mountainous ribbon of Tian Shan connects many oases, including Tourfan.

CENTER :

- Anshui, Hubei, Jiangsu, Sichuan, Zhejiang -

- Shanghai is the largest city in the country, the most populated, the most cosmopolitan, the most westernized... The city has been occupied by foreigners for several decades and its cultural identity has been deeply marked. After the Communist victory, it was muzzled, but since 1992, it has resumed its rise to become the financial center of China and host the World Expo in 2010. It is China's most cosmopolitan and modern city. It is an urban whirlwind. Not much remains of historic Shanghai and the old opium districts are just a memory.

• Because of its many canals, Suzhou is called the Venice of the East. Many traditional gardens scattered throughout the city also make it famous, as well as the culture of silk. In the surroundings, many lake villages like Zhouzhuang are worth a visit.

• East of Tibet, Sichuan has the same natural and cultural attractions. The valley of Jiuzhaigou is a natural reserve where giant pandas frolic between lakes and waterfalls. Touched by an earthquake of incredible violence, the region has suffered many human and architectural losses. The faces of the thousand Buddhas that populate the cliff of Qianfo Yà near Nanking were victims of the Cultural Revolution.

• The largest Buddha in the world is in Leshan and reaches 71 meters. It is reached by a dizzying staircase carved into the cliff. Going up the Yangtze and Changjiang rivers, many other Buddhist testimonies are offered to the eyes of visitors.

NORTHEAST :

- Henan, Liaoning, Shaanxi, Shanxi -

• Beijing (or Beijing) is the capital and one of the cultural centers of the People's Republic of China. Its old historical districts, the Hutongs, have been razed to the ground by the frenzied urban planning of recent years. It remains nevertheless to visit the Forbidden City, one of the oldest and best preserved palaces of the country. In front of it is the famous Tiananmen Square where every day thousands of Chinese and tourists come to greet the remains of Mao. You will be able to dominate the whole while going up on the "coal hill" of the Jingshan park. The Temple of Heaven and the Summer Palace are two jewels from the past that you should not miss.

• The Great Wall of China extends its 6000 km from the Gulf of Bohai to the southern Gobi Desert. Punctuated with watchtowers and bastions along its entire length, it sometimes shrinks and seems to be only an imposing earthen levee. The most frequented places are the passes of Juyongguan, Xifengkou, Jiayuguan and Shanhaiguan.

• Two other architectural sites are to be visited in the Beijing area. The thirteen tombs of the Ming Dynasty and their stone animal alleys are located at the foot of Tianshou Mountain. In Longmen are the Buddhist rock caves where many statues were carved into the rock between the 5th and 11th centuries.

• Shaanxi province is often considered the cradle of Chinese civilization. Crossed by the Huang He, whose color earned it the name of "country of the yellow earth", it spreads its landscapes until its neighbor Shanxi and its mountains take over. At the end of it stands the Wutai Shan, one of the four sacred Buddhist mountains of China.

SOUTHEAST :

- Guangdond, Guanxi -

• Embark on a cruise on the Lijang River, you will be able to admire, between Guilin and Yang Shuo, the sugar loaf hills that make the landscape a little supernatural, and make a stop at the caves of Guilin.

• In the southwest of the city of the same name, the "White Cloud Mountains" are waiting for you. The Baiyun Shan is a mountain covered with forests whose ascent will give you a breathtaking view of the city of Guangzhou (Canton) and the region covered with quality tea plantations.

• Guangzhou, like Beijing or Shanghai, is quickly covered with concrete and loses some of its former soul. Because of its geographical distance, its cultural and political integration came later. The city offers its visitors many extensive, beautifully designed and maintained parks as well as two zoos. Nevertheless, the city is especially famous for its shopping (its fair which takes place every two years is the most important in China and certainly in the world) but also for its cuisine. The street stands are innumerable and the Cantonese have the habit of snacking at all hours.

THE SOUTH :

- Yunnan, Hainan -

• Yunnan has landscapes of great diversity, from the arid plateaus of Tibet to the tropical forests of Xishuangbanna. Near its capital city, Kunming, the city of eternal spring, two types of landscapes await you: the rice terraces and the limestone columns of the "stone forest".

• Lijiang is probably the most beautiful city in the region. It is an ancient city, resulting from the dongba culture of the Naxi, which has kept all its charm with its 350 bridges and its maze of canals overhung by the Jade Dragon Mountain.

• The Tibetan monastery of Shangri-la, the three pagodas of Dali, and the Taoist temple of Kunming show the cultural diversity of the region. In the south of the region, many minorities have also preserved their customs.

• Hainan is an island province of China, famous for its tropical beaches. It has a thriving tourist industry and is being heavily promoted as "China's Hawaii ». Hainan is undergoing heavy tourist-oriented development with various international hotel chains establishing resorts, especially in the Sanya area. These days, many wealthy Chinese from the northern provinces own second homes in Hainan, where they move to in the winter to escape the bitter cold that characterises much of northern China. Haikou is the tropical capital of the island, while Sanya is the main beach resort. Other attractions include tropical forest national park and old villages of Hainanese culture.

HONG KONG :

Former English colony, retroceded to China in 1997, Hong Kong has long lived between two waters, like an open window on the Middle Kingdom. Now fully integrated into China (or even called to order by the central government when it grants itself too much freedom), Hong Kong has nonetheless retained its particularities. In the first place, its unbridled capitalism, its modernity and the widespread use of the English language. It is always easier to access Hong Kong than the rest of China, in all respects including visas (not required here for French visitors unlike the rest of the country). If Hong-Kong is resolutely apart, and cannot be compared to Beijing or Shanghai, the spirit of China is nevertheless very present there. For each ultra-modern shopping center there is a traditional market, for each futuristic neighborhood there is a fishing village on an island and at the foot of the buildings junks sway on the waters of the port. Hong Kong is a destination that surprises by its exoticism and diversity, that of an Asian urban whirlwind with Western influences, which is undoubtedly one of the most fascinating and dynamic metropolises on the planet. The visit is easy and outside of the urban madness of the city the western traveler will be more comfortable than in the metropolises of mainland China.

• Hong Kong is known for its large number of skyscrapers, space is limited and densities are so high that it was necessary to gain space in the air and on the sea. In the north of Hong Kong Island, the Central District skyscraper line dominated by Victoria Peak is the best known view of the region. Two of the most famous buildings are the Bank of China Tower, designed by I. M. Pei, and Cesar Pelli's Two International Finance Centre. You can go up to the 55th floor (about 250 m) of the second one to discover an exceptional panorama of the bay. Another spectacular view is the one you get by taking the funicular to the top of Victoria Peak.

• On the island of Hong Kong, you can't fail to visit the Aberdeen district to discover the floating villages, junks and sampans. Each neighborhood has its own particularities: Central where business is in full swing, Sheung Wan more traditional, Causeway Bay shopping kingdom, Mongkok or Yaumatei traveled by the crowds, Mid Levels much more residential, Lan Kwai Fong and Wanchai with wild nights. Several museums will also deserve your interest such as the Tea Arts Museum at Flagstaff House, the Oceanographic Museum in Ocean Park or the Tsui Museum of Art and the Space Museum.

• If you are looking for a real change of scenery, you have to cross the bay from Hong Kong Island to Kowloon and its colourful districts. The best illustration of this effervescence is Nathan Road, a gigantic shopping street going up from Tsim Sha Tsui to Boundary Street, for about 3 kilometers. Its frenetic activity spreads to the nearby streets, where one can find night markets, such as the one on Temple Street. Also, you can't miss the Peninsula Hotel, whose sumptuous décor echoes the Rolls-Royce cars parked in front.

• The New Territories include most of the mainland of Hong Kong as well as many islands where Chinese traditions are much more present. The region offers many opportunities for hiking. Don't miss the Ten Thousand Buddhas Temple which takes its name from the countless statues that populate the area, the Kadoorie Botanical Gardens, ideal for breathing after the urban diving that Hong Kong imposes, and the Tai Pau Kau Forest where birds and rare plants can be found.

• The Hong Kong archipelago also has many secondary islands including Lantau, Lamma, Po Toi, Cheung Chau and Peng Chau. These are dotted with natural parks offering many opportunities for walks. Moreover, these small islands populated by fishermen still offer the vision of traditional coastal communities and cars are not welcome. Many beaches also allow you to relax while admiring the spectacle of the bay.

MACAU :

Returned to China since 1999, Macau has not ceased to be the Asian capital of the Game. While there are still charming cobbled streets with colorful balconies and some buildings emblematic of Portuguese architecture, the city is growing vertically at full speed and casinos flourish there in the footsteps of tourists.

• If you like gambling, Macau is more than just a rival to Las Vegas, it has the largest **casino in the** world: the Venetian. This casino, located on the Cotai Strip, a land platform built on the water that connects Macau to the nearby islands of Taipa and Coloane, reproduces an artificial and overheated Venice. Slot machines, black jack, baccarat, roulette, boule, keno, craps are on the program, but also Chinese games such as fan tan, dai siu, pai kao and mahjong. The dancers on stage and the players in the hall form a fascinating spectacle. For the partygoers, bars and nightclubs allow to alternate pleasures. Of course, the Venetian is only one of the many casinos in the city. Just like Las Vegas, the city's casinos are sometimes attractions in themselves and the city's emblems, the most famous of which is the giant pineapple of Lisboa.

• For three centuries, Macao was one of the Portuguese colonial jewels, some monuments are there to testify of it. At the top of a hill on the peninsula is the lighthouse of Guia, the oldest of the entire Chinese coast. In the city center, the Leal Senado is covered with beautiful azulejos and hides a pleasant garden. From Largo do Senado square, you can visit the church of Sao Domingo and admire the ruined façade of the Sao Paolo church, which was once the largest Christian monument in Asia. To learn more about the History of Macau, don't hesitate to visit the new Macau Museum in the military buildings of the Fortaleza do Monte nearby.

• For a few moments of tranquility, several gardens offer themselves to you like the Praça Luis de Camoes and its belvedere, the Lou Lim Leoc and its miniature Chinese landscapes and the Sun Yat Sen park. Places of worship are also havens of peace, you will have the choice between the Chinese temples Kun Lam and Lin Fong Miu, the Buddhist temple

A-Ma and the churches Sao Lourenço and Sto Agostinho. The contiguous islands of Taipa and Coloane have 41 km of coastline with small beaches. Those of Hác-Sá in Coloane are the most popular.

TIBET :

The fascinating lands of Tibet were indexed by China in 1950 and officially renamed Xizang while the provinces of Kham and Amdo in the east and northeast were attached to Qinghaï and Sichuan. The Dalai Lama and the Tibetan government have since been in exile in Dharamsala, India. This mythical land remains nevertheless a destination in its own right that inspires travel. The formalities of entry in this Chinese province are particularly constraining, you will need a little organization to be able to discover its eternal beauties.

* Located on the Tibetan plateau, at the bottom of a valley surrounded by mountains, its altitude of 3 650 meters makes Lhasa one of the highest cities in the world. Mythical city, it was transformed gradually by the Chinese government, nevertheless by walking in the old city you will be able to measure all its spirituality. Follow the pilgrims (clockwise) on the Barkhor to Jokhang, the most revered shrine in Tibet. Climb the Potala, the palace of the Dalai Lama, the most emblematic monument of Tibet. The Ani Sangkoung Nunnery, Ramoche Temple and Norbulingkha Garden are also worth a visit.

* In the immediate surroundings of Lhasa, many excursions are possible. The monastery of Drepung, about ten kilometers west of Lhasa, still has several hundred monks. Five kilometers to the north is the monastery of Sera, a major center of Tantric studies. The monastery of Ganden is 45 km east of Lhasa and is a prestigious example of Tibetan high altitude monasteries. Although the Tibetan uprising in 1959 resulted in heavy repression and the destruction of most of the monasteries, the remaining places of worship are increasingly frequented.

* Green oases punctuate the desert plateau between Lhasa and Shigatse, the second largest city in Tibet located 350 km southwest of Lhasa. If Shigatse has lost some of its charm, you will have to visit in the surroundings the monastery of Tashilhunpo, the traditional seat of the Panchen Lama where countless statues of Buddha are gathered. Continuing on the road to Kathmandu, you can also stop at Gyantse where there are very large stupas, including the one with one hundred thousand figures.

* The Chomolongma camp is the base camp of Everest at the foot of the Rongbuk glacier, it offers views of Everest even more grandiose than in the N. épalDo not hesitate to make a detour to the monastery of Rongphu, from where the panoramas are exceptional or to the monasteries North and South of the monastic city of Sakya. From the villages of Shegar or Tingri, you can reach the base camp in three or four exhausting days before continuing your trek to the N, épalalong the Friendship Road.

* There are many other hiking possibilities in the Tibetan territory, sherpas and yaks will accompany you. The Central-Western region has countless turquoise lakes. The second salt lake of Tibet, Nam-tso, is 200 km north of Lhasa. More than 1,600 km west of Lhasa, Lake Manasarovar is a sacred place in Ngari Prefecture near Mount Kailash, considered by Tibetans and Indians as the throne of Shiva, a major pilgrimage site. Not far away, the mysterious and imposing ruins of the Gugé Kingdom and the Tirthapuri sanctuary are also worth a visit.

* East of the capital, the Kongpo region is a huge forest overexploited by the Chinese, and the Dakpo, the region of fruit trees. Kangding and Tagong have important monastic complexes. In the heart of the Kham region you will meet the Tibetan nomadic populations with their ancestral way of life.

East Timor

East Timor (or Timor Leste) consists of the eastern half of the island of Timor, Atauro and Jaco and Oecussi-Ambeno, an enclave located in the western part of the island of Timor, surrounded by West Timor under Indonesian sovereignty. Originally a Portuguese colony, East Timor was annexed by Indon following ésiethe invasion in 1975. The country seceded in 1999 and gained full independence in 2002. Following the serious incidents in Dili on February 11, 2008, unrest in the country cannot be ruled out. The Ministry of Foreign Affairs recommended that travel to East Timor be postponed until further notice.

• Despite the violence that followed the independence referendum in 1999, the old town of Baucau on the north coast has retained remnants of the Portuguese colonial era, including the Pousada de Baucau and the impressive municipal market. The city also has pleasant beaches and magnificent sea views.

• Suai, in the south of the country, was also one of the places of the massacres of September 1999, but it is there that the most beautiful black sand beaches are found, bordered by a sea that can sometimes be dangerous.

• Pantemakassar, in the enclave of Oecussi on the territory of West Timor, between the sea and the mountains, offers in its surroundings some beautiful swimming spots such as Pantai Mahata at 2 km or Lifau at 5 km.

• Mount Ramelau is the highest mountain of the island of Timor and the highest point of East Timor. It can easily be climbed in three or four hours from Maubisse, a small mountain town, ideal for refreshment, where a remarkable market is held every Sunday.

India

It is not an easy exercise to briefly summarize a country as large and complex as India. First of all, India is not an easy destination. It is even one of the most demanding journeys, except for countries in precarious situations. The country has the peculiarity of confronting the Western traveler with realities he does not know, extreme poverty, dirt sometimes filthy, food so spicy that it is inedible (and most often no known flavors on the horizon to decompress), and the most disturbing of all: death, well present, animal corpses, funeral rites ... To this must be added the oppressive crowd and the cultural gap that must be crossed to discover the country. All the mystery of India, however, lies in this decadent greatness, which makes many travelers try the adventure and the destination has largely democratized. Everyone has a different feeling about the country and this one depends among other things on the regions (the south of the country is perceived as easier, and rightly so). The paradox is also that, despite often chaotic travel conditions, India, a thousand-year-old country, reserves a thousand and one wonders for its visitors (palaces, historic cities, varied landscapes, unique natural sites, wildlife worthy of Africa, after all it is the country of the Jungle Book, and more than anything else, an unequalled dose of humanity). Adventure and exoticism are everywhere in this country that is teeming with incredible vitality, everywhere and all the time. Some become fans of it, others are washed away by the whirlwind. Access is easy, and so is travel, even if it often leaves memories (trains are a unique experience, just like buses, always crowded, and driving is totally anarchic, often frightening). The health situation is bad, especially far from the big cities. Safety is generally not a problem, but the less seasoned travelers may feel uncomfortable, both in the big cities, which are literally chaotic, and in the small country towns that make up the heart of this essentially rural country (contrary to popular belief). India is a truly special destination, one that is fundamentally upsetting, that is much closer to the sensory experience than to traditional tourism, but where you never know in advance whether it will be good or bad.

NORTH AND NORTHEAST :

• Bodh-Gaya is a village located about one hundred kilometers from Patna in the state of Bihar, it is the place where Siddhartha Gautama attained enlightenment and thus the state of Buddha. The Ficus religiosa, the tree at the foot of which this event took place, is still there and is revered with fervor. A Buddhist complex, including the Mahabodhi Temple and its diamond throne, was built nearby and is one of the largest Buddhist pilgrimage centers in the world.

• Calcutta is a huge, totally chaotic agglomeration on the banks of the Hûghlî river where wealth and poverty seem to clash at every street corner, all wrapped in a very strong spiritual atmosphere. If you arrive by the Howrah train station, you may not get over it. In the rush, go to Dakshineshvar, the temple of Kali, and the market on Mahatma Gandhi Road. For a break, choose the Victoria Memorial, Indian Museum or Botanical Garden in the south of the city.

• Two hundred Buddhist monasteries are scattered throughout the state of Sikkim. Even if tourism is not yet very developed in the region, the Indian government has imposed a permit to enter this territory. The monastery of Rumtek is the largest monastery in the Eastern Himalayas. The one of Pemayangtse is also worth a visit.

• Amritsar is a city located in the northwest of the Indian Panjab state. Holy city for the Sikhs, it can be proud of the Golden Temple, a majestic marble and copper construction with upper parts covered with gold plates and leaves, built in the middle of the Immortality Lake.

• Delhi is divided into two parts. In Old Delhi, you will visit the Red Fort of the Moghols, the Gandhi Memorial and the largest mosque in the country (Jama Masjid) before getting lost in the popular streets and the market of Chandni Chowk. In New Delhi, the federal capital of India, you won't wander through the long soulless avenues, but you will appreciate the brick minaret of Qutb Minar located south of the city. The India Gate and the Parliament are also two emblematic monuments of this crazy city.

• In the heart of Himachal Pradesh is Dharamsala where many Tibetan refugees live (in McLeod Ganj, the upper town). It is here that the Dalai Lama is currently in exile. This small village has become over the years the center of the peaceful struggle of Tibetans in exile and the meeting place for many tourists.

• The monasteries of Ladakh, the region nicknamed Little Tibet, are in perfect harmony with the surrounding relief. Those of Lamayuru, Tikse, Phuktal or Hemis are good examples. The festivals which take place there at various times of the year are very famous.

• Kaziranga National Park is located in the Golaghat and Nagaon districts of Assam State on the eastern edge of the Himalayas. Two-thirds of the Indian rhino population lives here, and it has the highest density of tigers in the world. Leopards, elephants and deer are also present. The Bengal tiger can also be admired in the Sundarbans Tiger Reserve, about 100 kilometers south of Calcutta.

• Take the Himalayan railway from Darjeeling (or the bus, it's faster) to get to Darjeeling, located in the hills at the foot of the Himalayas. The whole region is known for its tea. The plants are grown at 2750 meters above sea level on the mountainside. These 87 plantations are the only ones allowed to use the appellation of controlled origin.

• A land of peaks dominated by the 8,598 meters of the Kanchenjunga massif (the mountain goddess), Sikkim is nevertheless nicknamed the "rice valley". Here, extremes meet for the most brilliant marriage of climatic excess. In a few hours, one can go from the jungle to the fodder terraces, from the farms where tea is stored to the glaciers and the eternal snows of Mount Pandim. Trekking in the region of the Gocha pass will take you to sublime landscapes with multicolored orchids.

• Between the N épaland Kashmir lies Himachal Pradesh, which the most experienced hikers will be able to hike, even if the highest peaks such as Nanada Devi will be closed to them. In addition to an interesting flora and fauna, Tibetan monasteries will punctuate the walk. The surroundings of the Spiti and Parvati rivers are particularly pleasant.

• Still today, it is not recommended to venture into the Kashmir valley. Nevertheless, the city of Srinagar, capital of Jammu-Kashmir, gives a good idea of the wooden architecture of the whole region. Don't hesitate to stay in one of the boats that lie along the Dal or Nagin lakes for a moment of pure relaxation in the middle of nature.

NORTHWEST :

• Rajasthan, country of kings, is located in the west of the India. Renowned for its traditions and colorful monuments, it is in Jaipur, the capital, and in Udaipur that you will find its jewel. The Hawa Mahal, or palace of the winds, of the first has a delicate pink color while the palace of Ra Ra on the edge of Lake Pichola radiates the second of light. In the same region, the Amber Palace and Jodhpur Citadel are among the sites not to be missed. On the road of the caravans of the Thar desert, take time to discover Jaisalmer, fantastic ochre city, or Bikaner and their surroundings.

• The Taj Mahal, symbol of the country, is located in Agra in Uttar Pradesh. This white marble mausoleum was erected by Mughal Emperor Shah Jahan in memory of his wife in the seventeenth century. It is an unmistakable monument that lives up to everything you have ever imagined about it. The Red Fort of Agra and nearby Fatehpur Sikri are also listed as World Heritage Sites.

• Benares, today Vârânaçî, is located entirely on the left bank of the Ganges, facing the rising sun, the other bank being devoid of any construction. The city, dedicated to Shiva has more than 1500 temples and attracts pilgrims from all over the country. The banks, called ghats, are covered with stone steps that allow Hindu devotees to descend to the river to practice ablutions and pûjâs.

• In Rajasthan is the Ranthambore National Park, reputed to be one of the best places to observe wildlife in India. Beware, this former hunting ground of the Maharajas of Jaipur is closed between June and October. The Sariska National Park and the Bharatpur National Park are two other reserves in the region also conducive to the discovery of local wildlife.

• In Uttar Pradesh, two beautiful national parks will allow you to observe several varieties of deer, as well as tigers and other felines. These are Corbett National Park, the oldest of the national parks in the country, and Dudhwa National Park.

CENTER :

• Hyderâbâd and Secunderâbâd are twin cities, capital of the new state of *Telangana*, separated by the Husain Sagar, an artificial lake. The Charminar is the emblem of the first one, it is a triumphal arch surmounted by four luxurious minarets. Many other monuments (Mecca Masjid, Golconda fort...) make the city an interesting stopover. Eight kilometers away are the ruins of the Golkonda fortress.

• Ahmedabad is the main city of Gujarat. Devastated by the 2001 earthquake, it nevertheless remains a flagship destination in the region because of its cultural richness. The celebrations and popular festivals that take place there throughout the year are particularly lively. Crafts and gastronomy are also very well cared for. And the monuments that make up its architectural heritage are each worth a small visit.

• The sacred mountain of Palitana in the same region is one of the high places of pilgrimage of Jainism. The two acropolises where more than 863 temples are gathered can be reached by climbing a staircase with 3950 steps.

• Khajurâho is a village in Madhya Pradesh where there is a religious complex of more than twenty temples. This place is known to tourists for the explicitly erotic bas-reliefs that adorn the facades of the temples. In the same region, the fort of Gwälior and the Great Stupa of Sanchi are worth a visit.

• Ajantâ is a village in Maharashtra famous for its group of 29 artificial caves dug out of hard basalt to shelter monks during monsoons or to host meetings and prayers throughout the year. Beautifully colored frescoes still adorn the walls of some of them.

• Ellora is another troglodytic site in the region. Thirty-four sanctuaries have been excavated from a vertical wall of the Charanandri Hills. Some caves are Hindu, including Kailasanâtha Temple, some Buddhist, including Vishwakarma Cave, and some Jain, and all are worth a visit.

- Mumbai is the capital of Maharashtra state. The standard of living there is higher than in the rest of the country, and the social and cultural diversity is even richer. Bombay is known worldwide for its Bollywood film production. After a long stroll along the Marine Drive, feel free to enter one of the hundred cinemas in the city. Ten kilometers away is the island of Elephanta known for its temples carved into the rock. Bombay is also the most frenetic city in India, a title that is difficult to obtain. It is an endless amalgam of modern districts and slums, a giant anthill that leaves visitors often exhausted.

- Orissa is a region bordering the Bay of Bengal. There are many places of interest: Bhubaneswar and its many temples, Purî and its Jagannâtha Temple, Konârak and its Sûrya Temple, Hirapur and its Yoginis Temple, the Jain Caves of Udayagiri and Khandagiri and the Buddhist sites of Lalitagiri.

- The coasts of Andhra Pradesh, where Goa, Daman and Diu are located, have welcomed since the 1960s many travelers in search of sunny beaches and wild nights. Vagator is located 22 kilometers from Panaji, the capital of Goa, and is one of the most famous spots in the area where the Full Moon Parties take place every month. Markets, beautiful tropical beaches and colonial architecture are the attractions of *Goa*, the most relaxed state of the country.

- The only place in the world where you can see Asian lions is Sasan Gir National Park. If they don't show up, don't worry, you'll still see some of the 2,375 species of animals found in the reserve. The best time? From the beginning of November to the end of March.

- Kanha National Park and Bandhavgarh Reserve are two natural areas in Madhya Pradesh where you can observe all kinds of animals in the wild.

- Along the Arabian Sea are the Western Ghats, a mountain range that separates the Dekkan Plateau from the coast. The spectacle of these black and red cliffs is impressive. In the heart of its landscapes, you will find the temple of Bhima Shankar, a high place of Shivaism.

- The fine sandy beaches around Puri, in Orissa, are a pleasant place to relax. You can swim there fully dressed (as is often the case in India) and enjoy the activities of the locals in the late afternoon. An experience to do: going north just before sunrise will allow you to see hundreds of fishing boats taking to the sea at the same time.

SOUTH :

- Mysore is located in Karnataka and is famous for its Indo-Muslim palace and especially the way it is lit at night, a sight that rivals our most beautiful Christmas lights.

- Hampi is an Indian village located within the walls of the ruined city of Vijayanâgara, once the capital of one of the largest Hindu empires. If the village is modest, the ruins that are linked to it are all the more impressive. In the middle of a set of pavilions and sanctuaries of pink sandstone, rises the superb Virupaksha temple. Nearby, the four sanctuaries of Badami were carved into the cliff at the time of the Hindu kingdom of Chalukya.

- Cochin and its peninsula are known for these Chinese squares with which the fishermen of the region catch fish. The historical heart of the city is located on the peninsula of Mattancheri.

- 60 km from Chennai, the ancient Madras, is the archaeological site of Mahabalipuram on the ocean shore. The descent of the Ganges River, probably the largest bas-relief in the world, was carved here in honor of the river. The temple of the shore and the five ratha of the south are the other important monuments of the site.

- Other places of interest in Tamil Nadu are the Ranganatha Swami in Srirangam, the great temple of Shiva Brihadisvara in Thanjavur, the Ranganatha Temple in Tiruchirapalli and the Temple of Minâkshî in Madurai. As you can see, the state of Tamil Nadu is characteristic for its temples. *Tiruchirapalli* and *Madurai* inevitably form the keystone of organized stays in the state.

• Pondicherry, former chief town of French India, has a certain charm and a gentle way of life rare for an Indian city. It is a city with a different atmosphere from the rest of the country, much less frenetic. Not far from there, Auroville, the city of dawn, is a community founded in 1968 by the "Mother", the spiritual companion of Sri Aurobindo, Indian thinker of the new man. A utopian city in the forest, it is more of a mystical experience than true tourism because there is, as such, nothing special to see there.

• The Andaman and Nicobar Islands comprise more than 500 islands off the coast of Burma. Here, it is already Southeast Asia. The beaches are idyllic and the seabed is beautiful. Here is a small dream spot, far from the turmoil of the subcontinent, that you probably did not foresee in your itinerary. If you add it to it, you may meet on the Andaman Islands very small groups of native hunter-gatherers speaking languages that are not related to any other. The destination requires a special permit to be explored, and only a few islands are open to foreigners.

• In Karnataka, the Kâverî River splits into two arms to form the island of Sivasamudram before arriving at the Kaveri Falls, 100 m high, often considered the most beautiful waterfalls in the country.

• As for the wildlife of Karnataka, you will be able to observe it in the Kudremukh Park in the north of the region or in the Bandipur Park in the south. On another islet of Kaveri is the Ranganathittu Bird Sanctuary.

• From Kottayam to Allepey, in the state of Kerala, you can embark on a cruise on these small floating houses that slide along the back waters. Its narrow canals cross very green landscapes and the coconut groves of Kerala, passing through traditional small fishing villages.

• The long Kerala coast is home to many beautiful beaches including Kovalam 16 km south of Thiruvananthapuram, or Varkala. In the north of the state, Cannanore is another pleasant beach. Off the coast of Kerala, the Laquedives Islands are coral islands full of diving spots.

• The Nîlgîri Mountains are a haven of freshness in the tropical atmosphere of the south of the country. Starting from Udhagamandalam (Ootacamund) or Coonor, numerous hikes allow the traveler to discover the eucalyptus, tea and coffee plantations. A short elephant ride in the Mudumalai National Park will allow you to observe the very rich fauna of the region.

Indonesia

The most populated and the largest archipelago in the world, Indonesia is a universe to discover and it is a magnificent destination. The diversity of its cultures, ethnic groups and religions make that there are many facets in this country which as a whole is blessed by the deities of tourism. The exuberant tropical nature is certainly its most beautiful attraction, with the majesty of the volcanoes, the strangeness of the meeting of the dragons of Komodo or the jungle and the totally wild mountains of Borneo and New Guinea as highlights. Of course with so many islands, Indonesia also has its share of fantastic tropical beaches, some well established to welcome visitors but most of them are totally deserted. The interest of the country is that it is never impossible to go somewhere, and the slightly (or very) experienced traveler will be able to freely discover the whole country, including the most remote areas, even if it is sometimes necessary to ask for a permit to access them (New Guinea for example). The less seasoned traveler will not be outdone, especially on the island of Java, which concentrates the population, for example in the urban jungle of Jakarta without too many tourist interests but an experience to be lived, and the historical or cultural sites. All of them meet in Bali, the real pearl of the country, a small island where the softness of the welcome is equaled only by the attraction of a well marked culture and the beauty of the landscapes of volcanoes, rice fields and beaches. In the tourist areas the infrastructures are very good, although the sanitary system is of average quality. The quality/price ratio is in any case very high, at the level of Thailand. Off the beaten track, the situation is different. Indonesia has some of the most isolated corners of the planet, where infrastructure is at best very limited and even if, as we have seen, access is always possible, one should expect nothing less than an adventurous trip when one decides to explore, for example, the impenetrable forests of Kalimantan (the Indonesian part of Borneo). It should also be pointed out that the country as a whole is influenced by Islam and that if it is rather moderate, its customs should be respected.

SUMATRA :

Sumatra, the largest of the entirely Indonesian islands, is located in the west of the archipelago.

* Lake Toba, in the north of the island, is the largest volcanic lake in the world. Surrounded by high mountains and waterfalls, it is truly a magical place. You will be able to bathe there, go to the island of Samosir which is in its center (where you can visit traditional Batak villages), and relax at the hot spring of Pangururan.

* In the center of the country is another lake, Lake Maninjau. Its beauty and mild climate also attract travelers. On the shores, in the villages Maninjau and Bayur, you can meet the Minangkabao people and observe the work of the fishermen. It is also a famous site for paragliding.

* In the region of Padang and Bukittinggi, it is the Minangs who will welcome you. The big houses (Rumah Gadang), buffalo fighting, saluang (music), rendai (theater), silat (martial art) and richly spiced gastronomy are typical of this art of living.

* At 125 km west of Sumatra, Nias Island is famous for its surf spots (Sorake Bay, Hinako Islands, Banyak and Batu Islands). The inhabitants have managed to preserve their way of life (despite the 2005 earthquake). Sculpted megaliths representing their ancestors are erected in different places of the island. The Sakkudeis people with flower tattoos, from which they get their nickname of Flower-Men, are waiting for you on the island of Siberut, in the Mentawai archipelago.

JAVA :

In the south of the archipelago, the island of Java is the most populated in Indonesia.

* The temple of Borobudur, the largest Buddhist monument in the world, is the emblem of the island. Built in the ninth century, it is a place of worship and pilgrimage very busy especially between May and October when the actors of the Ramayana meet. The bas-reliefs of the four floors of the gallery tell the lives of Buddha. 72 stupas surround the main one and compose a mandala, visible from the sky.

* Other temples on the island are also worth a visit. The 240 Shivaite temples of Prambanan are also classified as World Heritage Sites. 8 temples in the Dieng Highlands have survived volcanic activity, but this region, north of Magelang or Wonosobo, is best known for its small sulfur geysers.

* Java is indeed famous for its volcanoes, 25 of which are still active. Hiking and eruption observations are on the program. The easiest routes are the Bromo with its sea of sand and the Kawa Ijen with its acid lake. The most difficult are the Merapi, the most active volcano of the island, and the Semeru, the highest.

* Prefer Yogyakarta to Jakarta. It is the cultural center of the island where traditions such as th, éâtre d'ombres wayang kulitand handicrafts (batik) are remarkably highlighted. Kota Gede, the goldsmiths' district, is worth a detour. 20 km from the city is a curiosity: the church of the Sacred Heart of Jesus in the village of Ganjuran.

* Madura is a small island near Java. We come there to watch karapan sapi, a traditional bull race. The town of Sumenep was the seat of the princely court of the island, there is a mosque, a palace and the royal cemetery of Asta Tinggi. From the port of Kalianget, one can embark to the other islands of kabupaten (Poteran, Kangean, Sapeken and Masalembu).

THE LESSER SUNDA ISLANDS :

These small islands connect Indonesia to Australia.

* On the island of Flores, the most touristic attraction is the cratère du Kelimutu with these three colorful lakes in the kabupaten of Ende. On the west coast, one can still observe the Komodo dragon in freedom. The fishing villages and the ethnic groups of the inland have managed to keep their traditions despite the religious impact of the Portuguese colonization.

* The landscape of the island of Lombok is dominated by the Rinjani volcano. On its slopes is the crescent of the Segara lake from which emerges the smoking crater of Baru. Superb hikes are to be made in this national park. The beaches of the island are also famous, those who like idleness will choose Sengigi, surfers will go to the south coast and divers will love the Gili Islands.

* Sumbawa Island is also known for its beautiful scenery, rugged terrain, fertile valleys and beautiful white sandy beaches. South of the kabupaten of Dompu, surfers meet on the beach of Hu'u. The diving sites of the island Ie de Komodo (that of the famous dragon) and the marine national park of Moyo are superb. In Sumba, in the south, traditional houses in the Bondokodi area and the ikat weaving process are among the attractions of the island.

* East Timor or Timor Leste, a land of adventure, covered with jungle, where tourism is almost non-existent.

BALI :

Bali is also part of the Lesser Sunda Islands but is a destination in its own right.

* The cultural heritage of Bali is one of its greatest treasures. The traditional dances (barong, kechak, legong) performed to the sound of gamelan have become one of the most popular performances by tourists. Religious festivals (processions, ceremonies and cremations) are done without complex in front of all visitors. Ubud is the cultural and artistic center of the island, the city is known for its paintings and galleries.

* The layering of rice fields makes Bali's landscapes the most enchanting of the entire region. This one is also marked by the two holiest volcanoes of the island: Mount Batur and Mount Agung (still active). The former is known for its spectacular caldera and lake, but both are great experiences for all hikers.

* The beaches of Bali are famous for their waves very popular with surfers. In the south, beaches such as Kuta Beach, Legian Beach and Sanur are flooded every year by tourists. For more tranquility, you will have to go to the north. Lovina Beach is the main seaside resort, but the entire coast offers magnificent diving and snorkeling sites.

THE NORTHERN ISLANDS :

In the north of Indonesia are the islands of Kalimantan, Sulawesi, Moluccas, and Irian Jaya.

* Kalimantan shares its territory with Malaysia. The rivers that run through it (Kapuas and Malakam) are the subject of pirogue descents that take place over several days before ending with hikes in the jungle to discover the dayak villages. The orangutans of Tanjung Pating National Park, the pile dwellings of Banjarmasin, and the market of Tamianglayang are the other attractions of the island.

* The tropical forest of Sulawesi (or Sulawesi) covers a large part of its territory in the shape of an octopus. The main interest of the island lies in its population, the mysterious Toraja civilization. Its funerary traditions, the tombs dug in the cliffs of the cemeteries of Londa and Lemo and their wooden effigies, and its sacrificial rites (farewell buffaloes, pigs) are impressive. Set on bamboo stilts, their houses, the Tongkonans, are remarkable and carefully decorated. The slender roofs in the shape of a ship's bow reach a height of 15 meters. Apart from these improbable encounters, you will find many trekking possibilities around Lake Posso and in Lore Lindu's park as well as beautiful seaside (but not touristic) spots on the Togian Islands.

* A thousand islands and islets are scattered over about 1200 km to form the Moluccas, one of the least known destinations in Indonesia. In addition to a common paradisiacal nature, each island differs from its neighbor by its traditions

and culture. For centuries, this archipelago, rich in spices, was the only source of nutmeg and cloves in the world. Numerous ruins here and there are a reminder of this era of great trade.

• Irian Jaya, also known as Western New Guinea, is bordered by Papua New Guinea with which it shares many similarities. Its remote location, cultural, historical and geographical features make it a region apart from Indonesia. With a little courage and a good pair of shoes, you can set off to meet the sublime nature where the Papuans live. It is a harsh land, shaped for adventurers. The small town of Wamena and the valley of Baliem, connected to no road, are the gateway to the world of the Papuans. It is not an easy trip but it is an experience that cannot be forgotten. The Teluk Cendrawasih National Park is home to coral reefs, coastal ecosystems, mangroves and Indonesia's largest marine national park. The thermal springs of Mioswaar Island, the underground cave at Tanjung Mangguar and the birds of paradise of the Biak Archipelago reinforce the unusual side of the whole region.

Iran

The traveler generally does not know well how to situate Iran in all respects. We know that its history is rich, it is the ancient kingdom of Persia. We know that it is a country where Islam is strict, the morality police is watching. We know that it is a country of desert, between Central Asia and Arabia. It is generally thought that traveling to Iran for a Westerner is an impossible thing. Times are changing and as for other destinations that we still believe to be inaccessible (Colombia, Nicaragua) it is now possible to travel to Iran which, at least for its central part (the classic circuit), can now be visited without too many complications but with a good preparation. However, it should be noted that certain regions remain strongly discouraged (and notoriously dangerous, especially border areas), and that the inexperienced traveler who wants to discover the destination will be well advised to contact a tour operator. What we do not know about Iran is everything else, its traditions, culture, monuments, architecture, mountains (snow-covered and skiable), landscapes. The opening and especially the end of the embargo have generated an important development for the country, which already has a good level of infrastructure, but the cultural shock is still largely at the rendezvous. In Iran, the traveler is confronted with the very idea of a change of scenery, for the better and sometimes for the worse. No McDonald's but Mash Donald's, no possibility to use a bank card (for foreigners all payments must be made in cash, but the destination is rather cheap), Iran is a world apart in today's globalized world. You will have understood it, beyond the treasures of Persia, it is this unusual exoticism that curious travelers come more and more to look for in the country. It is not a very simple destination, but it is one of the most exciting destinations where you can still find the magic of the Thousand and One Nights.

• The architecture of Esfahan, drowned in well-irrigated greenery, offers a sumptuous contrast with the desert expanses that surround it. In spite of the threat of a modern urbanism in full proliferation, the atmosphere of the city, in particular by its market and the surroundings of its mosques, reflects the traditions of the country. Naghsh-e Jahan Square, one of the largest squares in the world, is lined with important historical monuments from the Safavid era.

• Tabriz is best known for its bazaar, reputed to be the longest in the world. About twenty covered courtyards follow one another there and the diversity of stalls and stalls makes it the most active shopping center in the region. The Shah Goli and its swimming pool as well as the Blue Mosque and its glazed ceramic decorations are the two most visited sites in the city.

• Mechhed welcomes every year millions of Shiite pilgrims who come to gather at the silver mausoleum of Imam Reza. In Qom, another holy city of Shiism, is buried Hazrat Fatimah Ma'sumeh. His tomb and the theological center of the city attract millions of people. In the central south of the country, the mausoleums and mosques of Shiraz, Kerman and Yezd are among the most beautiful monuments in Iran.

• In a deserted landscape rise the ruins of the mythical Persepolis burned by Alexander the Great in 330 BC. The site, of Greco-Egyptian inspiration, is however well preserved. The monumental staircase, the Palace of the Hundred Columns and that of the Apadana give an idea of what the capital of the Achaemenids built by Darius I twenty-five centuries ago was like. Five kilometers away are the tombs of the Achaemenid kings at Naqsh-e Rostam.

• Evidence of the medieval period is also scattered throughout the country. Bam, in the south, is famous for its citadel, a city of clay built 2,000 years ago and pleasantly restored in recent years. Alamut, in the north, has a ruined fortress where the sect of the Assassins had found refuge. There are 23 other fortresses from the same period in ruins in the same region.

• Iranian landscapes are just as fabulous as its historical heritage. To the north, a spectacular road once established by Shah Reza Khan runs through the Elbourz Mountains to the maritime city of Chalus. The coast of the Caspian Sea is a popular area for the people of Tehran who come here in search of a little rest even though the climate is not always ideal.

• The landscape of the western part of the country has been carved out of the lava that has been rejected by the volcano of Sahand. Gradually shaped by the wind and rain, they formed cones that the inhabitants could then easily dig and transform into troglodyte houses as in Kandovan. A little further south, the Ghar Parau abyss is the deepest cave in Asia.

• In the southeast, the Zagros massif, whose folded slopes abound with rivers, is always traveled by nomads. A guide will help you, in addition to the logistic organization, to go to meet these populations. A little further east, the desert begins. From Kerman, discover the dunes of Dasht-e Lut.

Iraq

Let's be clear, few destinations rival Iraq. It is one of the cradles of human civilization, an ocean of archaeological sites (estimated at more than half a million) that we owe to the ancestral Sumerian civilization, the Assyrians and of course Babylon, a mythical city whose hanging gardens were one of the seven wonders of the ancient world. Badgad has always been the most influential city in the Arab world. The possible discoveries in this country are innumerable, and its desert nature gives it some magnetic landscapes. However, to be perfectly clear, it must be added that Iraq is NOT a travel destination of any kind. After two wars, the country is in a state of total turmoil. Not anarchic, but not far away, Iraq is quite impossible to cross outside the northern provinces of Kurdistan. It is a country within the country, but although security there is more or less assured, this region, in the front line of terrorist organizations' positions, should also be totally avoided. The infrastructure is in the worst shape, the state of health is very poor, the roads are very dangerous and insecurity is widespread. If Iraq emerges from its bad situation, travelers will certainly find their way back, and with great interest, even if the extent of the destruction is already a blow to the heart of humanity.

• In Baghdad, the precious National Museum of Archaeology has suffered a lot of damage since the invasion of the American forces of the museum's enclosure, which is considered a very easy target for any attack due to its location in the center of the capital, right in front of the main railway station. More than 20,000 pieces have disappeared as well as thousands of plaques with very important Sumerian engravings. The Abbasid palace, built around 1179, and the al-Mustansiriyah school, a large law college founded in 1232, also transformed into museums, had already been bombed in 1991.

• Not far from the south of Baghdad is the city of Ctesiphon which was the capital of the Persians under the Sassanids and may be the first village in history. It has the largest brick arch, thirty meters high, which has remained in its place for more than 2,000 years. Buttresses were installed in 2007 and the right wing has been partly reconstructed to preserve this unique testimony.

• Samarra, north of Baghdad, had a large mosque with a unique spiral minaret. Following the invasion of Iraq in 2003, the city became the object of numerous attacks between Sunni and Shiite communities. The dome of the Golden Mosque was destroyed by a first attack on February 22, 2006, and another attack hit its two minarets on June 13, 2007.

• The 1991 bombing caused extensive damage to the wonders of world architecture. For example, the ziggurat of Ur (3rd millennium B.C.) was hit by four hundred shells (the Iraqi army had set up planes nearby, prejudging that Abraham's birthplace would not be attacked). The Assourbanipal Palace in Nineveh and a tenth-century church in Mosul also suffered from the conflict. Ancient villages converted into military sites were destroyed, such as Kirkuk, whose traditional houses in the citadel were razed to the ground, or Tell El-Lahm (south of Ur), whose ruins were crushed by bulldozers before being looted.

• In the south of the country, sites such as Larsa (now Senkerah) or Obeïd were completely closed because of the major damage they suffered.

Israel

Israel is a country that does not leave one indifferent. An illegal state for some, a Promised Land for others, this small piece of Middle East land unleashes passions inversely proportional to its size. In practice, Israel is by far the most developed, the richest and, because of its importance, the most militarily powerful country in the region. The omnipresence of the army is a fact, but in practice it is a very safe destination, at least in times of "normal" tensions (which are never neutral), and for the traveler it is an easy and exciting journey ahead. Indeed, Israel is not a land disputed for nothing and the country is home to incredible historical treasures, the most sacred sites of the three great monotheistic religions of humanity and landscapes that can only be described, no pun intended, as biblical. The Neguev Desert is a splendor, the corals of the Red Sea are home to an extraordinary multicolored fauna, the hills around Lake Tiberias evoke an exotic Provence, as for the sunsets of the Dead Sea, they are among the most beautiful on the planet. In front of these natural assets, the cultural attractions have nothing to be ashamed of, quite the contrary. Tel Aviv is aptly nicknamed the New York of the East, the beach and the sun. Nazareth, St. John of Acre, the historic cities are numerous, but of course the highlight is Jerusalem, one of the oldest cities in the world, where religious fervor and the power of symbols will carry away even the most atheist of visitors. Optimal infrastructure, in all areas, ease of travel, the destination remains penalized by a very complicated and volatile geopolitical situation. Before going there, the traveler must keep himself informed of the current state of affairs. Another drawback is that it is an expensive destination.

• Jerusalem holds a prominent place in the Jewish, Christian and Muslim religions. The monuments attached to these different cults are each of extreme importance for believers and make the city an open-air museum. The Temple Esplanade and the Wailing Wall (the only remnant of the Second Temple) are revered by Jews for its proximity to the Holy of Holies, located on Temple Mount. The dome of the Rock of Omar Mosque dates from the seventh century and is the oldest Islamic monument. It stands on the same esplanade as Al-Aqsa Mosque, the largest in the city and sacred to Muslims. For Christians, Christ's tomb at the Holy Sepulcher and the Via Dolorosa, marked by the stages of Calvary, is an important place of pilgrimage. Jerusalem also has an exotic, historic neighborhood where religious influences rub shoulders, as well as historical legacies (traces of the Roman city, including the Cardo).

• The entire Holy Land attracts pilgrims and curious travelers throughout the year. In Nazareth, the Basilica of the Annunciation is the largest church in the Middle East. Around Lake Tiberias many episodes in the life of Jesus took place. In Capernaum, one can meditate on the house of Peter and in the remains of the synagogue where Jesus came to preach. On Mount Tabor, the Basilica of the Transfiguration was built to celebrate the event of the same name.

• In the north of the Mediterranean coast, vestiges dating back to the time of the Templars make Saint Jean d'Acre a city classified as a World Heritage Site. Slightly to the south is Mount Carmel, which overlooks the waves and is home to the Mausoleum of the Báb, a very important place in Baha'i, in the student city of *Haifa*.

• The Dead Sea straddles the territories of Israel and the West Bank. It is 400 meters below sea level and its density is such that a human being can float there without any problem. Its high concentration of minerals is universally known for its therapeutic virtues. Nearby, you can visit the fortress of Masada where the remains of the constructions of Herod the Great are located.

• In the south of Israel, the Neguev conceals several geographical curiosities. Three large cirques (the Ramon crater, the large crater and the small crater), the red gorges, the pastel-colored stones and the work of erosion embellish the ancient Nabataean Perfume Road that crosses it.

* Eilat, at the southern tip of the country, is very popular for its climate and its exceptional sunshine, but especially for its diving sites. The coral reefs and the thousands of extraordinary fish make its international reputation.

Japan

Impossible to evoke the destination Japan without talking about a change of scenery. This is the common thread of a trip to the land of the rising sun because Japan is a world that does not share much with the West except for the cultural influences that it sends there, manga, anime, video games ... The motivations for a stay in Japan are multiple but they very often pass first through this cultural base that attracts travelers. On the spot they then discover the futuristic grandeur of Tokyo, to be classified among the craziest cities on the planet, the beauty of the Kyoto temples or the beautiful landscapes of the country with the perfect cone of Mount Fuji in mind. The country is neither easy nor complicated to explore, you just have to leave your landmarks and habits behind, and be carried away by the overall experience of the destination. The language is a border in itself, and the same goes for the gastronomy and customs, but it is also what makes Japan so attractive. The exoticism is even found in the basic infrastructure of tourism such as hotels, which often have nothing to do with what we know in Europe. A successful trip to Japan is the prerogative of a visitor who will not try to master everything at all costs. The culture shock and the very high cost of the trip are the two obstacles to Japanese exploration, which otherwise proves to be very well organized. A country of tradition and modernity, Japan is a fascinating destination with an unsuspected diversity that surprises visitors, from the snowy mountains of the north to the tropical islands of the Okinawa archipelago.

* Now extinct, Mount Fuji remains the symbol of the Japanese nation and an extremely popular place of pilgrimage for all Japanese, whether Shinto or Buddhist. In the center of the country, it is bordered to the north by the five Fujigoko lakes which offer a remarkable view of the volcano, at its feet lies the Aokigahara forest. The ascent of Mount Fuji is relatively easy, the four routes give access to historical sites such as Murayama or Yoshida. The descent is through trails covered with volcanic ash that can be used by mountain bikes. Until the end of May, Mt. Fuji offers various ski touring routes on its northeast slope.

* Mount Aso is the largest volcano in Japan, but also one of the most active. Its caldera is one of the largest in the world. Many tourists visit it every year for its thermal areas and viewpoints despite the danger posed by its fumes and projections.

* The Japanese Alps consist of a chain of volcanic peaks that runs from north to south through the central and largest part of Honshu. Their beauty and irregular structure have often made them compare to the European Alps. The northern part is in the heart of the Chubu-Sangaku National Park. Nearby, Nagano is the resort that hosted the 1998 Winter Olympics. The very cold winters on the island of Hokkaido in the north of the country also give the opportunity to practice winter sports and ice sculpture (Sapporo Snow Festival).

* Matsushima, an archipelago on the Sendaï side, is one of the most beautiful landscapes in Japan. 260 pine covered islands are scattered in the bay where a cruise is more than recommended. The islands of Ogi-ga-tani, Tomi-yama, Otaka-mori and Tamon-zan are the most famous. It is possible to take a ferry from Shiogama to Matsushima to admire the islands from the sea.

* In Kyushu, the island in the south of the country, is the city of Beppu famous for its 3000 hot springs with extremely varied properties. Twenty minutes by bus from the city, you will be confronted with the eight hells including the Umi Jigokua of boiling water, the Chi-no-ike Jigoku with its red color or the Tatsumaki Jigoku and its powerful geyser.

* The sacred sites and pilgrimage routes located in the Kii Mountains have been declared a World Heritage Site. Three sacred sites of Shintoism and Buddhism, Yoshino and Omine, Kumano Sanzan, and Koyasan, are connected by pilgrimage routes to the ancient capitals of Nara and Kyoto. There is no better place to commune with nature.

* The Okinawa archipelago, in the extreme south-west of the country, is the region of the seaside vacations of the Japanese. These islands offer a tropicalized version of traditional Japan. Beaches, hot springs, and the seabed are the main attractions.

* Tokyo is known worldwide for its ultramodernity. But in the same city where skyscrapers such as the Tokyo Tower or the Akihabara Electronic Town have grown, there are many Shinto shrines and traditional Buddhist temples, particularly in the districts of Chiyoda, Shibuya and Minato. The Imperial Palace is very close to Ginza, the shopping and entertainment district. Other monuments are worth a visit such as the Meiji Shrine and the Asakura Temple. The Tokyo National Museum will make its small effect with the fans of Japanese traditional art.

* Kyoto is considered the cultural center of the country because of its 2000 temples (including the Golden Pavilion), its palaces, its Zen gardens, its architecture. In Uji, a neighboring city, is the Byodo-in Temple and the Ujibashi Bridge. The nearby Otsu is part of the same group of historical monuments of ancient Kyoto.

* Japanese castles were built of wood, only three have survived until today. In Himeji, there is Himeji-jo Castle, known for its white exterior color. The one of Matsumoto, near Tokyo, is famous for its black color. Kumamoto Castle on Kyushu Island is the most fortified castle in the country.

* Buddhism is very present in Japan, and like Shintoism, it gave birth to many places of worship. The most important temple in the country (and the largest wooden temple in the world) is located on the sacred mount of Koya, south of Nara. In the area, there are many inns temples in the area that will accommodate you for the night. Nearby is Horyu-ji Temple, the oldest wooden construction in the world. Buddha is also very present in Kamakura, a seaside town with a long and busy beach. In the Seto Inland Sea, Itsukushima (or Miyajima) Island is famous for its temple and its famous floating torii (gate).

* In Hiroshima, the ruins of Genbaku Dome and the Peace Museum bear witness to the events of August 6, 1945. Numerous testimonies related to the bomb (objects, photos, scale models of the city, survivors' testimonies, paintings...) make it a very striking visit.

Jordan

The Kingdom of Jordan is a very beautiful destination and certainly the only one in the tormented Middle East region that offers at the same time regional authenticity, infrastructure and above all security and political stability for an easy trip in good conditions. This country of colors, Red Sea, pink city of Petra or white of Amman, ochre of the desert, is a symbol of the magic of the East. Very hospitable, the Jordanians welcome visitors with open arms, which pleasantly changes the sometimes tense atmospheres found in their neighbors. Over the centuries, the country has been home to many civilizations, Canaanite, Greek, Roman, Byzantine, but it was the Nabateans who left Jordan its most remarkable site, the fantastic troglodytic city of Petra. It is by far the tourist engine of the country, but the kingdom is not limited to this destination and offers many other attractions, from the coral reefs of the Red Sea to Aqaba, through the superb desert landscapes of Wadi Rum, the ancient city of Jerash or the hypnotizing Dead Sea and its spectacular sunsets. Complete and rather simple, as much to access it as to apprehend it, the destination must be at the top of the list of those who are looking for a beautiful trip in the exoticism of the East.

* Petra is an ancient troglodytic city in the heart of a basin bordered by mountains. Even the pink or red sandstone cliffs, numerous monuments with monumental facades make this 3 km long rocky cirque, the highlight of a stay in Jordan. Funerary temples and tombs bear witness to the Nabataean kingdom (4th - 2nd century B.C.). Take the long parade of the Sîq to reach the most famous of these constructions: the Khazneh. Nearby, 800 steps will take you to Deir Monastery, the largest of the buildings on the site.

* The ancient city of Gerasa is today surrounded by the modern city of Jerash in the north of the country. At first Roman (forum, theater, temples of Artemis and Zeus), it then had a Christian influence (churches of St. John the Baptist, St.

George, and Saints Como and Damien). The sand that covered these ruins for many centuries and the restoration work of the last few years have made it possible to offer today's visitor a sumptuous spectacle.

• In Al-Karak, there is a famous fortified castle dating back to the Crusades, the Moabite Krak. Around the site is the town where many 19th century Ottoman buildings have been restored. Along the road of the kings which runs along the western border of the country, you will also find the mosaics of Madaba.

• In the Jordanian desert there are many castles that served as second homes to the Umayyad caliphs. Qusair Amra's frescoes make him one of the most famous.

• The Wadi Rum desert lies to the south, on the border with Saudi Arabia. Its sandstone djebels ranging from black to light yellow, with a predominance of red, including the one called the Seven Pillars of Wisdom, stand tall and sublime the most beautiful desert in the Near East.

• The Jordan River is famous for its waters that baptized Christ. On the left bank, a tower near the north shore of the Dead Sea, is the place where St. John the Baptist preached: Bethany. The cave itself was transformed into a church with a drinking water canal running through it and can be visited today.

• Mount Nebo is also a famous place in terms of religion. From its summit, Moses contemplated the Promised Land and it is traditionally the place of his death. From these heights in western Jordan, you too can observe the course of the Jordan River, and the lands across the river to Jericho, or even Jerusalem on a clear day.

• The Dead Sea is about 50 kilometers west of Amman. Its warm, very salty waters and therapeutic mud have attracted tourists since ancient times. The mountains to the east and the hills of Jerusalem to the west offer a superb panorama.

• Around Aqaba, in the south of the country, the Red Sea offers underwater bottoms rich in coral reefs and multicolored fish. North of the border with Saudi Arabia, Yamaneh is known to be one of the most beautiful spots in the world.

Kazakhstan

Whoever announces that he is going on a trip to Kazakhstan will often get some surprised remarks in return. The destination is totally unknown in Europe, and its tourist image is close to nothing. This very large country (five times the size of France), which is further away than we imagine (to the east we are on the borders of China), gained its independence from the USSR in 1991 and like all former Soviet republics, it is marked by this past (especially in its "massive" architecture). Nevertheless, Kazakhstan is rich in particularity: Cultural on the one hand with its population descended from nomadic horsemen who knew how to adapt to its immense steppes between West and East. Geographical on the other hand. Overlooking the steppes, forests, lakes and desert, the Celestial Mountains or Tian Shan form a mythical landscape. The Khan Tengri culminates at more than 7000 meters and is one of the most difficult climbs in the world, but very experienced trekking adventurers can reach its base camp in one of the most beautiful sites of Central Asia. The Altai and Zailiyskiy Alatau Mountains are easier to access and there open their arms to hikers who are not necessarily experts. The latter find in Kazakhstan a very beautiful playground. The country also offers the attraction of the Baikonur cosmodrome, the Soviet Cape Canaveral, which offers guided tours and allows to attend, by organizing oneself, the space rocket launches. In practical terms, the country has an average standard of living and access is fairly simple, especially since visas are no longer necessary for tourist stays of the French. On the other hand the sanitary situation is not excellent without being alarming (non-drinking water) and the infrastructures are rather average in general. Transportation in the country must be well prepared, trains are not considered very safe and airlines are blacklisted. A destination that has potential for the somewhat discerning traveler, but is very confidential and expensive.

• If you don't let yourself be fooled by the imposing Soviet architecture of Almaty, you will enjoy strolling around this airy city, where parks, gardens and squares occupy an important place. The downtown park is dominated by one of the tallest wooden buildings in the world, the Orthodox Zenkov Cathedral, which remarkably did not need a single nail to be built. It is now a concert hall, which is not anecdotal in this city where culture is well established with many theaters and museums.

• In the south of the country is Djamboul (formerly Taraz), one of the trading cities that dotted the Silk Road. All the archaeological finds relating to it have been gathered in the Museum of Regional History. In the surroundings of the city, you will have the opportunity to meet a multitude of old forts, castles and mausoleums. Those of Aisha Bibi (12th century) and Babadji Khatoun (11th century) have preserved beautiful decorative architectural ornaments, such as mud bricks, covered with more than fifty different patterns.

• The most famous mausoleum of the country is located in Turkestan, still in the south of the country, it is the mausoleum of Khoja Ahmed Yasavi, the first Kazakh heritage to have been registered in the World Heritage of Humanity. Unfinished, this Timurid construction is the best preserved that has come down to us. Its domes, including the largest ever built in Central Asia, have a beautiful decoration of green and golden tiles.

• A cable car line connects downtown Almaty to the top of Mount Kok Tobe. From this place of relaxation in altitude, one can admire the panorama of Almaty and the Ala-Taou Mountains. The Olympic winter sports resort Medeo has a huge ice rink. Built for the training of Soviet athletes, today it is one of the favorite gathering places of the inhabitants of Almaty. 500 meters upstream, one can ski from November to April on the slopes of Chimbulak, the most famous resort in Central Asia. But the ski fans will be able to be satisfied in all Kazakhstan, all specialized travel agencies offer to discover the mountains of the country by helisky.

• The surroundings of Chimbulak, Medeo and Kokshoky are also a paradise for hikers and mountaineers. The valleys of the Tien-Chan mountain range and, to the north of these, the Zailiyskyi Alatau mountain range are also ideal for trekking and discovering unspoiled nature. Between the two regions, the desert expanses of Sari-Ichik Otraou will allow you to ride your horse to meet the Kazakh nomads.

• Still in the same region, the river Ili will welcome your rafting or canoeing trips between lakes Balkhach and Qapshaghay. While the former is not an ideal resort due to the many industrial complexes on its banks, the latter is more pleasant. But the prettiest lake in the country is the turquoise lake of Bolshoye Almatinskoye. Surrounded by majestic ridges, it extends its kilometer not far from Almaty.

- The Charyn canyon, 200 km east of Almaty, was carved by the river of the same name. The landscapes there are splendid, even recalling those of the American Grand Canyon. The valley of the castles is the part where the rock formations are the most surprising.

Kuwait

Gulf War and oil, these are about the only images we have of Kuwait in the West. This small emirate, located between Iraq and Saudi Arabia, presents the same physiognomy as its southern neighbors, Qatar or Bahrain. It also has more or less the same attractions, a large desert (monotonous but still remarkable), rather beautiful beaches (with luxury hotels), a very modern capital rich in buildings, and great follies (amusement parks, unusual architecture). Mostly frequented by business travelers, Kuwait is not really on the list of destinations in the region, largely exceeded by the reputation of Abu Dhabi or especially Dubai. Nevertheless, for those who appreciate the genre (and the scorching or even hot temperatures), Kuwait is in the same register, but more discreet.

• Buildings, large hotels, avenues, large parks... Kuwait City is home to the majority of government services as well as the most important banks and companies in the country. Don't miss to go up to the top floors of the three futuristic towers which are the symbol of Kuwait City. The Great Mosque and its two blue bulbs are also worth a visit.

• Several amusement parks offer a wide range of entertainment such as Aqua Park, the first and largest water park in the Arab Gulf region, and Entertainment city, one of the largest amusement parks in the Middle East located in the Al-Doha region, 20 km from Kuwait city.

• On the coast, various water sports can be practiced (be careful, ask for information, as there may be mines). Of the nine islands added to the territory, only Failakka is inhabited. One goes there from Salmiya by dhows. It contains three archaeological sites: a habitat of the IInd millennium before J.-C., a Hellenistic fortress and the vestiges of a paleochristian basilica.

• Neither mountains nor rivers, the flat country of the Gulf is mostly made of a desert that slopes gently down to the sea. You must see it in spring, when it is covered with vegetation and camel races are organized.

Kyrgyzstan

Kyrgyzstan (or Kyrgyzstan) is a small country in Central Asia, a former Soviet land dominated by mountains and the horses that populate them. In this adventure destination, which despite its modest size evokes above all the great outdoors, live the Kyrgyz, semi-nomadic, renowned for their life in yurts, simple and without materialism, and for their extreme hospitality (please indicate immediately that you do not drink alcohol if you do not wish to spend the whole of your stay drinking free vodka). They are the first attraction for discovering the country, as well as the spectacular mountain scenery. Nomadism, horses and mountains are the determining marks of the destination. Culture, environment, everything is very exotic, and the trip is not really complicated, without being within the reach of all travelers. The infrastructure is still limited, the local situation is not very stable, and you have to know how to manage the omnipresent corruption, so the majority of travelers go there through an agency. Curious travelers really need to consider this destination, especially hiking enthusiasts.

• To the east, the Yssik Kul Lake forms a small inland sea at 1600 meters above sea level. It is the second largest mountain lake in the world after Titicaca. It became a popular holiday resort during the Soviet period and continues to welcome tourists to its shores today. The northern resorts, such as Cholpon-Ata, are frequented in summer by tourists from border countries. The southern shore, less equipped, offers wild and picturesque landscapes of great beauty, as well as easy access on foot or on horseback to the summer pastures (which are populated by shepherds' yurts from the beginning of the transhumance) and the high plateaus located above 4000 m.

• Karakol is located at the tip of the Yssik Kul Lake and is the last town before the Karkara Pass which borders Kazakhstan. Apart from the Orthodox church and the mosque-pagoda, both built entirely of wood, the town is also a good logistic base for mountaineering expeditions to the Khan-Tengri massif.

• Lake Son Koul, located in the Tian Shan massif, is another much smaller mountain lake (3016 meters) which is only accessible through passes at more than 3100 m. Every summer, its shores serve as pasture for more than 50,000 head of cattle and one meets a population with an authentic way of life and a surprisingly friendly welcome. The beauty of the panorama on the mountain ridges and the richness of the wildlife make it an exceptional place.

• The village of Arslanbob is located at the foot of the sumptuous Babach-Ata mountain range, and is a starting point for hiking excursions in the heart of an immense walnut tree massif. Immediately near Arslanbob, two very impressive waterfalls are easily accessible. The village and the waterfalls are the site of an Uzbek pilgrimage, organized around the tomb of Arslanbob, a revered figure in Uzbek Islam.

• The Burana Tower is the subject of an excursion from Bishkek, the capital. This Qarakhanide minaret is all that remains of the ancient city of Balasagun, a former stop on the Silk Road.

• The archaeological site of Saimaluu-Tash gathers the largest collection of petroglyphs in Central Asia. It is located near the Kugart Pass, northeast of the Ferghana ridges, in the Kazarman district, Jalal-Abad region, in a gorge, at an altitude of 3000 meters. More than 90,000 symbolic drawings have been engraved on the basalt stones of the site.

• In the region of Naryn, is the site of Tach Rabat. This important stone fortress was a Nestorian temple of the tenth century before being transformed into a caravanserai that served as a stopover for travelers on the Silk Road. Four kilometers away is the Chatyr Kul lake adjacent to the Chinese border.

• Osh has been a trading city since antiquity, a stopover on the Silk Road, located at the eastern end of the Ferghana Valley. It still shelters in its center one of the most famous markets of Central Asia. Before going there, ask about possible tensions with Uzbekistan ékistanbecause the region is sometimes unstable.

Laos

In the Southeast Asian region, Laos is the least known country. Away from the main tourist routes, and in the shadow of its imposing neighbors, Thailand in the first place, Laos is a very poor but very welcoming country, where the pace of things is as quiet as that of the Mekong, its backbone. The adventure is there, but there is nothing perilous here. Its landscapes are soft prints, between rice fields and karstic reliefs, punctuated with temples and elephants. After all, the country calls itself the kingdom of a million elephants. Endowed with a well marked culture and a strong identity, Laos still reveals some vestiges of the French colonization. Vientiane, the capital, still looks like a provincial prefecture and you can see bakeries and pétanque players. Nevertheless, the true base of Laos remains Buddhism, particularly in its former capital, Luang Prabang, the country's flagship destination. The trip itself is not very complicated but it requires time and a good dose of letting go. The infrastructures are deficient and we are a thousand miles away from the well established circuits of neighboring Thailand but as everywhere in the region, the kindness of the population is the guarantee of a quiet stay. A very beautiful destination for the curious.

• Luang Prabang is the former royal capital of Laos and has retained its original appearance. Symbol of Buddhism in Asia, a third of the city is occupied by temples and the streets are filled with thousands of monks dressed in simple yellow-orange togas. The glass decorations of Vat Xieng Thong, the carved doors of Vat That Luang, the ornamental figures of Vat Siphutthabat, the leaf gilding of Vat Mai, the golden arrows and sanctuaries of Vat Chom Si... have made the city a World Heritage Site. The many markets also make the wealth of the city.

• By taking a slow-boat (motorized pirogue) from Luang Prabang to the north, you will come across the two caves of Pak Ou, an important place of pilgrimage. More than 4,500 Buddhas were deposited there by pilgrims.

• East of Luang Prabang lies the province of Xieng Khouang where the famous Plain of Jars is located. Imposing megalithic vases, whose meaning and origin are not yet fully elucidated, dot the fields of the region.

• If the small town of Vang Vieng, located between Luang Prabang and Vientiane, is of little interest by itself, its surroundings are really worth the detour. Its sugar loaf mountains are full of amazing caves: Tham Jang and Tham Phu Kam to the west and the Tham Sang triangle to the east. The Nam Song River which borders the city is descended by tubing or kayaking.

• On the banks of the Mekong River, Vientiane, the capital, also has some beautiful monasteries (Pha That Louang, Vat Phra Kèo, Vat Ong Teu, Vat Simuong...). The wooden houses and colonial villas recall the double cultural heritage of the country and will charm the visitor.

• Between Paské and Paksong, the Boloven Plateau is home to several coffee farms where hikes to meet the ethnic minorities of the region are punctuated by tastings. In the heart of the lush forest, the Tad Fan and Tat Yuang waterfalls offer walkers views and natural pools as a reward.

• Further south on the Mekong River, between Pakse and Champassak, you will find the Si Phan Don district, the "four thousand islands", where the Khone Falls and their rapids divide the river to form dozens of small islands and beautify the landscape. Keep your eyes open, you can see the giant Mekong catfish or the Irrawaddy dolphin gliding through the river's eddies.

• Just over the border with Cambodia is the Vat Phou Temple, a Hindu temple built by the Khmers overlooking a hill in the Pasak Mountains. In addition to the beauty of the ruins and the surrounding area, the superb view of the Mekong River offered by the site will delight all visitors.

Lebanon

On its small territory, Lebanon concentrates a wide range of landscapes and attractions, from the shores of the Mediterranean to the snowy mountains, through the vestiges of History. In times of stability, the country is one of the most attractive destinations in the Middle East. Unfortunately, stability is not the strong point of local geopolitics and the country has been through long years of war. Nevertheless, Lebanon has serious assets to offer to travelers.

* Beirut has recovered from the war to become one of the trendiest capitals of the East. You don't have to look far to discover the stigmata of a tormented past (and present), but the image of a ravaged city is to be put away.

* The Mediterranean coast that stretches above Beirut offers the most trendy spots with seaside resorts such as Jounié or Byblos. All along, the mountains drop down to the sea, offering a panoramic view of rocky coasts and colorful sunsets. Byblos is also known for its medieval walls with barrels of ancient columns and its archaeological site where there are ruins of all the populations that have inhabited the area since its foundation.

* Tripoli had the reputation of being the peaceful city par excellence. Today, it is not recommended for travelers because of the great local instability. Its medieval history, its Mamluk architecture (whose jewels are the Taynal mosque, the Al-Qartawiya madrasa and the Al-Burtasiya madrasa...) and the Arab charm of its alleys and souks will have to wait for the moment before being admired again. The St. Gilles citadel erected by the Crusaders in the 12th century will continue to watch over them in the meantime.

* Heading west from Tripoli, the road winds through a sumptuous mountain landscape, along spectacular gorges. Olive groves, vineyards and red-roofed villages make the whole thing shine. The town of Bcharré is home to the Gibran Museum and the artist himself is buried in the old monastery overlooking the town. Downhill and cross-country skiing can be practiced in the region in winter. On the way to the Cedars, the road crosses the last remaining Lebanese forest of biblical cedars. Do not hesitate to make a detour to the Qadisha cave. Superb hiking trails will lead you to the tombs of the first Maronite patriarchs and to monasteries dug into the rock.

* The Orontes River crosses the desert plateau that connects the Lebanese Bekaa to Syria by digging a real canyon 50 to 90 m deep. At the source, Aïn es Zarqa, water gushes spontaneously from an artesian well of the most beautiful effect. Further down, on the slopes of Mount Lebanon, is the site of the Afqa cave. From the depths of the reddish rock escapes the Nahr Ibrahim whose waters cradled the loves of Adonis and Venus. Nearby, the 6 km of galleries and concretions of the Jeita cave can be visited by boat, an extraordinary experience.

* Baalbeck was the most important city of Roman Syria in ancient times. A remarkable ensemble remains, with the temples of Jupiter, Bacchus, and Venus displaying their sumptuous columns. This acropolis is one of the largest in the world, and its ruins suggest the importance of the place during the reign of the Caesars.

* Tyre, south of the Mediterranean coast, also preserves important Roman remains. On the peninsula, a well-preserved road passes under a monumental arch and runs along an aqueduct and several hundred stone or marble sarcophagi. The site, surrounded by the sea on all sides, is sumptuous, but is in a risky area that is not safe from Israeli artillerymen. From Tyre to the north, one passes by the 'Ain Babuq spring, then by the 'Ain Habrian hot spring, and finally arrives at the Nahr el Qasmiye, the lower part of the Nahr el Litani.

* Sidon, or Saida today, is largely built on an island and offers a multitude of sites to visit. The construction of the temple of Eshmoun dates back to the seventh century B.C., the castle of the Sea and that of the Land were built by the Crusaders, while the fortress Khan el-Franj, the caravanserai of the French, was put into operation in the seventeenth century.

* The village of Beiteddine, a little further north, is famous for its palace of the Emir Bashir. The vast courtyard, the sculptures, the woodwork and mosaics and the hammam make it an exceptional place that really deserves a visit.

Malaysia

Malaysia is made up of two very distinct territories, each of which responds to a different travel desire. Adventurers will choose East Malaysia north of Borneo while more "classic" tourists will head for Peninsular (or Western) Malaysia south of Thailand. In either case, Malaysia is a country that offers travellers an explosion of nature.

EAST MALAYSIA :

- Not far from Sandankan is the Sepilok Sanctuary, a rehabilitation center for orphaned or injured orangutans. At several times during the day, visitors will be able to approach the food platforms and see the ballet of the Lords of the Jungle. The Semenggoh center in Sarawak is renowned for the same reasons.

- Mount Kinabalu, at 4,095 meters, is one of the highest peaks in Southeast Asia. Different trekking possibilities will give you the opportunity to discover its phenomenal biological diversity including carnivorous plants and orchids. Its ascent will lead you (along with many other hikers) to a gigantic granite slab, gently sloping and overhung by superb spikes. If the weather is good, you will be offered to your eyes a panorama of the forest and the Crocker Massif.

- Not far from Mount Kinabalu are the Poring Hot Springs which are actually large bathtubs where water flows very slowly from a tap. It is rather the surrounding forests that are worth the detour, as they hide the largest flower in the world: the rafflesia.

- Just minutes from the town of Kota Kinabalu, on the northwest coast of Sabah, the five islands of Tunku Abdul Rahman Park are famous for their coral reefs and the varied species that live there. Gaya, Manukan, Mamutik, Sapi and Sulug also have beautiful white sand beaches where many tourists flock.

- The island of Sipadan, in the Sulawesi Sea, is one of the richest marine habitats in the world. The island is surrounded by vertical walls plunging to 600 meters and serves as a sanctuary for many turtles. Became a nature reserve in 2005, it is no longer possible to stay there and you will have to reside on one of the neighboring islands to discover this spot.

- The Gungung Mulu National Park is famous for its exceptional tropical fauna and flora, but especially for its caves. Indeed, immense cavities populated with limestone concretions and impressive colonies of bats await the explorers. The Sarawak Cave is the largest natural closed enclosure in the world.

- Those who are fascinated by the underworld will be overwhelmed by this region, for nearby on the west coast are the Niah Caves where human remains dating back 40,000 years have been found. The site is also famous for its many swallow's nests which the Chinese are fond of.

- The jungle of Sarawak is part of the primary forest of Borneo and the flora and fauna are equally diverse. Sumptuous trekking tours will allow you to go from discovery to discovery. Another way to meet the region and its inhabitants is to take a pirogue on one of the brown rivers that criss-cross the forest (such as the Rajang River). Do not hesitate to stay in one of these community long houses that border the banks (long-house) where the Ibans tribe will be happy to welcome you.

- The coast of the South China Sea has recently seen the traditional wooden villages on stilts making room for large resorts, the most famous of which are located around Damai Beach. Following the coast northward, you can stop in Brunei, an Islamic monarchy landlocked in Malaysia where oil wealth contrasts with the rest of the coast.

WEST MALAYSIA :

- The center of this part of Malaysia is the Cameron Highlands from which the panoramas become exceptional. The Taman Negara Park is home to an astonishing variety of flora and fauna. Orchids, caves (Gua Telinga) and waterfalls (Lata Berkoh) are there. Continuing eastward, it is the turn of the tea plantations to sublimate the landscape.

* Kuala Lumpur is a green and orderly city whose suburbs extend as far as the eye can see to the sea. From the towers of the city center, you can admire the patchwork, but don't forget to visit especially the great mosque, the Sultan-Abdoussamad palace and the old train station with its Moorish Indian architecture. Away from the city are the Batu Caves and their Hindu shrines.

* The mixture of Dutch and Portuguese colonization in Melaka, to which a strong Chinese presence is added, makes it a particularly interesting southern city to visit. Do not miss the huge Chinese cemetery of Bukit China where some monuments are true masterpieces.

* In the other state capitals, such as Kuala Kangsar (Perak) or Kota Bharu (Kelantan), the sultans' palaces are always admirable and the different districts offer endless possibilities for strolls.

* The island of Penang is located on the northwest coast of the country. If its capital, Georgetown, is one of the most active cities in the country, one can easily find some peace and quiet by taking the funicular that climbs from the Air Hitam district. At the top, the colonial houses, the lush vegetation and the altitude offer a haven of peace to visitors.

* The tourist success of this island since the 70s has rubbed off on the other beaches and archipelagos of the coast. It must be said that the beaches of Malaysia, and particularly on the islands, are perfectly representative of the clichés of tropical paradise, where turquoise waters, white sands and lush jungles often mix. Langkawi and Pangkor are two good examples where the high-end equipment and shopping possibilities know how to delight the crowds. The east coast is not to be outdone and offers the same kind of pleasures, although less developed, on Tioman Island or the Perhentian Archipelago for example.

Maldives

The Maldives is a true paradise for divers from all over the world where the coral beds and the extraordinary clarity of the waters offer a magnificent setting for the ballet of multicolored fish. **Of the** 1199 islands, only 202 are inhabited and less than half of them are accessible to tourists. The dominant concept of tourism in the archipelago is that of the hotel islands. These complexes, often luxurious, isolate the visitor from the locals but plunge him in return into idyllic landscapes. For some it is paradise and for others it is a type of travel that they do not even consider, it is up to you to choose your camp. The 2004 tsunami severely damaged this prosperous economy by drowning for a few hours nearly 95% of the territory and some islands could not be completely rehabilitated. Nevertheless, this destination continues to be a dream of high-end idleness and an ideal choice for many honeymooners. In the paradisiacal picture of the destination, one should not pass over in silence a rigorous political and religious drift which, for some years now, has made more and more foreign tourists react.

* Male is a surprising capital city entirely built on an atoll with a large reinforcement of embankments, dikes and sand drawn from the ocean floor. Overpopulated (it is home to 2/3 of the Maldives' inhabitants), the city is unique of its kind. The pleasant park of the sultan, the great Friday mosque and the Singapore Bazaar market are pleasant places to visit. Male is the only place in the archipelago where you can be an independent traveller and not get ruined for good.

* The three atolls closest to the capital, North Male, South Male and Ari, are home to many club hotels without losing their wild side. Diving sites as in the rest of the country are great and surfing is a pleasure on the North Male atoll.

* Diving is indeed the primary activity in the Maldives. Whatever your hotel island, numerous outings will be proposed to you to discover the seabed and its inhabitants. A wreck like the one of Halaveli (a cargo ship sunk in 1991) in the North Ari atoll is only one example among dozens of others, not to mention the fact that you just have to leave the beach with your mask and snorkel to be amazed. Stingrays, moray eels, turtles and all kinds of fish are waiting for you in water with ideal temperature and clear as it is hard to imagine.

* For those who want to vary the pleasures, all water activities are possible. Catamarans, windsurfing, water skiing...

There is something for everyone. Fishing, especially deep-sea fishing, is also one of the activities that will be proposed to you and you will be able to taste your catches in the evening. On land, white sandy beaches, jungle gardens and luxurious spa will delight those who stay at the quay.

- In the south of the archipelago, on the atoll of Addu, is Seenu, the second largest city island of the Maldives. It contrasts with the rest of the country because of the English influence still present today at the very heart of its culture. It is a good starting point to meet the traditional populations of the atoll.

- Fuamulaku is another island apart because of the fertility of its land. All kinds of tropical fruits grow there, which is not the case in the rest of the archipelago. Located outside the tourist area, it will be difficult to find a seaplane or hydrospeed to get there. Nevertheless, more and more mini-cruises are developing to allow you to go from one fishermen's atoll to another and discover a little more of these paradisiac confetti lost in the Indian Ocean.

Mongolia

A trip to Mongolia usually does not leave you unchanged. If there is one country that symbolizes the great outdoors, it is this one. Mongolia is immense and immensely deserted. The shock is all the greater with the capital Ulaanbaatar, its skyscrapers, shopping malls and huge yurt shantytowns where former nomads come to run aground on the lights of modern society. Nevertheless, many Mongols still live like their ancestors, with the pride of Genghis Khan rooted in their hearts. A people of a kindness as infinite as the landscapes they inhabit, Mongols are the authentic highlight of the destination. We discover their way of life, in yurts and with their families, accompanied by their animals and especially their horses. The trip to Mongolia is not always easy, the distances are long, the infrastructures are not very developed, but for the prepared and curious visitor it is a beautiful adventure that is quite feasible.

- Ulaanbaatar is a capital city that is both timeless and totally surprisingly modern. The roads leading to it could be more accurately described as tracks, the Soviet-inspired high-rise buildings, surrounded by brand new buildings and luxurious shopping centers, quickly give way to yurt neighborhoods all around the city, where cars still mingle with stray goats and cows. Two buildings stand out from the rest: the Tibetan Buddhist monastery of Gandantegchinlin and the winter palace of Bogdo Khan. From the surrounding mountains, the view of the capital is surprising and disconcerting.

- The four peaks surrounding the capital are considered holy places. Tsetseegum, Chingeltei, Songino Khairkhan and Bayansurkh are all four suitable for hiking. A particularly rich fauna lives in these larch forests where you can come face to face with an ibex or sable. From what remains of the Manzshir Khiid Monastery near Zuunmod, you can climb Tsetseegum Uul, the highest and most spectacular peak of the Bogdkhan range.

- Taking the Trans-Mongolian Railway from Ulaanbaatar to Beijing can be a way to discover the landscapes of the Gobi Desert. Treks and horseback riding are also a good way to become one with the landscape and to meet the Kazakh nomads. Covering a third of the country's surface, this desert is one of the largest deserts in the world. We find there heterogeneous landscapes where plains, mountain ranges and dunes succeed one another, all under a blue sky and a brilliant sun 250 days a year. One can meet bears or rarer animals such as the snow leopard or Przewalski's horse. Przewalski's horse has also been reintroduced in protected areas of the Khustain Reserve.

- The horse is one of the emblems of the country. Although Przewalski's horse is completely wild and cannot really be approached, the equestrian tradition is flourishing with the arrival of new visitors. The Orkhon valley offers a magnificent setting for hikes along the water's edge. Don't miss the ten meter wide and 20 meter high waterfall formed by one of its tributaries, the Ulaan Tsutgalan. It is a popular destination for tourists, as is Khövsgöl Nuur Lake, a high altitude lake of breathtaking beauty. 775 km northwest of Ulaanbaatar, it is a sacred place where yaks, ibexes, elk and sheep graze. Its waters are full of fish and if in winter the trucks cross them frozen, in summer they offer the possibility of kayaking.

- In 1220, Genghis Khan established the capital of his vast empire at Karakorum, whose traces today border the city of

Kharkhorin in the province of Övörkhangai. On its ruins (and with its stones) was built the monastery of Erdene Zuu which has crossed centuries, ravages and communism to reach us. Another important monastery in Mongolia is Amarbayasgalant Khiid. Its beauty is accessible only if the doors are open to you (some agencies have contacts, the most resourceful travelers can ask there).

Myanmar (Burma)

Myanmar is the new name given by the military junta to Burma when it took power in 1989, referring to the country's mythical former inhabitants and breaking with its recent history. Authoritarian regime, the State of Myanmar is ruled by a military dictatorship. However, and against all expectations, the country has opened up abruptly in recent years, allowing the development of a real tourist industry. However, tourism is still preserved, still far from the development of neighboring countries (Thailand, Malaysia). Several states of the country remain inaccessible to foreigners, and it is better to be well informed of the situation before undertaking a visit. However, travelers who discover the country generally come back enchanted, because the magic of Asia operates intact there, the beauty of the temples is incomparable, and the kindness of its people could one day take away the title of "country of smiles" from its Thai neighbor.

• Rangoon (Yangon) has the largest number of colonial buildings of any city in Southeast Asia. Its Bogyoke Aung San market was built by the British and is today one of the must-see places. Its interior paved streets will take you from surprise to surprise. Built on a very strict plan, the city is especially worth visiting for its pagodas including the sumptuous Shwedagon pagoda and its golden dome, the Sule pagoda, and the Botahtaung pagoda. If bicycles, motorcycles and rickshaws are forbidden in the city itself, cars are starting to be more and more numerous. Since 2007, Rangoon is no longer the capital of the country in favor of the city of Naypyidaw located more in the center of the country, in the division of Mandalay.

• Bagan (formerly Pagan) is a city of the same province and was the ancient capital of the kingdom of Pagan, destroyed by the Mongols in 1287. These 5000 religious buildings, including 2000 pagodas, follow one another over 42 km and are impressive. Thatbyinnyu is the highest monument of the site and the most representative. Pagodas, monasteries, temples and stupas testify of this ancestral Buddhism, but still very alive.

• Many other cities in the country have beautiful pagodas. In the southwest, Sagaing is a religious and monastic center. A 90-ton bell (the largest in the world still capable of ringing) was transferred there from Mingun where the largest pagoda ever built was destroyed by an earthquake in the 19th century. In Pegou, in addition to very old pagodas, the Buddha of Shwethalyaung, 60 meters long, has been lying since the 10th century. In Mandalay, further north, the teak Shwenandaw Monastery is the only remnant of the royal palace that was bombed by the British during World War II.

• One of the most beautiful natural sites in the country is Inle Lake and its floating islets in the mountains of Shan State. Its calm waters at an altitude of 1,328 m are crossed by the boats of the Intha fishermen who row in a unique way at the back of the boat. The local market proposes a very interesting craft (bags, silks, carved objects…) and is itinerant, it rotates over five days in five different places including the lake in floating market mode. September and October are the best time to visit. The festival of Hpaung Daw U pagoda, which lasts almost three weeks, is followed by the festival of Lights of Thadingyut.

• Myanmar has many other surprises in store for you, such as the Pindaya caves and its thousands of Buddha statuas, the Salouen canyon, one of the largest in the world, or the huge golden rock of Kyaikto. Mount Popa and its surroundings are covered with a particularly dense vegetation, contrasting with the rest of the center of the country, due to the fertile volcanic ashes and the numerous streams that water the region. Many monkeys have found refuge in these volcanic chimney landscapes.

• The country is crossed from north to south by the Irrawaddy River. The backbone of the country, it remains today the main axis between the most important cities and most of the population lives in its watershed. Embarking with the locals on its waves can be a good way to discover the region.

Nepal

Without being very extensive, the territory of Nepal has a very wide variety of landscapes, the most famous of which are the mountains that adorn the north of the country. Indeed, it is in Nepal that eight of the ten highest mountains in the world, including Everest, which marks the border with Tibet, are found. A paradise for hikers, Nepal is also the country of the jungle and the tiger. Two facets that share a unique cultural environment and traditions. Unfortunately, natural disasters, political tensions, ethnic grievances and the persistence of guerrilla warfare can make the journey difficult. It is not, like India, a destination to be taken lightly, but it is a journey full of promise and a real experience.

* Kathmandu, the political and religious capital of the country, has been a dream come true for long distance travelers since the 1970s. The old city, the Thamel, is remarkable for its many 17th century Buddhist and Hindu temples and palaces, despite the damage caused by pollution and earthquakes. Its doors, its carved wooden balconies and its stalls still have an undeniable charm. Six kilometers south of the city center is Patan, a former royal city. Many monasteries are scattered around the main square, Durbar Square. 13 km east, Bhaktapur is also a museum whose jewel is the Golden Gate.

* Throughout the Kathmandu region there are many other treasures. Swayambhunath, west of the capital, is one of the oldest and holiest Buddhist sites in the region. The Buddhist shrine of Bodnath is famous for its giant stupa also crowned with a pair of eyes and its many Tibetan refugees. The double-roofed gilded bronze temple of Pasupatinath, and its shrine of Shiva, is a Hindu shrine. The archaeological site of Lumbini in Rummindei is considered the traditional birthplace of the Buddha and has become an important place of pilgrimage.

* The Annapurna tour is one of the most beautiful and best known treks in the country. With a great diversity of landscapes, one goes from a hot and humid subtropical climate where banana trees reign, to an arid, dry and cold universe, where ice and rock reign, in only a few days. It is not a question of reaching the summits at more than 7,000 meters, but of being able to appreciate its majesty, it is nevertheless necessary to be in excellent physical condition and to count 15 to 20 days of trek.

* The Dhaulagiri massif is located just west of the Annapurna massif, separated by the valley of the Kali Gandaki River descending from the Mustang kingdom further north. Going around it will allow you to discover the secret Hidden Valley and even to climb Thapa Peak (6,000 meters). You will need to be in better physical condition than for the previous trek, but the reward of the scenery will be worth your effort.

* To see the roof of the world, you will only have to walk a few hours (33 km) from Kathmandu to Nagarkot, the only place in the valley where you can see the Everest range at any time. Some travelers choose to spend a night at the Everest base camp at 5,380 m altitude on the southern slope of Everest. From Namche Bazaar, capital of the Sherpas (two days walk from Lukla, which is linked by air to Kathmandu), you will have to walk another 6 to 8 days to reach this unlikely and touristy place. As for the ascent of the major mountain, it is an extraordinary adventure, reserved for explorers and very experienced mountaineers (and rather fortunate because expeditions never cost less than 70.000$). Mount Everest leaves no margin of error for those who try to climb it, the success rate is low and more often than not lives are left behind.

* In an absolutely different register of tropical jungle, the Royal Chitwan National Park in the Terai is home to more than 400 rhinos, 80 tigers, about 50 species of mammals and 400 species of birds. To observe them, you will have the choice between elephant trekking, 4x4, canoeing or walking. Less known and therefore much wilder, the Royal National Park of Bardia, in the southwest of the country, is rich in elephants, monkeys and dolphins of the Ganges.

North Korea

It is difficult to approach the last iron dictatorship on the planet as a real tourist destination. Oppressed people, Stalinist regime, to get there you have to close your eyes to many principles of freedom and democracy. However, the country is not as compartmentalized as one might think, and a few tourists, meticulously supervised (in a mock guided tour), visit it every year. This country is so anachronistic, so far from the reality of the modern world, that it becomes intriguing. If one day tourism becomes a reality there, this aspect of experiencing another world will undoubtedly be its greatest attraction. However, the oppression of its people is a much more important issue today than a possible opening of tourism in the distant future. The supervised trips, escorted by government guides, show an idyllic image of the country that does not correspond in any way to the daily reality of its inhabitants.

* In Pyongyang, there are many palaces, frescoes, monuments and museums illustrating the war and the regime. In particular, you will not fail to bow (obligatorily!) before the giant bronze statue of the respected President Kim Il Sung and admire the Tower of Juche, a giant obelisk more than 150 meters high representing the official ideology. The Children's and Students' Palace is a gigantic building that welcomes thousands of children every day with the aim of making them the future elite of the country. You can also visit the former presidential palace of the Great Leader, which became his mausoleum after his death, the Korean War Museum and the Monument to the Martyrs of the Resistance War against Japan, from where you can enjoy a beautiful view.

* In the outskirts of Pyongyang, in Mangyongdae, is the house where Kim Il Song was born, revered as the holiest site in the country and a must for all visitors to the country. It is obviously only a staging. A little further on, at 2:30 am drive, near Kaesong is the tomb of King Kongmin, thirty-first king of the Koryo dynasty (14th century). The royal tombs of Koguryo are inscribed on the World Heritage List.

* In the south, the DMZ - the Demilitarized Zone - on the 38th parallel is the last global remnant of the Cold War. You will visit the site of Panmunjom, where the armistice was signed. You will see North Korean, South Korean and American soldiers, there since 1953. The Concrete wall (wall built by the South Koreans) and the tunnels that connect North and South speak for themselves.

* Southeast of Pyongyang, the Kumgang Mountains or "Diamond Mountains" (so called because of the glitter of the mountains at sunrise) rising to 1,638 m, have been sacred to Koreans for thousands of years and have many hiking trails.

* To the northwest, the Myohyang Mountains are crossed by trails from which you can visit about twenty Buddhist temples, including the famous Pohyon Temple, built in 1042. This region is also home to the International Friendship Exhibition where the various gifts offered to North Korean leaders are displayed.

* In the northeast, on the border with China, Mount Paektu, the highest point of the whole Korea, at 2,744 m, has magnificent summit lakes and is also suitable for beautiful walks. It is said that the sunrises from the summit are particularly sumptuous from August to September.

Oman

A sort of antithesis to Dubai, yet nearby, the Sultanate of Oman, at the extreme south-east of the Arabian Peninsula, has been an independent monarchy since the mid-18th century. Country of Sinbad the sailor and the Counts of the Thousand and One Nights, Oman is a plunge into happy Arabia, this somewhat mythical country, with a powerful exoticism, land of the famous incense tree and the Queen of Sheba. Like Yemen, the Sultanate of Oman is a magnificent destination, authentic, but unlike its tormented neighbor, it is a safe, comfortable trip where the welcome is warm. A little-known nugget where the landscapes alternate between arid mountains, oases with lush palm groves and sandy beaches, all dotted with fortified villages that seem to be one with nature. In reality, Oman is a top destination but very few travelers are aware of it.

• The 1,700 km of coastline are still little frequented by tourists. The most accessible beaches are in Salalah and the surroundings of Muscat, the most beautiful being always on the edge of the big hotels. Diving enthusiasts will discover on the north coast of the island a beautiful seabed. The most important dive sites are in Musandam in the Gulf of Oman, in the Strait of Hormuz, in the Arabian Sea, and along the tropical coast of Salalah. To welcome divers and travelers, beautiful luxury hotels have been built, respecting the environment and far from the overbidding of the neighboring emirates.

• The Musandam peninsula owes its beauty to its fjords, do not miss a mini-cruise in dhow for example from Khasab to go up towards the fjord of Khawr Ash Shamm. It is by 4x4 that you will best discover the coast of the Gulf of Oman between Quriyat and Sur, dotted with wadis and nesting places for large sea turtles (Ra's al-Hadd). The coast of Dhofar presents an alternation of cliffs, creeks and long white sand beaches, an ideal place to observe the spectacle of dolphins, but dangerous for swimming.

• Along the east coast, the Wahiba Desert is made of ochre and reddish dunes, but it is in the north that the landscapes are the most breathtaking. The Jebel Akhdar is a succession of canyons, cliffs and fortified mountain villages as in Bahla (classified as a World Heritage Site) or the oasis of Hamz. From Muscat, the Wadi Bani Khalid is a natural basin located in a narrow valley that attracts many curious people. In 4x4, you can cross the Hajar through the Sumayl valley and open into the plains of Nizwa, in the west, and the Sharqiyah, in the east.

• In the south, Dhofar manages to bring together spectacular canyons and the most luxuriant vegetation maintained by the monsoon from July to September. The legendary incense- and myrrh-scented trees (Boswellia sacra) can be found in Jebel al-Qamar. Many hikes are possible, some of which will lead you to Rub'al-Khali, the great desert of Arabia among the most inhospitable in the world and nicknamed the Empty Quarter.

• Oman has more than 500 forts scattered along the coast and in the heart of the desert. The fort of Nakhl is the largest of the Sultanate and dominates from the top of its rocky promontory, the foothills of the Western Hajar and the plain of the Batinah. Do not miss the hot spring of the palm grove at the back of the construction. The Citadel Road, at the foot of Jebel Akhdar, passes by three other prestigious forts (Bahmla, Birket-el-Mouz and Nizwa). The hundred ksour of the country, the souks of Salalah and the great Sultan Qaboos Mosque of Muscat are other architectural ensembles not to be missed.

Pakistan

Pakistan has much to offer to travelers. Its history is rich and its heritage, especially religious, is immense. Rightly associated with Islam, Pakistan is one of the birthplaces of Hinduism. Its exotic and animated cities, its superb landscapes, particularly in the northern mountains with the famous K2, the second highest peak in the world, as a bridgehead, are a formidable field of exploration for the adventurous traveler. Unfortunately the situation in the country, the political instability and religious fundamentalism prevents from envisaging a serene voyage there. Not all regions are formally advised against but the traveler will have to be careful everywhere.

• When the political situation allows it, the north of the country occupied by the Himalayas is one of the major meeting places for hikers and mountaineers. The Karakorum massif has famous peaks, including the K2. The Nanga Parbat Massif itinerary will take you through the lakes of Kaghan Valley before reaching Chilas and the Karakorum Highway to continue in the Rupal Valley around the Nanga Parbat Massif. From Gilgit, you will go north on the Karakorum Highway towards the Khunjerab Pass: after crossing the Naltar Gorge, you will be able to hike to the Hispar, Biafo or Batura glaciers (among the largest in the world), or to the Shimshal Valley. Southeast of Gilgit starts the Balistan route, while in the west you can hike to the Hindu Kush massif via the Shandur Pass or the Lowari Pass.

• Pakistan has seen the Great Moghols reign (Lahore, their city, is the cultural capital of the country), pass the merchants of the Silk Road and blossom the *Indus* civilization. The state of conservation of the archaeological sites of the two cities of the Indian Bronze Age of Mohenjo-daro and Harappâ is not extraordinary but their importance makes them all the same major stages. The organization of the cities around the river, the brick of the constructions, the art of pottery and the statuary of this time made it possible to better understand this civilization discovered late. The boatmen of Malla and the Mohana fishermen perpetuate certain traditions. Sehwan, the Mecca of Sufism, Taxila and its Greco-Buddhist vestiges, the museum of Peshawar devoted to the art of Gandhara and the monasteries of the Swat region (and more particularly the sites of Butkara, Nimogram, Jehanabad and Barikot) also reinforce the archaeological interest of the country.

Palestinian territories

Palestinian Territories consists of two territories, the West Bank and the Gaza Strip, separated by the State of Israel. Promised Land of the Jews, Holy Land of Christians, Sacred Land of Islam, Palestine is at the center of the three great monotheistic religions. Places of worship and veneration are scattered throughout this historic territory that will undoubtedly attract travelers once the situation has stabilized.

• Jericho, on the west bank of the Jordan River, is considered one of the oldest inhabited cities in the world, and archaeologists have unearthed the remains of more than 20 successive settlements dating back 9,000 years. The archaeological excavation sites of the biblical city are rather unspectacular in spite of their historical charge. The ramparts and the round tower are nevertheless to be noted, as well as the Palace of Hisham, 2 km north of the new city, and the synagogue of Jericho located between the two. In the surrounding area, the remains of five monasteries remain out of the 90 listed, such as the Byzantine Monastery of St. George perched on a hillside in the heart of a nature reserve.

• Bethlehem, 10 km from Jerusalem, is separated from it by a concrete wall built by the Israelis along the border with the West Bank. It is an important religious center. The Jewish tradition makes it the birthplace and coronation place of the king of Israel David. It is considered by many Christians as the birthplace of Jesus of Nazareth. The cave and the Church of the Nativity are a very important place of pilgrimage. Bethlehem is also the seat of a holy place of Judaism, the tomb of Rachel, located at the entrance of the city. A few kilometers away is the Mar Saba Monastery, one of the oldest Christian monasteries.

• Hebron, about 30 kilometers south of Jerusalem, is one of the oldest cities in the Near East still inhabited. It is home to the tomb of the Patriarchs, where according to tradition, Adam and Eve, Abraham and Sarah, Isaac and Rebekah, and Jacob and Leah lie. A monument was built around the tomb in the time of Herod the Great. The Muslims then transformed the monument into a mosque known as the Ibrahim Mosque.

• The soil of the Gaza Strip keeps the memory of six millennia of Egyptian, Assyrian, Greco-Roman and Islamic civilizations. The Roman temples of Beit-Lahiya, the vast Romano-Byzantine necropolis near Jabalya and Al-Nazla, that of Deir-al-Balah, the fortress of Khan-Yunis among others are patiently waiting for the end of the conflict to bear witness to this important past.

Philippines

The Republic of the Philippines is an archipelago of more than 7,000 islands in the Pacific Ocean. With 17,000 km of coastline, the Philippines has to offer sumptuous beaches associated with coral beds of infinite beauty. Inland, you will also find many surprises worthy of the most beautiful postcards.

LUZON & NORTHERN ISLANDS :

• The north of the island has the most beautiful landscapes of the country. The rice terraces of the Banaue mountainous region have been a World Heritage Site since 1995. Created by the ancestors of the Ifugaos ethnic group 2000 years ago, they continue to feed people and beautify the landscape. The Moutain trail is a road that connects Baguio to the top of the mountains of the same name in Bontoc. The highest road in the country will allow you to contemplate the most beautiful panoramas of the Cordillera.

• From the Spanish colonial architecture of the historic district to the American buildings, Manila is a city full of contrasts with an intense pace of life. Don't miss its cathedral, churches and palaces, but also the Makati business district. The Chinatown, Rizal Park and the Pistang Pilipino market will give you a different view of the city.

• The Philippines has about thirty volcanoes and the landscapes that go with them. South of the capital, the spa Los Baños is famous for the sulphurous hot springs that bubble at the foot of the inactive volcano Makaling. To the west, the eruption of Pinatubo in 1991 transformed the region into a desert of ashes that hikers have taken over. In the southwest, the Taal volcano forms a perfect cone in the middle of the lake of the same name that we never tire of admiring.

• For relaxation, the most beautiful sandy beaches are in Boracay, on the islet of Inanuran or on the almost private island of Pamalican. For diving and water sports, the sites around Batangas, Puerta Galeraà Mindoro and the Mindoro Strait are famous. On this island, take a day to get away from the beaches and go to the city of Taal where the volcano of the same name is located. It is a very large caldera containing a lake, Lake Taal, which contains an island, Volcano Island, which contains another lake.

VISAYAS & CENTRAL ISLANDS:

• It is in the center of the archipelago that seaside tourism has developed the most. The beaches and the lagoon of the island of Palawan are among the most beautiful in the Far East. In addition to the countless reefs where thousands of marine species live, there are wrecks such as those of the Japanese fleet in Coron. Around Cebu, the great metropolis in the center of the country, do not hesitate to embark on a banca to discover the miraculous beaches of the 167 islands of the region. The most famous beach of Bohol is Alona Beach on the peninsula of Panglao, you can learn to dive in Balicasag and observe dolphins near the island of Pamilacan.

• In Bohol, in the interior of the country, the landscapes offered by the chocolate mountains are absolutely incredible. More than 1000 conical hills shape the landscape which from green to brown in the dry season (January to May). On your way there, you can visit the baroque churches of Baclayon and Dauis or take a mini cruise for lunch on the Loboc River. On Palawan, it will be the turn of the underground river of Saint-Paul to dazzle you with its limestone karst landscapes.

MINDANAO :

The island is home to a strong Muslim minority traditionally in rebellion against the government. It is advisable to inquire before traveling to the Zamboanga Peninsula and the southwestern part of the island.

• In Davao, a city in the south of the country nicknamed "the basket of fruits and flowers", don't miss the Greenhills & Derling orchid gardens and the huge fruit and fish market. Nearby you can climb Mount Apo (2954 meters) to meet the exceptional fauna that has made its home there (270 species of birds, 100 of which are endemic).

• To the north of General Santos, the Sebu Lake and its eight islets are invaded by tilapia cultures. The women of the Tboli tribe who live there have a special relationship with the music that they play in their daily lives.

• At the southwestern tip of Mindanao is the romantic Zamboanga City with its 17th century Fort Pilar walls. The atmosphere here is different from that of the other cities on the island, the Islamic influence is more pronounced, but the beaches and reefs of the surroundings are like the rest of the country: superb. You will be able to do snorkeling on the island of Santa Cruz.

Qatar

Like Bahrain and the USmirats arabes unis, Qatar is one of the Gulf countries that offer travelers a privileged latitude of coastline. Mostly visited by businessmen or expatriates in the Gulf, Qatar remains a marginal tourist destination despite its opportunities for scuba diving, desert trekking and a particular blend of architectural modernism and Islamic tradition.

• Al-Khor, 57 kilometers north of Doha, on the east coast, is conducive to seaside activities such as para sailing, water skiing and jet-skiing. The island of Shara'o has remarkable beaches and has the same seabed and variety of tropical fishes as in the Red Sea. Uninhabited, the islets of Al Shafliyeh and Shafliyah are accessible from Doha in a day trip by dhow. The excursion is rewarded by the beauty of the beaches and the spectacle of migratory birds.

• The desert covers most of the country alternating pebbles and dazzling white dunes. In the company of a guide, you can discover new sensations in 4x4, you will cross at full speed the sand canyons and go down in "free fall" the dunes. In the south, the desert borders the salty las of Khor al-Udayd, an arm of the Arabian Gulf on which the setting sun plays a sumptuous show every evening.

• Doha, the capital, is a city where westernization is widely felt through the wide highways and buildings. At the same time, the white houses, the mosques, the camel market and the souk are a constant reminder of its traditions. Don't miss to visit the Great Mosque, Al-Kut Fortress and the National Museum.

Saudi Arabia

From the Red Sea to the dry spaces of the Rub Al Khali, the Kingdom of Saudi Arabia possesses the largest territory of the Arabian Peninsula and offers travelers extraordinary sites. However, apart from the pilgrimage to Mecca, obligatory once in a lifetime for every Muslim, or an expatriation in the western ghettos of the oil cities, the visitor remains very rare in this ultra conservative country. The cities of Medina and Mecca, located in the sacred perimeter, are absolutely inaccessible to non-Muslims (under penalty of heavy sanctions and, until recently, the death penalty), but this does not mean that the rest of the country is an open door. Access is, in practice, very simple (numerous air links, direct flights from Paris) but in theory it is almost impossible. No tourist visa, no visa for Jews, no visa for non-religious people (it is mandatory to declare a religion to enter the country), many sites forbidden to non-Muslims, obligation to have a Saudi "sponsor" in all cases, the obstacles are multiple. For this reason, travel to Saudi Arabia has long been the object of a certain fantasy among Western travelers. Richard Burton undertook his famous "Journey to Mecca" in 1853, under the identity of a fake Pakistani religious. Here we are in front of a unique destination, with limited but remarkable attractions (starting with Madahine Saleh), but probably the least accessible of the whole planet (no tourist visa possible, nor for people without religion whatever the reason of the trip). On the spot, the level of development acquired thanks to oil guarantees a very comfortable trip, with excellent infrastructures. For the vast majority of travelers, the prospect of Saudi Arabia today remains limited to a possible stopover at an airport. Needless to say that for non-Muslim Western women, it is better to avoid any contact with the country. Women's rights are non-existent there.

• In the desert, between Jordan and Iraq, the ancient Nabataean city of Madahine-Saleh is the most interesting tourist site in the country, which could be compared to Petra in Jordan. Less spectacular, but better preserved, you will be able to discover its remains at the wheel of a vehicle, so great are the distances. Don't miss Qasr Farid, the most important tomb and the Diwan, the r. éunionhall.

• Half of the country is occupied by one of the largest and most arid deserts in the world, the Rub al-Khali, the famous "empty quarter" of Arabia, so inhospitable that no tourist expeditions are organized there and even the Bedouins make only very rare incursions. It is in the northwest, in the vicinity of the Hijaz, around El'Ula, that the possibilities of hiking begin to develop. This ancient crossroads of the incense route is also worth a visit for its museum and the remains of an ancient temple, as is Tayma, nearby, whose ancient palace, fortifications and necropolis are of great interest.

• Further north, on the edge of the Nefud desert, the small towns of El Djof and Sakakah offer vestiges sometimes three to four thousand years old. Jubbah contains treasures that are rarely visited and difficult to access, including rock paintings that date back more than 5000 years. Nearby, Domat al-Jandal is an important but under-exploited archaeological site. You can also visit Qasr Marid for its Nabataean ruins and Omar for its ancient mosque.

• In contrast, the Gebel Asir region, in the southwest of the country, offers vacationers the freshness of its mountains, vegetation and national park. The Saudis themselves have made Abha, for example, one of their favorite vacation spots. Be sure to visit the mountainside ruins of the village of Habella, 60 km away. In addition, At Ta'if and its mountains, east of Mecca, is also a pleasant place to relax.

• At the southern end of the Gebel Asir, Najran, an ancient oasis at the crossroads of the incense route and Jizan and its very old souk are really worth the detour for their architecture. On the way, you will cross traditional villages with colorful houses.

• Riyadh, the capital, is a modern city that has to offer its souks, its old town and its National Museum. At 30 km from the city, the camel market, which is held daily, is one of the most important in the Middle East. Do not miss also at the same distance to the north, the ruins of Dir'aiyah, first capital of the al-Saud family.

• Around Djedda, it is scuba diving that is in the spotlight. Tourism has never been really developed in this region, so the sea bed is still immaculate. In the city, you can visit the Municipal Museum for its architecture, and take time to discover the souks of al-Alawi. The Gulf of Aqaba is also famous for its sea bed.

Singapore

Singapore is known worldwide for its extraordinary economic success. Located between Malaysia and Indonésie, Singapore is also a success story in terms of ethnic diversity. Chinese, Malays, Indians and Westerners blend together in the greatest harmony. Singapore is at the same time a state, a city, a main island and 63 other small islands and islets.

If there is one word that sums up Singapore perfectly, it is "unique". In this dynamic city-state, rich in contrasts and colors, you will find a harmonious blend of culture, cuisine, art and architecture. First and foremost known as a first-class business center, Singapore is becoming a true tourist destination. Between the hustle and bustle of the business district and the soothing calm of the tea rooms, between the impressive skyscrapers and the charm of the small Buddhist temples, Singapore offers a fairly complete picture of the charms of Asia. To this, we must of course add the futuristic aspects of the country, such as the Changi airport and its waterfall which will not fail to impress you, or the incredible site of Gardens by the Bay, which seems to come straight out of the movie Avatar. Land of contrasts, Singapore will seduce you during a getaway, a shopping stopover, or to rest from the sometimes hectic rhythm of Asia.

South Korea

In the collective imagination of travelers, South Korea is a bit like an annex of Japan. If the two countries share the same exoticism, it should however be remembered that Korean culture is ancestral and has as many particularities as its neighbors. This very modern country, with customs that are confusing for a European, is still far from the main tourist routes of the Far East, but it is surrounded by a fashion effect that makes it an increasingly popular destination for lovers of this part of the world. From a purely tourist point of view, South Korea cannot compete with its neighbors, but its temples, the historical remains of past kingdoms, the mountains of the east or the island of Jeju, a sort of Korean Hawaii, are notable attractions. If there is still beautiful countryside in South Korea, the country has an image above all urban, which is of course surpassed by Seoul, the emblematic capital and one of the great Asian megacities. Both hyper modern, with its huge shopping malls and skyscrapers, while preserving the heritage of its rich past, Seoul is the country's major destination. A trip to Korea is first of all an experience, the impression of landing on another planet. An experience made easier by the calm, security and order that is typical of South Korean society. The infrastructures are of excellent quality and the trip is simple, apart from the cultural shock and the language barrier. The climate is quite harsh, icy in winter and very humid in summer (with a risk of typhoon), as well as a very high cost of living.

- Seoul is the former capital of the Li dynasty. The palaces of the Li dynasty have now been transformed into museums. Yesterday's shrines and today's markets will allow you to better understand the origins of this country and its customs. To get back in touch with the present, all you need to do is a little shopping. Entire districts are dedicated to electronics or fashion.

- Forty Buddhist temples are open throughout the country to foreigners who wish to learn more about this culture. The most important is the one in Songgwongsa where many illustrious monks have been trained. To name a few others, you will find not far from Nonsan, the temple of Kwanch'oksa where the largest stone Buddha of the East rises to 18 meters, and in the national park of Songnisan, the temple of Beopjusa where it is the turn of a bronze Buddha to unveil himself.

- Gyeongju is the capital of the ancient kingdom of Silla and thus inherited a very rich architecture where royal tombs, pagoda remains and Buddhas are found. In the area, the Pulguk temple and its terraces are to be visited, as well as the Sokkuram cave and its white Buddha and the astronomical observatory of Cheomseongdae.

- On the east coast, the Taebaek Sanmaek Mountains extend to the sea and offer their slopes to hikers and even skiers in the resorts of Yongp'yong Valley. In the west of this massif, the Soraksan park is also a good playground for all the fans of walking.

- In the south, the island of Cheju is conducive to idleness, but few Westerners know it yet. Very beautiful beaches await you there, dominated by the Hallasan volcano at the origin of the formation of the island.

Sri Lanka

The effects of the 2004 tsunami are slowly fading, but unfortunately the same cannot be said of the tensions between Tamil activists and the government. If traveling to the north and northeast is strongly discouraged, the rest of the country will delight you with its beauty. History and nature have been generous with this small island where cultural interest and seaside interest are perfectly combined. Sri Lanka is a magical destination, as refreshing as a cup of tea.

- Several cities have preserved jewels of Sri Lankan religious architecture. On the map is a real cultural triangle between the ancient capitals of the country: Anuradhapura, Polonnaruwa and Kandy. Temples and stupas rise to the glory of Buddha and for the greatest pleasure of the visitor.

- Buddha would have come to preach three times in Sri Lanka in different places which today welcome pilgrims from all over the world. Every full moon (poya), dazzling celebrations take place such as the one in April at Adam's Peak where there is a mysterious imprint left by Buddha, Adam, Shiva or St. Thomas, according to the beliefs of the people.

• Sri Lanka is a seaside destination where the climate is idyllic all year round. From the beaches of the southwest (Negombo, Kalutera, Bentota, Mount Lavinia) to the natural aquariums of the northeast (Batticaloa, Trincomalee), don't forget your bathing suits and diving masks!

• Ceylon tea has kept the old name of the island, but continues to delight the taste buds all over the world. The best vintages come from the Nuwara Eliya region and the province of Uva. You can visit plantations and renowned factories.

• With 12 national parks and more than 3500 wild elephants, Sri Lanka is also called "Elephant Island". Gal Oya, Wilpattu and Yala are the most famous parks where you can admire these beautiful animals. You will also be able to meet them during the parades that animate cities and villages.

Syria

"Every individual has two homes, his house and Syria" said a former director of the Louvre Museum in Paris. A land of history, Syria has indeed vestiges from thirty different civilizations. Traces of the oldest alphabet in the world were found in Ugarit in northern Syria. If more than 50% of the surface is covered by desert, the variations in the landscapes of the other half of the country compensate for their diversity. High mountains covered in snow until spring, hills populated by green orchards, basaltic landscapes disarming from eternity, the Mediterranean coast with its wild reflections, everything is there to alternate culture and nature. Of course, bogged down in years of civil wars, Syria is no longer a tourist destination and the extent of destruction is probably enormous.

• The colonnades of Palmyra are part of our imagination. An Arab castle overlooks the ruins of the city of Queen Zenobia (2nd - 3rd century AD). These are composed of superbly decorated temples such as that of Bêl, an agora and a Roman theater, and a set of impressive funerary architecture.

• The Haurel and the Druze djebrel, in the south of the country, saw the birth and death of the Roman period. Many vestiges of this period remain in the region. In Bosra for example where the Roman theater were mixed over the centuries a cathedral then an Umayyad mosque, fortifications and medersas.

• The Mesopotamian city of Mari, the Hellenistic ruins of Doura-Europos, the villages of the first Christians of the Qualamoun massif testify to the empires which crossed this country.

• The citadels left by the Crusaders tell a story closer to us. Do not miss the Krak of the Knights at Qala'at al-Husn, the great port of the Templars at Tartous, the Saône Castle and the Marqab, nestled in the heights of the Gebel Ansariye.

• Damascus was elected Cultural Capital of the Arab World in 2008. Jewel of the first great Islamic empire of the Umayyads, it was previously under the influence of Assyrians, Persians, Greeks, Seleucids and Romans. The great mosque, the citadel, the ramparts, the tomb of Saladin, the old Christian quarter, the convent of Soliman: so many architectural pieces not to be missed under any pretext. The Damascenes continue today to make their city an unprecedented place of welcome.

• Aleppo is one of the oldest inhabited cities in the world. Its magnificent citadel was restored in 2008 by the Aga Khan Agency for Culture. A labyrinth of alleys and souk connects its promontory to the great mosque dating from the same period. Like Damascus, Aleppo is marked by the richness of its craftsmanship.

• Latakia is an extremely dynamic port city. By taking the road to the north, you will discover beautiful beaches such as Shatt el-Azraq. Make the detour to Ras Shamra cape on the tracks of the ancient Ougarit.

Taiwan

Taiwan is an island located southeast of mainland China, with a status that varies between "independent territory" of the Republic of China and "province of mainland China" under the authority of the People's Republic of China. More known destination for businessmen than for tourists, it nevertheless offers a great variety of landscapes, a mosaic of peoples and a most animated capital.

* Taipei is a lively capital without much tourist reputation in spite of the amusing contrasts which it proposes between modernity (Taipei 101 is the highest tower in the world) and Chinese traditions. Don't miss the world's largest collection of Chinese art at the National Museum of Art. The Chiang Kai-shek Memorial, the Lung shang temple and the Confucius temple are also worth a visit between shopping and massage.

* The sometimes high relief of the eastern part of the island has created the most beautiful Taiwanese sites in Chungyang Shanmo. Starting from the coastal town of Hua-Lien, you will take a road that will lead you to the Taroko Gorge, a wonderful site and a road marked out with remarkable stages (sanctuary of the Eternal Spring, Swallow Cave, tunnel of the Nine Curves, Tiansiang, bridge over the rivers Tatzuchili and Tasha, Pudu temple).

* The relief then softens to make way for a greener nature and beautiful lakes such as the Lake of the Sun and Moon where the surrounding mountains are gracefully reflected. In the north, you will find Shihmen Lake and the forests of camphor trees where Chiang Kai-shek rests for eternity. There is also the Coral Lake where mystical hikes are also a must.

* The island of Taiwan is dotted with a hundred hot springs of volcanic origin excellent for your health. Beitou, 13 kilometers north of Taipei, and Wulai, also in the district of Taipei, 27 kilometers south of the capital, are the main ones.

* Although beach tourism is not yet widespread in Taiwan, the beaches in the south remain paradisiacal. The most beautiful are in Oluanpi, the cape of Mao-pi T'ou offers a coral landscape, while in Chialoshui, the beach is made of blocks of coral looking like sponges. To the north, the beautiful jagged coastline is dotted with friendly villages such as Jioufen and Yeliou.

* Do not hesitate to go to the Pescadores archipelago whose 64 islands have beautiful beaches and pretty fishing villages. The three main islands, Penghu, Paisha and Siyu, are connected by bridges.

Tajikistan

Tajikistan, which emerged from the former Soviet Union, had to face a civil war that made it one of the poorest countries in the region. Mountainous like its neighbors, it offers to the brave hikers, who have chosen it as a destination, the superb panoramas of one of the highest mountain ranges in the world.

* To the southeast, the Pamir mountain range cuts the country in two. Its high plateaus and glaciers provide an unprecedented playground for fans of mountaineering and high mountain trekking. The ex-Pic Kommunizma (Ismail Samani) and the ex-Pic Lenin (renamed since the fall of the USSR) dominate the whole country. The seven colorful lakes of Koulikalon punctuate a vast plateau at the foot of the impressive north face of Mary Peak. The road that crosses the Pamir from Khorog to Kyrgyzstan is the highest in the world, with passages at more than 4000 m.

* Gateway to the Fergana Valley, Khodjent, founded by Alexander the Great, has many remains, such as its 10th century citadel, a lively bazaar, a mosque, a medersa and a mausoleum. Dushanbe, the capital, is located on a pleasant site, at the foot of the snowy Hissar mountains, but is not of great tourist interest.

* In Pendjikent, in the valley of Zeravchan, the Sogdians had built a large city made of temples, seigniorial houses of

wood and dried brick, traces of which can be found today on the site. The country also preserves the Buddhist monastery of Adjina-tepe and ruins of cities of ancient Bactria (ancient region of the Bactrian people, later conquered by the Greeks).

Thailand

Exceptional destination that the elephant country (because of its shape), which combines the charm of the landscapes, the exoticism of its culture, the kindness of its people, the comfort of its infrastructure, all at ridiculously low prices and bathed in the tropical climate. If the Indonesian island of Bali succeeds in distilling a similar sweetness and appeal, no country in the world has arrived at the tourist alchemy created by Thailand. Everything here is soft, colorful, flowing, exotic and welcoming. And the variety of attractions is spectacular, from the paradisiacal islands of the south, to the mountains and rice fields of the north, through temples, palaces and jungles, natural or urban, with Bangkok as a highlight, the craziest metropolis on the continent. Easy to get to, very well equipped, very welcoming, cheap, safe and without major health problems (as long as you stay informed), Thailand is open to all travelers, experienced or not, and everyone will find something for everyone. Needless to say that the country is, by far, the most touristy country in Southeast Asia. The only shadow in the picture to be taken into account is a far southern region plagued by troubles, but little visited in all cases, and a problem of overexploitation sometimes palpable and questionable (Pattaya, Patong).

THE NORTH :

• Bangkok includes 350 temples, each one more incredible than the other (such as Vat Phra Keo or Vat Arun), dozens of markets of all kinds open day and night and more than 10 million inhabitants who are agitated in the middle of it all. You can walk or take a boat as you have done for centuries, but also take the subway of the future (the Skytrain), a pink cab or a tuk-tuk. Let yourself be carried away by the crowds, you are not at the end of your surprises. Near the capital (80 km), the floating market of Damnoen Saduak is one of the tourist attractions of the region.

• Take a cruise on the Chao Phraya or travel through its valley by train to discover the architectural wealth of several cities. Going north from Bangkok, you will cross the many temples and stupas of Ayutthaya and then the ancient cities of the kingdom of Siam like Lopburi (and its monkeys) or especially Sukhotai, real regional pearl.

• In the north, you will find the peaceful and authentic city of Chiang Mai, second city of the country and endowed with a strong power of attraction. Further on, at the Burmese border, you can hike in the famous Golden Triangle to meet the mountain minorities. In the west of the country, jungle, rice fields and rivers dominate the landscape. The famous bridge over the Kwai River is visible in the town of Kanchanaburi, in the heart of one of the most beautiful corners of the country.

• In a country that alone represents all the exoticism of the tropics, it is not surprising that nature is luxuriant. One can discover it in all its splendor, as well as its inhabitants (monkeys, elephants, birds) in some natural parks, the most famous of which are Khao Yai, near Bangkok, and Khao Sok which offers a real postcard jungle. In the north, the environment is more mountainous and the landscapes are just as remarkable, especially in the northwest around Chiang Mai and Chiang Rai.

THE SOUTH & THE ISLANDS :

• The west coast recovered from the tsunami it suffered in 2004 and whether you go to Phuket, nicknamed the Pearl and which is the most touristic island, or in the other islands and nooks of the Andaman Sea (*Koh Phiphi, Koh Lanta, Phangna Bay* comparable to Halong Bay, *Railay* beach near Krabi) you will find a very high quality tourist infrastructure and magnificent seaside landscapes.

- On the side of the Gulf of Thailand the islands have a different personality but are just as beautiful. Koh Samui, the largest and most developed island, and its neighbors (Koh Phangan, Koh Tao) will welcome you whether you are a beach, nature, diving lover or partygoer.

- If you are looking for islands a little wilder, a little less touristy, then again you will be spoilt for choice. Ko Chang, the elephant island on the northeast coast, is famous for its jungle, while the marine park of Ko Tarutao in the extreme south of the country certainly offers the most beautiful beaches (and diving) in Thailand.

- Which beach to choose? The time of the year when you go to Thailand can influence your choice: between the end of October and the beginning of December is the rainy season on the archipelago of Koh Samui while the weather from Phuket to Krabi is fine at this time of the year. This region has its monsoon period from July to September while the weather is fine in the Gulf Islands.

Turkmenistan

With a history of 5,000 years, Turkmenistan is not easily visited. The majority of these mountains are inaccessible and its dictatorial regime is one of the most autocratic in the world. This destination is therefore still largely unknown to travelers.

- The Karakum desert, the takyrs, these large basins surrounded by dunes, and the oases (Tedzhen, Murgab, Kerki, Chardzhou, Tashauz) draw an unusual landscape that alone deserves the trip. There live the Koumlis and their sheep caraculas from which the astrakhan is made.

- In the vicinity of Ashgabat, the capital, where the cult of the head of state is omnipresent, you can visit the ruins of Nisa, 15 km to the west, between green mountains and desert, and those of Anau, 10 km to the east.

- On the Silk Road along the Caspian Sea, you can stop at the several thousand year old city of Merv. Don't hesitate to make a detour to the beautiful gulf of Kara-Bogaz or to the port city of Turkmenbashi.

United Arab Emirates

Mostly we know Dubai, a bit of Abu Dhabi, but these are just two of the federal states of a country that has seven. To these two must be added Ajman, Sharjah, Fujairah, Ras el Khaimah and Umm al Qaiwain (certainly the least known of all). They form the United Arab Emirates. This country, like most federal states (e.g., Usa and Canada), is approached primarily by its states rather than as a whole, and while there are no borders between them, they are often approached as separate destinations. In absolute terms this is not the case, each emirate is based on the same economic base, a great wealth provided by the oil industry, and each has the same cultural and geographical characteristics (desert environment). The nuances come from each emirate's own political choices, and at this level, Dubai has clearly hit the nail on the head to put itself in the spotlight. To do so, the emirate first established itself as a hub for air transport and large business gatherings, before offering travelers a series of experiences worthy of an amusement park (gold souk, dizzying skies, ski slopes in the middle of the desert, gigantic shopping centers). Superficial, certainly, but undeniably entertaining, Dubai has also succeeded in forging an image of luxury while not excluding less well-off visitors. Nevertheless, in this city where money is flowing freely, it is better not to plan a budget too tight to take advantage of it. For its neighbors, the idea is finally about the same, but on a more moderate scale. Certain emirates, more conservative on the religious level, are still reluctant to sell their souls to the sirens of Western-style consumerism. Abu Dhabi, the country's capital, however, is following the path laid out by Dubai and today offers more or less the same attractions (major airlines, shopping centers, architectural innovation and large luxury hotels by the sea). Next to this, one finds there what is certainly the most beautiful asset of the destination, the desert in all its splendour, that of the famous Empty Quarter of Arabia (the Rub al Khali). Equipped with excellent facilities and infrastructure, the emirates are one of the world's best destinations to enjoy the magic of the desert, its landscapes, its starry nights, in remarkable comfort. So is a trip to the Emirates interesting? Certainly yes, on the condition that you understand a minimum of its workings before going there, do not forget that it is an oriental society, and do not leave without your well heated credit card. Travel there is very simple, travel is also very easy, hotels are among the most luxurious on the planet, security is optimal and the general infrastructure is excellent despite a two-speed society, where immigration (which is the main provider of labor) is often forced to a laborious life. The only downside often comes from the overall superficiality of the destination, to which seasoned travelers won't even pay attention and which quickly wearies them out, but also from the climate. The sun is scorching in this region and the pools are air-conditioned to avoid turning into soup. Winter is much more pleasant, with mild temperatures, but it does not last long.

* Dubai, the leading financial center in the Middle East, embodies commerce in all its splendor. In the heart of the city, don't miss its souks, its gold and spice markets and overdo the shopping in its many luxurious discount shopping malls. Its fame is also due to the media coverage of tourist projects such as the Burj-Al-Arab Hotel, the most luxurious and "star" hotel in the world, to the gigantic real estate projects such as the Palm Islands, an artificial palm-shaped peninsula, The World, an artificial archipelago that reproduces the world map, the Dubai Marina with its particular and disproportionate architecture, without forgetting the highest building in the world, the Burj Dubai and the largest indoor ski resort, Ski Dubai. The old quarters (Bastikiya), the Al-Fahidi fortress, the palace of Sheikh Said and the old port (Creek) are pleasant to discover.

* Abu Dhabi as a political capital has long been very quiet and conservative, while Dubai was innovating economically and architecturally. It has now entered into competition with the latter. A forest of ultramodern buildings has already grown and many other projects are underway. A new city, Masdar, the first 100% ecological city, will soon emerge from the desert near the international airport. A 5-hectare construction site has been opened in the heart of the city: the central market will replace the old souk in 2010. The island of Saadiyat is being developed with the establishment of a cultural district and several museums (Guggenheim Abu Dhabi, Louvre Abu Dhabi, etc.) aiming for world renown. As in Dubai, one can embark from the city's port for mini-cruises in dhows.

* Sharjah is one of the most conservative emirates in the country and has favored the construction of low-rise houses to the detriment of the skyscrapers of its neighbors. In the historic center stands the King Faisal Mosque, the largest of the seven emirates. It also has the most interesting souks in the whole country, don't hesitate to get lost in the alleys of Al-Borj Road. In Ras al-Kaimah, you can see the fort (Julfar), but especially the archaeological site of Shimal and its tombs in the 3rd millennium BC.

* The entire territory of the Emirates is desert or semi-desert. The south of the country consists of part of the Rub' al Khali (the desert of deserts), while the east and north are occupied by mountains. Some oases (Al Ain, Manama...) allow to maintain a life in the desert. The first, with its camel markets, is the most spectacular. Sebkhas (salt plains) occupy the south and west of the country, especially along the coast west of Abu Dhabi. On the program: hiking, camel or 4x4 rides, dune skiing and falcon training. Don't miss the Liwa Oasis, 220 km southwest of Abu Dhabi, where a traditional palm grove provides shade.

* The fine sandy beaches bathed by the sapphire blue waters of the Persian Gulf welcome more and more tourists every year. The most popular are around Abu Dhabi and Dhubai (Jumeirah). Divers will love the site of Fudjayra. Deep-sea fishing and golf are also in the spotlight. In addition, the United Arab Emirates has a thousand islands. The island of Sir Bani Yas, property of Sheikh Zayed, has been erected as a nature reserve where Arabian oryx, gazelles, antelopes, bustards and flamingos live.

Uzbekistan

Throughout its history, the territory of present-day Uzbekistan was mostly dominated by the great surrounding empires of Persians, Greeks, Arabs, Mongols or Russians, and finally became a full-fledged state only in 1991. Nevertheless, it is this mixture of influences that makes the destination the real must of all Central Asian countries. Despite rather compli-

cated travel conditions (no or few foreign languages spoken, poor infrastructure, geopolitical unrest) in which the independent visitor must have a spirit of adventure, Uzbekistan is incredible for its cultural heritage and landscapes. The highlight of the trip are the cities of the Silk Roads, especially Samarkand, but also Bukhara and Khiva, which alone deserve the trip.

• Emir Tamerlan adorned Samarkand with prestigious buildings in the 14th century. The necropolis of Chah-e Zendeh, the Gur-e Mir and the madrasas make it a turquoise and golden destination with an exhilarating atmosphere of bazaar and adventure. Less well known, Bukhara is an important center of Islamic art. Khiva, a fortified city in the heart of the Kyzyl Kum desert, was also an important stop on the Silk Road. Tashkent is a cosmopolitan city, aerated by wide green spaces and refreshed by numerous fountains, which is the current cultural center of the country. Its eastern district and the Museum of Applied Arts are well worth a visit.

• In addition to these cities, which make Uzbekistan one of the most touristic countries of the former USSR, there are many archaeological sites. Northeast of Samarkand, on the site of Afrassiab, visit the necropolis of Chakhi-Zinda, composed of several richly decorated mausoleums. 70 km southeast of Samarkand, the archaeological site of Pendjikent is discovered through a fertile valley of cotton fields. 7 km west of Bukhara, one can admire the monumental complex of Chor-Bakr.

• First foothills of the Himalayas, the Pamir mountains dominate Samarkand and reach the borders of Pakistan and India. At their feet, the steppes cover an immense territory. The rocky plateaus and the dunes of the Kyzylkoum desert are part, like the Fergana valley, of the most beautiful regions of Central Asia.

Vietnam

At the extreme east of the Indochinese peninsula is the territory of Vietnam, whose dragon shape is a harbinger of the strength of character that this nation is capable of. It took 30 years of struggle to achieve independence. Since its reunification in 1975 and in spite of communism, this country has not ceased to catch up, opening itself more and more to the world. Due to its many contrasts due to its history, its 54 different ethnic groups, and the diversity of its landscapes, Vietnam is a particularly rich destination for the visitor in search of a change of scenery and encounters.

• The Halong Bay is one of the major attractions of the country. 2,600 rocky islets with surprising shapes emerge from the waters and are part of those emblematic images that make us all dream. The bay is generally visited during cruises of varying lengths on hotel boats.

• The Mekong Delta is to be discovered by sampan. By admiring the silhouettes of the peasants in their hoods, which are cut out along the rice fields and gardens, the traveler feels in the heart of Asia.

- Ho Chi Minh City (formerly Saigon), is the youngest and richest city in the country. The colonial district is one of the most charming and Cholon, the Chinese district, is full of life and bicycles. To better understand the country, a visit to the History Museum is recommended.

• On the opposite side of the country is Hanoi, a city famous for its pagodas, monuments and housing. Historic heart of Vietnam, four districts make up the city, two of which are worth a visit: Ba Dinh and Hoan Kiem.

• In between, the former imperial city of Hue is a stopover that is usually on the traveler's agenda. On the exotic Perfume River, Hue is famous for its superb imperial city and a remarkable set of pagodas.

• In the center of the country, the large city of Danang is gradually becoming a famous seaside destination with the construction of large hotels and resorts. The attractiveness of the region lies nevertheless in the small town of Hoi An, a jewel of exoticism, a preserved city where one can travel by bicycle and famous worldwide for its tailors and its streets lit with Chinese lanterns.

* Minorities such as the Mongs, Nungs or Daos live in the mountains of Tonkin in the north of the country, especially around Sapa. Hiking and visiting the markets allows you to meet these populations and their traditions, while enjoying the beautiful landscapes.

* 3000 km of coastline stretches along the South China Sea. The center and the south of the coastline already look like postcards of the beaches of South Asia. Many seaside resorts such as Vung Tau, Mui Ne, Phan Thiet or Nha Trang will allow you to rest between the various adventures offered by the rest of the country. At the extreme south of the country, the island of Phu Quoc is worthy of the Thai islands but tourism is still quite confidential.

Yemen

Either Yemen hasn't changed for centuries, or it has just emerged from the ground... Villages intermingled with landscapes in a thousand shades of brown, vestiges and hills dotting the horizon, the impression is such that one is left speechless. An ideal setting to observe the ancestral traditions that punctuate the life of the country. Kingdom of the Queen of Sheba, this territory has a magical aura that the political turmoil and wars of recent years prevents from radiating.

* From the capital Sana'a the tone is set. At 2,350 m, the ramparts of the oldest architectural complex in the Middle East encircle a city of finely crafted buildings whose windows boast glass tile half moons called qamariyas.

* Mountain villages such as Hodeida, Baraqich or and Ta'izz offer themselves to the eyes of hikers along picturesque roads. At more than 3000 m above sea level, the stone, brick or adobe constructions are part of the high plateaus that welcome them.

* Tihama, the coastal plain - almost a desert - plunges into the Red Sea in wild and overheated beaches. For adventurous divers, a paradise that is difficult to reach: the islands north of As Salif.

* On the other side, the Arabian Sea also has its treasure: the island of Socotra for which any botanist would be damned. More than 800 species of plants grow there, 200 of which do not exist elsewhere.

Denmark Strait

ARCTIC CIRCLE

Akureyri
ICELAND
Vatnajokull
REYKJAVIK
2119 ▲
Hvannadalshnukur

Lafoten
Vestfjorden

Trondheimsfjorden
Trondheim
1796 ▲
Alesund
NORWAY
2469 ▲ Galdhopiggen
Bergen
OSLO ★
Drammen
Norrkö...

Faroe Islands
(Denmark)
Suduroy

Shetland Islands
(UK)

Stavanger
Kristiansand
Skagerrak
Goteborg

Orkney Islands
Wick
Isle of Lewis

NORTH
SEA

DENMARK
COPENHAGEN ★
Malmo

Rockall

Hebrides
SCOTLAND   Aberdeen
Perth
Glasgow
Edinburg

British
Isles
ULSTER
Belfast
IRELAND
DUBLIN
Cork

UNITED
Newcastle
KINGDOM
Liverpool Manchester
WALES   ENGLAND
Birmingham

Frisian Is.
Hamburg
NETHERLANDS
AMSTERDAM ★
Rotterdam   Berlin ★
Dusseldorf
GERMANY
Leipzig
PRA...
CZE...

NORTH

ATLANTIC

CELTIC SEA
Cardiff
Plymouth

Southampton
LONDON
English Channel
Le Havre   Lille
Brest   BRUSSELS ★
BELGIUM
Rennes   LUX.
PARIS ★
Frankfurt
Stuttgart
Strasbourg
Danube
Munich
VIEN...
AUST...

Nantes
FRANCE
BERNE ★
Geneva LIECHT.
Lyon   SWITZ.
Mt Blanc   4810 ▲
A   SLOVENIA
L   LJUBLJANA
P
S   Milan
Venice
CROAT...

Bay of
Biscay   Bordeaux
Massif
Central
Turin
Florence
S.M.

OCEAN

Toulouse Montpellier
Pyrenees   Marseille
Bilbao   3404 ▲   Nice
Vigo   Aneto   AND.   Gulf of
Valladolid   Liona   Corsica
Douro
Porto   Zaragoza
Coimbra   Ebro   Barcelona
MADRID ★
PORTUGAL **SPAIN** Balearic Is.
LISBON ★   Tage Valencia   Menorca
Ibiza   Mallorca

M.C.
ITALY
VAT. ★ ROME
Naples
Sardinia

Azores
(Portugal)

Sierra Morena
Cordoba
Seville 3482 ▲
Mulhacen
Gibraltar (U.K.)
Strait of Gibraltar Ceuta (Spain)
Tangiers   Melilla(Spain)

MEDITERRANEAN SEA
ALGIERS ★   Annaba TUNIS ★
Chlef   ★
Oran   Constantine
TUNISIA
2236 ▲

Palermo
3323 ▲ Etna
MALTA
Sfax

Map of Eastern Europe, Russia, and surrounding regions showing:

Countries/Regions labeled:
Lapland, Finland, Estonia, Latvia, Lithuania, Kaliningrad (Russian Fed.), Belarus, Ukraine, Moldova, Romania, Bulgaria, Serbia, Kosovo, Montenegro, F.Y.R.O.M., Albania, Greece, Turkey, Cyprus, Syria, Iraq, Georgia, Armenia, Azerbaijan, Russian Federation, Kazakhstan, Uzbekistan, Turkmenistan, Slovakia, Hungary, B&H

Cities:
Kiruna, Lulea, Umea, Oulu, Vaasa, Tampere, Pori, Turku, Helsinki, Tallinn, Riga, Vilnius, Minsk, Warsaw, Krakow, Bratislava, Budapest, Belgrade, Bucharest, Sofia, Skopje, Tirana, Athens, Salonica, Corfu, Izmir, Bursa, Istanbul, Ankara, Konya, Antalya, Adana, Mersin, Kayseri, Gaziantep, Aleppo, Al Mawsil, Kirkuk, Nicosia, Rhodes, Peloponnesus, Olympus (2911), Musala (2925), 2542, 3088, Nar'yan Mar, Vorkouta, Murmansk, Arkhangel'sk, Petrozavodsk, Syktyvkar, St Petersburg, Novgorod, Pskov, Vologda, Viatka, Kudymkar, Perm', Iaroslavl, Kostroma, Ivanovo, Nizhniy Novgorod, Yoshkar-Ola, Izhevsk, Yekaterinburg, Tver, Moscow, Vladimir, Cheboksary, Kazan', Smolensk, Kaluga, Ryazan', Tula, Saransk, Simbirsk, Ufa, Chelyabinsk, Tol'yatti, Samara, Orenburg, Bryansk, Gomel, Orel, Penza, Saratov, Ural'sk, Koursk, Lipetsk, Tambov, Kharkiv, Belgorod, Voronezh, Aktyubinsk, Lviv, Chisinau, Dnipropetrovsk, Donetsk, Volgograd, Odesa, Rostov-na-Donu, Atyrau, Sevastopol, Krasnodar, Elista, Astrakhan', Stavropol', Maykop, Groznyy, Makhachkala, Tbilisi, Yerevan, Baku, Turkmenbashi, Nukus, Urgench, Ashgabat, Mary, Turkmenabat, Mashhad, Gorgan, Tehran, Tabriz, Qom, Mt Ararat (5137), 4810, 5671

Physical features:
Kola Peninsula, Chesha Bay, Arctic Circle, White Sea, Gulf of Bothnia, Aland, Gulf of Finland, Lake Imandra, Lake Oulu, Lakes Region, Lake Ladoga, Lake Onega, Lake Beloye, Lake Peipus, Rybinsk Reservoir, Nijni Reservoir, Kama Reservoir, Samara Reservoir, Saratov Reservoir, Baltic Sea, Carpathians Mts., Danube, Dnieper, Don, Volga, Oural, Ural Mountains (1895), Caspian Depression, Aral Sea, Caucasus, Elbrus 5642, Black Sea, Sea of Azov, Krimea, Caspian Sea, Kara-Kum, Bosporus, Anatolia (Asia Minor), Aegean Sea, Lake Van, Lake Urmia, Tigris, Euphrates, Salt Desert, Pechora, Mezen, Severnaya Dvina, Sukhona, Pripet, Kama, Crete

EUROPE

Albania

Forty years of fierce communism kept Albania out of the picture. Today, it is still one of the poorest countries in Europe that few travelers have ventured to explore. Chronic political instability in the Balkans has helped to keep tourists away from the area, but Albania's cultural richness is not least of all. Between the Mediterranean Sea and Eastern Europe, this rugged territory in every sense of the word has known the influence of all the great neighboring ancient civilizations and has managed to preserve many traces of this heritage. If we add to this the 362 km of sunny coastline and the very cheap aspect of the destination, Albania will not remain "the last secret of Europe" for long.

- Tirana, the capital, is the most interesting city in the country. The imposing communist buildings lined with squares and gardens with disproportionate volumes have not necessarily been restored and spread this atmosphere typical of countries that survived such a regime. Take a walk, beautiful surprises await you like the National Library or the old bazaar. To get an overview of the city and the plain that stretches around, take the cable car from Mount Dajti 25 km away.

- The Adriatic coast is almost deserted except for the seaside resort of Durrës. The lack of tourist facilities will allow you to discover natural shores that can rival those of Gr èceor Italy where summers are also always warm and sunny. To the south, towards Saranda, the meeting of the Ionian Sea and the land gave birth to beautiful beaches.

- The vestiges of Greek cities like Appolonia of Illyria or Greco-Illyrian cities like Butrint make Albania an almost obligatory detour for all fans of archaeology. All the more so since traces of Roman, Byzantine and Turkish occupation can be found throughout the rest of the country. This is the case in Berat, for example, a small town where history is on the walls.

- The Black Drin river valley in the north of the country is difficult to access, but offers the adventurers a succession of splendid gorges. At the source of the Black Drin, Lake Ohrid, one of the oldest in the world and the deepest in the Balkans, is known for the diversity and richness of its fauna.

Andorra

The Principality of Andorra, whose origins date back to the reign of Charlemagne, is one of the smallest states in the world. With an exceptional natural setting in the heart of the Pyrenees, it is above all its advantageous tax system that attracts tourists in search of savings.

- More than 6,000 stores are waiting for you to make tax-free purchases. Photo, video and hi-fi equipment, or more prosaically, alcohol bottles and full tanks of gas are at unbeatable prices.

- The sun and snow cocktail makes Andorra an ideal destination for skiers. The Grand Valira, which combines the Pas de la Case and Soldeu-El Tarter, is one of the largest ski resorts in the Pyrenees. The Vallnord ski area follows it closely and La Rabassa is specialized in cross-country skiing. In the summer, it is the turn of mountain bikes, horses and hikers to take over.

- In Caldéa, a spring of thermal water has led to the creation of a spa center offering balneotherapy activities that attract many tourists. The futuristic glass architecture of the building does not go unnoticed in the landscape.

- The religious architectural heritage bears witness to the fervor of the population. About twenty churches and chapels with beautiful paintings of Romanesque inspiration are scattered throughout the country and reflect the different terroirs. Those of Sant Cerni de Nagol and Sant Joan de Caselles are worth a visit.

Armenia

Armenia has gone through many years of suffering and misfortune. This small, mountainous and landlocked territory has been in conflict with its Turkish and Azerbaijani neighbors several times, and the seismic activity in the region has repeatedly caused major disasters. Despite these many difficulties, Armenia has been able to maintain a rich cultural heritage. The Armenian civilization is one of the oldest in the world, from the first kingdoms to the invention of the Armenian alphabet and the Christianization of the country, it has taken advantage of every event as a tool or inspiration for its cultural work.

• The capital, Yerevan, was founded in 782 BC and is one of the oldest cities in the world. With Mount Ararat as a backdrop, this pink city with its hilly relief is full of monuments, each more precious than the next. Known for its Matenadaran Library and the ten thousand very old Armenian manuscripts preserved there, it is also known for its fortress, its mosque, its market, its theater and its museums.

• In Echmiadzin, west of Yerevan, is the seat of the Armenian Apostolic Church and some of the oldest religious buildings in Christendom. It is nicknamed the "Armenian Rome" and deserves more than a detour. St. Etchmiadzin's Cathedral is classified as a World Heritage Site.

• To the east of Yerevan, it is the monastery of Saint Lance of Geghard which is likely to surprise more than one. Its chapels carved into the rock and its location are simply sumptuous. Continuing east, you will find Lake Sevan, a huge natural reservoir. All around the lake, you can visit various monasteries built on its shores, including Noradouz, Sevanavank and Ayrivank.

• Even further east, it is the temple of Garni that will attract the curious. The only Greek monument in the country, it was erected in 77 BC, with ramparts and solemn buildings. Built in basalt, it was devastated by an earthquake, but is now restored.

Austria

For a waltz or a slalom, Austria is a country that has a lot to offer. It is easy to think of a romantic weekend in Vienna or a musical trip to Salzburg, 1000 km away... Then you are in the land of Mozart, Strauss and Schubert. But you shouldn't forget the rest of the country and its great possibilities for snow sports and other sports activities, as well as the nature that takes you by storm.

• Vienna is one of the most beautiful cities in Europe. Crossed by the Danube, it is at the heart of Central Europe and has a cultural influence that goes beyond its borders. It is difficult to summarize all its attractions in a few lines: almost sixty museums, endless Baroque facades, cafés and bakeries on every street corner... and of course the omnipresent music from the famous Staatsoper (the national opera house) to Beethoven's house.

• Salzburg's Old Town, its fortress, museums and musical heritage can rival the capital. The facades of Linz, where the oldest church in Austria is located, are also worth a visit, as are Innsbruck and Graz, which to the west and east each have proud monuments with memorable roofs and bell towers.

• But if you only spend a weekend in Vienna, let yourself be tempted by a nearby excursion that sums up all the splendors of the country: Schönbrunn Palace. A Habsburg summer residence, it has more than a thousand gleaming rooms, about 40 of which are open to the public. The park and its formal gardens, but also the oldest zoo in the world, will perfectly complete a day out of modern times.

• Austria is three-quarters mountainous and is one of Europe's skiers' paradises. Every winter, there is a wide choice of places to go down the slopes on this side of the Alps and get a good breath of fresh air. To name but one, you will find in

Kitzbühel the most difficult and prestigious slope in the world: the Streif. You can ski until spring by practicing the "figl", a powder ski in full melting, practiced for example on the slopes of the Hafelekar-Spitze mountain.

• In the summer, Tyrol and Vorarlberg offer a wide range of sports activities such as mountain biking, hiking and canyoning. All this in dreamy landscapes where small flowery villages alternate with forests and high altitude lakes.

• The south of the country is not to be outdone, Carinthia and its national parks can be discovered on foot by hikers of all levels.

Belarus

Independent since 1990, Belarus is still deeply marked by its Soviet past, Russians represent 20% of the population, Russian is the second official language after Belarusian and the economy has not been thoroughly reformed. Its territory has one of the lowest population densities on the continent, with the majority of Belarusians living in urban areas. The 1994 constitution makes Belarus a secular state, but the life of Belarusians is deeply marked by the Orthodox religion. These three aspects, the Russian cultural heritage, the great wilderness and the Orthodox fervour make Belarus a land to discover.

• Minsk was almost completely destroyed during the Second World War, so it was rebuilt in the Soviet style: similar high facades, green spaces and wide avenues, all giving an impression of space. The main pre-1945 monuments are churches, generally very renovated, but there are still a few old houses and buildings, concentrated in the upper city east of the Svislach River.

• Hrodna (Grodno), 280 km west of Minsk, is much more picturesque, as it has managed to preserve its architectural heritage. You can visit the Farny Cathedral, the church and monastery of the Bernardins, the wooden church of St. Boris and St. Hlib, but also the museum of the History of Religion, the old castle and the new castle (Stari and Novi Zamak).

• On the Polish border is Brest. The most famous monument of the city is the memorial of the 1941 battle between Nazis and Soviets. Nearby is the fortress, partly rebuilt since the last war. It houses several museums, including the War Museum and the Archaeological Museum. The Church of the Resurrection of Christ is the largest religious building in Belarus. 70 km north of Brest, the Bialowieza Forest National Park is an exceptional nature reserve that is home to European bison. There are many possibilities for hiking and camping to discover this territory.

Belgium

Belgium is one of those small European countries that has to offer the cultural and architectural richness of its cities and the romanticism of its countryside. Besides beer and chocolate, Belgium has a lot more to offer.

• Brussels is the greenest capital of Europe and one of the most cosmopolitan cities in the world. Strolling along the Grand-Place to admire the ornamental richness of the guildhouses, dropping by the Manneken Pis and taking a break in the light of the stained glass windows of the Saint-Michel cathedral are the favourite stops for tourists. You can also go shopping in the luxury boutiques of the Galeries Royales Saint-Hubert, in the antique stores of the Sablon, or in the famous flea market of the Marolles. The Parc du Cinquantenaire, the Laeken Park and the Bruparck add to the many museums in the city, making it a destination in its own right.

• Bruges, in the north of the country, has many canals surrounding and crossing the city to the point of having earned it the nickname of "Venice of the North". The Belfry of the Main Square, the monuments of the Burg (Burg Square) and the beguinage are the main attractions. The numerous festivals and museums make it a cultural stopover with undeniable charm.

• Antwerp is less frequented than the previous ones, but it has nevertheless many assets. Apart from the Main Square, the highlight of the city tour is the Cathedral of Our Lady. Its 123-meter-high north tower in the flamboyant Gothic style is a real jewel, to which three monumental paintings by Rubens, major masterpieces of Flemish painting, can be added. For fans of painting, the city is home to numerous museums in addition to Rubens' house.

• The architectural heritage and museums of Ghent, the churches and warm atmosphere of Liege, the mixture of Gothic and Baroque art of Leuven and the beautiful natural surroundings and the collegiate church of Dinant are all exciting stops on a stay in the flat country. The many festivals and fairs that take place throughout the year will also liven up the stay.

• Excursions into the Belgian countryside will also offer you many surprises. In the south, hikes will take you to the heart of the forest landscapes of the Ardennes or to the peat bogs of the Natural Park Hautes Fagnes-Eifel. In the north, the charm of the North Sea and its vast beaches, as well as the dikes and canals around Damme will delight the most romantic among us.

Bosnia and Herzegovina

Bosnia and Herzegovina is a republic composed of two entities: the Federation of Bosnia and Herzegovina, and the Serbian Republic of Bosnia. Successively Roman, Slavic, Hungarian, Ottoman, Austro-Hungarian and Yugoslavian, this territory was torn apart by an inter-ethnic and religious war from 1992 to 1996. This conflict left many human and material after-effects.

• Sarajevo, the capital, was devastated by the civil war. Nevertheless, it has preserved a certain architectural heritage dating from the Ottoman period of its history, particularly in the city center in the Bascarsija district. From the Austrian protectorate, it has kept a few churches, a good number of administrative buildings and some rich private residences. Since the end of the war, tourism has resumed, especially around the various cultural events organized there or the winter sports possibilities offered by the surrounding mountains.

• Mostar, about 100 km south of Sarajevo, was completely destroyed during the conflict and has been rebuilt identically since. This has helped to preserve its appeal and charm. The Old Bridge District of the Old City of Mostar is a World Heritage Site. This bridge cuts the city in two: the modern districts of Mostar-West Mostar inhabited by a Croatian and Catholic majority and the Old Town of Mostar-East Mostar inhabited by a Bosnian and Muslim majority.

Bulgaria

What do you know about Bulgaria? Maybe not much, except the fame of their famous yoghurt and some memories from your geography or history classes. Now is the time to bring this destination back to the foreground and to evoke all its hidden beauties. Contrary to neighboring Romania, the 44 years of Bulgarian communist regime did not destroy the architectural and landscape heritage, each region has preserved its qualities and today invites the tourist to come and enjoy them.

• Sofia is one of those capitals where it is good to live. The markets are numerous there, the smiling inhabitants, and the architecture... disparate. Between the old cobbled streets lined with 19th century houses and the large avenues with Soviet style buildings, you will find jewels of neobyzantine architecture such as the Alexander Nevski Cathedral.

• To the south of the capital is one of the prettiest monasteries in all of Eastern Europe: the Rila Monastery. All made of wood, perched in the heart of the mountain, it is still active but opens its doors to hikers. If you like it, go down even further south to admire the frescoes of the monastery of Batchokovo a few kilometers from Plovdiv or go back up north to visit the monastery of Trojan.

• Numerous mountains are scattered throughout the country and will delight hikers in search of wild and unspoiled nature. In the southwest, between the Rila and Pirin mountains, a magnificent scenery of forests, emerald lakes and limestone ridges awaits you. Near Blagoevgrad, you can visit the Dancing Bears Park in Belitsa, one of the largest bear sanctuaries in Europe. In winter in the same region, skiing takes over. In the surroundings of Bansko, 65 km of ski slopes are waiting for you.

• To better understand Bulgarian history, nothing is better than spending a day and a night in Veliko Tarnovo, former capital of the Bulgarian Empire. Opposite the town on the hillside stands the ancient fortress Tsarevets where a sound and light show tells the history of the town at nightfall.

• The Black Sea coast has long made Bulgaria a favourite destination for communist regimes. Varna, the "pearl of the Black Sea" was marked by this period and remains today with the whole "Sun Coast" a very pleasant spot for those who are looking for a good substitute to the Mediterranean, but cheaper. For more authenticity and less nightclubs, go down to Nessebar built on a rocky peninsula.

Croatia

In recent years, Croatia has become one of the leading destinations in the Mediterranean. The beauty of the Dalmatian coasts and islands has nothing to envy to that of Italy or Greece èceand tourists are increasingly numerous. It is a truly fascinating country, with many wonders including the Palace of Split and the old city of Dubrovnik. Of all the former Yugoslavia, Croatia is the most interesting destination both by its coastline and its monuments and landscapes. The teams of the cult American series Game of Thrones have made no mistake in making Croatia their main source of scenery. One of the most beautiful destinations in the world.

• The coasts of Dalmatia and Istria are a geographical jewel. With the Dinaric Alps in the background, the landscapes of pine forests, creeks, gulfs and bays take on their full extent. This coastline with a very marked cut-out is surrounded by more than a thousand islands, each one more beautiful than the next. By sailboat or schooner, landing on uninhabited islets is a pleasure that is renewed each time.

• In the south of Dalmatia, Dubrovnik was the most popular destination before the conflict that shook the country from 1991 to 1995. Today the whole region is trying to regain the interest of tourists, Dubrovnik has received the help of UNESCO to restore its coat of arms and its fortified site shines again. The whole Makarska Riviera is once again welcoming tourists en masse. The islands of Brac, Hvar and KorÄ ula have both seaside and architectural attractions.

• A little further north, you will find the city of Split built on the remains of Diocletian's palace. It is the cultural and economic center of the region and offers the visitor a multitude of activities. Its neighbor, Trogir, with its medieval alleys lined with high stone houses is just as charming.

• Continue along the coast and you will arrive in Sibenik. The region is one of the most beautiful national parks of the country, that of Krka, crossed by the river of the same name and dotted with its waterfalls. The city itself has a magnificent cathedral dating back to 1434. Still in this northern part of Dalmatia, you will still have Zadar to visit. The rival city of Dubrovnik will delight you with its medieval churches and remains of fortifications.

• The west coast of Istria also has some coastal treasures less known to French tourists. Sport and idleness are however also on the program in Porec, Rovinj or Umag. In Pula, in addition to the sumptuous amphitheater left by the Romans, you will find these islands that were used as resorts by the entire Yugoslav intelligentsia, including Tito. Here you can visit his summer residence.

• The Opatija Riviera on the east coast of Istria was home to Austro-Hungarian high society in the 19th century. Beautiful nature surrounds the beautiful residences of that time, which have now often been converted into hotels.

• The Dinaric Alps extend from the northwest to the southeast of the country parallel to the coast. They are traversed by several hiking trails that allow to penetrate into a grandiose nature, between mountains and vast plains. Numerous caves and rocks with surprising shapes will delight speleologists and mountaineers.

• The Plitvice Lakes National Park located east of the Dinaric Alps was one of the main battlegrounds during the Serbo-Croatian War. Today, it is a wonderful place for hiking where 16 lakes with transparent waters shimmer in the sun and where waterfalls are born non-stop. A geological phenomenon of limestone dissolution transforms the landscape every day and arouses the admiration of tourists.

• Zagreb, the capital city, is far away from the most beaten tourist paths. Nevertheless, its museums and art galleries will make it a pleasant cultural stop, especially as it is a lively, young and cultural city.

Cyprus

Since 1973, Cyprus has been divided in two by the Green Line or "Attila Line". The Republic of Cyprus is the only one internationally recognized, however, it practically controls only the southern part of the island, as the northern part is occupied by the Turkish army and has declared itself the Turkish Republic of Northern Cyprus. To this division can be added the two British enclaves Akrotiri and Dhekelia, two military bases kept by the United Kingdom in the south of the country, but the same sun shines over the whole territory and the traveler can spend a peaceful vacation discovering the multicultural heritage of the country.

• Sand is rare on the Cypriot coasts which are more often covered with pebbles. However, the climate allows bathing until November and the cliffs are cut into the sea, which embellishes the landscape. If Limassol has been disfigured by mass tourism, the surroundings of Paphos (Coral Bay) and Aghia Napa are very busy, but have managed to preserve their environment. The beaches of Polis on the Akamas Peninsula in the northwest are the wildest. On the coast, do not miss also the set of rocks and cliffs Petro Tou Romiou where would have been born from the foam, Aphrodite, the goddess of Love.

• The mountainous and forested setting of the volcanic chain of Troodos as well as the freshness offered by its altitude (2000 m) gives the opportunity to make pleasant hikes to discover the small Byzantine churches that hide there (Asinou, Aghios Nikolaos and Panaghia tou Arakou), the small typical villages (Omodos) and the Greek Orthodox monasteries like the one of Kykko. In winter in this same region, it is possible to go skiing (in Platres for example). On the way back down to the west coast, you will cross the Cedar Valley (not to be missed during the flowering season between September and October).

• Many archaeological sites are scattered on the island. On the Greek side, don't miss Khirokitia (reconstitution of the circular huts of the first Orientals), Kourion (ancient Greco-Roman city) and Paphos (houses decorated with mosaics of Dyonisos, Theseus and Aiôn). On the Turkish side, do not hesitate to go to the south of the port of Kyrenia to visit the castle of Saint-Hilaire and the abbey of Bellapaïse. The medieval part of Famagusta and the ancient city of Salamine are also worth a visit.

• Nicosia, the capital, has been divided in two since 1974 and has suffered a lot from inter-community violence. Since 2004, relations have become more flexible and one can move from one side to the other. This will allow you to visit the old Greek quarter, its museums and Byzantine churches, but also the mosque (former Saint Sophia cathedral) and the Lusignan house.

Czech Republic

Since 1993 and the "Velvet Revolution", tourists have discovered Prague, one of the most beautiful European cities. But the Czech Republic is not only its capital, the ancient kingdoms of Bohemia and Moravia have many other surprises in store for you.

• Prague is called the "City of a Hundred Spires", but it actually contains 550 towers that contribute to the magic of the capital. The majestic Vltava, the statues of the Charles Bridge, the beautiful Baroque residences (including the Wallenstein Palace or the Clam-Gallas Palace), the buildings of the Viennese secession (such as the Municipal House) sometimes make it look like a theater set. The Old Town (Staro Mesto), the Lesser Town (Mala Strana, Kampa Island), the Castle Quarter (Hradcany), the Old Jewish Quarter (Josefov) and the New Town (Novo Mesto) are all worth exploring to unravel their mysteries.

• Bohemia and Moravia have nearly two thousand castles. In the vicinity of Prague alone, at least five can be seen: Troja, Zbraslav, Krivoklat, Konopiste and Karlstejn, one of the most famous. To the north, on the road to Bohemia, one must stop at Terezin, where the city's two fortresses were transformed by the Nazis into a Jewish ghetto and prison. To the northwest of Jicin, the Bohemian paradise is particularly famous for its sandstone "rock towns", such as Prachovské skály, whose fantastic shapes and picturesque names appeal to the imagination. On the border with Poland, the Giant Mountains offer hiking trails in the summer and ski slopes in the winter.

• To the west, Karlovy Vary is a very old spa resort where Goethe, Marx, Beethoven and Pushkin stayed. Equally famous is the town of Mariánské Lázne (Marienbad) with its rococo palaces, parks and fountains. Don't miss the Gothic and Baroque houses of Cheb and, on the border with Germany, the Soos reserve, whose soil gives off carbon dioxide fumes. To the south, near Austria, lies the small medieval town of Ceský Krumlov, which is a World Heritage Site.

• In the south-east, Moravia is less visited than Bohemia, although it is more authentic and has many interesting sites. Brno, the country's second largest city, is worth a visit for the Špilberk Fortress and the old St. Peter's Cathedral. Together with it, Olomouc is the historical, political, religious and university center of the region. In Trebic you can visit the Jewish quarter and the St. Prokopius Basilica. Telc has preserved an important medieval heritage and Slavkov u Brna is the site of the Battle of Austerlitz commemorated by the Peace Monument.

Denmark

Denmark is the smallest of the Scandinavian countries despite its almost five hundred islands, of which only 72 are inhabited. Between the Baltic Sea and the North Sea, beautiful landscapes and charming villages are waiting for you to discover another north.

• Copenhagen is a young city and culturally speaking, this means a certain dynamism. The capital's museums (the National Museum, the Museum of Fine Arts and the Glyptotek), but also the Dansk Design Center and the Carlsberg Visitors Center, as well as Louisiana, about 30 kilometers north of the city, will delight art and culture enthusiasts. For the stroller, the canals that crisscross the city, the emphasis on bicycle use and the lively city center make Copenhagen an ideal city for a weekend.

• The Danish royal dynasty is 1000 years old and its architectural heritage illuminates the country's landscapes. More than sixty castles await you all over the country. Frederiksborg Castle in Hillerød, built on three islets of Slotssø, is considered the masterpiece of the Danish renaissance. The castle of Kronborg located near the town of Elsinore is the one where the action of Hamlet takes place.

* Roskilde was the capital of Denmark from the 10th century to the 15th century; on the edge of a fjord, Viking ships used its strategic position to control the bay of Kattegat. Today, a museum recalls this period and the city's cathedral, where most of Denmark's kings and queens are buried, bears witness to the city's past importance.

* The island of Møn is located south of Sjælland Island and east of Falster Island. It is known for the chalk cliffs of Møns Klint. Do not hesitate to take the thousand or so steps down to the beach to admire them from the ground.

* In the far north of Jutland is the small village of Skagen, a favourite place of the country's painters at the end of the 19th century. Nearby, go to the tip of Grenen to admire the meeting of the North Sea and the Baltic Sea. The moving dune of Råbjerg Mile is the second largest in Europe and has been moving over the centuries. In the middle of the pines you will find a church that the elements have silted up over time.

* For those who would be tempted by a short dip in the salt water, the most suitable beaches for swimming are located in the east of the country. The coasts of Fionie, the southern Seeland, Loland and the small island of Bornholm are covered with fine sand that attracts visitors.

FAROE ISLANDS :

The Faroe Islands are a group of 18 islands that belong to Denmark and lie between Scotland and Iceland. A volcanic relief bristling with basalt cliffs, cut by fjords and beaten by the winds, constitutes the landscapes of these islands of the far north.

* A 12 km hike starting from Oyrabakka will allow you to discover the landscapes of the island of Streymoy dotted with lakes, waterfalls and impressive cliffs before going down to the village of Leirvik. On Vagar, don't miss to go to the lake Fjallavatn or the Bøsdalafossur waterfall. For those who like climbing, you can choose the Slaettaratinfur or the Gráfelli on the island of Eysturoy. Koltur, the smallest island of the archipelago, is also an island to be discovered on foot after a helicopter ride.

* The coasts are also sumptuous, you can walk along the south coast of Vagar to the village of Sandavagur known for its two-colored church, admire the panorama offered by the west coast of the same island between Sorvagur and Bour on the island of Mykines and the neighboring islets of Gasholmur and Tindholmur, or discover the canyon dug by the sea in the cliffs of the northeast coast of Eysturoy in the vicinity of Gjov. Numerous species of birds will offer you an aerial show during the whole trip.

* South of Streymoy, Thorshavn, the capital, is worth visiting for the lively port and the narrow streets of its historical district. To the southwest of Bordoy, Klaksvik is the second largest city in the Faroe Islands and its setting is dominated by the impressive slopes of Kunoy, across the arm of the sea that separates them.

GREENLAND :

One cannot really say that Greenland is a tourist destination in the classical sense of the word. There is not really any infrastructure, starting with roads (the most common means of land transportation is still the dog sled), the climate is harsh (summer exists but it never gets over ten degrees) and the landscape is logically not very varied. To be honest, in the register, Antarctica is a much more grandiose trip, however it is unaffordable for many travelers (both in time and money). So Greenland, even if it is ultimately a rather different place, is a less complex alternative for those who wish to discover the icy spaces of our planet. It is a wonderful experience, rather than a trip, the opportunity to discover a unique culture, spectacular landscapes and a very special place, without forgetting to touch the immense problem of melting ice pack, which Greenlanders live every day. The aurora borealis, a magical spectacle that deserves the trip, the glaciers and icebergs, the Nordic fauna or, to the astonishment of the visitors, the colorful villages, are the main assets of this immense island, which is not a country but a dependency of Denmark. Obviously everything is quite complex in the tourist register and it is often expensive, but without risks (except for the unwary). Travelers who like expeditions, who know what to expect and who have an attraction for the far north, will try the adventure. It is highly recommended to use a travel service provider.

* The Northern Lights are a fascinating spectacle. It is in the south, during the darkest nights of autumn, that you can

see the most beautiful. As for the midnight sun, it is visible at the latitude of Jacobshavn (west center of the island) during the whole month of June. In winter, the total polar night only affects the northernmost parts of the island (and are in a way even stranger than the midnight sun).

• The glaciers that cover most of Greenland descend to the ocean before giving way to icebergs scattering the waters. It is generally from Disko Bay, a typical Arctic village on the west coast, that one can embark on a mini-cruise between the blocks of ice. On the east coast, in Tasiilaq, don't miss a boat tour in the Sermilik Fjord.

• The spectacle of the colonies of walruses, narwhals, seals, penguins and terns can be enjoyed both by boat and on foot. The possibilities of excursions are numerous towards the approaches of the Icelandic, the lakes and the mountains. The south coast is the most suitable for discovering the spring and summer vegetation.

• From Qaqortoq, one of the prettiest cities in the country, you can take a boat to Hvalsey, one of the best preserved Viking ruins in the region. Do not hesitate to go for a swim in the hot springs of Uunartoq Island, close to the icebergs.

• The lack of roads or railroads to get around requires the use of new means of transportation such as dog sledding or kayaking. Today, one can go as far as the Thule polar base region, an expedition that is obviously reserved for well-prepared travelers.

Estonia

Estonia is the smallest of the Baltic countries and the northernmost of the three. Having regained its independence in 1991, it is now outward-looking. At the forefront of new technologies, it has offered software such as Skype to Internet users around the world. But what does it have to offer visitors?

• The capital, Tallinn, has managed to preserve its architectural heritage despite the bombings of the Second World War. A medieval city surrounded by ramparts dating back to the 13th century, it was also a trading post of the Hanseatic League (association of northern European merchant cities) for several centuries. From the citadel of the upper town to the Gothic Town Hall of the lower town, you will cross a meander of lively cobbled streets. The Dominican monastery and the Kadriorg Palace are worth a visit.

• To the north of the Estonian territory is the Lahemaa National Park where a thousand lakes are hidden in a dense forest. Near the eastern edge of the park, the Baroque Palmse Manor House is popular for its period furniture and large grounds.

• The island of Saaremaa is the most important island in the country and has become a leading destination for the neighbouring Finns. It is the most pleasant place in the country when the good weather arrives. The Episcopal castle of Kuressaare is worth a visit. Also look for the meteorite crater in Kaali.

• Located in the village of Kuremäe in the northeast of the country is the Pühtitsa Monastery built on a former pagan shrine. It is still active, but you can still spend the night there. This monastery welcomes thousands of pilgrims every year.

• On the coast, you will have to go to Pärnu. First fishing port of the country, it is also a charming seaside resort with its wooden houses from the beginning of the century. Haapsalu, another "Venice" (from the Baltic this time), is also worth a visit.

Finland

Finland has taken up the challenge to make its inhabitants live in perfect harmony with nature, and the same will be true for the traveller who comes to discover its territory. Through various activities, he will see all the beauty of the country's forests, lakes, marshes and beaches.

• Beyond the Arctic Circle lies Lapland, which seems to be still untouched by tourists despite the craze it experiences every autumn during the Indian summer and every winter. It can be discovered on skis in Levi, Ylläs, near Kittila, or Saariselka, near Ivalo, but also by snowmobile, dog or reindeer sled, toboggan, snowshoe or cross-country skiing. The polar night (and the Northern Lights) is followed, from mid-May to the end of July (depending on the location), by the fabulous midnight sunlight.

• In winter, you can also discover the Gulf of Bothnia Sea by snowmobile, as it freezes enough to travel safely on its surface. Departing from Kemi, have the incredible experience of going from island to island in this way. You will also be able to embark on a huge icebreaker that will make you sail on this icy sea. In the original winter experience section, you can even spend the night or have dinner in a real ice castle that is built every year in Kemi.

• In the summer, you will discover the wonderful landscapes of Mount Saana on foot or by bike in the Lemmenjoki and Pallas Ounastunturi national parks and in the vicinity of Lake Inari where the sacred island of Uko and a Lappish cemetery are located. In the south-eastern part of the country and in Karelia, nature reserves more than two hundred thousand lakes hidden in the heart of the forest. Isolated wooden cottages on the islets welcome nature lovers. There are many activities to practice: canoeing, hiking, fishing, swimming and gold panning.

• Along the southern coast, the "Route of the Kings" once used by kings, bishops and notables on their way from Norway to Russia, offers visitors numerous historical monuments and charming little wooden villages. Do not hesitate to stop in Kotka, Loviisa, Porvoo, Karjaa, Kirkkonummi, Pohja, Inkoo and Turku. Opposite the latter, the Åland archipelago (6,000 islands and granite islets) punctuates the Baltic Sea with its forested landscapes where castles, stone churches and windmills are hidden.

• Helsinki is especially noteworthy for its location on a peninsula that offers the possibility of beautiful sea trips. Nevertheless, don't miss the small islands of Suomenlinna, a former fortification in the city's harbour, the Orthodox Uspenki Cathedral, the Temppeliaukio church dug into the rock and the museums of the Suomenlinna fortress, a quarter of an hour away by ferry. Tourism in Helsinki is largely dominated by culture and as in all Nordic countries, architecture and design are of great importance.

France

France is the most visited country in the world, Paris, its capital, is the first tourist city in terms of attendance and the Eiffel Tower is the monument that sells the most tickets on the planet. The great variety of landscapes, the length of the coasts, the number and diversity of monuments without forgetting the prestige of the French culture as well as the richness of the heritage explain the craze of the visitors.

THE NORTH :

• Paris is one of the world's great capitals, full of all kinds of activities, exceptional museums, historic monuments and unmissable districts filled with famous Parisian cafés. From the Champs-Élysées to the Latin Quarter, the Butte Montmartre, the Louvre and Notre Dame de Paris, the City of Light is sure to dazzle you. But the Ile de France is not limited to Paris, don't hesitate to make a few excursions to visit the Palace of Versailles, the Palace of Vaux le Vicomte, or the Basilica of Saint-Denis, have fun at Disneyland or discover the Chevreuse Valley, Auvers sur Oise, the Forest of Saint-Germain or the medieval town of Provins.

- Between the Marne and the Somme, the Picardy region offers multiple facets. On the art side, take the road to the gothic cathedrals of Amiens, Beauvais or Laon, and make a royal stop at Chantilly or Compiègne. On the nature side, walk along the bay of the Somme and its floating gardens, follow the Chemin des Dames and discover the Aisne bocage. You can also observe the birds of the Parc du Marquenterre or visit the creuttes, the typical troglodytic dwellings of the Laonnais region.

- The Nord-Pas-de-Calais is visited for its "Belle Époque" seaside resorts such as Le Touquet or Merlimont, the architectural wealth of its cities such as Lille or Arras, the importance of the port cities (Calais, Dunkirk) and the bocage landscapes in Avesnois, the slag heaps around Lens and the 120 km of beaches of the Opal Coast. The street fairs, carnivals and festivals are added to the culture of beer to make the daily life of the North a surprising festival.

THE WEST :

- The Brittany peninsula has the largest seafront in France and each portion of this coastline has its own identity that you can discover by taking the customs officers' path (today GR34) from the port of Saint-Nazaire to the gates of Mont-Saint-Michel. Several islands punctuate the Gulf of Morbihan like the Ile aux Moines, a small paradise full of flowers, the island of Arz to be discovered by bike or Belle-Ile-en-Mer with its magnificently steep relief. Several circuits will allow you to admire the beauties of Brittany's inland lands and their architectural surprises, such as those of the Route des enclosures (Landerneau, Landivisiau and Morlaix). Big cities like Rennes or Nantes, and small towns often largely pedestrian will reserve you many encounters with the past at the bend of a street or a staircase. The architectural heritage of Brittany also has to offer you several megalithic monuments, including the alignment of Belz.

- The cathedral of Le Mans, the castle of the Dukes of Brittany and the abbey of Fontevraud, which hosts the Cultural Center of the West, are the major buildings of the Pays de la Loire. The Loire Valley, listed as a World Heritage Site, is partially contained within this region. The Loire Valley castles located in the region are the castle of Montreuil-Bellay, the castle of Montsoreau, the castle of Saumur, the castle of Brissac, the castle Le Lude, the castle of Baugé, the castle of Serrant, the castle of Angers and the castle of Plessis-Bourré. The medieval city of Guérande, located on the Guérande peninsula, is known for its salt marshes while the Puy du Fou is one of the most popular French amusement parks. On the lazy side, the seaside resorts of Croisic, Pornic, La Baule, Saint-Brévin-les-Pins or Sables d'Olonne are very popular. The landscapes of the Marais Poitevin, the "Green Venice" and those of the Regional Natural Park of Brière can be discovered by bike or by barge.

- With 600 kilometers of coastline, Normandy offers the tourist an astonishingly varied landscape. The cliffs of the Albâtre Lake, including those of Étretat, are followed by the tourist highlights of the Côte Fleurie (Deauville, Trouville, Honfleur and Cabourg), the historical testimony of the D-Day landing beaches and the wild nature of the Cotentin, the coast then ends in apotheosis with the Mont-Saint-Michel. The Church of Saint-Nicolas in Caen, the cathedral of Bayeux and the abbeys of Lessay and Cerisy la Forêt are other important testimonies of the Norman architectural school where the Gothic style, nourished by the traditions of Romanesque architecture, reached perfection. Le Havre is the only city whose modern architecture is classified as a World Heritage Site for its downtown. the southwest :

- No less than 450 kilometers of coastline line the Charente coast, beaches, cliffs and islands promise visitors beautiful hours of sunny rest. Royan, with its five beaches, is its seaside capital. Off the coast of La Rochelle, the pines, vineyards and salt marshes of the Ile de Ré are easily discovered by bicycle. Oysters and fine sand are the key words on the Ile d'Oléron. Past Royan, the Gironde estuary offers the spectator unusual landscapes where caves and small coastal villages invite to stroll. The fortified city of La Rochelle, the arsenal of Rochefort, the zoo of La Palmyre are all worth a visit. Inland, in the Marais Poitevin, you can discover the vineyards surrounding Cognac or follow the meanders of the Charente. Angoulême, city of comics and Poitiers and the Futuroscope offer a lot of entertainment.

- Bordered on its entire western side by the Atlantic Ocean, Aquitaine is bathed in the mild oceanic climate and the Gulf Stream. Between the famous seaside resorts, 250 km of coastline offer as many fine sandy beaches suitable for relaxation, but also for surfing. Biarritz and Arcachon are seaside resorts with a longstanding reputation, but Hendaye, Saint-Jean-de-Luz, Cape Breton, Hossegor, Biscarrosse-Plage or Lacanau are also very popular. The gastronomic and wine-producing reputation of the territories of the Basque Country, the Périgord, the Dordogne and the Bordeaux region is well established. The natural areas of the Dune du Pilat, the limestone plateaus of Quercy, the Landes de Gas-cogne and the Pyrenees offer equally delicious landscapes. Thermalism also has its place through eleven renowned thermal spas such as in Dax or Saint-Paul-lès-Dax.

• The Midi-Pyrénées is the largest region in metropolitan France and is very rich touristically speaking. The prehistoric sites of the caves of Niaux and Mas d'Azil, the Romanesque cathedral of Saint Lizier, the Cathar heritage of the castle of Montségur and the feudal fortresses of Foix and Tarascon-sur-Ariège, make Ariège a department full of emotion. Aveyron is the country of the Causses Noir, Larzac, the valleys of Ségala, Tarnet de la Dourbie, the gorges of Truyère and Jonte, the lake of Pareloup and Aubrac, as many landscapes which inspire respect among which hide bastides and cities of the Templars (Belmont sur Rance, Bozouls, Conques, Espalion...). The cathedral of Albi, the fortified city of Corde-sur-Ciel and the other sites of the Tarn are integrated into the imposing and varied nature of the Black Mountain, the forest of Grésine and the Gaillacois vineyards. The pink city of Toulouse, steeped in tradition and history but also a lively student city, and the Canal du Midi are the two stars of the Haute-Garonne. The gastronomy of the Gers, certainly the most authentic corner of the country, the legends of the Lot, and the sports activities of the Hautes-Pyrénées are also waiting for you. the south-east :

• Between Provence, Catalan country and Camargue, Languedoc-Roussillon cultivates its contrasts for the pleasure of travelers. The 200 kilometers of coastline are home to modern marinas such as La Grande Motte as well as small towns of character such as Sète or Aigues-Mortes. Of the five departments that make up this region, only Lozere does not have a seafront, it nevertheless has some small treasures such as the Aven Armand or the Tarn Gorges. The Cathar castles and the fairy-tale fortified city of Carcasonne, Montpellier the university, Nîmes the Roman, the hiking trails of the Canigou massif or the beautiful village of Collioure on the shores of the Mediterranean are beautiful destinations.

• The PACA region offers a wide range of activities always sunny. In the north, the Hautes-Alpes alternates between the joys of snow in winter and hiking in summer as in Serre-Chevalier or in the Champsaur Valgaudemar. The beauty of the Mercantour and the Verdon gorges also promises many sensations. On the coast, Cannes, Nice and Saint-Tropez are the great social events of the summer. Add to this the pleasures offered by Antibes "la Phocéenne", Grasse the capital of perfumers with its picturesque old town, Saint Paul de Vence a chic and quiet village, the islands of Lerins with its monastery and Menton with its superb site and unique subtropical vegetation. The Bouches-du-Rhône is also a destination in its own right. From the creeks of Cassis to the Baux de Provence in the Alpilles, from the Camargue and its manades to the islands of Frioul and the famous Château d'If, landscapes and cultures combine for your well-being, and even the big cities like Marseille, Arles and Aix-en-Provence have a unique atmosphere and a remarkable historical allure. In the more rural Vaucluse, Avignon, with its famous broken bridge and its superb Palais des Papes, Vaison-la-Romaine and the Provencal massif of the Luberon, dotted with typical villages, are very popular with tourists.

• The Rhône-Alpes is a sporting department. You will be able to canoe in the Ardèche gorges, go down the slopes of the 3 Valleys or Tigne-Val d'Isère ski area, hike in the Mont-Blanc massif or sail on the waves of Lake Geneva. Old Lyon, classified as a World Heritage Site, the Savigny Abbey, the castles and canals of Annecy, the spa resort of Aix-les-Bains, but also many other sites are to be explored in the region. Gourmets will be spoilt for choice among the specialties to be enjoyed accompanied by a Beaujolais or a Côtes-du-Rhône, and the many renowned tables.

THE EAST :

• The jewels of Franche-Comté's cultural heritage are the citadel of Besançon, the Royal Saltworks of Arc-et-Senans, the Château de Joux, the Chapel of Ronchamp and the Lion of Belfort. Don't hesitate to take the tourist trains of the Hirondelles line or the Horlogers line to discover the other beauties of the region. During the winter season, the Jura, in the resorts of Les Rousses and Métabief for example, gives pride of place to cross-country skiing.

• 1200 kilometers of rivers and canals will allow you to discover Burgundy along the water. The towpaths along the waterways, disused railroads, vineyard paths and small country roads have made it possible to set up a loop of about 600 kilometers of cycle routes and greenways. But it is wine that is without a doubt the most famous ambassador of the region. Chablis, Nuits-Saint-Georges, Beaune, Mercurey, Pouilly-Fuissé... 5 tourist routes will allow you to taste the best vintages. The hill of Vézelay and the basilica of Sainte-Madeleine are the starting point of one of the four routes of the Way of St. James of Compostela which then passes through the priory church of La Charité-sur-Loire. The other great architectural ensemble of the region not to be missed is the Cistercian Abbey of Fontenay.

* The towns, sites, monuments and religious buildings of Champagne-Ardenne bear witness to the region's rich past, whether in Reims, City of the Rites of the Kings of France, in Sedan with its imposing fortified castle, the largest in Europe, in Langres, a fortified citadel surrounded by ramparts, or in Troyes, the capital of the mesh and a historic stopover for the Champagne fairs. Most of them are located in Reims, Épernay and Châlons-en-Champagne, the Champagne Houses unveil their cellars, of great beauty or of particular historical value where you can taste the renowned bubbles of the Champagne-Ardenne region.

* Lorraine has admirably preserved and enriched its heritage. The grandiose archeological sites of Bliesbrück-Reinheim or Grand and the fortifications of the Maginot Line are its most outstanding examples, but the Saint-Etienne Cathedral in Metz, the Basilica of Saint-Nicolas-de-Port and the Stanislas Square in Nancy are other examples. The region's castles are the setting for magnificent achievements, such as those of Lunéville, Fléville and the Monthairons. In the Vosges, downhill and cross-country ski areas set in beautiful surroundings add to the appeal of the thermal spas of Bains-les-Bains, Contrexéville and Vittel.

* Alsace is the richest region in Europe in terms of the concentration of feudal castles, witnesses of its eventful history, the most famous of which is the Haut Koenigsbourg castle. From North to South, the Romanesque Road of Alsace invites you to discover a major aspect of the regional religious heritage and at the same time allows you to appreciate the richness of the region's landscapes. The jungle of the Ile de Rhinau, the abundant forest of Erstein, the Little Alsatian Camargue and its biological diversity, but also the panoramas of the Grand Ballon, the legends of the Cascades du Nideck or the vestiges of the Massif du Donon are the highlights of a visit in the region.Strasbourg, European capital, is a city of Art and History where the charm of the old districts and its cathedral is added to an excellent beer production.

THE CENTER :

* The Centre region is known for the architectural treasures of its heritage. The enchantment of Chambord, the purity of Chenonceau or the proud silhouette of the castle of Amboise overlook the Loire and make the happiness of tourists. Discover the royal river while taking a river walk, contemplate the colorful landscapes from the top of the towers of the cathedrals of Chartres and Bourges, find, during a visit to Nohant, the atmosphere of the novels of George Sand... The possibilities of strolls are more than numerous. The nature of the region is protected by three regional natural parks: the Brenne, country with a thousand ponds, the Perche and its sunken paths punctuated by green hedges, and Loire-Anjou-Touraine, jewel of the Loire Valley. To the north of the Loire, the Orleans forest is the largest state-owned forest in France and to the south of the valley, the Sologne is renowned for the beauty of its forests, moors and heather dotted with water bodies.

* Limousin is not one of the French regions most frequented by tourists. Nevertheless, it offers a large number of activities. You can canoe down the 120 km of the Dordogne valley, rich in castles and picturesque villages, hike in the Plateau de Millevaches or in the mounts of Blond or discover Creuse with a donkey. The site of Oradour-sur-Glane, a martyr village, the castles of Sédières, Val and the towers of Merle, but also the Cascades of Gimel or the national porcelain museum of Limoges are worth a visit.

* Scattered with lakes and forests, Auvergne offers its visitors the largest group of volcanoes in Europe. The Parc Naturel Régional des Volcans d'Auvergne watches over the five groups that make up this unusual land: the chain of Puys (or Monts Dômes), the Massif du Sancy (or Monts Dore), the Artense and Cézallier plateaus and the Monts du Cantal. More than 500 Romanesque churches, nearly 50 castles are to be visited on the Historical Road of the Castles of Auvergne and the 10 water towns heir to the charm of the Belle Époque, including Vichy, are as many welcoming stops along the tourist circuits. The "Via Podiensis" starting from Le Puy-en-Velay is one of the four routes described as early as the 12th century to reach the Spanish sanctuary of Santiago de Compostela, a hiking trail that today continues to reveal its beauties to those who choose to take it.

CORSICA :

Corsica has been known since ancient times as one of the most beautiful islands in the Mediterranean. The Greeks named it "Kallisté": the most beautiful, and we call it today "the island of beauty". Its assets and its strategic position within the Mediterranean geopolitical space have made it a territory that several great nations have sought to appropriate over the centuries. French since 1768, the island is one of our most beautiful and proudest departments, and there is reason to be. Thanks to its one thousand kilometers of coastline, including about 300 kilometers of fine sand, Corsica is a dream place for yachtsmen, divers and other lovers of the deep blue sea. For those who are more attracted by the green, they will be delighted by the inland where the green mountains are home to a very ancient culture.

- The Cap Corse is a kind of peninsula about 40 km long where each village has its own small port. Going around it will allow you to admire multiple landscapes while giving you pleasant stops on the small pebble creeks that dot the east coast.

- Located in the north-east of Corsica, at the base of the Cap Corse, Bastia is the main port of the island and its main commercial city. Listed as a City of Art and History for its museum, its old palace and its fortress, it is its gentle way of life that makes it such a friendly city.

- Porto Vecchio is one of the favorite cities for tourists, as it has some of the most beautiful beaches in the country such as Cala Rossa, Palombaggia and Santa-Giulia. The animation of its alleys and the luxury of its hotels reinforce this idea of an ideal destination.

- Bonifacio is located at the extreme south of Corsica. The narrow streets of the old fortified town, the limestone cliffs over 60 meters high, but also the windswept desert plateau that occupies all the surroundings make it an unmissable stopover. This sentinel city has been facing since ancient times the archipelagos of the Lavezzi and Cerbicales islands, famous for their seabed.

- Ajaccio is located on the west coast of Corsica, at the bottom of the gulf of the same name. The yellow facades of the buildings, the alleys and the numerous café terraces contribute to give the city a pleasant atmosphere. The "sentier des Crêtes" (ridge path), which starts from the city center, allows an easy hike and offers splendid panoramas on the gulf. The shores of the gulf are dotted with a multitude of beaches and small coves ideal for swimming and scuba diving.

- The gulf of Porto, on the west coast, is listed as a World Heritage Site. The Genoese tower of Turghiu, which overlooks Capo rosso, offers a breathtaking 360 degree view of the entire region. The nature reserve of the Scandola peninsula offers sumptuous landscapes populated by numerous seabirds and endemic and protected plants. The calanches of Piana are also part of the most beautiful panoramas of the region.

- Calvi occupies a privileged position in Corsica. Located at the end of the Balagne, it can boast of its mild climate, its blond beaches, the mountain range among the highest in Corsica that surrounds it, its proud citadel, its historical past, its ports and its international airport.

- The hinterland of Porto (the Deux-Sevi) stretches east to the Vergio Pass. Isolated from the coast, this region has kept its freshness and authenticity and nature has kept its rights. Don't hesitate to walk from village to village (paying attention to the herds that wander freely on the road) and you will have some nice surprises such as the Spelunca gorges and the Aïtone forest.

- In the middle of the regional park, the aiguilles de Bavella are among the most beautiful places of the Corsican interior. Jagged peaks, large rocky walls and wind-bent pines are the ingredients. The GR 20 passes at the foot of the aiguilles in the Asinao valley but a variant called "alpine" allows to approach the towers of Bavella.

- Balagne is located on the northwest coast of the island and is one of the first wine-growing regions of Corsica. In order to defend their heritage and make their villages live, craftsmen have founded the association "Corsicada" to promote the discovery of Corsican craftsmanship. Potters, engravers, organ builders and violin makers await you in Pigna and Sant'Antonino for example.

* Castigniccia takes its name from the chestnut tree, castagnu in Corsica, of which the whole region is dotted. Situated in central-eastern Corsica, it is one of the greenest and most wooded corners of the island. In addition to nature, its exceptional religious heritage will thrill you at the turn of villages such as La Porta, Carcheto, or Piedicroce.

* Calacuccia is one of the most important villages of Corsica and draws its fame from its lake. This lake provides the electricity that feeds the whole island and will be for you a very pleasant holiday resort where water activities are added to the multiple possibilities of hiking. In winter, the village allows you to reach the ski resort of the Vergio pass quite quickly.

* All hikers will find their happiness in the Asco valley. The Asco river flows from the highest point of the mountain into numerous gorges, and beautiful panoramas of the island's peaks are offered to hikers.

* The archaeological site of Filitosa is one of the biggest tourist places of Corsica. Megalithic monuments, menhir statues and dolmens emerge from the past to form one of the most important prehistoric complexes in the world.

* Starting from Corte, in the heart of the island, the Restonica gorges offer multiple possibilities for swimming and hiking. A winding road leads to the Grotelle sheepfolds which are the departure point to the lakes of Melo and Capitello, two grandiose sites that are well worth the effort to reach.

Georgia

The problems of rationalism in several Georgian autonomist provinces worsened in the 2010's in South Ossetia leading to a conflict between Georgia and this separatist province supported by Russian troops. While the situation has returned to normal in the rest of the country, this region, as well as Abkhazia, remains formally inadvisable for travelers. The surroundings of the Great Caucasus and the country's religious architectural heritage nevertheless make it a destination that may one day open to the general public.

* The capital Tbilisi, often the gateway to the country for tourists, is imbued with an oriental atmosphere that makes the first walks along the wooden houses and the Mtkvari river pleasant and relaxed. The Zion Cathedral and the very old Antchiskhati Basilica are among the most important monuments of the city. But many other religious buildings adorn the city. Near the Metekhi church (one of the most famous in Georgia) there is a mosque and a synagogue built next to each other.

* For fans of religious art, the country has several churches and monasteries that have made its reputation. The red drum dome of the Church of Zion in Ateni, the Bagrati Cathedral in Kathmandu, and the Ghelati Monastery are just a few examples.

* Gori is the birthplace of Stalin and his birth house has now been turned into a museum. The last unbroken statue of the dictator is here. The town is dominated by the medieval fortress of Goristsikhe. Opposite it rises a hill where there is a nice little church.

* Ouplistsikhe, founded in the 1st millennium BC is one of the most touristic places in the country. It is a troglodyte town where caves are connected by alleys and stairs. The result is quite magnificent. One of these caves contains a basilica from the 9th century.

* On the road leading from Tbilisi to Vladikavkaz in Russia, you will cross the Darial Gorge which has been carved by the Terek River whose valley contains sumptuous landscapes. At the northern border, the mountainous regions of the Great Caucasus could one day be suitable for skiing, but for the moment the most courageous will be able to discover them on foot.

• The beaches of the Black Sea have an almost Mediterranean atmosphere and the coastline is punctuated by small rather pleasant seaside resorts such as Batumi, Gagra and Sukhumi. Each one has its fortress, they still have to make their reputation.

Germany

In 2019, reunified Germany celebrated its 30th anniversary. It is therefore an historic country, but one with a young and original character. As a major European power, Germany is not one of the continent's major tourist destinations. However, the urban planning of the big cities, the charm of the countryside and the open-mindeness of the inhabitants are contrary to all the preconceived ideas we might have. Because Germany is a federal country, each region has its own identity, with its small (always dynamic) capital city and picturesque landscapes. It's up to you to choose your trip: discover Bavaria and the Black Forest for a nature vacation, go on a high level cultural adventure in the big cities, or explore lesser known corners of the country, such as the northern coast for example.

• The Bavarian Alps offer breathtaking panoramic views. The Bayerisher Wald National Park with its European brown bears and lynx is not to be missed.

• The German Alpine Road will take you to the many lakes in the region and will lead you to the extravagant romantic castles of King Ludwig II of Bavaria, including Neuschwanstein, the madness that was the inspiration for Walt Disney's Cinderella's Castle.

• Visiting the Rhine Valley by boat is a romantic journey through vineyards and castles, culminating in the small town of Heidelberg.

• The 17 spas towns in the Black Forest (southwest) offer a wide range of hiking opportunities in a beautiful landscape and a relaxing atmosphere.

• Berlin is the capital of Germany, one of the greatest cities in Europe, and is incredibly rich in monuments and museums. State-of-the-art architecture and a lot of alternative places make it a city not to be missed.

• Dresden is one of the most beautiful cities in the country. Completely baroque, it is known as the "Florence of Elba".

• Cologne, Germany's oldest city, is crossed by the Rhine and has a magnificent cathedral, certainly the most beautiful monument in the country.

• Munich and Hamburg, at both ends of the country, are also worth a visit. The former for its old center and its famous Oktoberfest (Oktoberfest). The second for its canals and its vibrant atmosphere of historic port.

Gibraltar

Gibraltar has been an overseas territory of the United Kingdom since 1704. It is located south of Spain, bordering the Strait of Gibraltar, which connects the Mediterranean Sea to the Atlantic Ocean.

• It is a preferred port of call for cruise ships, as goods and services are sold without value added tax. Feel free to go shopping on Main Street.

• Between scrubland, scrub and pine forest, a large part of the territory is occupied by the immense Rock of Gibraltar, a nature reserve populated by Berber macaques, the only wild monkeys in Europe. In addition to these, there is the interest of discovering the unique views of the Bay of Gibraltar, the Isthmus, Spain and Morocco, which are offered by the network of galleries dug into the rock.

Greece

White houses on a blue background, vestiges of sunny temples, creeks and heavenly beaches, Greece is the image of its mythology, polymorphous and fascinating. It is made up of three distinct geographical entities: mainland Greece, the Peloponnese peninsula and the islands that make up one fifth of the total surface area of Greece.

CONTINENTAL GREECE :

* The Roman ruins of Philippi correspond to an ancient city in eastern Macedonia. The theater, the forum and the baths are among the best preserved remains of the site, but it is the early Christian basilicas that attract the most attention, such as the Basilica of Paul, one of the oldest buildings of Christian worship, surely dated.

* The Monasteries of the Meteors form a superb ensemble of seven buildings suspended on top of huge grey rock masses, sculpted by erosion. The tour starts from the city of Kalambaka. A circuit of about 17 km allows to go around the monasteries.

* Delphi is one of the most famous and grandiose archaeological sites of the country. One finds there the sanctuary dedicated to Apollo to which the believers could ask their question through the famous Pythia which made its oracles. In addition to the temple, the theater and stadium tell a story that leaves visitors astonished. The geographical location is equally sumptuous.

* Athens, the capital, has as its emblem this fabulous acropolis that rises above the city. It is so large that it seems to be under constant renovation. The most visited monuments are the Propylæa at the entrance, then the Parthenon and the Erechtheion. Do not hesitate to take a tour of the museum where a rich collection will complete your visit. The museums in the rest of the city are also worth a visit for all fans of archaeology. And the city itself, with its narrow streets and lively atmosphere, reflects the Greece of today.

* Chalkidiki is that peninsula of Macedonia that the Greeks call "the secret paradise of Greece". Its beaches do not seek to compete with those of the Cycladic islands, but it is nevertheless an equally pleasant seaside destination. Ouranoupoli, for example, is a very popular resort for tourists. From Tripití, one can reach the coves of Ammouliani, the only island of Chalkidiki.

* Le Pinde is a mountainous massif of Epirus, in the north of Greece. Small villages populate the region of Zagoria and small paths connect them to each other. Towards Kipi and Koukouli, you will find superb arch bridges. The Vikos Gorge, the deepest canyon in Europe, is one of the other attractions of the region. To the east, the Pelion Massif is the setting for your hikes.

* Mount Olympus is the highest mountain in Greece and was in Greek mythology the domain of the gods. The total ascent of the mount is generally done over two days starting from Priona.

PELOPONNESE :

* Corinth was one of the most important cities of ancient Greece and remains a significant city today. The vestiges of the Acrocorinth (including the magnificent archaic Doric temple of Apollo) dominate the city and remind anyone of its exceptional past.

- Mycenae is the kingdom of the Homeric hero Agamemnon, who led the Greek army in the Trojan War. The remains are succinct, but once past the famous Lion's Gate, one can still get caught up in imagining the past splendor of the Mycenaean palace.

- Nafplio is a historical city located on the seafront near Mycenae. It is dominated by two fortresses (Acronauplia and Palamède), respectively Greek and Venetian. The Bourdzi fortress, on an islet, guards the entrance to the port.

- Epidaurus is famous for having been a Mecca of Greek medicine during antiquity, but it is visited especially today for its theater, which has been magnificently preserved over the centuries. Do not hesitate to test its acoustics, it is considered particularly good there. During the summer, shows without sound system are given there on weekends.

- Olympia was the site of the first Olympic Games more than 2500 years ago. Traditionally, the Olympic flame is lit a few months before the opening ceremony of the Olympic Games, both in winter and summer. The temple of Zeus dominates the other vestiges (gymnasium, palace and stadium).

- In the south of the peninsula is the citadel of Mystras. From the summit, the view extends on one side over the entire valley of the Eurotas and on the other, over two gorges sinking into the Taygetos massif. The Byzantine monasteries, convents, palaces, fortress, and churches make this place a magical place where time seems to have stood still.

- The Gulf of Corinth separates the Peloponnese from mainland Greece. The Charilaos Trikoupis Bridge was built in 2004 to facilitate traffic between the two parts of the country. The roads that weave between the sea and the mountains will lead you to charming little ports away from the tourist paths.

- From Nafplio, the coastal road carved into the cliff to Leonidion is beautiful. For example, you will pass through Astros and its famous beach, but there are many other small spots that may catch your attention during your trip.

- The Peloponnese ends in the south with three "fingers". Remaining very traditional, this splendid region reserves, sea side as well as land side, the possibility to stay in charming guest houses, especially in the medieval city of Monemvassia, one of the most beautiful stages of the Peloponnese, from which one explores the small creeks and the fishing ports of the region. The tormented relief of the Magne region dotted with small Byzantine churches and defense towers will seduce more than one.

CORFU :

On the west coast of Greece lies Corfu, the entry point to the Ionian Islands. This archipelago offers in the Ionian Sea a pleasant alternative to the Cyclades for the tourist in search of sunny beaches, but also wild nature and archaeology.

- Fortified since ancient times, the city of Corfu is surrounded by castles. The Spienada, the ancient fortress, the church of Saint Spyridon and the Archaeological Museum are the main attractions of the colorful city. It is in the latter that you can admire the famous Gorgon pediment of the temple of Artemis.

- Nature has been kind enough to offer Corfu sumptuous natural sites such as the triple bay of Paleokastritsa, the first region of Corfu to have experienced a tourist boom. The northwest of the island sees its coast here plunging steeply into the sea and forming charming little creeks. If one goes down there easily by winding small paths, one should not forget to climb to the top of the hill where the monastery of Paleokastritsa is hidden and where there is a breathtaking view.

- Most of the hotels, campsites and discos on the island are lined up north of Kerkira in the villages of Dassia, Ipsos and Pyrgi. The campsites scattered in the shade of lemon and pine trees are particularly pleasant. For swimming, you can choose between the long pebble beach of Kassiopi and the small creeks of the village of Sidari. Don't forget to go there to test the benefits of clay (and the legend) of the Canal de l'Amour. To the west of Kerkira is the beautiful site of the village of Pelekas and the famous beach of Glyfada.

- Along the south coast, off Kanoni, there are two islets to visit. From the first one, where the Vlachernes monastery is located, we reach the second one, the Mouse Island, by boat to discover a small 13th century church and especially to admire from the platform one of the most beautiful views of Corfu. In Benitse, the beaches are very busy, for more tranquility, go to Haghios Ioannis or Messongi.

- The Achilleion is a neoclassical palace of Pompeian style located on the outskirts of the village of Gastouri built at the request of Sissi the Empress. Residence of Kaiser William II of Germany at the beginning of the 20th century, it was later transformed into a military hospital, occupied by Axis troops, turned into a casino and is today a museum retracing its own history.

- A last site makes Corfu a surprising and interesting destination. On the west coast, next to Lakonès, there is the Byzantine fort of Angelokastro clinging to a 160 m high rock, which is surrounded by the sea and is connected to the mainland only by a narrow passage.

IONIAN ISLANDS :

- Paxos and sister Antipaxos have a nature of rare beauty. It is an ideal place to hike and discover its secret caves and secluded beaches. Opposite the main town Gaios there are two islets not to be missed : Agios Nicolaos and Panagia. Mongonissi and Kaltsonissi, south of Paxos, and Exolitharo and Daskalio near Antipaxos are also worth taking the sea to discover its hidden treasures (especially the underwater fauna).

- Lefkada is a mountainous island where vegetation flourishes. If to the east the coasts are soft, sheltered from the wind and punctuated by small green islets, the most famous of which are Skorpios, Madouri and Sparti, the west coast is steeper and interspersed with immense golden sandy beaches. Tourists have a preference for the first and the small fishing villages of Ligia and Nikiana and Nidri but you should not miss to go to the south of the island to admire the white cliffs of the Cape of the Lady or the jump of Lefkada.

- Ithaca, where Penelope waited patiently for Ulysses, seems to consist of two islands connected by a narrow strip of land. This beautiful, quiet and mountainous place has picturesque villages and beautiful, peaceful beaches. Ithaca has indeed managed to preserve its authenticity better than its neighbors.

- Kefalonia is the largest and most mountainous of the Ionian Islands. The ruins of the 13th century castle of Haghios Georgios, the Katavothres chasms sucking water from the sea, the strange stalagmites of the Drogarati lagoon, a natural concert hall, and the century-old olive trees of the Livathou plain are the main attractions.

- Zakynthos is famous for its fine sandy beaches and emerald green waters which make it second only to Corfu in the favorite sites of tourists in Heptanese. The most famous beach is Navagio. A mixture of Greek and Italian architecture, the villages of Zakynthos are emblematic of the entire region.

- Kythera, located between the Peloponnese and Crete, is said to have seen the goddess Aphrodite born from its waters. The island is dotted with numerous villages and hamlets, the prettiest of which are Chora, Levadi, Fratsia and Milopotamos. It is bordered by many beaches including the red sand beaches of Firi Ammos, near Agia Pelagia.

CRETE :

Crete was attached to Greece at the beginning of the 20th century, but remains a destination in its own right. On the program: multiple possibilities of hiking in the mountainous heart of the island, days of absolute idleness on the sunny beaches and a Minoan civilization that has left archaeological traces not to be missed.

- Agios Nikolaos is a city on the east coast of Crete. Its small pebble and fine sand beaches and the warm temperature of the water make it one of the most touristic places of the island. In the center of the city is the Voulismeni Lake, famous for being one of the favorite bathing places of the goddess Athena, but especially for its small taverns that make the tour more pleasant. Nearby, the seaside resorts of Elounda and Sitia are also very popular. The beach of Vaï, to the east, is the most beautiful example.

• The plateau of Lassithi has been nicknamed the "valley of the 10,000 mills". Coming from Heraklios, the walk to the pass is decorated with the remains of its last ones sometimes transformed into small stores. Nearby, lemont Dicté hides on its slopes the cave of Psychro, where Zeus was born.

• The municipality of Ierápetra, on the southeast coast, is made up of several villages and hamlets, as well as the island of Chrissi. The latter is uninhabited, but every year it welcomes many tourists who come to relax on the few sumptuous white sand beaches and small paths that are allowed to them.

• The southern coast, where sand and tourist infrastructures are becoming scarcer, offers the traveler a haven of peace a little further away from mass tourism. In the southwest, the village of Paleochora is one of the examples of alternative rest from where one can reach the Greek island of Gavdos. The one of Agia Roumeli is only accessible by sea or by the Samaria Gorge Trail.

• Indeed, only walkers will be able to appreciate all the treasures of the island, as roads are still rare in some areas. For all hiking fans, Crete is an ideal destination. Take the E4 European trail which passes through the towns of Kissamos, Loutro, Rethymno, Anogia and Kato Zakros. High plateaus with majestic relief, deep gorges and several thousand caves are waiting for you. Small lost villages, monasteries and shepherd's huts (Milatas) will punctuate your walk.

• The most sumptuous spectacles are those hidden in the region's gorges. The Gorges de Samaria are among the longest gorges in Europe and walking between the rock faces is a most fascinating experience. The Imbros Gorge from Komitades is also very popular. For more tranquility, visit the Aradena Gorge, which is a little more difficult to access, but just as beautiful.

• The most important archaeological site of the country is that of Knossos, not far from Heraklion, where the palace of king Minos is located. Its very complex architecture is undoubtedly at the origin of the mythological stories about the labyrinth of the Minotaur. After discovering its ruins, the archaeologist Sir Arthur Evans wanted to restore the main lines of the palace by raising the walls and painting them with bright colors. If these works are disputed today by the archaeologists, the result is nevertheless striking. For more authenticity, the observation of the frescoes and the high earthenware jars will allow you to imagine your version.

• Phaistos is the second most important site of the island. The palace, but also the remains of dwellings and workshops cover an important area where to wander. To complete your visit, go to the Heraklion museum where you will find the famous clay disc with enigmatic symbols that was found there as well as many other objects testifying to this civilization.

• Heraklion is the main city of the island and there is a very surprising mixture of architecture. Between the Byzantine church of Aghia Aikaterini, the Venetian monuments like the Koules fortress, the Turkish fountains and the concrete buildings, there is something to lose one's mind. Fortunately, part of the city center is now pedestrian, which makes the walk more pleasant.

• Gortyn, located 45 km southwest of Heraklion, is another important site. In addition to the Basilica of Agios Titos, where the shrine of St. Titus, patron saint of the island, is venerated, and many other remains (excavated or not), the Code of Law of Gortyn is found there. It consists of twelve stone tablets written in the Cretan Dorian dialect which are the basis of a complex judicial system.

• Chania (Hania) is the second largest city on the island and is considered to be one of the prettiest city stops. The old Venetian port with its 15th century lighthouse and the Janissary Mosque are the highlights. Discovering the covered market and the Splantzia district will allow you to appreciate its special atmosphere. Halfway between Chania and Heraklion lies Rethymno, a city with Turkish charm not to be missed.

CYCLADES :

From Piraeus in Athens, embark for one of the prettiest destinations in the Aegean Sea: the Cyclades archipelago. 2,200 islands, islets and rocky islets of which only 33 are inhabited await you, forming a circle around the sacred island of Delos. Every year, hundreds of thousands of tourists sail from island to island in search of the one that will definitely delight them. They come back perplexed, because all have their attractions and the choice is impossible.

* Makronissos, a rocky island 3 km long and 400 to 500 m wide, is nowadays uninhabited and is considered as a memorial of the civil war, because opponents of the regime of that time were deported there. This was also the case on the island of Gyaros, which is now closed to the public. Between the two is Kea where Athenians come to seek rest because of its proximity to the capital. The small port of Korissia, the fishing village of Vourkari and the upper town of Loulis are the main places of life between sea and orchards.

* Pretty villages and splendid beaches are also in place in Kythnos. In addition to the fishing port of Merichas, you can visit the village of Driopída divided in two by the valley and the church of Kanála lost in the pine forest. Don't miss the warm sulphurous and ferruginous waters of Loutrá, ideal for relaxation. Then come the uninhabited islets of Piperi and Serfopoula, before reaching Serifos. The latter, away from tourism, has to offer its creeks with transparent waters and the white city of Chora clinging to the mountain. Off the east coast is the islet of Voys.

* Sifnos is still little known although Kamares, its main port, and the beaches of Platy Yialos and Vathi are attracting more and more tourists. To the east of the island, on a steep rock with a beautiful panoramic life towards the sea is the medieval village of Kastro. Facing the bay of Platis Gialos is the small island of Kitriani where fish are king.

* Kimolos, like its neighbors, is a mountainous island with beautiful beaches. These, like Aliki, Klima and Ellinika, are mainly located on the south and southeast coasts. It is surrounded by the uninhabited islets of Agios Georgios, Agios Efstathios and Polyaigos, property of the Orthodox Church.

* Nearby is Milo where the famous Venus was discovered. It is one of the most beautiful islands of the Cyclades where you can find the largest natural bay of the archipelago and incredible beaches. 20 km away is the uninhabited island of Antimilo. Of volcanic origin, its deserted coves await sailors in search of solitude.

* Folegandros is one of the most authentic islands of the Cyclades. You will be charmed by the beauty of Chora, built on the edge of a cliff and whose church of Panaghia overhangs the 300 meters of emptiness. The beaches are also numerous, that of Ambeli, on the northwest coast is one of the wildest and most beautiful. After two uninhabited islets, Kardiotissa and Kalogeri is the peaceful Sikinos. Poorly served, the island lives at its own pace and its beautiful landscapes patiently await those who will visit it.

* The archipelago of Santorini is one of the most touristic destinations in the Cyclades. The spectacular cliffs where the hanging village of Oia and the lively town of Fira nestle contribute to its reputation. In the center of the archipelago, one can observe the sunken crater from which emerges the volcanic cone of Nea Kameni and its neighbor, Palea Kameni, which is regularly closed to tourists. Unusual beaches, such as Red Beach, await you and the thousands of other tourists who flock there every year. In the south of the archipelago, the Christiana Islands are small uninhabited islets.

* True cone of stone rising from the sea, Anafi is the southernmost island of the Cyclades. Its remoteness makes it a peaceful place sheltered from the tourist paths. The most beautiful beaches are located on the south coast of the island and the inland remains very wild. Pachia and Makra are two sublime and deserted islets located in the south of the island.

* To the north of the island, the island of Ios is on the opposite side. It is known for its beautiful beaches such as Mylopotas, but also and especially for its summer animation which ruins any hope of tranquility.

* Amorgos owes to its very rough contours and its virgin landscapes the reputation of being one of the most beautiful islands of the Cyclades. Tiny coves await you there to offer you a few hours of rest lulled by the waves and the inland has many hiking possibilities to offer you. Discover one of the most fabulous monasteries ever built, the monastery of Panaghia Hozoviotissa, which shines bright white on the cliff above the cove of Aghi Anna where some passages of the Big Blue were turned. All around the island there are uninhabited rocky islets such as those of Nikouria and Gramvonis-

si, ideal for scuba diving, or, at the southern tip, that of Gramvoussa which is more difficult to reach.

* To the west, in addition to the two small uninhabited islands, Keros and Kato and Ano Antikeros, belonging to the Greek National Heritage (which prohibits them to tourists), the archipelago of the Little Cyclades awaits you. This one is composed of multiple islets and rocks: Iraklia, Schinoussa, Phidoussa, Glaronissi, Kalo and Epano Koufonissia, Donoussa and Makares. Each of them has surprises in store for you, such as the Aghou Ioanni cave in Iraklia or the natural pools of the Koufonissia. It's up to you to go and find them, you are more and more numerous every year.

* Naxos is the largest and highest of the islands of the Cyclades archipelago. Famous for the monumental gate that stands on an islet connected to the main city by a pier, Naxos is rich in archaeological sites as evidenced by its archaeological museum. The beaches of the west coast and the sailing clubs and other nautical activities that have settled there, but also the beauty of its contrasting landscapes dotted with small villages make it a most pleasant destination.

* Paros and Antiparos are also highlights in a journey around the archipelago. In the heart of the archipelago, these islands have golden beaches offered to the waves of the Aegean Sea and to tourists. As in the rest of the archipelago, one eats there deliciously well, one rests there with pleasure and one always finds something to visit whether it is the church of the Panaghia Ekatontopiliani on the first one or the Venetian castle of the second one. All around, the islets of Vriokastro, Gaidouronissi, Dryonissi, Pantieronissi, Glaropounta, Despotiki and Strongyli animate the sea with their silhouettes and invite the holidaymaker to swim.

* Syros differs from the rest of the islands of the archipelago by its neo-classical architecture and Catholicism. A little scorned by tourists, it has nevertheless to offer very beautiful beaches, the most beautiful of which are located on the north coast. The cultural and spiritual life of the island is also worth noting. To the east are the two tiny islets of Didymi and Aspro.

* Just in front of the island of Rhinee, Delos is also uninhabited, but the island has the most important historical testimony of the archipelago: the great sanctuary of Apollo. It is one of the most complete complexes in the whole of Greece and is well worth a visit.

* Then comes Mykonos, one of the most touristic islands of the archipelago. The beaches of Paradise, Super Paradise, Ftela, Psarou and Platis Yalos welcome every year hundreds of thousands of tourists who at night have a wide choice of nightclubs to vary with the pleasures of idleness. Nevertheless, the alleys of the main city and the church of Panaghia Paraportiani are part of these postcards of the Cyclades that nothing can spoil. To the east, the islets of Dragonissi and Chtapodia are uninhabited, as is Praso to the west.

* Tinos, in the north, is still unknown to tourists, perhaps because the beaches are less sandy and windier. On March 25 and August 15, thousands of pilgrims make the exception and invade the island, because for the Greek Orthodox, it is an important Marian pilgrimage, the virgin would have appeared there where the church Panaghia Evangelistria is built today.

* Andros is the greenest of the Cycladic islands. It hides in its heart sublime villages and offers to the sea beautiful beaches gilded by the heavens. Because of its proximity to the second port of Athens (Rafina), the island of Andros has become one of the favorite weekend destinations for the majority of Athenians.

EUBOEA & THE NORTHERN SPORADES :

Euboea is the largest of the Greek islands in the Aegean Sea facing Attica and Boeotia. The Northern Sporades extend to the east and southeast of the Pelion Peninsula, on eleven islands only Skiathos, Skópelos, Alonissos and Skyros are inhabited.

* Evia offers lush green valleys, wooded hillsides or mountains that will be appreciated by mountaineering enthusiasts, magnificent well-developed coastlines or secluded, magical beaches. To the north, traditional villages and mountain rivers call for hiking. The south is home to important towns such as Chalcis and archaeological sites such as Eretria. The

old captains' residences, now listed, and the seaside towns along peaceful beaches are real gems.

* Only 2 hours from the city of Volos by ferry, Skiathos boasts 70 bays and coves that attract many tourists every year. Long sandy beaches and intense nightlife combine to give life to a new destination in the heart of the Aegean Sea. Nine uninhabited islets surround it and offer many possibilities for a getaway.

* The second favorite destination of the Sporades, Skópelos is a mixture of picturesque bays, golden sand and olive groves. The island is dotted with huts, churches and monasteries whose white walls contrast beautifully with the blue sky. The beaches are mostly located on the southwest and west coast of Skopelos, in a landscape of pine and plane trees.

* Alonissos with few tourist and road infrastructures is the ideal place to rest in complete tranquility, the beach of the village of Rousoum is considered the most beautiful and certainly the most popular of the island. The surrounding area is a splendid marine park that is home to dolphins and Mediterranean seals. In Psathoura, a neighboring islet, hide the remains of an ancient city. The famous Cyclops Cave is decorated with multicolored stalactites and stalagmites.

* In Skiros, beautiful beaches and low hills, caves and waters suitable for underwater fishing make up the landscape. Remains from the Byzantine period, churches from the Middle Ages, houses with the air of small folk museums, specific local architecture give the island a special charm. Do not miss the landscapes of Yalo, Achylli, Vrachia and the beautiful beaches of Nyfi, Tris Boukes, Fanari, Diapori.

LESBOS, CHIOS, SAMOS :

Off the coast of Asia Minor are the Greek islands of Lesbos, Samos and Chios. These three sisters, very close to the Turkish coast, offer a green and mountainous nature in the blue Aegean Sea.

* Among the islands of the eastern Aegean, Lesbos is certainly one of the most famous. The city of Mytilene tells its eventful history through the visit of the Kastro, a Byzantine fortress built to repel Saracen incursions and then rebuilt in the fourteenth century, before being enlarged by the Ottomans. At the end of the island, near the small port of Sigri, in a place where curiously the sea winds have nowadays prevented any trees from growing, lie on the ground the petrified remains of a gigantic forest from another age. Do not hesitate to go to the small town of Plomari, the Greek capital of ouzo, or to the typical village of Haghiassos from where you can enjoy a magnificent view of the island. Three important pilgrimages attract crowds on festive days: the monastery of Madamados, near the northeast coast of the island, the tombs of Saints Raphael, Nicholas and Irene near Mytilene, and the monastery of Lemoni near Kalloni. Lesbos also has many beaches that can satisfy all tastes, the wildest are at Tarti in the southern end of the island, at Melinta west of Plomari and further north at Lapsarna, Tsonia and Lagada.

* The island of Chios, where Homer is said to have been born, is dominated by mountains of volcanic origin. There are beautiful green landscapes, beautiful beaches and picturesque villages that have kept their medieval appearance as those of Pyrghi and Mesta in the region of Mastichochoria. The latter takes its name from the production of mastic (extracted from a shrub of the pistachio tree family) that can be tasted in candy or chewing gum. The one in Pyrghi is really worth a visit for its tight constructions like a fortress around an old defense tower whose facades are decorated with black and white geometric designs (xysta) and embellished with beautiful flowers. Chora Chios is the main port of the island, there are several neo-classical buildings, mosques dating back to the Ottoman occupation, the remains of a Byzantine castle built by the Genoese and very picturesque winding streets. Karfas is an ideal beach for swimming, very touristy, just like Agia Fotia, Komi and Eborios (Mavra Volia).

* Samos, the easternmost island of the archipelago is also the most touristic. Its lush vegetation contrasts with the sea to give it a purely idyllic appearance. The capital, Samos, is built in an amphitheater on the eastern side of the island, inside the large bay of Vathy. The liveliest part of the city is the Pythagoras Square with its palm trees and numerous cafes. Don't miss to visit the archaeological museum located in the lower town on St. Syrion's Square, considered one of the most important in all Greece for the understanding of archaic sculpture. From the monastery of Zoodochos Pigis, located 9 kilometers from Vathi, you will enjoy a magnificent panorama of the Strait of Samos, Cape Mycale and the

Turkish coast. The oldest ancient sanctuary of the island is located 6 km south of Pythagorion. Following the road to Karlovassi, you reach the charming village of Kokari surrounded by clear waters and white pebble beaches. This type of beaches, hidden in isolated coves, can be found all along the northern coast of Samos. A little further on, from the village in the hamlet of Platanakia, you can go into the "Valley of Nightingales" and enjoy the singing of thousands of birds whose songs fill the mountain after midnight.

RHODES :

• Rhodes has a bewitching and secular character, between vestiges of the Middle Ages and modern comfort of tourist structures. Don't miss the ramparts of the old town, then entering the city through the Freedom Gate, you will encounter the remains of the temple of Aphrodite, the Auberge des Chevaliers d'Auvergne, the Arsenal, the Museum of Decorative Arts and the Byzantine Museum. The acropolis of the ancient city was located on the slope of Mount Smith which dominates the city. The Stadium, the square Odeon and the ruins of some temples can still be visited today. 3 km away from the city of Rhodes is the Rodini Park and, nearby, the Tomb of the Ptolemies and the ruins of a Roman aqueduct. On the eastern coast is the picturesque town of Lindos, built at the foot of a steep rock on which an acropolis still stands. In the vicinity, the village of Koskinou, the ancient spa town of Kalithea, the seaside resort of Falikari, the beautiful beach of Ladikou and the ancient Fodien village of Afandou deserve some moments of your summer. From the beach of Kolimbia, go to the oasis of freshness that is the site of Epta Pigés before going to admire the monastery of Panagia at the top of Mount Tsambika then sunbathe on the beach of Haraki, a beautiful fishing village dominated by the medieval fortress of Feraklos, which extends to the bay of Vliba.

• On the west coast, between Rhodes and Trianda, is the largest majority of hotels on the island. Then there is a succession of architectural ensembles not to be missed, such as the ancient Lalyssos, at the top of Mount Filerimos, or the ancient Camiros, and natural curiosities such as the famous Valley of the Butterflies. The western road runs along the sea up to the village of Skala Kamirou from where you can reach the island of Halki by boat. While discovering then the hinterland, you will learn that Rhodes still reserves you many other idyllic sites.

SOUTHERN SPORADES :

The Dodecanese (also known as the Southern Sporades) is an archipelago in the Aegean Sea comprising more than 160 Greek islands and islets, most of which are uninhabited.

• Off the Turkish coast, the small island of Patmos boasts an eventful religious past. Do not hesitate to visit the magnificent 11th century presbytery of St. John the Theologian before following in his footsteps to the Sacred Cave of the Apocalypse.

• Leros is a mountainous island with beautiful beaches, lush deep bays and picturesque toothed coastlines. The port of Laki, designed in 1923 by the architects of Benito Mussolini, is one of the best examples of Art Deco architecture in Greece.

• Astypalea is a butterfly island quite popular with Greeks, but little known to foreign visitors. The deserted bays, the white houses of the main town and its Venetian castle, the windmills and the fish market of the small port of Maltezana will immediately plunge you into the heart of Greece.

• Renowned as the homeland of Hippocrates, father of medicine, Kos has become a seaside resort. The main city is a garden city enhanced by medieval fortresses of the 15th century. Do not miss to dive at theBubble Beach, in the south of the island, where you will feel like you are in a huge marine jacuzzi.

• Karpathos is known for its karpathian houses made of carved rocks, like lace in a decor of forests, bays and mountains. You can discover many secluded and quiet beaches, but don't forget to go inland to discover the traditions of the island like those of the mountain village of Olimpos.

• Kassos is one of the quietest islands of the Dodecanese with little tourism. Kastelorizo consists of an amphitheater port and about fifty houses with welcoming inhabitants. Kalimnos is known as "the island of the sponge fishermen". Its volcano and the serenity of its daily life are the two main attractions of the island of Nissiros.Lipsi is one of its small islands with white houses and churches with blue domes. The port of Symi looks like a charming Venetian village. Far away from the stress of modern life, the beaches and churches of Chalki offer a true moment of rest for body and mind.

Hungary

Apart from Budapest, Hungary surely has secrets to reveal to the traveler who would venture outside the capital. Wedged between two Europes, crossed by one of the most legendary rivers of the continent, this country has some beautiful landscapes to offer you and cultivates an art of living to discover.

* Budapest is an ideal city for a long weekend. Its architecture is a cocktail of neoclassical, baroque and art nouveau and it is along the Danube that the capital has chosen to exhibit its most beautiful pieces. Budapest is actually composed of three cities and each one will try to seduce you. The old town of Buda has for it the palaces and quarters of the royal palace while Pest, more modern, competes with its parliament. The city is immense, fortunately the hot springs of the city have been skillfully used to make famous baths. Go to the Kiraly or Széchenyi baths to recharge your batteries, and you will leave the capital's bridges in style.

* Other cities in the country have buildings with breathtaking architecture. In Gödöllö, north of Budapest, is the largest baroque castle in Hungary. In Eger, in the east, a 17th century Turkish minaret and an imposing basilica emerge from the streets with Baroque buildings. In the west of the country is the Esterházy Palace in Fertöd, it is nicknamed the Hungarian Versailles.

* Lake Balaton is the largest freshwater reservoir in Europe. It is a popular holiday resort throughout Central Europe. Swimming and water sports make the southern shore famous, for example in Siofok. The northern shore is more reserved for spas, such as Balatonfüred. The Kis-Balaton is an ornithological reserve with various species of herons, egrets and other water birds.

* North of Budapest, the Danube, which flows from west to east, makes a sharp turn to the south, this is called the Danube loop. Here you will find several places not to be missed under any circumstances. The ruins of the Visegrad Palace offer a superb panorama of the river. The ecclesiastical capital, Esztergom, is famous for the Basilica of St. Adalbert. Szentendre is famous for its museums, art galleries and artists. The region produces a famous wine called Tokaji, which Louis XIV called the "wine of kings, king of wines".

* The Hortobágy National Park has made it possible to inscribe the Puszta, the largest steppe in Europe, on the World Heritage List. In these wild landscapes dotted with pendulum wells, many horses are bred.

Iceland

The secret of Iceland lies in its nature. It is the geographical characteristics of this island which are at the origin of the most beautiful phenomena that tourists come to admire. Geysers, waterfalls, glaciers and aurora borealis... nature here unfolds a spectacle that has the strength of the great American spaces, the mystery of Scandinavian history, and the magic of the regions of the far north.

• 60 km from Reykjavík, Geysir is the Icelandic geyser that gave its name to all the others, but it is no longer active since the beginning of the last century. A few hundred meters away is the Strokkur geyser, one of the most famous in the country. Every five to ten minutes it sends columns of boiling water up to twenty or thirty meters.

• At 6 km from this first show, we find the Gullfoss Falls. A succession of falls, 35 meters high and 70 meters wide, produce a rainbow. Together with the geysers of the Haukadalur valley, they form the Golden Circle, one of the most touristic places in the country. Other impressive waterfalls dot the island like Goðafoss or Dettifoss.

• Vatnajökull is the largest glacier in Iceland, but also in Europe. In the southeast of the island, it occupies 8% of its territory. Under the glacier are many active volcanoes and sub-glacial lakes. The numerous trails in the Skaftafell National Park allow walkers to access many places and panoramas such as the glacial valley of Mórsárdalur, the Svartifoss waterfall surrounded by basalt organs, the Salt House, the Kristínartindar Needle and the glacial valley of Thorsmörk.

• Numerous lakes dot the island. The lake of Mývatn, in the north, offers superb volcanic landscapes. The Skútustaðir pseudocraters that emerge from the water are due to steam explosions dating back 2000 years. As for the hot springs (Grjótagjá and Stóragjá), they are too hot to bathe. Fortunately, in the rest of the country there are plenty of opportunities. In the south, for example, in the Landmannalaugar region, hot and cold streams flow at the foot of the Laugahraun lava field.

• In the southwest, on the Reykjanes peninsula, is one of the most important spas in the country, the Blue Lagoon. This artificial lake in the middle of lava and lichen fields has dermatological virtues and is of rare beauty.

• Without reaching the fame of their Norwegian counterparts, the Icelandic fjords are just as majestic and spectacular. That of Ísafjörður, in the northwest of the country, is one of the most beautiful thanks to its stack of very old basalt flows. Hvalfjörður, in the west, is known for the large number of whales that frequent it.

• The Hekla volcano, in the south, is a popular hiking destination. Following the path of the last eruption, you can reach the summit in 3 to 4 hours. In spring, skiing is possible on short routes around the crater rim. In summer, easy climbing trails are accessible near the crater and in early winter, snowmobiling is possible.

• Reykjavík is the capital of Iceland and was for a long time the only city on the island. It is not necessarily of great historical interest and is obviously less typical than the small villages on the peat-roofed island. But when the weekend arrives, the streets come alive, the bars fill up and the party is in full swing.

Ireland

Ireland is this green island with steep cliffs right next to Great Britain. It is this country whose bad weather is said to be largely compensated by the warm welcome of its inhabitants. Ireland is above all a very endearing land, with an exciting culture and superb landscapes.

* In Connemara the most majestic landscapes await travelers in search of wild peninsulas and sheep by the thousands. Whether you take the scenic Sky Road around the Kingstown Peninsula or drive through the peat bogs of Connemara National Park, a strange sense of freedom will take hold of you. All the Celtic soul in landscapes.

* The highest cliffs of the west coast are those of Moher located on the town of Liscanor. Their vertiginous slopes plunge into the ocean to let the walker admire it unleashed at his feet. Opposite, the Aran Islands are home to thousands of sea birds and the maze of stone walls will lead you to several forts dating from the Iron Age.

* To the extreme southwest is the province of Kerry, famous for its mild climate and the views offered by the Ring of Kerry route. The lakes around Killarney and the beaches around Inch are very pleasant places to relax. The golf courses of Waterville and Tralee are well known. In the same region, the Gap of Dunloe starts at Kate Kearney's Cottage, crosses five small lakes, and ends downhill in the Black Valley. The ride can be done on horseback.

* To the north, it is the turn of the Slieve League cliffs, the highest in Europe, to make the walker dizzy. The rest of County Donegal is steeped in history with the tombs of pre-Christian farmers alongside the remains of the Vikings. To the south of the area, in County Sligo, is the Ben Bulben, which offers a great view of the surrounding area if you climb it (to be done on the south side).

* The county of Waterford, in the south-east of the country, is criss-crossed by several rivers. A mini-cruise on the Blackwater, for example, will allow you to discover the charming landscapes of the region. For those who love fishing, you should know that the waters of the river are full of salmon.

* The alleys and pubs of Dublin make the charm of this European capital. There are three routes to discover the city: the Georgian Trail, the Old City Trail and the Cultural Trail. Many squares and squares have preserved treasures of Georgian architecture (St Stephen's Green, Merrion Square, Ely Place, Fitzwilliam Square). In the evening, the Temple Bar district, in the historic center, is at the heart of the animation.

* Kilkenny is a medieval city with beautifully preserved architecture. St. Canice's Cathedral and the castle of the Butler d'Ormonde family make the city a major Irish tourist attraction. Do not hesitate to make a detour to see the beautiful ruins of the Cistercian Jerpoint Abbey.

* The surroundings of Cork do not lack sites to be discovered: Blarney Castle, famous for its Blarney stone, Cobh, emblematic city which saw millions of emigrants leaving for America and Kinsale, charming small port town famous for its gastronomy.

* To the west, the Burren massif is home to more than 60 funerary monuments dating from 3000 to 2000 B.C., the most famous of which is the dolmen of Poulnabrone. Not to be missed in the county of Mayo: Ceide Fields. It is the largest and most impressive Neolithic monument in Europe that has been preserved.

Italy

Rome, Venice, Capri... Italian cities are known by the lyricists of the French song, but especially by tourists. Every year, millions of us visit them and succumb to their charms, not to mention that outside the big cities, the countryside remains very attractive and the coasts sublime. Culturally, naturally, culinary, Italy is a fantastic land, and we must admit that the beautiful paese, "the beautiful country", is certainly the most beautiful tourist destination in the world.

* Rome is an exceptional city, an open-air museum of history. The Palatine was inhabited as early as the eighth century BC. Imperial Rome built the Colosseum, the Pantheon, the Trajan Column, the Baths of Diocletian and those of Caracalla. Emperor Constantine then had major places of Catholicism built such as the Basilicas of St. John Lateran and St. Law-

rence Outside the Walls. The Renaissance produced the Palace of Venice, the beginnings of the Sistine Chapel, the reconstruction of St. Peter's Basilica and the Farnese Palace, before Baroque art gave birth to Piazza Navona. Some of the most famous painters and sculptors (Raphael, Michelangelo, Bernini) have made the city a true work of art.

• Venice is famous all over the world for its labyrinth of romantic canals, its narrow cobbled streets with gingerbread buildings, and its fantasy carnival. The pigeons in St. Mark's Square and the facades of the Doge's Palace complete the myth. The aim is to wander randomly and discover some of the 100 churches hidden in the nooks and crannies of the city, to refresh oneself at the wells of the inner courtyards, to enjoy watching from another bridge. The vaporetti will allow you to do the same without getting tired.

• Florence developed considerably architecturally and artistically between the 12th and 16th centuries. This heritage is such that everything seems unavoidable: the palaces (Palazzo Vecchio, Palazzo Medicis, Palazzo Pitti) and the churches (Santa Maria del Fiore, San Marco, Santa Croce de la Novella). The Uffizi Palace, where the Medici collections are located, is one of the most beautiful museums in the world. To admire Florence, nothing is better than climbing to the top of the Boboli garden: the silver thread of the Arno, the Ponte Vecchio, the hills of Tuscany will offer themselves to you.

• Many other cities of the country are worth the detour. Besides Romeo and Juliet, Verona (the beautiful Verona) is famous for its Roman amphitheater still in operation during the summer. Pictures of Pisa and its leaning tower have traveled around the world. The curved shape of Piazza del Campo in Siena is a spectacle even outside the Palio delle Contrade race. The monuments of Assisi, Bologna, Padua, Vicenza, Ravenna, Turin and Trieste offer each city highlights that punctuate every stroll.

• Naples is one of the largest Mediterranean cities. If art is also present in the various monuments of the city, it is the hectic and colorful life that has taken over the streets. In the surrounding area, there is of course the ash city of Pompeii, but also the site of Herculaneum, Ostia and Paestum.

• In addition to the archaeological interest of the Naples area, the surrounding Mediterranean coast is full of picturesque nooks and crannies to relax in the sun. The islands of Capri and Ischia are known for their beauty, which cannot be overshadowed by luxury tourism. The Amalfi Coast, in the south, is classified as a World Heritage Site, villages like Positano or Ravello are exceptional sites.

• The coast of Tuscany, heading north, boasts a beautiful spot on the Ligurian Sea: the 10 km of sandy beaches of Viareggio have a worldwide reputation. Then comes the Italian Riviera, an extension of our French Riviera, which is divided into two parts. The Riviera of the Ponant, where you can find seaside resorts with authentic, sometimes rustic charm (we can mention for example Ventimiglia, with its famous market, Bordighera, appreciated by painters, San Remo, a chic seaside town, Imperia, Alassio, Albenga, Finale Ligure, Varazze...), and the Riviera of the Levant with its steep coastline, a superb panorama where tiny fishing villages are hidden, which can be reached on foot or by train (the Cinque Terre).

• Tuscany is one of the beautiful regions of Italy. Its light, its gentle way of life, its harmony are such that many have fallen in love with it and would not exchange for any beach the peaceful calm they have found there. The gastronomy of the region is just one more good reason to spend a week of absolute relaxation.

• The valleys of Valle d'Aosta are made up of a thousand hamlets and a hundred or so castles, such as those of Fénis, Verrès and Saint-Pierre, which are scattered along the valleys. The region is best known for its winter sports resorts. Courmayeur at the foot of Mont Blanc, Breuil-Cervinia, near the Matterhorn, Gressoney-La-Trinité at the foot of Mont Rose and Cogne in the Gran Paradiso massif where downhill skiing, cross-country skiing and heliskiing are popular with tourists.

• In northern Italy there are many lakes, each one more sumptuous than the next: Lake Maggiore with its enchanting islands and shores, Lake Como, a source of inspiration for poets, writers and filmmakers, and Lake Garda bordered by the Riviera of Olives.

SARDINIA :

To the south of French Corsica, Sardinia is an Italian region full of beauty. If you like hiking in the scrub, sunny beaches, Mediterranean gastronomy and wild nights, this island is for you.

* The Costa Smeralda is the northwest coast of Sardinia, 55 km long from the north of Olbia to Palau. The resorts of Baia Sardinia, Porto Cervo and Porto Rotondo are the most frequented by day and night. If you are looking for a little more authenticity, don't hesitate to take the ferry from Palau to the Maddalena archipelago. The island Caprera, which is part of it, is a nature reserve whose creeks will offer a superb setting for your bathing. Lovers of large sandy beaches and water sports will choose to go to Santa Magherita di Pula in the southwest of Sardinia.

* On the west coast of Sardinia, the bay of Porto Conte ends with the Capo Caccia, a vertiginous promontory whose base is home to the amazing Neptune Cave that can be reached by climbing the 656 steps of the Cabirol staircase or by boat from Alghero. The latter is one of the only Italian cities to have kept about 70% of its fortifications and the most beautiful city of the island. In the surrounding area, don't miss the many extra-urban archaeological sites (the necropolises of Anghelu Ruju and Santu Pedru, the villa Santa Imbenia, the Purissima place and the Nuragic complexes of Palmavera and Santa Imbenia).

* The Gennargentu is a mountainous massif in the center of the country that offers multiple possibilities of hiking through these holm oak woods between vertical rocky walls and limestone canyons away from any human life. To enjoy this preserved nature as much as possible, don't hesitate to spend a night in one of the huts that were once used as refuges for shepherds. In the heart of the Supramonte, don't miss a stopover in the village of Orgosolo, known for its abundance of mural paintings. Nuraghic remains are present around the village: stone village, dolmens, troglodytic tombs and so-called "giant" tombs.

* In the south of the island, Cagliari is worth seeing for its via Roma lined with arcades, its cathedral which can be reached through small alleys and its bastion of Saint-Rémy which dominates the Old Town with its massive silhouette. Don't miss also its National Archaeological Museum, the most important in the world regarding the Nuraghic civilization. To see its most beautiful remains, the site of Barumini, classified as a World Heritage Site, and the impressive ruins of Santa Cristina are to be visited on the way north.

SICILY :

Sicily is the largest of the Mediterranean islands and a tourist destination in its own right. The remains of ancient Greece will delight fans of archaeology, the landscapes of Etna will delight hikers, while the sunny coasts will delight those who love to relax.

* Situated on the north coast, at the foot of the Rocca, a rocky promontory 270 meters high, Cefalù was founded by the Greeks and then successively occupied by the Romans, Arabs and Normans. Today it is one of the main seaside resorts in Sicily. To enjoy a breathtaking view of the bay, don't hesitate to climb to the top of the Rocca rock before relaxing on the beaches of Spiaggia Mazzaforno and Spiaggia Settefrati to the west of the city.

* Palermo, the capital and largest city of the region, brings together the Latin, Greek and Muslim cultures. The ancient center offers an exceptional architectural heritage, both in terms of its abundance and diversity. Don't miss the Palatine Chapel, the Byzantine Church of the Martorana, the churches of San Giovanni and San Cataldo and the Cathedral of William II in the southwest. The Abbey of Monreale with the mosaics of its cathedral and the arcades of its cloister is also worth a visit. Palermo is also known for its many markets with a unique and exotic atmosphere.

* On the west coast, Taormina combines the beauty of its bay with the quality of its historical testimonies. The city, dominated by its fortress, forms a balcony on the sea facing Etna and enjoys an exceptional microclimate. The pedestrianized city center, with its medieval alleys, where you can discover splendid viewpoints or vestiges of the ancient city, gives an intense feeling of calm. The city's gardens are unparalleled havens of peace, especially in high season when tourists number in the thousands.

- In Agrigento, on the west coast, there are many archaeological remains. In addition to the ruins of the great sanctuary of Olympian Zeus, one of the largest in ancient Greece, the Valley of the Temples offers visitors the grandiose remains of Heracles, Juno, the Dioscuri and Concord. About thirty kilometers away, visit also Eraclea Minoa where a splendid theater has been preserved.

- Bordered by long sandy beaches, but also enamelled with creeks, the south coast is a little further away from the tourist routes. Do not hesitate to make a small stop in the small town of Sciacca which has managed to preserve its charm of yesteryear. The port, the market, and the cornice walk make it a very pleasant stopover.

- Syracuse was presented by Cicero as the largest and most beautiful of Greek cities, its historic center is now part of the World Heritage of Humanity. Its amphitheaters, the temples of Apollo in Ortygia, as well as the fortification of the Epipoli, the Beneventano Palace and the necropolis of Pantalica are all masterpieces to be admired. To deepen the visit, do not hesitate to spend some time in the collections of the Archaeological Museum.

- Catania was built in the 8th century B.C. on the coulees of Mount Etna. The best way to discover the history of the city is to walk up Viale Vittorio Emanuele II punctuated by ancient ruins, churches and baroque palaces. Don't miss the Cathedral of St. Agatha, Piazza del Duomo and the Greco-Roman theater before taking a rest in the Bellini Garden from where you can admire Etna or mingle with the crowd stretched out on the black sand of the Little Rade of San Giovanni Li Cuti.

- Etna, in the east of the island, is the highest volcano in Europe (3350 m) and one of the most active in the world. From Catania, reach the Rifugio Sapienza to begin its ascent between ashes and rocks, up to the Tower of the Philosopher at 2,920 m. Here you can follow the activity of the southeast crater and see the latest results of the 2002 eruption.

- In the center of the island, you will find a beautifully preserved countryside. At an altitude of 900 m, Enna is one of the beautiful inland towns, which has remained away from the major tourist circuits. Don't miss to climb to the Castello di Lombardia, one of the largest and most important castles on the island. Nearby, the village of Pergusa, on the shores of the lake of the same name, is worth a visit.

AEOLIAN ISLANDS :

Of volcanic origin, the Aeolian Islands include seven inhabited islands: Lipari, Panarea, Vulcano, Stromboli, Alicudi, Filicudi and Salina. It is a World Heritage destination that attracts many tourists every year. Excursions, hikes, thermal cures and swimming are the activities on the program of this archipelago.

- Lipari is the largest of the Aeolian Islands, all the history of the latter can be discovered with the visit of its archaeological museum whose value is recognized worldwide. The historical center of Lipari is dominated by the Castle, built on a promontory. The small square of Marina Corta is a meeting place around its bars and restaurants just a few steps from the sea. Behind the port, the lower town stretches out with its corso Vittorio Emanuele, a place for a stroll punctuated by characteristic stores and alleys.

- The pumice stone quarries in Porticello, whose exploitation has formed beautiful white sand dunes overlooking the sea, are worth a visit. One of the favorite pastimes of swimmers is to climb the dunes, cover themselves with pumice powder and throw themselves into the sea. Inland, many paths will lead you to the top of the craters where you will discover fumaroles escaping from the ground. You can also take advantage of the natural springs for a spa treatment.

- Salina is the second largest island of the archipelago in terms of both surface area and population. Formed by six ancient volcanoes, it has the highest relief of the archipelago and is the most fertile and lush island. Precious grapes are cultivated here to produce the "Malvasia delle Lipari", a very sweet wine, as well as capers that are exported all over the world. The most beautiful beach of the island is located in the small village of Pollara, a natural amphitheater with suggestive colors where the famous house of the movie The Postman is located. Don't miss also the ancient sanctuary of the Madonna del Terzito, which dates back to the 15th century.

* Between Lipari and Stromboli, the tiny island of Panarea is a very popular place for Italian high society. The nature is preserved, the seabed is very beautiful and the view of the Stromboli volcano leaves you dreaming. Going up the mule tracks, you can dive among the thousand colors offered by agaves, prickly pears, capers in bloom, red, pink, purple, orange bougainvillea and, of course, heather.

* On Stromboli is the active volcano of the same name, also called the "lighthouse of the Mediterranean". In addition to the night hike to the summit, it is also possible to observe, from the sea, the fall of the incandescent projections along a kind of natural slide, the Sciarra del fuocco located on the northwest face of the island. If you are looking for peace and quiet in an unusual environment, this small piece of land is for you.

* To the southwest is Vulcano, on which another active volcano is located. 2 trails (one of which passes very close to the fumaroles) will allow you to reach the summit and have a rather impressive view of the crater itself, the fumaroles of a very bright yellow and in the distance the other islands of the archipelago. At the seaside, there are black sand beaches and thermal waters with a very strong smell of sulfur, but with therapeutic virtues not to be missed.

* Wild and picturesque, away from the tourist trails, Alicudi has very few infrastructures to welcome travellers, no roads and no sandy beaches. Its highest point is the stratovolcano Monte Fillo dell'Arpa, which rises to 675 meters above sea level, on its heathery slopes, but also vineyards and olive trees on terraces color the volcanic landscape.

* To the west of Lipari, Mount Fossa Felci dominates the island of Filicudi from its 774 meters above sea level. Next to seven other volcanoes eaten away by erosion, Filicudi is inhabited by a few hundred people, divided between three villages connected by winding paths and a single road. An interesting archeological site dating back to the Bronze Age as well as marine caves of great beauty are worth a visit.

SAN MARINO :

The Serenissima Republic of San Marino is landlocked within the territory of Italy between Emilia-Romagna and the Marches. This small independent state is one of the oldest republics in the world and has become a very popular place for tourists who do not hesitate to make a detour to spend a few moments or to take refuge there when the mists fall on the Adriatic coast.

* The historical center of the Republic of San Marino develops around its three towers and is characterized by its alleys that go up and down continuously and lead visitors to discover ancient buildings, small shops and unusual corners. Don't miss the opportunity to visit the great Piazza della Libertà where Palazzo Pubblico stands. 92.3% of the population is Catholic, and only 3% of the inhabitants declare themselves to be without religion. This predominance of the Catholic Church is reflected in the architectural landscape of the Republic, which has several monumental churches or cathedrals.

* Paths cross the 61 km² of this micro-territory. The Monte Cerreto Park Trail, which is very easy to walk along, nevertheless allows you to enjoy superb panoramic views of the fields that extend to the Adriatic Sea, the Rock of Montalbo, whose wall houses the "Sacello del Santo" place of worship that overlooks Mount Titan, the valley of the San Marino Torrent and part of Valmarecchia.

* The itinerary of the woods, small waterfalls and mills of Canepa will take you on a tour through the green surroundings of Montecchio and Canepa to meet the Grotta di Canepa and the ancient water mills. The Castellaccio Trail will take you through unspoiled nature to the ruins of a medieval fortified castle at the top of Mount Seghizzo. The itinerary of the ancient Railway and Lavala follows a portion of the ancient railway network that connected Rimini and San Marino, do not hesitate to visit the arboretum of Ca' Vagnetto along the way.

VATICAN :

The Vatican is the smallest state in the world, but its fame extends far beyond its borders. In the heart of Rome, the monuments and museums that populate the 44 hectares of the Holy See are among the most grandiose in the Catholic world.

* Enter the Vatican City through Piazza Pio XII to access Via della Conciliazone, which leads to the beautiful St. Peter's Square, its elliptical double colonnade, obelisk and crowds of tourists. At nightfall, the square empties and the spectacle becomes completely mystical.

* At the end of the square is the largest basilica in the world, St. Peter's Basilica. Its marble-clad interior contains eleven chapels and forty-five altars. The gilded bronze baldachin designed by Bernini, Michelangelo's Pietà, and Canova's funerary monument to Clement XIII are the most important pieces in the basilica. It is possible to climb to the top of the dome from where one can enjoy a superb panorama of St. Peter's Square and the city in the background.

* The Vatican Palace offers visitors many architectural curiosities, but above all the collections of the museums that are among the richest in the world. Egyptian and Etruscan archaeology, Greco-Roman antiquities, Gregorian and Christian art add to the sumptuous treasures of the Pinacoteca (including paintings by Raphael, Titian and the unfinished anatomical study by Leonardo da Vinci).

* Of course, the Sistine Chapel is the crowning glory, and the murals of Perugino, Botticelli, Ghirlandaio, Signorelli and Michelangelo are such masterpieces that you will inevitably leave with a stiff neck. To recover, don't hesitate to take a stroll in the palace gardens.

* From the Papal City via the Vatican corridor, known as the passetto, you can reach the Castel Sant'Angelo through the Borgo district. This imposing fortress dominated by the statue of Archangel Michael was originally the mausoleum of Emperor Hadrian and was to serve as a refuge for the Pope in case of invasion.

Kosovo

Following the violent conflicts between Serbian authorities and Albanian separatists in the late 1990s and the ensuing severe humanitarian catastrophe, Kosovo was placed under UN administration in 1999. Since the Kumanovo Peace Accords, dated the same day, a NATO force, KFOR, has ensured peace and order in the region. On February 17, 2008, the parliament of Kosovo proclaimed the independence of its territory, which not all countries, including Serbia, recognize. However, the new government of the Republic of Kosovo does not exercise real control over the northern part of the country, as the Serbian population is in the majority in some municipalities.

* Priština, the capital of Kosmet, was hard hit by the war of 1998-1999. It still retains its oriental character with its small white houses, above which the minarets of its mosques rise. Do not miss the clock tower erected in the 19th century, the imperial mosque and the old Turkish hammam.

* At the extreme south of Kosmet, Prizren is located in an area with many small churches nestled in the mountains. Picturesque town located at the exit of a gorge, Prizren is made of green hills where are hung many mosques, low houses of oriental type and some monuments of the Serbian Middle Ages.

* Several monasteries of the Serbian Orthodox Church with strong spiritual value are located on its territory: Banjska Monastery, Devia Monastery, Gracanica Monastery, Patriarchate of Pec, and Visoki Decani Monastery. Several of these monuments have been placed on the World Heritage List.

* Brezovica, a Serbian enclave in Kosovo, is the largest ski area in the country located on the territory of the Šar Mountains National Park. From November to May, the resort offers skiers good quality snow, but the ski lifts do not always work.

Latvia

Like the other Baltic countries, Latvia is not among the most popular countries for travelers. However, the architectural richness of its capital and the beauty of its countryside more than make up for any preconceived ideas you may have about the country's climate. Although the years following independence from the USSR were difficult, Latvia is now well on its way to catching up economically and, who knows, in terms of tourism.

* Riga, the ancient city of the Hanseatic League, is a real open-air museum crossed by the Daugava River. In addition to the historic center, the city is also worth a visit for its testimonials of Art Nouveau. The century-old German buildings in the Vecriga district and the view from the bell tower of St. Peter's Church are among the city's attractions. At the foot of the church, the Doma laukums square is most pleasant in the summer when all the terraces take it by storm. Parks and wide boulevards have completed the city over the years. Don't hesitate to stroll along them to feel the atmosphere of the capital, just as you will have to make a detour to the central market installed in former airship hangars from the First World War.

* Cesis is a 13th century city at the entrance to the Gauja National Park. Its castle has been transformed into a museum that tells the history of the country. Nearby there are the ruins of the Sigulda castle, a small spa resort that turns into a ski resort in the winter (known for its toboggan runs). In the heart of the forest, the ruins bear witness to the country's past and offer a beautiful view of Turaida Castle. In the same region, the ruins of Krimulda castle, but also the Gutmanis and Viktors caves are worth a visit.

* Mazsalaca is one of the centers of Latvian folklore. This small town of Vidzeme hides in the surrounding hills the famous werewolf pine which has the ability to turn you into a monster of the same name during the full moon, the staircase of dreams which will reveal to lovers if they are made for each other, and the Devil's Cave whose source has healing properties.

* In its setting of lakes and forest, in the Laglave region, the basilica of Aglona (8 km from the town of the same name) is a Latvian Catholic landmark. Under the two 60-meter high bell towers, you will find ten wooden altars where a miraculous icon (the Virgin of Aglona) is hidden. At the edge of the lake gushes a sulphurous spring appreciated by pilgrims and walkers.

* Bauska, 65 km south of Riga, is known for its 15th century castle, but it is the Palace of Rundale, 12 km away, that is really worth the trip (by bus). Nicknamed the "Versailles" Léton, it owes its architecture to one of the masters of Italian Baroque, also creator of the most beautiful buildings in St. Petersburg.

* Jurmala is the seaside resort of the country. On about forty kilometers on both sides of the city, the beaches alternate with pine forests. The colors of the Baltic Sea, the numerous restaurants and bars on the coast and even the water temperature (up to 20 ° in summer) can make this area a pleasant place to relax.

* Kuldiga is located in the west of the country, in the Kurzeme region. Its religious buildings and ancient fortress make it a picturesque spot. Nearby, on the river Venta, is the widest waterfall in Europe: 2 meters high and 275 meters wide.

* To the northwest is Dundaga famous for its castle. It is said to have been haunted by a young woman who was walled up there alive as punishment for attending a gnome wedding. The surrounding countryside, crossed by the river Pádce, is very pleasant.

Liechtenstein

Liechtenstein is a very small country wedged between Switzerland and Austria. While it attracts multinational companies with a very favorable corporate tax, the same is not true for tourists who have not made it one of their favorite destinations. However, the mountains and castles of the region are worth discovering for all those in search of luxury, peace and quiet.

* Vaduz, the capital, has two sites not to be missed. The 12th century princely castle surrounded by vineyards overlooks the modern city. Still inhabited by the princely family, it is not open to the public, but you can follow the path that leads to the "Känzeli" from where you can admire the panoramic view of the city and the Rhine valley. In the heart of the city is the Kunstmuseum Liechtenstein. This black cube made of tinted cement and basalt stone has an important collection of international modern and contemporary art.

* Near Balzers in the south of the country, the Gutenberg Castle built more than 800 years ago and its grounds are open to visitors. The village is an ideal starting point for hiking and for exploring the beautiful mountains of Liechtenstein and the neighboring Heidiland.

* The peaks at the western end of the Voralberg and the slopes of the massif are ideal for hiking in summer or skiing in winter. The resort of Malbun, at an altitude of 1600 m, is perfect for families in search of fresh air.

Lithuania

Lithuania was the first Soviet republic to seek freedom from ties with the USSR and is now part of the European Union. The medieval architecture of its cities, the ancestral charm of its countryside, and the unusual seaside resorts on its coast make it a new destination in Northern Europe.

* From its tumultuous history, Vilnius has managed to keep a cosmopolitan atmosphere and preserve the architecture of its old town despite the various events it has gone through and the new constructions that have sprung up in recent years. The city is dominated by the ruins of the beautiful Gediminas Castle located on a hill overlooking the city. At the foot of the latter, the Catholic Cathedral of Saint-Stanislas is one of the many churches that dot the city, the most famous of which is that of Saint-Pierre-et-Saint-Paul. The artists' district (the Uzupis district), the Rasu cemetery, the university, the presidential palace, the observatory, the old quarter and the Jewish ghetto are all worth a visit. In the new city, the Museum of the Genocide of the Lithuanian People will mark your visit.

* In the vicinity of the capital there is another interesting museum relating a part of the country's history. It is the Grutas park-museum where you can see the monuments dedicated to the heroes of the Russian Revolution of 1917 and the unblocked statues of Lenin. North of Vilnius, in the village of Purnuskes, is the Europos Parkas where according to some calculations the geographical center of Europe is located.

* About thirty kilometers to the west is the medieval capital of the country: Trakai. It has two castles, one of which is the island castle, a gigantic Gothic-style building located on Lake Galve, one of the 200 lakes in the region. Following the Neman River westward, the second city of the country appears along the banks, Kaunas. The numerous museums of this one, its baroque city hall and its old buildings (like the house of Peruno) are the occasion of pleasant visits.

* The Curonian Spit is a narrow sandy tongue that connects the eastern shore of the Baltic Sea with the Curonian Lagoon whose territory is protected by two national parks. In the middle of dunes and pines, there is Neringa, accessible only by ferry, which includes several popular seaside resorts such as Nida, but also Preila, Pervalka and Juodkrante.

* Not far away, at the northern end of the isthmus is Klaipeda, a charming Baltic port that does not freeze in winter. Other sites are popular with tourists, such as the nice spa and seaside resort of Palanga. Its botanical garden and amber museum are two interesting attractions.

Luxembourg

Located in the heart of Western Europe between Belgium, France and Germany, Luxembourg is not a very exotic destination, it must be admitted. Nevertheless, this small country is a true haven of rest for any traveller in search of greenery and castles.

* The heart of the city of Luxembourg is perched on the steep cliffs of the narrow valleys of the Alzette and Pétrusse rivers, which are crossed by numerous bridges and viaducts. The old quarter and the fortifications of the city are listed as World Heritage Sites, but it is above all the contrast between this and the modern districts that makes the charm of the capital.

* The Oesling is the region that covers the north of the Grand Duchy and belongs to the Ardennes massif. Its main ranges of hills are intersected by picturesque valleys covered with spruce trees and formed by rivers such as the Blees, Clerve, Our, Wiltz, and Sûre. The town of Clervaux, in the heart of the latter, is a picturesque village known for its Saint-Maurice and Saint-Maurice abbey and its superbly restored medieval castle dating from the 12th century.

* To the south, in the canton of Vianden, is the town of the same name and its castle whose most remarkable rooms (the chapel, the Petit Palais and the Grand Palais) were built towards the end of the 12th century. The town is crossed by the river Our. Upstream, an artificial lake is located on the Mont Saint-Nicolas.

* Close to the German border, Luxembourg's Little Switzerland dominates the whole. In the region, the Mullerthal castle (and the Schiessentümpel waterfall), the abbey of Echternach, the medieval fortress and the Renaissance-style castle of Beaufort, and the sandstone cliffs are the sites not to be missed.

* The Moselle valley, from Remich to Wasserbillig, is pleasant for summer walks. Whether you take the waterway for a mini-cruise, the wine route through the vineyards or the cycle path, you will discover a peaceful and endearing region. Not far, south of Remich, the resort of Mondorf-les-Bains is famous for its thermal center and casino.

* A national hiking trail runs through the Eisch valley, called the Valley of the Seven Castles, where meadows and forests are dominated by impressive castles. This walk will make you discover the castles of Mersch, Schoenfels, Hollenfels, the old and the new castle of Ansembourg, the castle of Septfontaines and the castle of Koerich.

Macedonia

Macedonia, which came out of the former Yugoslavia, is still experiencing internal tensions because of the claims of the Albanian population present on its territory. The displacements in the border area at the level and the north of the cities of Tetovo and Kumanovo are always disadvised. The rest of the country nevertheless has many attractions that will one day tempt travelers.

* Skopje, the capital, was almost completely destroyed by the earthquake of 1963. The Turkish quarter was partly spa-

red and its alleys and walls follow a 2000 year old pattern. The Mustafa Pasha mosque and the St. Panteleimon lemon monastery are jewels of the country's eastern architectural heritage. The caravanserais (Karpan An, Kuršumli An and Suli An), the hammam Daut Pasha, the dilapidated but still active bazaar and the Turkish bridge Kameni Most are also worth a visit. The city is dominated by the Kala fortress and its park, which is ideal for walking. About 15 kilometers from the center, the lake and the Matka Canyon form a wild and sumptuous landscape.

• Ohrid is a small town in the southwest of the country, located on the edge of the lake of the same name which is the oldest lake in Europe. Its lake, its landscapes, its medieval heart, but above all its many archaeological sites (including the ancient theater) and its monasteries and churches (St. Clement, St. John of Kaneo, St. Sophia) make it the tourist center of the country. In the surroundings, a few kilometers from the Albanian border, is the monastery of Saint Naum. The numerous springs that punctuate the region, the small rock chapels, the fauna and flora of the Galitchitsa National Park offer it an exceptional setting. Nearby is the Prespa Lake, whose surroundings are also worth a visit.

• The rest of the country, rich in Orthodox churches, Ottoman mosques and Byzantine monasteries, will delight fans of oriental architecture. The frescoes of the Sveti Pantelejmon church in Nerezi are superb. The mosques of Tetovo, Prilep and Bitola and the monastery of Treskavec near Prilep are places worth visiting and admiring. To go back a little more in time, we will not miss the archaeological site of Stobi, 80 kms south of the capital. This city of Hellenistic Macedonia was abandoned in the fourteenth century, but churches, synagogue and ancient ramparts still remain.

• Macedonia is also famous for winter sports and the infrastructures at the disposal of the skiers are particularly numerous there. Whether it is in Popova Sapka, west of Skopje, in Mavrovo on the Bistra mountain, or in Krusevo, near Prilep, you will find your happiness in the snow. Another tradition of the country has developed around the sites of Katlanovo, Negor, Debar, Kosovrasti and Bansko, these are spas known for their benefits.

Malta

Between Sicily and Tunisia, lies the archipelago of Malta that many civilizations have coveted over the centuries. From the passage of the Phoenicians, Romans, Arabs, French and English, Malta has been able to preserve the best and build a unique identity where everyone can find their interest between seaside and cultural tourism.

• Valletta is a 16th century city with many buildings from the time of the Knights of the Order of St. John of Jerusalem, who ruled the island for two and a half centuries. The military architecture of its seafront with its golden colors immediately makes the visitor dream whose imagination bubbles from the gate of the past city. The Cathedral of St. John, once called the Church of the Knights, the former Palace of the Grand Masters, the Inn of Castile, the Upper Barrakka Gardens and the objects of the National Museum of Fine Arts will definitely make you fantasize.

• The small medieval town of Mdina is the ancient capital of Malta. Its ramparts are home to only 300 inhabitants and no cars, hence its nickname of the "city of silence". From the top of the rocky promontory on which Mdina is built, one can enjoy a breathtaking view of the rest of the island. Along its cobbled streets, you can admire many Norman and Baroque buildings.

• The fishing villages of Marsaxlokk and Marsaskala. The typical boats of the first one (luzzu) and its fish market on Sundays make it an interesting stopover. The second one has a pleasant walk, but is especially famous for its diving spots and the fortifications overhanging it (the Fort Leonardo and its towers to the north and the St-Thomas tower on the end of Il-Hamrija).

• Tarxien, a village north of Valletta, is known for its megalithic temples, the oldest of which dates back to 2,800 BC. Numerous statues and animal reliefs tell the story of this vanished civilization and its cult of fertility. The Hypogeum of Hal Saflieni (near Paola south of the capital) is a large structure dug into the ground at the same time, which became a necropolis in the Bronze Age.

* In Ggantija on the island of Gozo, two other temples dating from the Neolithic period have survived until today. These are the two oldest complex religious constructions in the world that have survived on the Mediterranean rim without having been almost completely looted, demolished or buried.

* Sandy beaches are rare in Malta. Mellieha Bay in the north-west of the island and Golden Bay in the west are the only ones to boast with the Ramla Bay in the north of the island of Gozo. But the small wild creeks will welcome those in search of relaxation and calm. Moreover, if the sand is lacking, it is to the benefit of the sea caves whose amazing show will delight divers. The most beautiful one is located on the south coast of Gozo and is called "Blue Hole".

* Still in Gozo, you will find one of the most beautiful beaches of the Mediterranean even if it is covered with pebbles. The high cliffs that surround it and the clarity of the water that bathes it make the west coast of the island along the Inland Sea, an unmissable spot. Near Dwejra Point stands a gigantic arch carved in the cliff.

* Other caves, on land this time, attract tourists. It is indeed on the island of Gozo, in the cliffs overlooking the bay of Ramla, on the northeast coast, that legend has located the cave where Calypso held Ulysses for many years. Speleologists, do not miss the alabaster caves accessible from the village of Xaghra on the same island.

* If the island of Gozo also lends itself to hiking, it is the small island of Comino, wedged between it and the island of Malta, that holds the record for tranquility and naturalness. In fact, cars are not allowed, only one hotel is built there and the green vegetation blends in perfectly with the bluest waters of the region.

Moldova

Moldova is a landlocked Eastern European country between Romania and Ukraine, independent since 1991, which has experienced various political problems. This has surely earned it to stay away from the tourist trails that run through this region. A confidentiality that will allow you to taste the good Moldavian wine in complete tranquility.

* Chisinau, on the banks of the river Bik, has kept the architectural mark of the Ottoman style despite the bombings of the Second World War which made two thirds of the Old City disappear. Pushkin's house and the Museum of Fine Arts are worth visiting.

* Fifteen kilometers north of the capital are the Cricova wine cellars which can be visited in the company of official guides from the Chisinau Wine Tour Office. 60 km of underground galleries await you for tasting sessions. About 15 km away, Cosujna also produces quality wines, such as the Straseni vineyard famous for its sparkling white wine. A little further on, the Romanesti wineries are the market leaders.

* The monastery of Capriana, located about seven kilometers southwest of Straseni, miraculously survived looting and destruction by the Soviets. Orheuil Vechi an archaeological site located near the towns of Ohrei and Trebujeni. There is also a medieval village, an ancient fortress and the Butuceni hermitage, a 13th century monastery.

Monaco

About 20 kilometers east of Nice is the Principality of Monaco. A particularly mild Mediterranean climate bathes this tiny state. Its Casino, Prince's Palace, Oceanographic Museum and luxury hotels make it a popular destination for tourists, not to mention the many international events that take place there.

• The oldest part of the principality is called "the Rock", the whole city seems to be built in an amphitheatre facing the sea. It is in this area that all the city's institutions are located. The palace of Monaco has been the residence of the princes since 1297. Every day at 11:55 a.m. on the square you can watch the changing of the guard. To prolong the magic of the fairy tale, one can go to the Cathedral of Notre-Dame-Immaculée where the Princes rest.

• The Oceanographic Museum of Monaco, which is located near the Palace, had Commander Cousteau as its director. Its aquarium, one of the oldest in Europe, offers the possibility of observing 350 species of fish (for more than 6000 specimens), 200 species of invertebrates, and 100 species of tropical corals. A great educational place, you can complete your visit with a visit to the Exotic Garden where more than 7000 varieties of plants are represented.

• The Casino de Monte-Carlo is one of the most prestigious and luxurious baroque-style casinos on the planet in the heart of Monte-Carlo in Monaco. Its architecture, gardens and fame attract the curious, but it is above all the unrepentant players who are deeply attached to it. Next to it stands the Hotel de Paris, a Belle Époque style palace that is among the elite of Monegasque hotels, along with the Hotel Hermitage, the Monte-Carlo Beach Hotel, the Monte-Carlo Bay Hotel & Resort, the Hôtel Métropole and the Loews.

• La Condamine is the commercial district of the principality. Famous for being the place of departure and arrival of the Monaco Automobile Grand Prix, it is pleasant to stroll there and linger at one of the terraces of the many small restaurants.

Montenegro

In the face of the well-deserved tourist success of neighboring Croatia, Montenegro now serves as an as yet unexplored little brother. Montenegro is a very small country, with a very marked relief and characterized by grandiose landscapes. The interior of the country remains very unknown and little explored, but the Adriatic coast has been attracting travelers for a few years now. The beauty of the mountains falling into the sea, the sandy beaches and the centuries-old villages are an undeniable asset. Still quite far from western tourism, the country has kept a strong Slavic soul and is already the premise of the eastern Mediterranean. The infrastructures are correct and in the great bath of tourism the destination has already earned its nickname of "new Côte d'Azur", which should guarantee the country a very promising future for tourism.

• The Mouths of Kotor are considered the southernmost European fjord. Here, the Adriatic Sea borders several inland gulfs connected by deep passes and the mountains form its natural borders with the rest of the country. An ideal naval base in the days of Yugoslavia, this place nowadays welcomes more and more tourists. Do not miss: the Savina Monastery in Herceg Novi and the beaches of the nearby villages, the Benedictine monastery on a small island facing the town of Perast and the Verige (the narrowest passage of the mouths), and of course the old town of Kotor and its impressive defense wall.

• The 300 km of coastline is dotted with fishing villages and charming little islands. St. George's Island and the Church of Our Lady of the Reef built in the 17th century on an artificial islet form a lovely site. The almost island of Sveti Stefan was converted into a hotel island in 1955 and Tito welcomed his distinguished guests there. The former summer residence of the kings of Montenegro, in Milocer, in the middle of its shady park, has also become a beautiful summer resort. The seaside resorts of Buvda, Ulcinj and Petrovac are developing more and more.

* Close to the Mouths of Kotor is the Lovcen Mountain National Park where nature is beautiful. The road from Kotor to its summit makes a series of 32 steep curves in the middle of a sumptuous landscape. From there, the whole Montenegro is embraced, from the Mouth of Kotor to the Adriatic Sea, from the Skadar Lake to the Durmitor massif. In the heart of the park, look for the village of Njeguši where the birth house of the Montenegrin royal family, the Petrovic, is located.

* A hundred kilometers to the north, the Durmitor massif and its exceptional fauna await you. Brown bears, wolves, chamois, birds of prey and heather roosters have made it their home. Capital of winter tourism in Montenegro, Zabljac is a well-equipped ski resort. A few villages are scattered in the park including Mala Crna Gora, the highest in the Balkans, located on the edge of the Sucica and Tara canyons. In addition to numerous hikes, the valley of the latter offers the possibility of rafting in a magnificent setting.

* Lake Shkodra is the largest lake on the Balkan Peninsula and one of the largest bird reserves in Europe with 270 species of birds, including the last pelicans on the continent. Do not hesitate to take the path from the village of Vranjina to the hill of the same name where a magnificent view awaits you. You will also come across a 15th century monastery on the road.

* But the most beautiful monastery of the country is that of Ostrog inlaid in the hill of the same name above the valley of Bjelopavlici. It is one of the most visited sanctuaries in the Christian world. Praying near the body of Vasilije would allow one to be healed and to face the difficulties of life. Monastic residences are located around the church, making this monument, in addition to the church and the beautiful landscape, a place of great beauty.

Norway

The territory of Norway has been carved to give the west coast of the Scandinavian peninsula its most beautiful landscapes. The mountains and glaciers of the interior have nothing to envy the fjords that cut the 2,500 km of coastline. The whole country will fill you with its impressive landscapes, but also with its peculiarities such as the Northern Lights and the midnight sun which make them even more fantastic.

* In the south, around Bergen, the most famous and beautiful fjords are to be found. The Sognefjord is the longest in Europe, extending inland for more than 200 km. Many cruises are possible to admire its beauty. Nordfjord is close to the Western Cape, Norway's westernmost territory, and the spectacular Briksdal Glacier. The Geirangerfjord is sumptuous, from its snow-capped walls flow superb waterfalls. The most complimentary adjectives are therefore appropriate to the vision of its glacial valleys, Norway's natural heritage. One of the best ways to discover the east coast is to take the Coastal Express, which links Bergen to Kirkenes in six days.

* Inland, it's the turn of the lakes to take over to amaze us. The National Park of Rondane, the oldest in the country, the lake Rondvatnet is surrounded by peaks that easily reach 2000 m and that can be reached in a day's walk. In mythology, the park of Jötunheim is the territory that Odin left to the ice giants at the Creation. The Hardanger Park is famous for all the skiing possibilities it offers. In the summer, hiking is a must and is also very enjoyable. The fisherman will be the most delighted, as the rivers and lakes of the region abound with trout and salmon.

* Going up to the north of the country will allow you to cross the Arctic Circle and admire the most beautiful natural phenomena that these remote regions have to offer. From mid-May to the end of June, the midnight sun shines on the landscape and never sets. From November-December until February, it is the turn of the Northern Lights to take over and dazzle you. And, as luck would have it, these are some of the most beautiful places in the country, which the region is

lucky enough to have, that will be magnified.

• The Lofoten Islands, off Bodø, like Alps rising out of the sea, are among the most beautiful islands in the world. Small fjords, needles, cirques and pastures make up the landscape. The whirl of currents (maelstrom), the colorful huts on stilts of cod fishermen, thousands of birds and Tysfjord killer whales (October) are the assets. They also have the advantage of a particularly mild climate in summer.

• The county of Finnmark, Lapland in the far north of the country, is the land of the Sámi and reindeer. You can discover its beauties by snowmobile or dog sled, but also experience diving under the ice or even fishing for the Kamchatka king crab (the most sought-after crab species in the world and the most expensive by weight). Tourist highlights of the region are the Alta rock art site, but especially the North Cape (an excursion is organized every day from Hammerfest). It is the northernmost point of Europe located on the island of Magerøy.

• West Spitsbergen is the largest island of the archipelago of the same name (or Svalbard) in the Arctic Ocean. Black mountains, glaciers, icebergs, but also hot springs (in the Northwest Spitsbergen National Park) make all the beauty of it. In the spring, a short but bright bloom brings back colors to the whole.

• Faced with all these wonders of nature, Norwegian cities find it hard to compete. One will note the medieval district of Bergen recalling its belonging to the Hanseatic League and the museums of Oslo (the Munchmuseet, the National Museum of Fine Arts, the open-air museum of the Froner park and the Viking museum in Bigdøy). Some of the country's villages, such as Heddal, Lom, Ringebu and Røldal, boast small churches made of so-called end wood. For a better understanding of Nordic habitation, the fresco in the Maihaugen Open Air Museum in Lillehammer is worth a visit.

Poland

Poland is a miraculous land that has survived difficult times to flourish today. At the meeting point of Western and Eastern Europe, this territory has a thousand things to offer to the traveler who has chosen it as his destination. Each village, each region has its own particularities and hides within them natural and human treasures.

• Krakow is one of the oldest cities in Poland, but also one of the most dynamic today. It has preserved its architectural heritage and since the end of the communist period, it has welcomed more and more tourists. Its main square (Rynek Glówny), its palaces (Baroque, Gothic and Renaissance), its eighty churches, its Jewish quarter (Kazimierz) and Wawel Castle will punctuate your itineraries. Take the time to enjoy a bagel or a pretzel and have a drink in one of the literary cafés that symbolize the cultural life of the city as much as its many museums.

• In the Krakow region is the Auschwitz camp, a symbol of man's barbarity whose visit will forever mark your spirits. The Wieliczka Salt Mine is also worth a visit for its entire chapel dug into the salt at a depth of about 100 meters. You can also visit Wadowice, the birthplace of John Paul II. Nearby is the most important place of pilgrimage in the country, Kalwaria Zebrzydowska, a church and monastery with chapels built on the hills.

• Warsaw aims to be the economic capital of the country, its business district is being renewed and transforming the face of the once Soviet city. The historical and medieval center was rebuilt after the Second World War and there is a high concentration of interesting buildings such as the Heroes' Monument, the Royal Castle, St. John's Cathedral, Lazienki Palace... From the ghetto, however, only a remembrance route remains. Gdansk (formerly Danzig) was also devastated during the Second World War, but the bourgeois houses along the royal road as well as the City Hall and the Basilica of Our Lady are now flourishing under the eyes of tourists.

• Other Polish cities all have something to offer visitors. Don't hesitate to visit the 13th century Teutonic Fortress of Malbork (Marienburg), the castle of the Dukes of Pomerania in Darlowo, the World Heritage city of Torun, the market square (Rynek) in Wroclaw, the old towns of Sandomierz and Poznan. The villages, all dressed in wood, are also an opportunity for interesting visits, especially for their churches and the welcome you will receive from the inhabitants.

* The capital of winter sports is Zakopane in the south of the country on the Zakopiana, just below the most important mountain range of Poland, the Tatras. There are not many ski lifts, but the resorts of Butorowy Wierch, Gubalowka, Kasprowy Wierch, Pardalówka, Polana Szymoszkowa, Witów Ski offer opportunities for natural skiing in winter, but also for hiking, climbing and rafting in summer.

* On the border with Lithuania, Masuria, the land of a thousand lakes, offers unspoiled nature to be discovered on a cruise along the rivers and canals that connect the lakes. You can also kayak, fish, and observe the living wildlife. To the east, the Warmie region offers many opportunities for hiking between forests and lakes, especially in the Olsztyn region where the Krzywe, Dlugie and Rejdykanyà lakes are located.

* To the south of this region is the Bialowieza primary forest, which has remained untouched by human influences. It is the oldest natural forest in Europe, with more than 5000 species of plants, 12 000 species of poultry, wolves, deer, lynx, tarpans and the last bison in Europe. Guided tours are organized to help you discover all their secrets, in winter these are done by sleigh.

* In spite of the coolness of the Baltic Sea, one seaside resort after another on the Polish coast. Let's mention Swinoujscie, Miedzyzdrokje (on the island of Wolin), Kolobrzeg, Gdynia and Sopot. The latter, with its beaches, pier (Molo) and forest in the background, is the most popular.

Portugal

Located on the Iberian Peninsula, Portugal is a country with multiple charms where medieval castles, dream landscapes and cosmopolitan cities rub shoulders in perfect harmony. Its proximity to the Atlantic Ocean has made Portugal a country with a rich maritime past and famous explorers allowing it to establish a true empire in the past. If the majority of tourists are nowadays attracted by the seaside resorts located on the south coast of the country, other regions abound with heritage treasures and Lisbon is riding on a wave of well-deserved tourist success.

* Lisbon alone deserves a few days of visits as there are so many tourist highlights in this capital. Three major historical districts compete with each other: Bélem, on the banks of the Taje, whose tower is the emblem of the city, the Alfama, whose Cathedral and the Castle of Saint George dominate the city, and the Baixa, where monuments and shops abound. To go out, go to vibrate to the sound of Fado in the Bairro Alto.

* Porto has an undeniable charm, the banks of the Douro are a spectacle that we never tire of admiring and that we are exhausted to survey. It goes up and down, enough to make your head spin as much as the city's wine specialty. The cellars of Porto generously open their doors to you on the bank of Nova de Gaïa.

* In addition to these two most famous cities, there are many spots in Portugal not to be missed, such as Evora and its Moorish heritage, Sintra and its castle with an explosive architectural cocktail, Obidos and its medieval ramparts, Coïmbra and its 11th century university and finally Guimaraes and its fortified castle.

* The road of the monasteries: At the end of the XVth century, the Manueline art (derived from the Gothic style) made hatch in the country many monuments to the glory of Catholicism. The Monastery of the Hieronymites in Lisbon, that of the Order of Sîto in Alcobaça, that of the Dominicans of Batalha or the Templar Castle of Tomar are masterpieces that leave no one indifferent. More recent, but just as impressive, Fatima welcomes believers from all over the world every year.

• Portugal is also famous for its seaside resorts, especially in the Algarve region with its 150 km of creeks and beaches. The weather is beautiful most of the year and it is without a doubt the most touristic area in Portugal. Don't miss Cape St. Vincent, the westernmost tip of Europe, with its cliffs and impressive waves - If Portugal is known for its cod, it is above all thanks to the large number of fishing ports. The most famous one is in Nazare, a charming town with narrow streets and white houses with red roofs - If the weather tells you, take a cruise on the Douro to admire the terraced vineyards of port and visit some quintas (properties). The scenery in this region is superb.

AZORES :

The Azores are a group of Portuguese islands located in the middle of the Atlantic Ocean, about 1,500 km from Lisbon and Morocco and 3,900 km from the east coast of North America. There are a total of nine islands divided into three groups. The Western Group consists of the islands of Corvo and Flores. The Central Group by the islands of Terceira, Graciosa, Sao Jorge, Pico and Faial and the Eastern Group by São Miguel and Santa Maria.

If the Azores are known above all for their anticyclone (but in reality it rains a lot there), the temperatures remain moderate throughout the year and the beaches are not sandy. You will therefore not find the seaside resort of your dreams, but nature in all its splendor and lushness. The hikers find their happiness in the volcanic origin of the place which offers multiple reliefs, ascents and descents around a very particular flora. To speak of the Azores is to speak of natural, wild spaces and virgin landscapes. A destination still little known but which deserves to become one.

MADEIRA :

Madeira is located in the Atlantic Ocean west of Morocco and is an autonomous region of Portugal. Its authenticity and exoticism make it a pleasant destination that remains an alternative somewhat apart from the great tourist flows oriented towards the Balearic Islands or the Canary Islands. A unique destination of its kind, closer to the exotic islands of the Pacific than to classic Europe, Madeira has long been in the minds of frequent travelers.

• Climb Pico Ruivo (3 hours from Santana) to admire the panorama visible from the summit, get lost in the Serra plateau between sheep and fog, discover the village of the Valley of the Nuns and taste its culinary specialties... Here are a few examples of hiking among the 2000 km of trails planned for this purpose. Don't forget to go to the Ponta de Sao Lourenço, in the south, where you can walk along the cliffs, an experience that will blow your mind!

• Funchal, the capital of Madeira, is the most populated and touristy city. Luxury hotels and nightclubs as well as gardens and religious monuments make Funchal a friendly city. Take the cable car to reach the village of Monte whose Botanical Garden overlooks the capital. The succession of tropical terraced gardens is beautiful. To taste the fruits and vegetables produced on the island, the best place is the Mercado dos Lavradores, Funchal's covered market.

• On the north-western tip of Madeira Island, Porto Moniz is famous for its natural pools formed in the volcanic reefs finely chiselled by the tide. An artificial beach has been built in Calheta, as Madeira does not have a sandy beach, although this does not prevent swimming and water sports. However, 9 km of fine sand await you on the nearby island of Porto Santo (40 km away).

Romania

24 years of Ceaucescu "reign" have marked Romania without nevertheless managing to extinguish this flame which makes the men friendly and the landscapes enchanting. To travel through Romania is to immerse oneself in the traditions of a vanished Eastern Europe and to discover the mutations that bring it into the third millennium.

• Take the monastery route: in Bucovina, the five monasteries of Voronet, Moldovita, Humor, Sucevita and Arbore constitute a mystical and colorful architectural heritage not to be missed.

* Follow in the footsteps of Dracula: from Sighisoara, the village where Vlad Dracul was born, through Sibiu, a Saxon town where the hero potentially lived for a year, to the castle of Brau, reputed to have served as his lair.

* Bucharest will allow you to discover the megalomania of Ceausescu. The People's Palace (2nd largest administrative building in the world after the Pentagon) and the alley leading to it have crushed the old historical quarters of the city. Fortunately, the huge parks will allow you to breathe and meet the inhabitants.

* More than 150 health resorts dot the coast and give this Black Sea coastline a not inconsiderable attraction. Sea, sodium, chlorine, salt and mud: here are the ingredients to give you back your health in Eforie, Neptua or Mangalia for example.

Russia

Straddling Europe and Asia, the territory of Russia is the largest on the planet. You will need more than one stay to discover all the richness of its cultural and natural diversity. In addition to the attractiveness of Russia's large cities, the opening of the country now allows the traveler to reach the most remote regions, some of which are among the most extraordinary sites of our planet, such as the Kamchatka region or the banks of the Amur river, the territory of the white tiger. A great way to discover the country, the Trans-Siberian Railway connects Moscow to Vladivostok on 9,238 kilometers in one week with 990 stops. Russia, because of its size and culture, is a world apart and discovering this country in its great widths is a true epic that can only be undertaken by the most adventurous travelers.

* Saint Petersburg is a city built on the Neva River and dozens of islets and canals conducive to a discovery of its baroque facades by boat. The eternal capital of the tsars, with its architectural, religious and literary heritage, has everything to amaze the visitor. Do not miss to visit the Hermitage Museum, one of the richest museums in the world. The best time of the year to travel to St. Petersburg is during the sleepless nights in June, when the days get so long that twilight merges with dawn.

* Moscow is a dynamic city where culture occupies a privileged place, several of its 150 museums are world-famous such as the Pushkin Museum, and its 40 theaters offer performances all year round. Behind its high red walls, the Kremlin is a city within the city of more than thirty hectares full of palaces, cathedrals and churches. In front of it lies the Red Square always full of tourists who flock to visit the mausoleum of Lenin and the Cathedral of Basil the Blessed.

* Northeast of Moscow, the Golden Ring region gathers the ancient cities of the tsars and princes of Holy Russia. In Suzdal, the exceptional medieval monuments (Kremlin, Nativity Cathedral, monasteries and wooden churches) mingle with the streams, rivers and farm animals within the city itself. The Old Town of Yaroslavl, the Ipatievsky Monastery of Kostroma, the Citadel of Rostov, the Golden Gate of Vladimir and the Monastery of the Trinity-St. Sergius Sergius of Sergei Possad all bear witness to this flamboyant era.

* Other cities also have architectural gems that are worth a visit. In Peterhof, near St. Petersburg, Peter the Great built a series of palaces and gardens that form the "Russian Versailles". Novgorod, on the Volkhov River, is the oldest Russian city, as evidenced by the St. Sophia Cathedral, the citadel and the city's medieval churches. The Old City of Kazan, the capital of Tatarstan, is an architectural pearl blending Western and Eastern influences with one of the most beautiful Kremlin in Russia. The citadel, churches and convents of Pskov (near the Estonian border), the Novosibirsk opera house (in Siberia), the hermitage churches on the island of Kiji (on Lake Onega) and the Astrakhan kremlin (on the Caspian Sea) confirm that there is something to see all over the country.

* North of St. Petersburg, Karelia, has 60 000 lakes. Lakes Ladoga (the largest of European lakes) and Onega are worth a stop for their small wooden villages and islands. The still very well preserved forests of the surroundings take all their value during the Indian summer.

- The ideal way to discover the west of the country is to follow the course of the Volga waterway that connects the Baltic Sea to the Caspian Sea. The locks of the first one, the floating houses of the second one, the steep landscapes, and the fauna of the delta (beavers, otters, sea lions) form a permanent spectacle enriched by the city stages.

- In the south, the Great Caucasus is an impressive mountain range where Mount Elbrus, the main center of tourism and mountaineering in the region, culminates at 5,642 meters. On its slopes, many winter sports resorts are scattered, the one of Terskol is nicknamed the "Russian Chamonix". In the North Caucasus there is the spa resort of Kislovodsk.

- The Black Sea is the only place in the country that is really suitable for swimming. The resort of Sochi enjoys a surprisingly warm climate for its latitude. The country's celebrities and elite meet here, tourists come to take a Black Sea cruise, and the city hosted the 2014 Winter Olympics.

- Lake Baikal in Siberia has some of the richest and most original freshwater flora and fauna on the planet (600 plant species and 1,550 animal species, including dolphins and freshwater seals on the Uzhkany Islands). In winter, you can walk on the large layer of ice that forms on its surface and cross-country ski in the surrounding area.

- The Amur, Lena, Ob, Yenisei are all navigable rivers (except in winter) to discover Siberia, the most gigantic wilderness on earth.

- Kamchatka is a volcanic peninsula that juts into the Pacific Ocean. More than 200 craters animate the landscape, for example with the perfect cone of the volcano Kronotski. The natural and burning fountains of the "Valley of Geysers" were damaged by a landslide in 2007.

- Between this peninsula and Japan lie the Kuril Islands where the landscapes of volcanoes, lava deserts, waterfalls, hot springs, fjords, crater lakes and beaches are each more fascinating than the other. The archipelago is home to several million seabirds and seal colonies, and is also bordered by some of the richest waters in the Pacific Ocean.

Serbia

A crossroads between South Slavic civilizations and Western Europe, Serbia is a largely unknown destination, long devastated by the Yugoslav conflict. Nevertheless, it has managed to preserve its culture and today welcomes more and more tourists. Its large cities, the richness of its architectural heritage, and its large national parks make it a territory of surprising charm.

- *Belgrade offers the resources of a great international capital, with many museums (National Museum, Ethnographic Museum, Fresco Museum...) and buildings, public or private, which mainly illustrate the architecture of the 19th and 20th centuries when the stigmas of the conflict were erased. Don't miss the fortress built on a rocky spur in the Kalemegdan Park, at the junction of the Save and the Danube, where Celtic, Roman, Slavic, Turkish and Austrian architecture is mixed.*

- *One hour from Belgrade, Novi Sad, capital of Vojvodina, is nicknamed "Serbian Athens" because of its cultural influence. Gothic, Baroque, Art Nouveau and Neoclassical art blend together to make the heart of the city a most interesting stopover. Nearby, the medieval fortress of Petrovaradin, overlooking the Danube, was built by the Austrians to defend themselves from the Turks. Five kilometers along the right bank of the Danube, don't miss a stopover to visit the historic town of Sremski Karlovci, the spiritual center of Serbia, full of historic monuments and buildings from the 18th and 19th centuries.*

- *Built between the 12th and 16th centuries, the Orthodox monasteries of Serbia constitute an exceptional architectural* heritage containing priceless riches in terms of frescoes and religious icons in Byzantine style. The monasteries of Sopocani, Studenica and Decani are inscribed on the World Heritage List. South of the capital, the monasteries of Zica, Ravanica, Manasija and Gradac are also worth a visit. In the north of the country, the valleys of the Fruska Gora National Park are home to 18 monasteries built for the most part between the 15th and 16th centuries where Byzantine and Baroque styles merge. The most famous of the latter are the monasteries of Krusedol and Hopovo.

* The Derdap National Park in the southern Carpathians, near the town of Kladovo, extends on the right bank of the Danube from the Golubac fortress to the Sip Dam. It is particularly famous for its Iron Gates, a grandiose passage through the southern slopes of the Carpathians where the river widens majestically. In addition to a diversified and protected flora and fauna, there are important remains that testify to the activity and history of mankind (the Mesolithic archaeological site of Lepenski Vir, the medieval fortress of Golubacet and the Table of Trajan dedicated to the Emperor).

* The Kopaonik Mountains National Park, in the southern part of Central Serbia, offers several centers of interest. In winter, skiing and snowboarding is practiced there, especially in the resort of Kopaonik which offers the largest ski area in the country. In the summer, it is possible to go hiking or biking to discover the numerous churches built by Serbian princes in the Middle Ages, but also the Samokovska valley, just below the Suvo Rudište, where many rapids and waterfalls and important gorges in the mountains have been formed. For relaxation, the spa town of Jošanicka Banja awaits you.

* The Tara Mountains are located in the west, along the border with Bosnia. Eighteen fully signposted hiking trails crisscross the Tara nature park, many of which start in the hamlet of Mitrovac. The park is also suitable for bicycle touring and rafting is practiced in the Drina Gorge. Moreover, the Tara Mountains also have a certain cultural potential, with Roman and medieval ruins, traditional wooden houses and, above all, the Raca Monastery. Mokra Gora, located in the south of the massif, is the starting point of a tourist railway line, the Eight of Šargan.

Slovakia

Slovakia is one of those small European countries that formed a big front. In 1993, it amicably separated from the Czech Republic, but did not become a destination in its own right. Although cruises on the Danube sometimes take travellers as far as Brastilava, the rest of the country is still unknown to the general public. However, the mountains that make up 80% of the territory offer a real alternative to all those who wish to vary their pleasures and discover other peaks than those of the Alps or the Pyrenees. In the heart of Europe, superb walks in the middle of nature await you, as well as cities steeped in history.

* The High Tatras are nicknamed "the smallest high mountains in the world". Only 26 km long, a dozen peaks culminate at 2600 m. They serve as a natural border between Poland and Slovakia. A European long-distance hiking trail will allow you to discover the most interesting fauna and landscapes. It is also possible to ski there as in Trbské Pleso or Star Smokovec.

* The Slovensky Raj National Park located in the Low Tatras also offers beautiful hiking possibilities to discover the giant's pots. The Dobšinská Ice Cave is unique of its kind.

* At both ends of the country, in the Malá Fatra Mountains in the west and the Eastern Beksides in the east, you can also experience the protected nature of medium mountains.

* Bratislava, 60 km from Vienna, is the cultural heart of Slovakia. Theaters, museums, galleries, concert halls and cinemas punctuate the city along the Danube. The castle (now the National Museum), St. Martin's Cathedral, the Mirbach Palace and the Primate's Palace are all places to visit to get to know this discreet capital.

* The castle of Spis is the most imposing in Central Europe. The ruins of this fortified site dating from the 12th century are spread out above the village of Ehra and amaze more than 170,000 visitors a year.

* If Trnava, north of Bratislava, is one of the industrial poles of Slovakia, it is also a city where Gothic and Baroque churches are jostling for position. Further north, the Church of St. Jacob in Levoca is also worth a visit, as is the Bardejov Cathedral.

Slovenia

Preserved from mass tourism which forgets to think about these countries in the center of Europe, Slovenia is a small forest lung at the crossroads of Europe. Coming from the former Yugoslavia and a member of the European Union since May 1st 2004, this country has received many names such as "a Europe in miniature", "the sunny side of the Alps", "the green lung of Europe"... And they are all justified! Smaller than Brittany, the Slovenian territory is, in terms of architecture for example, both influenced by Rome or Venice, but also by Germany and Hungary. Outside the cities, a green nature awaits you where a particularly diverse fauna has made its home.

* The Triglav National Park and the surrounding resorts in the Julian Alps are a small paradise for hikers (or skiers in winter). Among the most beautiful sites, that of Bled, never the shores of a lake have never been so enchanting.

* The Kras (or Carso or Karst) is rich of thousands of caves of varying sizes. Those of Postojna (the longest in Europe) or Skocjan are worth the detour. On foot or by mountain bike, discover the bowels of the Earth.

* Slovenia is also famous for its spas, about fifteen in all scattered throughout the country. They all offer beautiful settings in the middle of nature.

* The streets and museums of Ljubljana make the Slovenian capital a great place to wander and stroll. Valentin Metzinger, a great baroque painter, and Joïe Pleãnik, a renowned architect, have populated the city with cultural treasures just waiting to be admired.

* The cathedral, the castle and the fortifications of Maribor make it the second most important tourist site in Slovenia. It has been selected to be the European Capital of Culture in 2012 together with the city of Guimarães in Portugal. In the meantime, it hosts numerous winter sports competitions every year.

* The coast on the Adriatic is tiny, wedged between Italy and Croatia, but it is becoming more and more popular. Koper, for its Venetian influence, Portoroz for its casinos and Piran for its medieval port are the main (and ultimately the only) stops on a journey along the coast.

Spain

Each region of Spain is a destination in its own right that will amaze you with its landscapes, monuments and traditions. Like France or Italy, it is one of those great destinations you can't get enough of. Here is a glimpse of the great regions that make it up to guide you on the roads of this fantastic country.

CATALONIA & COSTA BLANCA :

* The Costa Brava begins at the French border and spreads its beaches and tourist complexes for 200 kilometers. Its rocky and fragmented coastline has been completely transformed by promoters except in the more difficult to access corners. Thus, Cadaqués has been able to preserve its urbanism from the big complexes and remains today one of the most pleasant villages of the coast with Begur or Aiguablava.

* Salvador Dalí was born in Figueras and today there is an extravagant museum dedicated to him. For fans of the artist, continue the visit to the cove of Portlligat where the fisherman's cottage is located, where he lived and worked regularly from 1930 until the death of his wife Gala in 1982. Finally, visit the hamlet of Pubol, where Dalí bought a castle in 1969 and, after the death of his muse, transformed it into a mausoleum to his glory.

* Barcelona is the historical, administrative and economic capital of Catalonia. Stroll along the Rambla, admire the buildings of the Barri Gòtic, the jewel of the Old Town, choose between the Catalan architects at Passeig de Gràcia, relax in the Güell Park... but above all, let your steps guide you. Gaudí's legacy and the bodegas are there to make you lose your mind, don't resist.

* In the hinterland, a network of 3000 kilometers of marked trails allows you to discover on foot or by bike a fabulous region: the Sierra de Montseny. The monastery of Santa Maria de Montserrat in the heart of the massif is worth a visit. The lake of Banyoles and its houses on stilts offer a pleasant setting for vacationing. The volcanic landscape of La Garrotxa Natural Park is home to exuberant vegetation that will delight walkers.

* The Catalan Pyrenees also offer a wide range of walks. In winter, skiers take over and take to the slopes of La Molina and Baqueira-Beret.

* Valencia is no longer in Catalonia, but gives the opportunity to push south to visit another great city on the Mediterranean coast. As Spain third city, Valencia is a very animated place. The delicacy of its monuments combined with its natural areas (La Albufera Natural Park and the Dehesa del Saler) make it a pleasant stopover.

* South of Valencia, the famous Costa Blanca begins. Centered around Alicante, a vibrant coastal city (and the only truly Spanish place in the area), and Benidorm, a huge resort with more high rises than anywhere else in Europe, the Costa Blanca is a delightful region if you know where to look. Beaches are wonderful, the sun is guaranteed and white villages are still here (hence the name), like charming Denia, even if tourist overheating is never far away.

ANDALUSIA :

* Andalusia was the last territory of the Moors before they were expelled from Spain in 1492. In the eastern part of the region, a rich architectural heritage bears witness to this period. The most famous buildings are the Alhambra in Granada, the Mosque-Cathedral in Cordoba, the Torre del Oro and the Giralda in Seville, and the Gibralfaro in Malaga. Each of these cities is worth a visit and will reveal its secrets if you take the time to walk through its streets and alleys.

* The Sierra Nevada offers some of the most beautiful views in all of Spain. It is the highest mountain range in Western Europe after the Alps and you can sometimes see the African coast from its peaks. Numerous castles stand on the high plateaus of the region, including La Calahorra. The heart of the massif can be reached quite easily by the "highest mountain road in Europe". Starting from Granada, at 640 m, it winds its way up to 3,150 m above sea level.

* The Costa del Sol has been ravaged by excessive urbanization. Nevertheless, the most famous spots such as Marbella and Torremolinos continue to welcome a huge number of tourists every year who come both for the beaches and the nightlife of these resorts. For more tranquility, visit the natural park of Cabo de Gata-Níjar in the east of Almeria.

* The southeast coast, called Costa de la Luz, has also been spared. In Cádiz, you will find the beach of La Caleta, which stretches for several kilometers. For a refreshing break, don't hesitate to visit the Hospital del Carmen and the oratories of its churches.

* The phantasmagorically shaped limestone blocks of Torcal de Antequera, the olive groves of the province of Jaénet its renaissance towns (Úbeda and Baeza), the arid plains of the province of Almería where many spaghetti Westerns were

made, and the white villages of the region (Arcos de la Frontera and Ronda) are some of the surprises that southern Spain has in store for you.

CENTER :

* Madrid is the capital of Spain where torrid summers alternate with harsh winters. Whether you drink here to cool off or warm up, the nightlife is undoubtedly one of the highlights of the city. Those who love shopping will not be outdone as in all major European capitals. And those who prefer art and architecture will also find their happiness between the baroque monuments that adorn the streets and the various museums. Meet Goya, Rubens, Titian, El Greco and Velázquez at the Prado, the Impressionists at the Thyssen-Bornemisza and Dalí Foundation, Miró and Picasso at the Reina-Sofia Center.

* The Royal Site of Saint Lawrence of El Escorial is located 45 km northwest of Madrid. This monumental complex contains one of the largest collections of relics in the Catholic world. The Library, the Basilica and the Pantheons of the Kings and Infantes are sumptuous rooms where history continues its course.

* Cuenca is located in the autonomous community of Castilla-La Mancha, northwest of Madrid. It is one of the most beautiful medieval cities in Spain, where the houses of the old town cling to a rocky hill bordered by gorges.

* Aranjuez, 44 km south of Madrid, is located on the left bank of the Tagus river. Its royal palace and beautiful gardens are well worth a visit.

* To the west of Madrid, there are also two towns that will give visitors the opportunity to marvel at Spain's heritage. Segovia, at the foot of the Sierra de Guadarrama, has a cathedral, an alcazar and an aqueduct that are sumptuous both in themselves and in their geographical location. Avila is surrounded by a medieval wall, Romanesque style, completely preserved.

* Toledo, finally, is also built on a promontory around which the Tagus River winds for the pleasure of the eyes. Churches, synagogues and mosques reflect a period when communities lived peacefully together there. El Greco, who spent the last part of his life there, also left his mark on the city.

* In the heart of the country, you can walk in the footsteps of Don Quixote. Different stages in the plain of La Mancha will make you forget the sadness of its relief.

NORTH-WEST :

The Atlantic beaches exude a little more charm than the Mediterranean beaches and they are often immense. On the other hand, the water is much cooler. From west to east, the north coast is divided into the Costa Verde, the Santander coast and the Basque coast. The waves are often powerful and make the happiness of surfers and kitesurfers.

- Santiago de Compostela is the last stage of the pilgrimage of the same name and was, along with Jerusalem and Rome, one of the most important pilgrimages of Christianity in the Middle Ages. This route, which is still very popular today, leads pilgrims to a Romanesque style cathedral. In the same region, the stained glass windows of the cathedral of León are also on the pilgrims' route. That's a good thing, they are magnificent.

- Bilbao is the most important city in the Basque Country. An urban revitalization plan is in place and has completely revitalized the entire city, which was once very damaged by heavy industry. The Palacio Euskalduna and the Euskotren tramway system are the most remarkable achievements. Of course, for the visitors, it is the Guggenheim Museum that attracts all eyes. The picturesque and lively old town is also worth a visit.

- San Sebastian is an important seaside resort on the Cantabrian Sea, nicknamed "the pearl" because of its beauty, especially that of its bay, the famous Concha. If you add to this the walks and tapas bars that the city center offers, you get one of the most touristy cities in Spain.

BALEARIC ISLANDS :

The Balearic Islands are an autonomous community of Spain. Located in the Mediterranean Sea, the five islands that make up the archipelago are among the top destinations for clubbing and relaxing. Mallorca, Menorca, Ibiza, Formentera or Cabrera, you are spoilt for choice when deciding where to put your towel. However, it would be unfair to reduce the archipelago to this image because it is in fact above all a natural site of great quality, where the Mediterranean Sea expresses itself in all its splendor, between coves and pine forests.

MALLORCA :

* The beaches around Palma are long and beautiful, but above all very busy. Mass urbanization has contributed to the deterioration of the landscape and you will have to go to the creeks of the north coast to find a bit of tranquility. The government is increasingly trying to protect its heritage and culture and some areas have been declared Natural Reserves.

* Palma de Mallorca is best known for its nightlife, but you can walk there during the day to vary with the seaside pleasures. The Gothic cathedral and the Almudaina palace are among the monuments to visit in the crowded streets.

* Take the little train that crosses the countryside just outside Palma. You will cross beautiful olive groves to arrive at the Serra de Tramuntana and its beautiful views. From Sóller, there are many possibilities for hiking and there are many unspoiled agricultural villages where you can make pleasant stops.

* Between the Badia de Pollença and the Badia d'Alcùdia is the town of Alcùdia, which has preserved some vestiges of the Roman period that the latest renovation work has made somewhat artificial. From here you can also enjoy some beautiful walks or bike rides in the Albufera Natural Park.

* The Dragon Caves (Cuevas del Drac) are among the most touristy places on the island. They are located near Cristo, on the east coast, and are more than 2000 meters long. The 6 underground lakes, stalactites and stalagmites are a refreshing sight in the middle of summer (except on weekends, when the other tourists will keep you warm).

* Valldemosa and Deià are two other cities that have attracted different artists and today offer their pleasures to tourists.

MINORCA :

* 200 km of coastline await you on this island, less affected than its neighbors by the tourist affluence. The most popular beaches are Cala Pregonda and Vall, but you may find yourself alone in the world in the coves, sometimes accessible only by boat or long hours of walking.

* To the east, Maó, the capital, has kept alive the imprint of the long British presence on the island and presents an unusual mix of styles. The nights are less crazy there than on the rest of the archipelago. During the day, historical places invite you to take a walk, such as the market held in the cloister of a former convent annexed to the church of Carmen.

* Ciutadella is a small jewel located on the west coast of the island, an ecclesiastical and aristocratic city, where you can find sumptuous palaces around the medieval cathedral. Nearby, the plain opens up to an immense abyss, the Pedreres de S'Hostal. These sandstone quarries offer every day a sumptuous setting for sunsets.

IBIZA :

* Ibiza is famous for its summer festivals dedicated to electronic music and its nightly rites. Its discotheques, such as the Pasha, Amnesia, Privilege or Space, host every year the best DJs in the world and you can dance until you drop. Don't count on the beaches to rest, they are as crowded as the nightclubs. Only the hollows of the northern cliffs enjoy a peaceful and saving silence.

- The Tower of es Savinar in Sant Josep de sa Talaia rises on a hill 200 meters above sea level and offers an exceptional view of the island and the islets of Es Vedrà and Es Venadrell.

- The necropolis of Puig des Molins is the most important collection of Punic remains in the world. In these 300 hillside tombs have been found numerous figures and figurines representing Greek goddesses.

FORMENTERA :

- Formentera is the smallest of the four main islands of the Balearic Islands, you can cycle around it to discover its pine forests, salt marshes and stone walls. To refresh yourself, push on to the promontory to the north of the island, Platja de Llevant to the east and Platja de ses Illetes and their white sand await you there. To the north of the latter, Pas de n'Adolf is a paradisiacal tongue of sand.

CABRERA :

- Cabrera forms a small archipelago with the islands and islets of : Na Foradada, Na Pobra, Illot Pla, Na Plana, L'Esponja, Illa dels Conils, Na Redona, Illa de ses Bledes, Cabrera itself (the largest island), L'Imperial and the Estells de Fora (cities from North to South). It is a national park where hikers can discover another version of the Balearic Islands.

CANARY ISLANDS :

The Canary Islands, located in the Atlantic Ocean, are one of Spain's seventeen autonomous communities. Lanzarote, Fuerteventura and Gran Canaria form the province of Las Palmas. Tenerife, La Gomera, La Palma and El Hierro form the province of Santa Cruz. These islands each have completely different characters, all ready to surprise you.

LANZAROTE :

- Lanzarote is the easternmost, northernmost and most volcanic of the islands of the archipelago. In the southwest of the island, the Timanfaya National Park is a huge sea of lava dotted with hundreds of cones called the Mountains of Fire. These lunar landscapes are among the most beautiful of the archipelago, they are to be discovered by hang-gliding, camel riding, or by mini bus.

- In the center of the island is the town of Teguise, one of the oldest in the Canary Islands. In the surrounding area, the region of La Geria is home to vineyards protected from the wind by stone constructions that form an unusual landscape. Don't hesitate to taste the wine made from them. To the south lies Costa Teguise, a quiet area with fine sandy beaches and turquoise waters.

- Still on the coast, the resort of Playa Blanca has kept its charm. Throughout the island, building regulations help not to disfigure the local architecture, which is rare in the Canary Islands. Near Playa Blanca there are beautiful beaches like Papagayo and small coves completely wild.

- Lanzarote owes the preservation and enrichment of its heritage to Cesar Manrique, artist, painter, architect, sculptor and defender of nature. Many of his works can be found on the island, and if you want to learn more about his work, visit the Fundación César Manrique, his former home, which has been converted into a major cultural center.

- Other surprises await you such as the Jameos del Agua cave system in the north at the foot of the Monte de la Corona volcano. It is connected to the Cueva de los Verdes by the Tunnel of Atlantis, this lava tube of more than six kilometers is the longest underwater volcanic tunnel in the world.

FUERTEVENTURA :

- Fuerteventura has the most beautiful beaches of the whole archipelago if not of all Spain even if the water temperature is lower than in the balearics islands for example. You can sunbathe on kilometers of fine sand, discover turquoise seabed of a surprising beauty, and above all you can practice sailing and kite surfing with delight. Indeed, between April and October, the breath of the trade winds attracts connoisseurs from all over the world. The world championships take place in July-August on the beach of Jandia, in the southeast of the island.

* The desert landscapes of the interior evoke the American West, dotted with windmills and white villages. Betancuria, former capital of the island is the prettiest of the island's cities. The typical houses of Antigua, the oldest city of the island, also deserve to linger there.

* In the north of the island, Corralejo, a former fishing village, has become an important seaside resort. Superb dunes, sometimes reminiscent of those of the desert, extend to the south before opening onto a deep blue sea. Off Corralejo, the small isla of Lobos is a paradise for divers and windsurfers.

GRAN CANARIA :

* Las Palmas, in the northeast of the island, is the largest city of the archipelago. Starting from the Santa Catalina Park, discover the Vegueta neighborhood where the Casas Consistoriales, the Bishop's Palace and the Santa Ana Cathedral are located. Take the Paseo de las Canteras promenade that runs along one of the most beautiful urban beaches in the world, the Playa de las Canteras. The city's museums and castles give it a cultural aspect that should not be overlooked. Fans of shopping and nightlife will also find plenty to do in the heart of the capital. For a nature break, head to the Tafira neighborhood, where the Jardin Canario (or Viera y Clavijo Botanical Garden) is located near the Caldera de Baldama.

* In the north of the island, along the coast from the capital, you will pass through the municipalities of Guía and Gáldar before arriving in the green province of Agaete, an area full of sugar cane, banana plantations, coffee, mangoes, papaya and orange trees. In the region, the Necropolis of Maípais, the 300 Cenobio caves of Valerón and the natural monolith of El Dedo de Dios are sites not to be missed.

* Continuing along the coast, you can admire the impressive cliff of Andén Verde and the Tirma Mountain. At an altitude of 1007 meters is the Roque Faneque, a 70 meter high needle sacred to the Guanches. Then come the beaches of Veneguera, El Perchel, Tasarte, Güi-Güi and others of great beauty. Many of them are isolated and can only be reached by boat or on foot. Push on to the Mogàn valley, which enjoys a most exceptional climate.

* Maspalomas is the main seaside resort of Gran Canaria. Surrounded by beautiful sand dunes, its golden beaches and climate attract many tourists every year. Playa del Inglés is the most frequented zone with that of Puerto Rico in the west. In the southwest of the island, in the prolongation of Puerto Rico, Puerto de Mogan is a small traditional fishing port which also contrasts by its architecture, its beaches are nevertheless crowded in summer. For more tranquility, go to San Agustin to the east of Maspalomas.

TENERIFE :

* South of Tenerife, the old fishing village of Los Cristianos, together with Playa de Las Americas, is the most important seaside resort on the island. Its large sandy beach is extremely popular. For more tranquility, go to the Costa del Silencio where the charm of the small villages will comfort you. In Santa Cruz de Tenerife, the capital, the artificial beach of Las Teresitas, which extends over 8 km, is very popular. On the north coast of Tenerife, Puerto de la Cruz has kept its authenticity while having built the lago Martianez, a vast water park designated by Cesar Manrique.

* In the center of Tenerife, the Valley of the Orotava is composed of several towns, among which La Villa de la Orotava, a historical and artistic jewel. In the Parque Nacional del Teide, classified as a World Heritage Site by UNESCO, is Las Canadas, a volcano 16 km in diameter whose Pico del Teide, the highest peak in Spain, rises to 3718 m above sea level. A cable car will take you practically to the summit from where you will have an exceptional panorama of the island and the entire archipelago.

* To the north of Santa Cruz de Tenerife rises an oasis of freshness: the Anaga Mountains. Hiking trails will take you to the heart of a varied vegetation, a paradise for birds. The views, from the natural viewpoints of the Pic del Inglés and the Cruz del Carmen, are also spectacular. Nearby is the town of La Laguna, an old university town from the 18th centu-

ry, which is still very lively today.

• Although Tenerife may at first glance appear to be a highly urbanized island due to an ever-increasing amount of tourism, it is easy to find unspoiled nature within a short distance. For example, the superb cliff of the Giants overlooks the sea just in front of the buildings of Puerto de Santiago. If this contrast is not enough, go to the mountains: from the village of Mascas a 4-hour hike will take you to the beach of the same name. In Guarachico, a volcanic eruption formed natural swimming pools.

GOMERA - LA PALMA - EL HIERRO :

• The Island of the Gomera, the most visited of the three, makes the happiness of the hikers. The sumptuous landscapes of the "beautiful valley" of Vallehermoso between forest and mountains are surpassed by the enormous mass of lava of the Roque de Cano. The calm of the villages is the opposite of the atmosphere on the neighboring island of Tenerife. To the south awaits you the last virgin forest in Europe: the Garajonay National Park. Rocky peaks, terraced crops of the Gran Rey valley, the pebble beach of Playa de Santiago, basalt columns of Los Organos, the rest of the island has a few surprises in store for you.

• La Palma is an extremely mountainous island whose highest peak is the Roque de los Muchachos which reaches 2,432 meters. Numerous astronomical observatories are scattered in the heights of the island. In addition to the stars, you will be able to admire the landscapes of the Taburiente National Park where pines and streams play with each other in a huge crater. The beaches of La Palma are all covered with black sand, we will choose those of the south coast where the currents are less strong.

• El Hierro is the smallest and westernmost of the Canary Islands. Its volcanic origin explains the great variety of landscapes it has: fertile farmland in El Golfo, steep coastal cliffs in the north, incredible geological formations created by lava flows and volcanic cones in the south, not to mention the exuberant vegetation that abounds in the center of the island. The turquoise waters bordering the island are famous for scuba diving.

Sweden

In Sweden, nature still has all its rights. Large uninhabited spaces await you to practice all kinds of activities and discover a magical country. From the North Sea coast to the arctic regions, the landscapes will do their utmost to give you a unique and invigorating experience. If you feel like making a stopover in the city, the towns and their inhabitants will know how to welcome you. The Swedes are much cooler than their climate and they have given their cities a special atmosphere. Between the red wooden houses of Dalarna, the creations of the glassworks of Orrefors, and the districts of Stockholm, Swedish art is as varied as it is pleasant.

• Dog sledding in Lapland is an activity to be tried once in a lifetime. It is not only a means of transportation, but a fantastic way to discover a tradition and a country. Snowmobiles and cross-country skiing are also welcome to experience the Northern Lights.

• Åre is the largest downhill ski resort in Sweden and the whole of Northern Europe where all skiers can find pleasure. If you are looking for something out of the ordinary, climb up to Riksgränsen. Just 300 kilometers above the Arctic Circle and only 300 meters before the Norwegian border, off-piste spots await you for good skiers. In the middle of summer, you can even ski in the middle of the night at the midnight sun period (May-June).

• Numerous hiking possibilities are offered to you. You can choose between the lava plateau of Kinnekule near lake Värnen, the primitive forest of the Tyvesta national park, the island of Gotland and its limestone needles... - Between Stockholm and Gothenburg, you can take the Göta Canal for a cruise which will make you discover, from lock to lock, islands and lakes each more beautiful than the others.

* Stockholm is one of those cities that we compare to Venice because of its many canals dividing the 14 islands of the city. Its old districts, its royal castles (Drottningholm and Gripsholm) and its museums (in particular the Skansen open-air museum) make it a particularly interesting destination. Stockholm is also the center of the Skärgard, the Stockholm Archipelago, a wonderful area of hundreds of pristine islands and islets.

* In the south in the province of Skåne, you will find vestiges of the Middle Ages such as the old streets of Sigtuna or Kalmar Castle or Malmö Castle. In addition, the coasts of the region will give you the opportunity to make a small detour to the beach if you feel like it.

* If Lapland, county of Norbotten in Sweden, is famous for its wild nature, small villages with wooden houses will welcome you for a break among humans. Arvidsjaur, Jokkmokk and Östersund are typical of the region.

Switzerland

Wedged between Germany, France and Italy, Switzerland has been able to take advantage of its three big neighbors and cultivate a multicultural identity. In summer for hiking, in winter for skiing, Switzerland offers a wide range of open-air activities in a magnificent setting. It is also good to live in the big cities where it is the turn of culture to blossom serenely.

* Swiss ski resorts are the most luxurious in Europe. Zermatt, St. Moritz and Gstaad welcome every year many tourists in search of abundant snow and top-of-the-range facilities.

* In the Scuol region, the mineral water springs flow in abundance. About ten of them are already dedicated to your well-being. There are also carbonic acid mineral baths and cures in Leukerbad, Baden, Bad Zurzach and Weggis Vitznau Rigi.

* The shores of Lake Maggiore, Lake Geneva, Lake Neuchâtel, Lake Constance, Lake Lugano and the Four Cantons are highly appreciated for their beauty and their mouth-watering atmosphere.

* The old town of Geneva, the cathedral of Lausanne, the museums of Basel, the gardens of Lugano, the convent of Zurich… Each Swiss agglomeration can boast of a major attraction well preserved. Swiss cities are also to be discovered for their inherent chic.

* Three medieval cities are the pride of the Swiss: Schaffhausen has preserved the houses of 12 trade guilds, the facades of Stein am Rhein are decorated with interesting frescoes, and St. Gallen is known for its abbey library, which contains 2,000 manuscripts.

The Netherlands

The Netherlands have conquered part of their territory on the sea with this desire for openness that characterizes them. As a people of merchants and sailors, the Dutch have made their country a land of tolerance that holds many surprises in store for everyone.

• Amsterdam is the main destination chosen by tourists to discover the Netherlands. Coffee shops, girls in shop windows and bicycles are the clichés that dot the 165 canals of the capital. The romanticism of these canals can be appreciated during a simple stroll or a short cruise on a bateau-mouche. This will be an ideal activity to relax after visiting some of the most famous museums in the world such as the Rijksmuseum (Rembrandt, Vermeer, Frans Hals...), the Van Gogh museum and the Stedelijk museum, as well as the houses of Rembrandt and Anne Franck in the Jordaan. In the evening, you can listen to excellent DJ's in the city's clubs, stroll through the red light district and admire the city lights from the bridges of the Herengracht, Keizersgracht and Prinsengracht canals.

• Many international institutions have chosen The Hague as the location for their premises. The city's green spaces give it a calm and tranquil appearance that is belied by the activity in the city center around its former count's palace, the Binnenhof. Don't miss a visit to the Mauritshuis museum (Rembrands, Rubens, Vermeer). TheMadurodam is a park where everything that makes Holland is represented in miniature.

• Delft, between The Hague and Rotterdam, is known for its porcelain, but also for its canals, the charm of its houses, its Gothic belfry and its churches, a landscape often celebrated by Vermeer, a child of the city.

• Rotterdam was badly damaged by the conflict of the Second World War. In addition to the lively shopping areas of Linjnbaan and Coolsingel, you can also discover the city from the sea by taking a cruise along the shores. The Oude Haven, the warehouse area, the Sheepvaart district and the Maritime Museum offer a beautiful view of this port area, the largest in the world. Don't miss the Boymans-Van-Beuningen museum (Jerome Bosch, Van Eyck, Frans Hals, Rembrandt and Rubens).

• Haarlem is worth for Grand Place and its Frans-Hals museum, Leiden for its mill (De Valk) and the canal houses of Rapenburg, Utrecht for its canals and campanile (Domtoren) and Maastricht for its old town around the Saint-Servais basilica.

• In spring (March and April) you can admire the endless fields of tulips, but also daffodils, hyacinths, daffodils and hyacinths, along the routes between Haarlem and Leiden north of Hoorn, and in the surroundings of Den Helder, Anna Paulowna and Breezand. Near Lisse, the Keukenhof park has beautiful greenhouses.

• The eastern part of the country, consisting of the provinces of Overijssel, Gelderland and Flevoland, will delight nature lovers. The Weerribben National Park and the Wierden Reserve are among the most important wetland nature areas in Western Europe. In the Upper Veluwe Park there are huge wooded areas and heath heaths suitable for hiking. In the swampy plain around Kinderdijk there are 19 windmills not to be missed.

• The coast is dotted with seaside resorts that offer holidaymakers beautiful beaches such as Noordwijk, Scheveningen, Zandvoort and Katwijk. Even if the weather is not always good, the Dutch coast has a certain charm. The dunes of Zeeland Flanders, the Ijsselmeer Bay and the territory of Flevoland reclaimed from the sea are the most beautiful landscapes of the North Sea. Don't forget to visit the Wadden Islands as well. On the program: the car-free nature of the Schiermonnikoog and Vlieland islands, the birds of Terschelling, the long beach of Ameland and the seals that can be observed on boat trips.

Turkey

Turkey straddles two continents. Its bowhead, Istanbul is crossed by the Bosphorus, on one side Europe and on the other Asia. True crossroads of civilizations over the centuries, this city was in turn the Byzantium of the Greeks, Constantinople of the Eastern Roman Empire and the capital of the Ottoman sultans, it is now assimilated to a large European city. Cultural exception compared to the rest of the country, Istanbul, because of its modernity, nevertheless guides the whole country. It deserves to be visited, because it conceals unimaginable treasures in terms of art and architecture, as well as natural wonders.

* Istanbul is the largest city of Turkey and its main touristic place. Jewel of the Islamic art, one will find there the most beautiful mosques of the country (the Blue Mosque, the church Sainte Sophie, the Süleymaniye mosque...) as well as the Topkapi Palace which has become a great museum of Islamic art. The vastness of the Bosphorus magnifies its banks and the Galata bridge which connects them has become legendary.

* Heading east of Istanbul, the archaeological remains are more and more numerous including Ephesus and Aphrodisias where many traces of the Greco-Roman period have survived.

* On the south coast, in Antalya, Aspendos, Side and Myra, Roman antiquity meets Islamic art.

* On the Black Sea coast, it is the turn of the Byzantine civilization to be honored with the churches of Trabzon and the monastery of Sumela.

* Fairy chimneys and troglodytic dwellings, Cappadocia is a territory where lava from volcanoes has given birth to a superb landscape.

* In Pammukale, the Cotton Castle, one can admire incredible limestone cascading formations.

* Mount Ararat is a sacred place where Noah's Ark would have run aground at the end of the flood. A 3-day hike, often in the clouds, is necessary to get to know the place.

* Four seas, 8000 kms of coastline, it has been 30 years that seaside tourism has been a great success in Turkey. Even if the coast of the Aegean Sea is the most successful, the Turquoise coast, in the south, has beautiful panoramas.

Ukraine

Leaving the USSR in 1991, Ukraine, the second largest European country, still remains a confidential destination and few travelers know the beauties of this territory. The kilometers of Black Sea beaches, the still wild nature of the Carpathians and the architectural heritage of the big cities are still reaching out to you.

* Odessa, the "Russian Naples" is a crossroads city on the Black Sea that has preserved the traces of the many communities that have settled there. In addition to the cultural appeal of the seven museums dating from the early 19th century, the 40 km of beaches, the thermal waters and the gentle way of life inherent to the city make it a most pleasant destination. Prymorsky Boulevard offers a superb view of the port and has the famous Potemkin Staircase. In the suburbs, in the village of Nerubayskoye, there are the catacombs of the glory of the partisans of the Russian-Turkish war.

* Once the equal of Constantinople and the cradle of the Eastern Slavic civilization, Kiev preserves important historical testimonials despite the damage caused by the Second World War. The most remarkable of them is, of course, St. So-

phia Cathedral, but you should not miss St. Andrew's Collegiate Church, the famous Golden Gate, St. Vladimir's Cathedral and, above all, the Pechersk Lavra. The animation of larue Khreshchatyk and decelles of the Podol, the former district of merchants and craftsmen, make the city terribly endearing.

• 131 km north of Kiev, on the banks of the Desna river, is Chernihiv. From the 10th to the 12th century, Chernichiv was an economic and cultural center of similar importance to Kiev. At that time the most beautiful religious buildings of the city were built: St. Catherine's Church, the Cathedral of the Savior and the Borissoglibski Cathedral. 300 km west of Kiev, Pochayiv is home to the second largest monastery in Ukraine where the baroque of the Uspensky Cathedral radiates.

• Close to the Polish border, the city of Lviv boasts Renaissance facades and Italian-style courtyards around Rynok Square. Its religious heritage is also prestigious: the Catholic Cathedral, the Boimi Chapel, the Armenian Cathedral and St. George's Cathedral are all worth a visit. Do not hesitate to go to the Opera House to attend a performance in a sumptuous setting. Not far from the city, the spa town of Trouskavets attracts more tourists every year.

• Kamianets-Podilskyï, near the border of Moldova and Romania, is an old fortified city, built on a rocky promontory surrounded by the Smotrych river. It houses an old quarter with winding alleys and several beautiful 15th century churches and is dominated by a 16th century castle topped by 9 watchtowers.

• The Crimea, now part of Russia (but still disputed by Ukraine), is a peninsula located in the south of the country, plunging into the Black Sea. The region is known for its vineyards, orchards, resorts and tourist sites. The towns of Sebastopol, Simferopol and the famous city of Yalta are among the most famous. 50 kilometers of coastline with a Mediterranean climate offer the visitor the opportunity to relax, following the example of the tsars and the nomenklatura. South of Simferopol, the city of Bakhtchyssarai is home to the Hansaray, the former palace of the khans surrounded by sumptuous gardens.

• The Carpathian National Park in the southwest of the country is an ideal playground for hikers. Numerous trails connect the pre-Carpathian hills with the real mountains, including Mount Hoverla, the highest in the country, and those of the Gorgani region with its impressive rock formations. You can also explore the Skole Game Reserve on horseback with a guide.

• The Crimean Tauric mountain range is also very popular for walkers. The rocky sites of Chuft-Kale and Manhup-Kale, the gorges of Bolshoï, the waterfalls of Dzhur-Dzhur and Uchansu are as many wonders to be discovered in the heart of a luxuriant vegetation.

• From Kiev to Odessa, the Dnieper welcomes all summer long numerous cruises which allow to discover the magnificent landscapes of the central plain of the former "granary of the USSR" and to visit the "sitch" of the Cossacks on the island Khortytsia, in Zaporijia.

United Kingdom

ENGLAND :

London is the largest city in Europe and the main tourist destination in England. But in addition to possessing the capital of the United Kingdom, the English nation has to offer other cities of interest, but above all poetic landscapes and varied coastlines.

• In London, Buckingham Palace, the Abbey and Palace of Westminster, Big Ben, St. Paul's Cathedral, the Tower of London, Tower Bridge, but also the many museums (often free) of the city (British Museum, British Library, National Gallery, Tate Britain, Tate Modern ...) will satisfy and exhaust you. Fortunately, the beauty of the parks and the fresh beer in the pubs will be there to force you to take some well-deserved breaks. From Camden to Notting Hill, through Soho,

Mayfair and Piccadilly Circus, each district of London has its specificities. Don't hesitate to experience this city, certainly the most exhilarating in the world (but also, it must be said, one of the most expensive).

* The romantic Cotswolds region is famous for its rolling countryside, manor houses and small inns. Oxford, less than 100 km northwest of London, is the seat of the oldest English university, a special atmosphere emanates from the fine architecture of the buildings. Continuing north, you can discover Stratford-sur-Avon, Shakespeare's city, before heading to medieval Warwick Castle to discover its garden and towers, or to Ragley Hall Manor. To relax, the Roman spa town of Bath offers a contemporary spa set against the complex built during antiquity. Before leaving the area, take a detour to the picturesque village of Bibury.

* The best way to explore the East Midlands is to venture into the Peak District National Park or the Lincolnshire Highlands. All kinds of activities can be enjoyed here: horse riding, hiking, cycling, caving, hang-gliding, paragliding and rock climbing... In the region, the historic towns of Lincoln, Nottingham, Leicester or Derby are worth a visit. The latter, in addition to being the capital of ale, a top-fermented beer, has a very old cathedral dating back to 943. Around the village of Edwinstowe is the famous Sherwood Forest, where you can walk in the footsteps of Robin Hood.

* The East of England is a compendium of the best that the nation has to offer: a pleasant countryside dotted with old towns, manor houses, picturesque villages and towns, but also a seaside with the flavor of yesteryear, all sprinkled with a touch of eccentricity. Norwich is a harmonious blend of medieval city and bustling modern town, Cambridge offers the serenity of its universities and the splendour of its architecture, Colchester, the oldest Roman city in the British Isles, deserves some attention and the 12 medieval churches of Ipswich are little wonders.

* The Lake District (Cumbrian Lakes region), to the northwest, is of outstanding natural beauty. The waters glisten between forested, sometimes steep banks protected by shale walls. Their slopes, covered with heather, are often drowned in mist. Keswick, in the heart of the superb fell country, the "land of mountains", is the English capital of hiking. The other towns of the region are also not lacking in interest: ancient history in Chester, culture and music in Liverpool, shopping and outings in Manchester... there is something for everyone. On the coast, Blackpool is one of England's favorite seaside resorts.

* From Kent, the "Garden of England", to the beautiful Dorset coastline and the Isle of Wight, to the weathered villages of Oxfordshire, the south-east of England is a very pleasant destination. History has left sumptuous architectural testimonies, such as the Roman palace of Fishbourne, the cathedral of Canterbury dating from the 12th century, Windsor Castle, the official residence of the Queen, and Leed in Kent.

* From the cathedrals of cities such as Salisbury, Gloucester, Wells, Truro and Exeter to the waves lining the Celtic region of Cornwall and the wide open spaces of Exmoor and Dartmoor National Parks, the southwest of England is a land of contrasts. You won't want to miss the megaliths of Stonehenge, which have majestically kept their secret since the end of the Neolithic period. You can also follow in the footsteps of King Arthur at Tintagel in Cornwall and Glastonbury in Somerset.

WALES :

Wales is one of the six Celtic nations, and is part of the United Kingdom. Situated on a peninsula in the mid-west of Great Britain, Wales has an unsuspected natural beauty between mountains and coastline. The castles, legends and people only add to the positive aspects of this destination in full revival.

* Snowdonia National Park boasts some of the most beautiful mountain scenery in the country. There are many hiking trails around Llanberis, Betws-y-Coed or Beddgelert. One of the most famous is the one that leads to the summit of Snowdon at 1085 m. Don't be mistaken, in spite of an altitude not so high, the landscapes have the beauty of those of high mountains and the walk is difficult. In the area, the castle of Harlech, the mines of Blaenau Ffestiniog and the seaside resort of Barmouth are not to be missed.

* The other face of Gwynedd County, its seafront, is also worth a visit. The village of Portmeirion, where Sir Clough

Williams-Ellis built some surprising buildings, is a paying site, but its originality and setting are more than interesting. The peninsula of Llyn has preserved the beauty of its landscapes. Close to the western tip is Bardsey Island (Ynys Enlli), today a natural reserve for sea birds, yesterday a high place of pilgrimage for Christianity (monastery), and maybe forever the island of Avalon. The island of Anglesey is connected by two bridges to Bangor and has some pleasant beaches, important Neolithic monuments and one of the most beautiful castles of the nation: the castle of Beaumaris.

• The south coast, between Cardiff and Swansea, is very popular with the English who enjoy the long beaches that line it throughout the summer. Discover the fabulous Gower Peninsula whose beaches will surprise even the most jaded. To finish getting drunk, go to The Mumbles (Oystermouth) where the pubs are numerous. Further west, walks in the Pembrokeshire Coast National Park will take you to cliffs, moorlands and beaches that compete in beauty and attract climbers and surfers. The villages of Solva, Tenby, Marnorbier, Pembroke and Saint David's have an irresistible charm.

• The Brecon Beacons National Park, in the center of the nation, is worth for its wild landscapes. From Landovery, Abergavenny, Merthyr Tydfil or Haye-on-Wye, there are various hiking opportunities such as the Offa's Dyke Path that will take you through the Vale of Ewyas. Don't miss the ruined Augustinian monastery of Llanthony Priory in the heart of the Vale of Ewyas.

• At the end of the 13th century, King Edward I erected about twenty castles to preserve the power of the English. In addition to those of Beaumaris and Harlech mentioned above, you should not miss the one of Conwy (35 km north-east of Caernarfon), and especially the one of Caernarfon (north-west of the nation). In Cardiff, the Norman castle remains in the center of the city, which is also worth for its dynamic atmosphere, of which the trendy Cardiff Bay dock district is the figurehead.

SCOTLAND :

In the north of the United Kingdom are the lands of Scotland. Drowned in the mists, torn apart by the sea, Scotland has a romantic aura that attracts many travelers seeking to pierce its legends. Once there, the beauty of the landscapes, the simplicity of the encounters and the quality of the whiskies may provide them with some answers.

• Coming from England, the first landscapes of Scotland are those of the Borders, a border area that advances its ruined abbeys (in Melrose, Kelso, Dryburgh and Jedburgh) and castles (Floors Castle, Mellerstain House, Traquair House, Abbotsford House) as witnesses of its tumultuous history. The memory of the writer Sir Walter Scott is also celebrated here, as the Tweed Valley vistas were the cradle of the Tweed Valley.

• Next come the two main cities of Scotland: Glasgow and Edinburgh. If we think of Glasgow as a sad industrial city, it is because we forget the different museums it has to offer (Burrel Collection, Gallery of Modern Art, Kelvingrove, Hunterian), the buildings designated by Charles Mackintosh and the atmosphere of the pubs in the city. As for Edinburgh, it is famous for its Old Town, which makes it the second most popular tourist destination in the United Kingdom. The castle, which overlooks the whole at an altitude of 135 meters, is connected to Holyrood Palace by the Royal Mile where the most beautiful and oldest monuments of the city are located. Do not hesitate to venture into the alleys that cross this artery. For more modernity, go to the port area of Leith, in the north, the new trendy district of the city.

• The Lowlands (The Trossachs), between Glasgow and Edinburgh, has been the scene of the adventures of Scotland's most famous heroes such as William Wallace, Robert the Bruce, Bonnie Prince Charles and Marie Stuart. The town of Stirlinga with its castle and medieval old town can be visited like a fascinating history book. The site of Culzean Castle, on a cliff on the west coast, is the most impressive in the region. This one is also worth for its formidable natural heritage of which the most beautiful example is Loch Lomond, the largest lake in the United Kingdom.

• Going north from Loch Lomond, one crosses the peat bogs that dominate the Black Mount before going up the Glen Coe valley and admiring the surrounding peaks. Here we are at Fort William where is the departure of one of the prettiest trekking of the country to the assault of Ben Nevis, the highest peak of the United Kingdom (1 344 m). The Ben Path will be used by beginners, while the more experienced climbers will choose the route starting from Steal. The route that continues around the cirque to Càrn Mòr Dearg is very popular with the most enthusiastic climbers, but requires a great deal of attention in winter conditions. From the summit, if the weather is good, the panorama is immense and splendid.

* To the east, here is the famous whisky route that crosses the Speyside, located around the Spey Valley in the Highlands of Scotland, where there is the largest concentration of distilleries in the country. On the program, you will be able to visit those of Glenlivet, Tamnavulin, Glenfarclas, Glen Grant, Tamdhu, Cardhu, Macallan, Aberlour... One of the prettiest and most authentic is that of the Glenfiddich house. The panoramas of the Grampian Mountains region are a perfect accompaniment to the tastings.

* To reach the coast, take the road from Braemar to Aberdeen through the Royal Deeside valley, punctuated by some of the most impressive castles. The castle of Balmoral, one of the most sumptuous, is still the property of the royal family and is regularly visited. Austere and grey at first sight, Aberdeen, the third largest city in the country, is in fact very flowery and waits for the slightest ray of sunshine to shine. A few kilometers to the south, don't miss Dunnottar Castle, a ruined medieval fortress on its rocky spur facing the North Sea. The north coast of Aberdeenshire is punctuated by small fishing villages in the heart of beautiful countryside.

* In the heart of the Highlands, in the continuity of Loch Lochy and Loch Oich (the Great Glen), is the famous Loch Ness where everyone will try to catch a glimpse of the shadow of Nessie looming on the bottom of the water. The ruins of Urquhart Castle on the north shore are among the main attractions of the area. Continuing north, the pubs and bagpipes of Inverness await you. The town also has a castle and many churches, as well as the impressive painting collections of the Art Gallery on Schoolhill.

* The Western Highlands offer a particularly wild landscape. The peninsula of Caithness and Sutherland is the northernmost county of Scotland. From Inverness, drive up towards Dornoch and Wick to John O'Groats, the northern tip of Scotland. From there, you can reach the Orkney or Shetlands archipelagos, if only for the prehistoric remains of the former or the cliffs and birds of the latter.

* Go down by the west coast to meet Loch Assynt and the mountains surrounding it, and then the equally magnificent Loch Morartout. Then comes the fabulous Wester Ross region where the coast forms small sublime bays like Gruinard bay and where the inland is a series of incredible valleys and majestic lakes sometimes open to the sea. A simply magical region that only the midges (a swarm of voracious midges) come to disturb.

* Finally, you should not miss under any circumstances to go to the island of Skye and its cliffs. Linked to the mainland by the Bridge of Skye and numerous ferries, it is the best the UK has to offer. To discover this paradise for walkers, kingdom of heather, you can follow the road from Broadford to Portree along the Cuillin Hills. At the entrance to the Trotternish Peninsula, the Old Man of Storr stands 137 meters high like a natural lighthouse. In addition to this last one, the surprises will be numerous: the cliffs and the waterfall of Kilt Rock, the Staffin Island, the famous Talisker distillery or the castle of Dunvegan...

NORTHERN IRELAND :

Since 1922, six of the nine counties of Ulster have together formed what is known as Northern Ireland, one of the four nations of the United Kingdom. The atmosphere differs from the rest of Ireland, although medieval castles and extraordinary landscapes are also found there.

* The most important attraction of the region is the Giant's Causeway, on the north coast in County Antrim. Thousands of basalt prisms follow one another there and offer to the wind a beautiful instrument. Take the path that runs along the cliff to enjoy the unusual panorama. Along the coast, you can also visit the seaside resort of Portrush and the site of Dunluce Castle, a medieval fortress. Nearby, the world's oldest whisky distillery is located in the village of Bushmills.

* The Northern Irish landscape is dominated by lakes, the most beautiful example of which is the hourglass shaped Lough Erne. Do not miss to visit the charming town of Enniskillen at the bottleneck. 3 km south-east of this town, you

can visit the sumptuous interior of Castle Coole and its gardens. 18 km to the west, the Marble Arch Caves and their limestone formations are also a tourist attraction. In the middle of the lake is White Island where a Romanesque church was built as well as Celtic statues from the 10th century.

• The Mourne Mountains extend to the east of the region around Newcastle, and offer a very nice hiking area. From Kilkeel you can, for example, hike up the Silent Valley. Nearby, do not miss the dolmen of Legannany, on the Slieve Croob hill, the most imposing of all Northern Ireland. The Anglo-Norman fortress of Greencastle and the Newcastle station are also worth a visit.

• Derry is one of the most picturesque cities in Northern Ireland, it owes its charm to its medieval ramparts. Armagh is worth for its beautiful Georgian houses. Belfast has to offer the animation of a small capital and some monuments of Victorian or Edwardian style like the City Hall or the University.

CROWN DEPENDENCIES NOT PART OF THE UNITED KINGDOM :

CHANNEL ISLANDS :

A short distance from the Cotentin peninsula, the Channel Islands are directly dependent on the British Crown. The waters of the English Channel have been able to mix French and English cultures to give these islands a full-fledged identity. The omnipresent sea, the green nature, the mild temperature: these are the strong points of this destination which, during a weekend, will surely know how to change your scenery a little more than expected.

JERSEY :

• Stroll in Saint-Hélier, the capital. A pleasant city center awaits you there and you can take advantage of it to do duty-free shopping or drink a beer in a traditional pub.

• The best way to discover the Jersey countryside is to rent a bike and get lost in the 154 km of cycling network that criss-crosses the island. From the dizzying cliffs in the north to the immense beaches in the south, it's a good opportunity to take a breath of fresh air.

GUERNSEY :

• Here, Victor Hugo will be your guide. Discover Saint-Pierre Port, the capital that so seduced the writer. From the lively streets to the stairs leading to the top of the city, you will find many places where the presence of the writer is still felt, such as Castle Cornet or Hauteville House.

• The island's countryside also made his 15 years of exile less painful. In the north, Saint Andrew, Saint Sampsonou Houmet Pardis may be able to make you a poet in your turn. The rest of the island, especially the southeast, will offer many mystical places to your imagination.

OTHER ISLANDS :

• From Guernsey, you can take a ferry to Herm and explore the island in less than a day. It is only 2.5 km^2! The flowery gardens and turquoise waters of Shell Beach and Belvoir Bay are worth the detour.

• Serq is a little bigger, but just as quiet as the previous one. Motorized vehicles are prohibited. At your feet, your bikes, or your carts to discover the last lordship of Europe.

• To visit Alderney, ask the tourist office to organize a treasure hunt that will take you from military constructions dating back to the Roman era to those of the Second World War.

• If you want to spend a night completely isolated from the rest of the world, you will have to go to the island of Burhou. Only the birds will compromise the silence of your sleepy morning.

ISLE OF MAN :

The Isle of Man is a territory attached to the British Crown, consisting of a main island and a few islets in the Irish Sea, in the center of the British Isles. It sums up by itself all the landscapes of the latter between stratified cliffs and sandy beaches, passing by mountains and wooded valleys.

• Castletown, in the south of the island, has some remarkable buildings such as Castle Rushen Castle, King William's College, Buchan School and the House of Keys. The silver-grey color of the stones used in the buildings gives the town a certain charm. Feel free to take a walk to Rushen Abbey or follow the coastline cut with your nose to the wind.

• Port Erin is a seaside resort famous for its vistas, including the superb sunsets over the Port Erin beach or the Bradda Point and the frequent glimpses of the Mourne Mountains on the nearby Irish coast. You can go to Calf Island, offshore to observe grey seals, seabirds and even basking sharks.

• Peel boasts the only cathedral on the island. It also offers visitors its castle, originally built to guard against attacks from the sea, which today.

• The Isle of Man Railway is an historic steam-powered rail line linking Douglas to Port Erin via Castletown. Along the way, views of Bradda Head and Milner Tower follow those of the Irish Sea. Not to be missed. In Douglas, horse-drawn Victorian streetcars take visitors along the main promenade.

• In addition to visiting these towns and enjoying the beaches, you can also discover the world's largest waterwheel, the Laxey Wheel, by taking the Laxey Wheel and Mines Trail or go out to meet the birds and animals that inhabit the marshes of the Curraghs Wildlife Park. Cregneash Folklore Village is a living replica of a typical 19th century smallholder village in the Isle of Man Highlands.

Shaoguan
Meizhou
TAIPEI
Xiamen
TAIWAN
Canton
Shantou
Shenzhen
Kaohsiung
Macau
Hong Kong
Haikou
Hainan
Luzon Strait
SOUTH CHINA SEA
Da Nang
Luzon
PHILIPPINES
Quezon City
MANILA
Mindoro
Legazpi
PHILIPPINE SEA
VIETNAM
Samar
Spratly Islands
Puerto Princesa
Panay
Cebu
Surigao
Ho Chi Minh (Saigon)
Palawan
Negros
SULU SEA
Pagadian
Cagayan de Oro
Zamboanga
Davao
Mindanao
Kinabalu
Sandakan
Jolo
Sulu Arch.
General Santos
BRUNEI
BANDAR SERI BEGAWAN
Tawau
MALAYSIA
CELEBES SEA
Sibu
Kuching
Borneo
Manado
Moluccas
Gorontalo
Pontianak
Samarinda
Palu
Sula
INDONESIA
Belitung
Banjarmasin
Buru
Seram
JAVA SEA
Ujung Pandang
BANDA SEA
Semarang
Surabaya
Celebes
Flores
Yogyakarta
Malang
Java
Bali
Lombok
Sumbawa
Sumba
Timor
Kupang
DILI
EAST TIMOR
Tanimbar
Aru
Volcano Islands (Japan)
TROPIC OF CANCER
Marcus I. (Japan)
Northern Mariana Is. (U.S.A.)
Wake I. (U.S.)
Saipan
Guam (U.S.A.)
Micronesia
MARSHALL ISLANDS
Yap Is.
Ulithi
Fais
Ngulu
Sorol
KOROR
PALAU
Faraulep
Elato
Eauripik
Satawal
Namonuito
Hall Is.
Pulap
Chuuk
Mortlock Is.
Minto
Oroluk
Pohnpei
Mokil
Pingelap
PALIKIR
Ngatik
Kosrae
Ralik Chain
Majuro Atoll
Caroline Islands
FEDERATED STATES OF MICRONESIA
Kapingamarangi
PAPUA NEW GUINEA
YAREN
NAURU
Jayapura
Admiralty Is.
BISMARCK SEA
New Ireland
New Guinea
Puncak Jaya
Mt. Wilhelm
L. Murray
New Britain
Bougainville
Solomon Islands
Melanesia
PORT MORESBY
Woodlark
SOLOMON SEA
HONIARA
Guadalcanal
San Cristobal
Santa Cruz
SOLOMON ISLANDS
Louisiade Arch.
ARAFURA SEA
Torres Strait
Cape York
Milikapiti I.
Wigram Is.
TIMOR SEA
Bathurst I.
Darwin
Gulf of Carpentaria
Cape York Pen.
Arnhem Land
Groote Eylandt
Espiritu Santo
CORAL SEA ISLANDS TERRITORY
Great Barrier Reef
CORAL SEA
VANUATU
Wyndham
Wellesley Is.
Cape Leveque
Kimberley
Pinctada
Cairns
Efate
INDIAN OCEAN
NORTHERN TERRITORY
Norman
Townsville
Great Sandy Desert
Port Hedland
Barrow I.
Mount Isa
Great Dividing Range
Ouvéa
Pouebo
Tiga
Maré
North West Cape
Macdonnall Ranges
Noumea
New
TROPIC OF CAPRICORN
Barcaldine
Rockhampton
Gibson Desert
Mt. Liebig
Alice Springs
Simpson Desert
QUEENSLAND
Fraser
Lake Amadeus
Uluru
Dirk Hartog I.
WESTERN AUSTRALIA
AUSTRALIA
Brisbane
Gold Coast
Geraldton
Mount Magnet
Great Victoria Desert
Lake Eyre
Gray Range
Norfolk (Aust.)
Lake Barlee
SOUTH AUSTRALIA
Kalgoorlie
Nullarbor Plain
Lake Torrens
NEW SOUTH WALES
Lord Howe (Aust.)
Perth
Lake Gairdner
Broken Hill
Northam
Ceduna
Port Augusta
Newcastle
Ball's Pyramid (Aust.)
Bunbury
Esperance
Great Australian Bight
Darling
Sydney
Cape Naturaliste
Cape Leeuwin
Arch. of the Recherche
Port Lincoln
Cape Catnal
Adelaide
Wollongong
Albany
Murray
Bendigo
Albury
CANBERRA
Kangaroo I.
VICTORIA
Mt. Kosciuszko
Geelong
Melbourne
King I.
Bass Strait
Furneaux Group
NEW ZEALAND
TASMAN SEA
TASMANIA
Greymouth
Tasmania
Hobart
South Island
South East Cape
Mt. Cook
Invercargill
Stewart Island

Hawaiian Islands (U.S.A.)

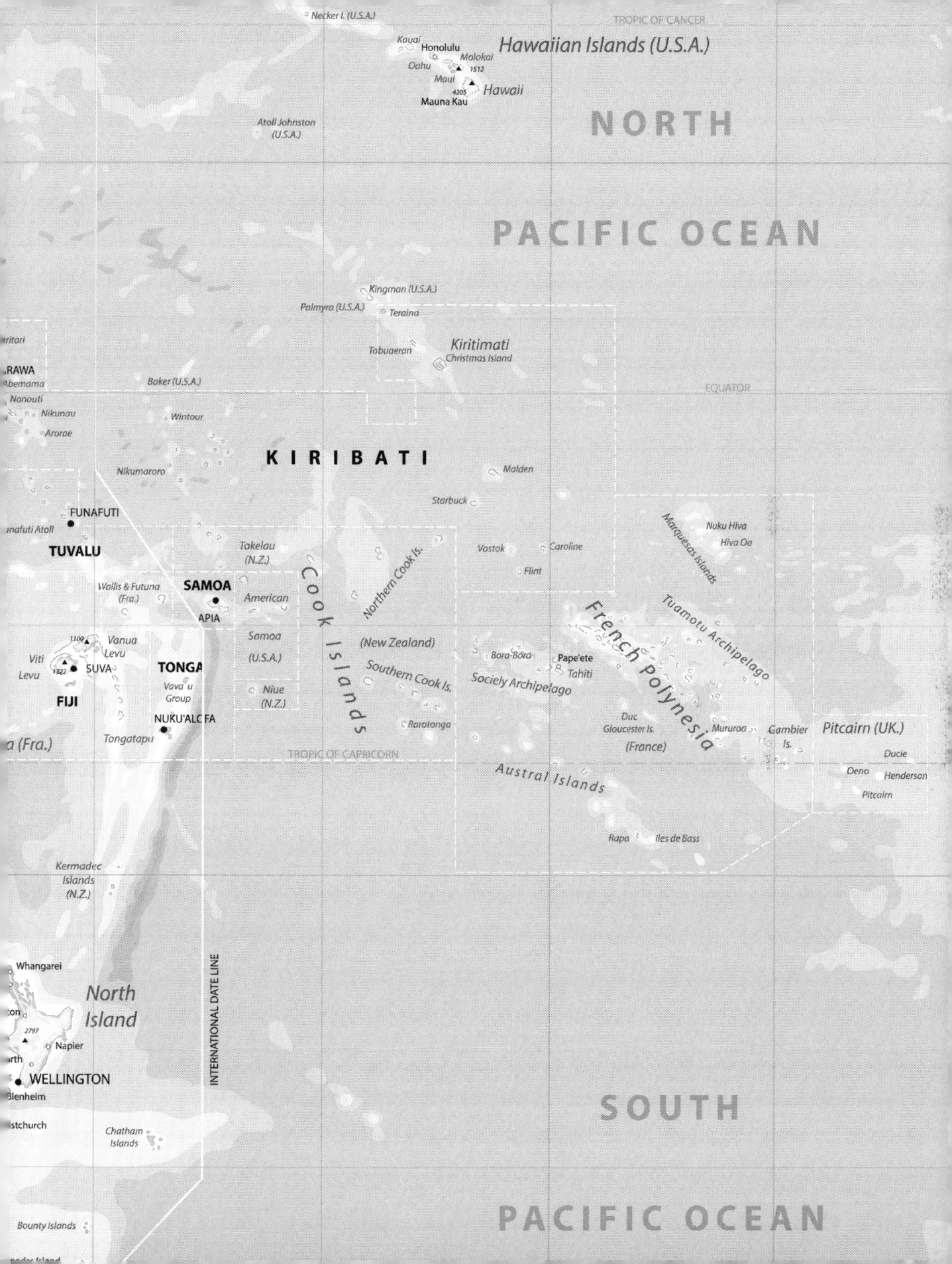

- Necker I. (U.S.A.)
- Kauai
- Honolulu
- Oahu
- Molokai 1512
- Maui
- Mauna Kau 4205
- Hawaii

TROPIC OF CANCER

NORTH PACIFIC OCEAN

- Atoll Johnston (U.S.A.)
- Kingman (U.S.A.)
- Palmyra (U.S.A.)
- Teraina
- Tabuaeran
- Kiritimati / Christmas Island

EQUATOR

- Maritari
- RAWA
- Abemama
- Nonouti
- Nikunau
- Arorae
- Baker (U.S.A.)
- Wintour
- Nikumaroro

KIRIBATI

- Malden
- Starbuck
- Vostok
- Caroline
- Flint
- Nuku Hiva
- Hiva Oa
- Marquesas Islands

- FUNAFUTI
- Funafuti Atoll
- TUVALU
- Wallis & Futuna (Fra.)
- SAMOA
- APIA
- Tokelau (N.Z.)
- American Samoa (U.S.A.)
- Cook Islands
- Northern Cook Is. (New Zealand)
- Southern Cook Is.
- Bora-Bora
- Society Archipelago
- Pape'ete
- Tahiti
- Tuamotu Archipelago
- French Polynesia

- 1100
- Vanua Levu
- Viti Levu 1322
- SUVA
- FIJI
- TONGA
- Vava'u Group
- NUKU'ALOFA
- Niue (N.Z.)
- Rarotonga
- Duc Gloucester Is.
- Mururoa
- Gambier Is.
- Pitcairn (U.K.)
- Ducie

TROPIC OF CAPRICORN

- Tongatapu
- (Fra.)
- Austral Islands
- Oeno
- Henderson
- Pitcairn

- Rapa
- Iles de Bass

- Kermadec Islands (N.Z.)

- Whangarei
- North Island
- 2797
- Napier
- WELLINGTON
- Blenheim
- istchurch

INTERNATIONAL DATE LINE

- Chatham Islands

SOUTH PACIFIC OCEAN

- Bounty Islands

OCEANIA

Australia

One could not better summarize the southern continent than by this nickname that suits it so well: Lucky Country. Australia is a fantastic destination, which uniquely combines great travel comfort with all that travel represents, both in terms of exoticism, a change of scenery, exploration and clichés. Impossible to reach without a long plane travel, Australia is the end of the world from pretty much anywhere else, and often it is considered the trip of a lifetime. If the cities are familiar, they are considered among the most pleasant to live in on the planet. Perth, on the Indian Ocean, Adelaide, city of cafes, Brisbane, tropical metropolis, or Melbourne, artistic and cultural capital, at the crossroads of America and Europe, but proudly Australian. Of course, the undeniable star is Sydney, one of the most charming cities in the world, carried by its symbolic opera and surf culture. However, it is at the gates of the cities that Australia reveals itself, in its nature, gigantic, often extreme. Outside the cities, it is the Outback, the infinite expanse of tracks and red earth that characterizes the largest island in the world. Between deserts, rocky massifs, temperate forests of Tasmania and the lush jungles of the Top End, the country offers a great diversity, but that one often reaches at the price of long journeys. This is here one of the few disadvantages of Australia, the endless straight lines in sometimes bare landscapes. There is the most desolate plain in the world, Nullarbor, and its fearsome endless road. Without contact with other lands of the globe since time immemorial, the country has seen the development of a culture, that of the aborigines, fascinating, the country of dreams. Also on the program, a unique flora and fauna. Among the animal discoveries, the marsupials are the emblems, kangaroos, koalas or the charming quokka at the head. On the other side of the coin, the destination is home (by far) to the most dangerous fauna on the planet (giant crocodiles, box jellyfish, red-backed spider, great white shark, taipan snake, among others), which should not prevent a stay in the country. The access is long but easy, as well as the movements. The infrastructures are of the best level, in all points, and it is a very easy destination. One should just not forget that in front of such a nature, humility is required and preparation is essential for the exploration of wild areas.

* Red earth and dry trees, welcome to the Outback in the center of Australia. The great Simpson desert, nicknamed the red center, hides in its heart the emblem of the country: Ayers rock ("Uluru"), this sandstone monolith, the largest rock in the world, is the sacred mountain of the Aborigines whose paintings and engravings adorn the caves.

* In the east of the country, west of Sydney are the Blue Mountains with plenty of eucalyptus trees, canyons, waterfalls and kangaroos. The Featherdale National Park is nearby, don't hesitate to get lost in it to meet the koalas that live there.

* Arnhem Land is located in the north of the country and is therefore called the "Top End". It is here, in the Kakadu National Park, that Crocodile Dundee was filmed. Venturing here is an unforgettable experience. In addition to the natural beauty, there are sites with an Aboriginal cultural impact, such as rock paintings at Obiri Rock and Nourlangui Rock.

* To the northwest is the Great Sand Desert, itself framed by the Gimbson Desert and the Tanami Desert. This is where the huge Wolfe Creek crater (875 m in diameter) is located, which a meteorite excavated 300,000 years ago.

* To the west, it is the turn of Karijini National Park to show off its shades of red in the sun. Dangerous gorges, heavenly waterfalls and natural swimming pools make the charms; kangaroos, wallaroos, echidnas, geckos, goanns, bats life.

* Tasmania is an island located 240 km from the south coast of Australia. It attracts hikers in search of the unusual and no one can be disappointed by the landscapes of the West Coast Ranges whose relief has been sculpted by glaciers of another era.

* The Great Barrier Reef stretches over 2000 km a short distance from the coast of northeast of the country. It is the largest coral reef in the world and it alone justifies the trip. For Australians, its thousands of islands, islets and atolls constitute the 9th wonder of the world. A simple mask and snorkel will allow you to admire 350 species of corals of different sizes, shapes and colors which, in luminous blue water, are home to more than 1,500 species of fish and crustaceans. Dream beaches where you can relax are, of course, part of the package.

* To admire the infinite rolls of the oceans and observe those that straddle them, you will be spoilt for choice. Torquay, in the south, is the world capital of surfing (Point Break, a mythical film if ever there was one, was shot there). The long beaches of Byron Bay, the easternmost city of the country, also attract surfers without falling into the crowd compared to the 30 km of sites scattered around Sydney. To the west, it is around Broome (on Cable beach) and Perth that you will be able to have a good time.

* In the south of the country, between Warrnambool and Cape Otway, it is the lovers of the Southern Right Whales who will be the most delighted from June to September. Take the Great Ocean Road, which offers magnificent views of the Bass Strait. Lorne beach is home to the famous platypus.

* To the north, the Tiwi Islands (Melville and Barthust) are home to the Tiwi tribe. After applying for a special permit to stay there, you can, between tropical forest and wild beaches, get acquainted with the aboriginal inhabitants and their millenary culture.

* On the north coast of Queensland, the Daintree Rainforest is home to a unique ecosystem, a jungle that extends to the ocean. Its exceptional landscapes both on land and at sea and its lush Amazon-like nature have earned it a unique designation as a UNESCO World Heritage Site on both land and sea.

* Sydney is the most interesting city in the country. Leisure facilities have gradually replaced industrial activity and the city now boasts many tourist attractions. Its green spaces, its old quarter (The Rocks), its bridge, its opera... make Sydney a pleasant and dynamic city.

* Melbourne is often referred to as the "sporting and cultural" capital of Australia because of the many events that punctuate its agenda. It is also called the garden city and the Royal Botanical Gardens are certainly worth a visit.

* Brisbane is the third largest city in the country, but with the most dynamic growth, Brisbane could be compared to a Miami with an Australian flavour. The mild climate, the economic vitality of the city and the natural wealth of its region (including the famous Gold Coast beaches on its doorstep) make it a favorite destination for travelers.

* Less famous than the country's other major cities, Adelaide is nevertheless one of Australia's most pleasant cities, often associated with the arts and its cafes. Located in the region of South Australia, a sort of local Provence, known for its beaches and vineyards, it combines the attractions of a metropolis with the charms of a provincial city.

* Alice Springs is located in the heart of the outback. A starting point for travelers in search of gemstones and unforgettable treks, it is worth the detour for its location. It is also a dive into the heart of the Aboriginal world. Perth on the West Coast is one of the world's most isolated cities, closer to Jakarta in Indonesia than to Sydney. It is however a lively city, where everything seems to justify the nickname of the country, the "lucky country". Ideal climate, sandy beaches, parks planted with palm trees, trendy neighborhoods, nothing can predict the isolation of this city. At the extreme north of the country, Darwin is a provincial but lively city, bathed in tropical languor, famous for its young and festive atmosphere, its night markets and the unbridled nature that surrounds it. Cairns, in the north of Queensland, is the tourist capital of the country and gives access to many wonders such as the Great Barrier Reef or the Daintree rainforest.

CHRISTMAS ISLAND :

Christmas Island is an Australian external territory located in the Indian Ocean, nearly two thirds of whose surface area has been declared a national park.

* Between the cliffs of the coast and the lush forest inland, the island, with thousands of birds, is a paradise for birdwatchers. It is also known for its 120 million crustaceans, including the red crab. The most impressive time of the year is at the beginning of November, when these crabs migrate from the forest to the sea to celebrate the mating season.

* On the east coast, the seaside resort of Waterfall Bay has a casino and some pleasant beaches named Greta, Dolly, Lily and Ethel.

COCOS ISLANDS :

The Cocos Islands are a coral archipelago in the Indian Ocean, formed around two atolls that have been an external territory of Australia since 1984. Only two of the 27 islands are inhabited: West Island and Home Island.

* The Cocos Islands owe their name to the thousands of coconut trees that cover them. To complete the postcard picture, you should know that they also have long white sand beaches, a magnificent turquoise sea and sublime seabeds. You can swim in the company of manta rays, turtles and dolphins.

NORFOLK ISLAND :

Norfolk, an island in the Pacific Ocean, is a self-governing territory associated with Australia. Formerly a prison island, it was long considered one of Australia's harshest and cruellest territories.

* Today, it is a pleasant resort where the ocean offers many opportunities for water sports (diving, surfing, fishing) and where the inland is full of hiking trails to discover the island's unspoilt nature and its tumultuous history.

Cook Islands

The Cook Islands are an independent state in the Pacific Ocean in free association with New Zealand. The archipelago is divided into two parts: the southern part and the northern part. All the islands that make it up form an absolute cliché of the South Seas, with a powerful exoticism. Coconut palms and abundant vegetation, azure blue sky and turquoise lagoon, white sand, multicolored fish, the Cook Islands are a picture of nature.

* The most visited islands are Rarotonga, the main island (but still small, you can go around it in an hour), and Aitutaki. The Muri Beach, on the first one, is particularly appreciated while the lagoon of the second one is considered as one of the most beautiful in the whole Pacific and therefore in the world. It is these two islands that also present the most interesting inland landscapes.

* Diving remains the main activity to be practiced in this archipelago where corals and wrecks have become a meeting place for all kinds of marine species. Don't miss also the underground limestone caves of Mitiaro and if you go to the atolls of Manihiki and Penrhyn, know that their specialty is the culture of the black pearl.

Fiji

If you are looking for the end of the world, here it is. This archipelago in the South Seas has its procession of clichés, like its neighbors. There is good and bad, and unfortunately the trend is to make Fiji a less pleasant destination than it used to be. The change of scenery is assured, especially by its population, cannibalistic just over a century ago and now considered one of the most welcoming on the planet. Yes, but until when? The social climate in Fiji is deteriorating as tourism grows. Highly prized by Americans and Australians, who tend to frequent compartmentalized hotel areas, the destination now inspires more mixed returns. Traditional ceremonies to welcome foreigners, a cultural anchor, known as kava *ceremonies, are becoming rare, and while the country is not at all dangerous, it is nevertheless advisable to be cautious, as everywhere else. It's a pity because about twenty years ago the only risk in Fiji for a tourist was to be overwhelmed with smiles and sincere bula. "Bula" is the classic greeting of the islands, but it is now a tourist tic, sometimes overplayed. It's just a remark and it's useless to see a darker picture than it is, Fiji is still a very beautiful destination, a very pleasant country and with a charming population. Its strong point is its diversity, the islands are among the largest in Oceania which gives them both a typical Polynesian coastline, with beautiful beaches, but also an interior with lush rainforests. The trip to Fiji is simple, the sanitary level is good, the hotels cover the whole range, the transportation is not complicated but the roads are generally bad.*

- The two archipelagos of the Mamanuca and Yasawa are the most famous in Fiji. The first are covered with blond sand while the second, volcanic, are overrun by thick vegetation. The transparency of the water in both cases only embellishes the whole.

- Fiji guarantees to every diving enthusiast pure happiness, especially in the surroundings of Taveuni Island. As a whole, they are among the ten most popular dive sites in the world. The world's largest reserve of soft corals, it is home to a thousand different species of fish and sharks, humpback whales, killer whales and sperm whales.

- Viti Levu is the most important of the Fiji Islands. Suva, the administrative and political capital, and Nadi, the tourist capital, are located at each end while the interior of the island remains very wild. In Nadi, you can walk through the sugar cane fields at Momi Bay, visit the colorful and bronze Hindu temple on the beaches of Wailoaloa Bay and Nadi Bay.

- The inland of Vanua Levu, Fiji's second largest island, has the same wild vegetation. The prettiest spots on the island are in Savusavu Bay but also on the Tunulua Peninsula and along the Hibiscus Highway.

French Polynesia

French Polynesia is a group of 5 French archipelagos located 6000 km east of Australia. These 118 islands at the end of the world are a real paradise, let's try to go around them to sketch their beauty.

SOCIETY ISLANDS :

- Tahiti is the largest island of French Polynesia and the most visited by tourists. Starting from Papeete, a 115 km long road goes around the island to admire the lush landscapes surmounted by the majestic volcanic relief of the Orohena, Aorai and Diadem mountains.

- The west coast of Tahiti Nui (the big island) offers many possibilities for excursions such as the Punaruu valley and the Orange tree plateau, the Vaihiria valley and the natural caves of Maraa.

- On the east coast of Tahiti Nui, diving enthusiasts will marvel at the coral beds surrounding the reefs of Teaauroa, Faratahi and Teauraa, located after Uturaufea Point. Young and old will enjoy the geyser caused by the sea rushing into the blower hole. The waterfalls of Faarumai, the bay of Matavai and its black sand at Venus Point, the double belvedere at Taharaa Point are all miracles of nature to be admired.

- The peninsula of Taiarapu is the wildest region of Tahiti. From Taravao, don't miss the Vaipoiri lagoon which seems to swallow the waters of the lagoon, the Pari coast where the last "nature men" live, the Taravao plateau and its agricultural landscapes and the black sand beach of Tautira.

- If Tahiti Nui reserves you many possibilities of excursions, Tahiti Iti, its discreet little sister, also abounds in treasures.

You will discover them by following the narrow shady paths between the sea and the Polynesian chestnut trees that go down into the Pari towards the petroglyphs of Vaiote to the drums of the God Hono Ura.

• Opposite Tahiti (only 17 km away) is the island of Moorea, which can be reached by the ring road in half a day. Numerous walking tours or 4x4 excursions will also allow you to discover this authentic island. Between the sumptuous Opunohu and Cook bays and the plantations of pineapple, grapefruit, papaya, sugar cane and giant bamboos, you won't know where to start.

• In the rest of the archipelago: Tetiaroa is a private atoll, but it can be visited, the opportunity to feel alone in the world by walking from motu to motu; Mehetia is now uninhabited and its access is regulated; Maiao continues its peaceful existence away from the rest of the world. the Leeward Islands :

• Bora Bora, called "pearl of the Pacific", sums up all the beauties of Polynesia. Its turquoise lagoon surrounded by coral reefs is considered one of the most beautiful in the world. Armed with a snorkel and a mask, you are ready to face the thousands of multicolored fish that live there. Among the many islets (motu) that punctuate the lagoon, don't miss the motu Tapu at the entrance of the Teavanui pass and the motu Tane. The most translucent waters are found at Matira Point.

• It is possible to go around Bora Bora in half a day by taking the ring road, but do not hesitate to go inland to climb Mount Pahia for example, from where you will have an exceptional view of the entire lagoon. Helicopter tours, hiking or 4x4 excursions, all means are good to make you discover the island and give you pleasure.

• Bora Bora has more than twenty ancestral places of worship, mostly coastal. Do not miss the lemarae Fare Rua, on Farepiti Point. Its altar, surrounded by erected slabs more than 3 meters high, is almost 50 meters long. On Faanui Bay, the Fare Opu marae presents madrepore slabs decorated with petroglyphs representing sea turtles.

• Anchored in tradition, Huahine is a vast tropical garden where nature and culture blend together to offer many possibilities for excursions. It is here that we find one of the largest concentrations of Maohi remains, the most numerous of which are found on the shores of Lake Fauna nui. Every year in October, Huahine is the starting point of the largest pirogue race in the South Pacific, the Hawaiki Nui Va'a.

• Surrounded by its emerald lagoon and its motus, Maupiti seems lost in the Pacific and is effectively away from the main tourist routes. In addition to its authentic character, you will appreciate its cultural (lithic monuments of the Haranai Valley, legendary Hiro dugout of the Vaitea Valley, red dugout cliff Nina Here and the marae Ofera on the motu of Tiapa'a) and natural wealth.

• Raiatea and Tahaa share the same lagoon, which is both a mecca for yachting and a giant aquarium. Between the magical spectacle of the lagoon and the tropical enchantment of the inland, these islands are like their neighbors, little jewels to be savored. The deep and multiple bays, the preserved and sometimes spectacular environment (craters, waterfalls) and optimal sailing conditions offer the possibility of unusual tours.

• In the rest of the archipelago : Maupihaa does not have any tourist infrastructure, you will have to go there by your own means to meet the fifteen or so inhabitants; Motu One is mostly uninhabited and can only be reached by whaleboat, the vegetation has regained its rights over the remains of the Japanese occupation ; In Tupai, it is the pigs that have taken over the island even if the bungalows of the former dependency of the territory remain; the atoll of Manuae is a nature reserve where green turtles come to lay their eggs on the beaches every year from November.

MARQUESAS ISLANDS :

• Nuku Hiva is the chief town of the Marquesas Islands, the basalt peaks of about a hundred meters high that stand there recall the volcanic origins of the island. Departing from Taiohae, you can explore the magnificent Taipivai valley by 4x4 or by boat. Opening to the sea towards the South, it stretches inland for several kilometers to reach a beautiful waterfall that feeds a river which in turn forms a small lake surrounding a green island shortly before flowing into the sea. The Hakaui falls, on the south coast, are also not to be missed. The ascent of Mount Muake will allow you to contemplate the bay of Taiohae in the south and that of Hatiheu (one of the most beautiful of the archipelago) in the north.

• Ua Pou, in the south, is characterized by the presence of four large basalt columns which all four dominate the surrounding mountains. Discover this spectacular scenery by taking the road that goes around the island. Do not miss on the east coast Hohoi Bay and its pebble and black sand beach. Starting from Hakahau, don't hesitate to take a boat trip along the wild coast, where cliffs and sea caves can be found.

• Ua Huka, in the east, benefits from a drier climate which makes the vast plateaus and hills arid. Nevertheless, the calderas of the volcanoes that forged this land shelter deep fertile valleys: the Vaipaee valley on one side and those of Hane and Hokatu on the other. The latter are the subject of a very beautiful day trip in 4 x 4 (beware of the many horses and goats in the wild). On the outskirts of the island, diving enthusiasts will have the opportunity to come face to face with the giant turtles of the Haavei bay and even sharks, dolphins and manta rays.

• To the north, the small islands of Eiao, Hatutu and Motu One are located on the same coral massif and are all three uninhabited. Erosion and iron in the soil of the first one give rise to landscapes worthy of the planet Mars where endemic plants and animals live. The second one is the nesting place of many sea birds, such as the red-footed booby or the brown booby. The last one is made up of two sandy islets of an atoll that has now disappeared where sea turtles can be found.

• Hiva Oa is the most famous island of the Marquesas Islands. The painter Paul Gauguin is buried in the Atuona cemetery. The landscapes of the island are, like the paintings of the second, extremely colorful, Hiva Oa is also nicknamed the "Garden of the Marquesas". The island has many other centers of interest, such as the archaeological sites of Puamau where you can observe the largest tikis in Polynesia, or the site of Ta'a'Oa, which has more than a thousand paepae. At this place, the Bay of Traitres is an ideal anchorage.

• Just south of Hiva Oa is the uninhabited island of Tahuata. Very mountainous, it offers small bays with white sandy beaches bathed in crystal clear water. It is the Marquesan island that has the most coral formations, the rest of the archipelago being almost completely devoid of them. 21 km east of Tahuata is another uninhabited island, that of Moho Tani. Together with the rocky islet Terihi (300 m to the southeast), it has been classified as "Motane Island Nature Reserve", in order to protect its ecosystem.

• The island of Fatu Hiva is very impressive, it looks like a cathedral with more than 1000 meters high for 10 km long and 4 km wide. The peaks fall almost vertically into deep blue water. Don't miss the Bay of Omoa and especially the Bay of the Virgins, which is overlooked by amazing rocky peaks and is one of the most popular anchorages in the Marquesas. Moreover, the richness of the vegetation is so rich that you will surely indigestion mangoes.

OTHER ISLANDS :

• The Tuamotu Archipelago is an archipelago of 78 atolls, some of which are grouped geographically and form the archipelagos of the Actéon group, the Islands of Disappointment, the Duke of Gloucester Islands, the King George Islands, the Palliser Islands or the Raevski Islands. The main atolls are Anaa, Fakarava, Hao, Makemo, Manihi, Rangiroa, Tikehau and Mataiva. This region is world famous for scuba diving, the coral is magnificent and you can meet all kinds of fish (loaches, groupers, barracudas, eagle rays, manta rays, hammerhead sharks, tiger sharks, pelagic sharks, turtles and dolphins...) - The Gambier Islands are one of the least visited archipelagos in French Polynesia despite a strong potential due to their climate, their environment and their unique historical past. 5 high islands, of which only one is inhabited (Mangareva) and 18 motu, offer breathtaking Polynesian landscapes bordered by a lagoon with extraordinary colors. It is here that pearl farming first developed. Moreover, the Gambier Islands are one of the high places of Catholic evangelization in Polynesia, there are many churches and cathedrals built in coral blocks on old traditional places of worship, maintained and restored with fervor.

• The Austral Islands consist of five main high islands (Tubuai, Rurutu, Rimatara, Raivavae and Rapa), the atoll of Maria Islands and the islets of Marotiri. Tubuai and Raivavae have a low tourist activity. Rurutu is mostly visited by tourists during the whale season (September to November) when whales come to give birth in its waters. Its cooler climate makes the land more fertile, grapefruits, oranges, lemons, lychees, coffee and miri trees grow here. The braiding of the latter, a fragrant and symbolic plant, is one of the important handicraft activities of the region.

Guam

Guam is an island located in the Pacific Ocean attached to the United States although it is part of the Mariana Islands archipelago. The atmosphere and infrastructure are very much influenced by American culture due to the omnipresence of US Navy and US Air Force bases.

- Guam's coastline is the island's tourist attraction. The transparency of the waters offers divers beautiful excursions in the company of multicolored fish in search of historic shipwrecks. Surfing, windsurfing and canoeing are popular in Merizo, for example, although surfers have a clear preference for the beaches ofalofofo Bay. Along the sea, you can go from one extreme to the other: from the very touristy Tumon Bay to the Chamorro village of Inarajan.

- Guam is a volcanic island, you will be able to climb to the top of the mount Jumullong Manglo (410 m) to admire the relief and the cut of the coast. Other trails will lead you to Sigua Falls, Tarzan Falls or Talofofo Falls in the heart of the jungle. Three botanical gardens can be visited to soak up the tropical scents of the island: Inarajan in the south, Nano Fall near the village of Santa Rita and the pineapple plantation in Yigo.

Kiribati

Kiribati, straddling both the equator and the international date line, is an island state composed of three archipelagos in the Pacific Ocean: the Gilbert Islands, the Phoenix Islands, and the Line Islands to which must be added the isolated island of Banaba. If the narrowness of the emerged lands makes it one of the smallest countries of the world (less than 811 km2), their dispersion allows Kiribati to claim a maritime zone of 3 550 000 square kilometers. Sandy beaches, coconut palms and a seabed enriched with wrecks from the Second World War are the assets that very few tourists have been able to experience.

Mariana Islands

The Northern Mariana Islands are part of the Marianas Archipelago in the Pacific Ocean, north of Guam. They form an American Commonwealth, in partnership with the United States, of which it is an unincorporated organized territory. The main islands are Saipan, Tinian and Rota. They have the deepest oceanic trench in the world, the Mariana Trench, which is 11,053 meters deep.

- This tropical paradise offers beautiful beaches and crystal clear blue waters that welcome every year one of the many tourists in search of its exceptional diving spots. In addition to the wrecks of the Second World War, divers can explore the "Blue Grotto" in Saipan, a natural cave that communicates with the ocean.

Marshall Islands

The Marshall Islands is a state of Micronesia. The 30 atolls and 1100 islands are divided into two groups, the Ratak Islands and the Ralik Islands. These volcanic islands and coral atolls are known to have been the site of American nuclear tests in the 50s and 60s and, less seriously, to have seen the birth of the bikini on the island of the same name. Apart from that, the archipelago remains a very little known destination for travelers. Ratak Islands: - The capital Dalap-Uliga-Darrit is located in the atoll of Majuro and is home to the largest port in the country. Without great tourist interest, it is used as a starting point to join the rest of the archipelago. The most beautiful beach of the atoll is theLaura Beach Park but all will prefer the beaches of the Arno atoll which is just in front of the one of Majuro.

• Diving is possible everywhere in the 28 °C waters that bathe the archipelago. The clarity of the water allows you to see at a depth of more than 50 meters. Coral reefs, rays, sharks, turtles, and all kinds of molluscs animate the depths. The Marshall Islands were one of the theaters of the Second World War where the Americans fought the Japanese. Numerous wrecks in Maloelap, Mili or Wotje bear witness to this.

• The atoll of Aur is particularly appreciated by divers for its particularly fishy waters. In addition to its trees and lake, the tiny island of Mejit promises its visitors waters without poisonous fish. Ralik Islands: - Kwajalein is the largest atoll in the world with its 97 islets and its inner lagoon. Occupied by American troops since 1944, you will be able to dive there (having obtained an authorization from the Majuro visitors' office) but it will be difficult to stay there. The same is true for the nearby atoll of Ebeye where the marshalian employees of the U.S. government live.

• The atoll of Bikini is world famous for two very opposite things : the bikini and nuclear bomb testing. It has been reopened to tourists and offers to those who visit it the most beautiful diving sites in the entire region. Indeed, the absence of fishermen and any human activity has allowed a proliferation of marine species and there are many wrecks. Nevertheless, you will be able to make tourism there on the condition that you sign a waiver indicating that you renounce any lawsuit in case of cancer.

• The atoll of Jaluit, the capital of the country during the German and Japanese colonizations, is nowadays famous for the water sports that can be practiced there.

Micronesia

The Federated States of Micronesia in the heart of Oceania are located entirely on the Carolinas Islands and consist of the four states, each with a large degree of autonomy. Nevertheless, it is with the same pleasure that the traveler diver will make the tour of each one to discover its underwater wonders.

• The Chuuk Islands (ex-Truk) are the most populated state of the country and are surrounded by a coral reef which constitutes a lagoon where aircraft carriers, cargo ships and Japanese submarines were sunk during the Second World War. If we add to this the incredible underwater life that reigns there (sharks, rays, barracudas...), it is a great diving spot. The city of Weno has its own airport.

• Kosrae is composed by the island of the same name and five smaller islands (Lelu, Malem, Tafunsak, Tofol and Utwa). In addition to scuba diving, there are numerous excursions on foot, mountain bike or canoe to discover the Mangrove Forest.

• In the central-eastern part of the country is Pohnpei (formerly Ponape) where the new federal capital Palikir and the old Kolonia are located. This state is home to the island of Nan Madol. It is a series of artificial islets where a real megalithic fortress city that looks like nothing known. A mystery that will intrigue whoever visits this end of the world.

• Yap is the last of the four states and certainly the most traditional area of the country where traditional dances and stone coins are still in use. One goes there especially to have the pleasure of diving in the company of manta rays or sailing in the company of dolphins. A part of the world that almost looks like another planet.

• Micronesia is a region that extends far beyond the sole territory of this state and also includes the Marshall Islands, Kiribati, Northern Mariana Islands, Nauru, Palau and Guam.

Nauru

42 kilometers south of the equator are the 21 km of the Republic of Nauru, an ancient volcano covered with coral limestone that has made its fortune from the extraction of phosphorus damaging its tropical forest and seabed.

• The population of Nauru is concentrated on the coastal strip of the island, forming an almost continuous urban ribbon without any cities as such. Nauru is moreover the only state without a capital.

New Caledonia

At 20,000 kilometers from France, New Caledonia is a small piece of France on the other side of the world. Around the main island, Grande Terre, are several sets of smaller islands: the Belep Islands in the north, the Isle of Pines in the south, the Loyalty Islands in the east and even further west the Chesterfield Islands archipelago and the Bellone reefs. All of them offer sumptuous lagoons for divers, heavenly beaches and unseen hikes.

GRANDE TERRE :

• Grande Terre is surrounded by an 800 km long coral reef which has given birth to the largest lagoon in the world where tropical fishes abound. From the south to the bay of Poum in the north, creeks and white sand beaches follow one another. Near Noumea, the capital, are the famous beaches of Anse Vata and the Bay of Lemons where swimmers, surfers and divers have a great time. The bay of Kuendu, at the western tip of the peninsula, is ideal for swimming and snorkeling.

• Five hours northeast of Noumea, Hienghène is famous for its animal-shaped black limestone cliffs. If you follow the coast up the mountainside to the northeast, the landscape alternates waterfalls, river mouths, coconut groves and lush vegetation. In addition to Club Med, you can stay in the tribes in a traditional habitat to meet the people. From there, take the Arabs' path to cross in three days the mountains from the center of the island to the west coast.

• Bourail, in the north of the southern province, is located 162 km from Noumea between mountains and sea. Although popular with tourists, beaches like Poé's have remained wild and welcome many surfers. At low tide, one can climb an unusual rock formation, the pierced rock, the rest of the time one can hope to see turtles in the Bay of Turtles.

• To the south of the island is the Rivière Bleue Territorial Park, characterized by the wild and often red beauty of its landscapes, by its ecological wealth and by the abundance of rivers and water reservoirs. A paradise for hiking and 4x4 excursions, you will admire the Yaté lake, the Madeleine waterfalls, the Wadiana-Goro waterfall and its very old pine forests. Le Mont-Dore hides in its bosom the rare cagou, bird emblem of the country.

OTHER ISLANDS :

• The Isle of Pines owes its name to the abundant presence of pines with their characteristic high slender silhouettes, it is also nicknamed the island closest to Paradise. Accessible by plane from Noumea, it is one of the most touristic places of the archipelago. Kuto Bay is famous for its large white sandy beaches and the colors of the lagoon that can be discovered by pirogue. Close to the Bay of Oro, behind a barrier of rocks, there is a natural seawater swimming pool. The island is also known for its prehistoric remains. The rock paintings, the Lapita pottery of the place called "Vatcha" in the village of Vao and the mounds in the center of the island attract the curious.

• The archipelago of the Loyalty Islands includes four islands. Ouvéa, the most beautiful of the archipelago, is bordered to the west by a large lagoon and a 25 km beach extended to the north and south by a group of islets. The deep forests of Lifou, its caves and its immaculate beaches also seduce the traveler who, if he chooses to be there during the southern winter, will also have the pleasure to observe whales and sperm whales in its surroundings. The coastline of Maré is hemmed in by bunches of coconut and pine trees and the lush vegetation that follows it inland makes Maré the wildest of the four islands. Tiga is the tiniest, only a tribe of 150 inhabitants resides there, but it offers some of the most miraculous diving spots of the archipelago.

• The Belep Islands are very little frequented by tourists because of its remoteness from Noumea. Only the main island Art is inhabited. One finds there the same paradisiacal beaches and the same sumptuous seabed as in the rest of the archipelago.

• Very far to the west of the territory, in the vastness of the ocean, the Chesterfield Islands are composed of several islets and outcropping reefs. At 60 km to the southeast are the Bellone reefs. These privileged places are only visited by a very small number of people each year.

New Zealand

New Zealand is a remote and isolated destination where nature has chosen to flourish in every possible way. The diversity of the landscapes, the richness of the flora and fauna and the originality of the culture make this country the most exciting of territories. New Zealand is made up of two main islands (the North Island and the South Island), and many much smaller islands, including Stewart Island and the Chatham Islands.

NORTH ISLAND :

• 4 national parks are located on North Island. South of Lake Taupo, the Tongariro National Park includes 3 volcanoes sacred to the Maori which are still active: Ruapehu, Ngauruhoe and Tongariro. The ascent of the latter (17 km) requires one day, the Tongariro Crossing will take you through the Blue Lake and the Emerald Lake. It is also possible to go hunting, fishing, mountain biking, horseback riding or even flying to contemplate the area. In the winter, it is the turn of snow sports to take over.

• In the center of the country, Lake Taupo, the largest lake in New Zealand, is located in the caldera of the volcano of the same name. Its shores are lined with pumice beaches and colorful cliffs. The surrounding volcanic landscapes are rich in thermal springs. The best known are in Rotorua on the shores of the lake of the same name. Don't miss the spectacular hike to the Waimangu Spa valley, 25 km away, where the lakes are boiling and the craters are glowing red. Nearby, the waters of the Champagne Pool sparkling like the wine of the same name.

• One of the prettiest coastlines in the country is located along the Coromandel Peninsula. Starting from Thames, the road borders a succession of creeks and rocky headlands. On the other side of the peninsula, Te Whanganui-A-Hei, Cathedral Cove, is a marine reserve where a particularly varied fauna lives.

• Wellington, the capital, is located on a magnificent harbour, an ancient flooded volcanic crater, at the southern end of the North Island. Don't hesitate to climb to the top of Mount Victoria by cable car to discover a breathtaking view of the city. Nearby you can visit the Botanical Garden and its sumptuous rose garden. A stroll along Jervoy Quay and a tour of the Parliament Ground will complete your visit.

• Auckland, to the north, is the urban hub of the country. It is a fascinating maritime city, almost completely surrounded by water and covered with volcanic hills. The Auckland Museum and its collection of Maori art, the Kelly Tarlton's Underwater World & Antarctic Encounter aquarium and the shops on Queen Street are the highlights of this cosmopolitan city. You can also take a mini-cruise in the Gulf of Hauraki to discover the islands that dot it and their populations of blue penguins, petrels and shearwaters.

SOUTH ISLAND :

• 8 national parks are located on South Island. In the south, the Nelson Lakes National Park presents a beautiful setting of lakes and rivers where it is pleasant to camp, walk and fish. From Lake Rotoiti, don't miss to walk along the Buller River Gorge to discover the caves and waterfalls that hide there. To the west, Mount Cook National Park is home to the highest peak in the country (3754 m). The snowy ridges and glaciers like the Tasman Glacier form a sumptuous landscape. The Abel Tasman National Park, at the northwestern tip of the island is the smallest in the country. Hikers will appreciate the Abel Tasman Coast Track which follows the meanders of the coast.

• On the south coast is the Fiordland National Park. From Te Anau, you can take the Milford Track for a 4 day hike through beautiful nature to Milford Sound Fjord. The slopes of the surrounding mountains (in some places more than 1,200 meters high) are covered with primary rainforest and the waters of the fjord are inhabited by whales, seals and dolphins. Along the west coast, from Haast to Westport, is also famous for its splendid views. Tauranga Bay, near Cape Foulwind, is great for surfing and seal watching.

• The southwest of the South Island has another asset: the adrenalin-generating activities of Queenstown. The shores of Lake Wakatipu indeed offer a superb setting for all kinds of activities: paragliding, parachuting, bungee jumping, rafting and jet boat rapids but also tobogganing, skiing and snowboarding in winter. It is the same in Wanaka, at the edge of the lake of the same name.

OTHER ISLANDS :

• At 2 hours by ferry from Auckland, Great Barrier Island, located in the Gulf of Hauraki, is famous for its white sand beaches particularly appreciated by surfers. In addition, there is a mountainous massif that offers great opportunities for hikers and the Great Barrier Forest nature reserve criss-crossed by panoramic trails dotted with hot springs.

• Stewart Island is located 30 km south of the South Island and can be reached by ferry from Bluff. The only village is Oban, located in Half Moon Bay. Off the coast of Stewart Island there are three large islands and many smaller islands. The best known are Ruapuke Island, Codfish Island and Big Cape South Island. Two groups of islands called Muttonbird or Titi are located one between Stewart Island and Ruapuke Island, and the other around the Big Island of Cape South. Other islands include Bench, Native and Ulva, and the islands of Pearl, Anchorage and Noble.

• The Chatham Islands are located about 800 kilometers east of the South Island and have a dozen islands about 40 kilometers apart, two of which are inhabited: Chatham Island, the largest, and Pitt Island. Tourism is almost non-existent there.

• Tokelau is an archipelago of three Polynesian atolls in the Pacific: Fakaofo, Nukunonu and Atafu, halfway between Hawaii and New Zealand. The coconut trees are kings there and less than 2000 inhabitants of Polynesian origin live there quietly. It is possible to visit the atolls, which offer the beauty of their paradisiacal site.

Niue

Niue is an island with a tropical climate, one of the largest coral islands in the world, located in the South Pacific Ocean, east of Tonga Islands, which has a free association agreement with New Zealand. This confetti of 260 square kilometers has been confronted for several decades with the exodus of its population, which leaves to settle in Australia and New Zealand.

• Farniente and diving are on the program. The place is indeed known for its impressive caves and spectacular dives. The water of the ocean that breaks against the imposing rocky cliffs is of an incomparable clarity and the marine life abounds. Corals, tropical fish and wrecks from the Second World War effectively embellish the bottom.

• It takes at least a week to travel around the island and walk the many trails through the rainforest. You can easily fill your days with all kinds of activities, but you will not find anywhere to go out in the evening, as the whole island goes dark around 7 pm.

Palau

Palau is an Oceanic state, located in the archipelago of the Carolinas Islands, comprising 26 islands and 300 islets. The main islands of Palau are Anguar, Babeldaob, Koror and Peleliu which are close to the same barrier reef. About two thirds of the population lives in Koror, the former capital. North of these islands is the atoll of Kayangel. An isolated group of six islands, the Southwest Islands, including Sonsorol, more than 600 km from the main islands, are also part of Palau. In the southern part of the archipelago, the Rock Islands can be counted by the hundreds. Some are hardly larger than a reef, others, several kilometers long, are covered with a thick mangrove. The marine flora and fauna (dolphins, turtles, manta rays, sharks, barracudas) of these archipelagos are among the most famous in Oceania.

Papua New Guinea

Papua New Guinea shares the island of New Guinea with Indonesia and has more than 600 other tropical islands, the most important of which are New Ireland, New Britain (main islands of the Bismarck Archipelago) and Bougainville Island. This destination spreads a strong scent of exoticism as one of the most remote and inaccessible territories in the world occupied by ethnic groups with a way of life opposite to western ones.

• Three-quarters of the country's surface area is covered by primary or secondary forest where two-thirds of the world's orchid species, 9,000 types of plants, 700 groups of birds, 250 styles of frogs, 450 species of butterflies, 200 varieties of reptiles and more than a hundred different snakes live. You can take a cruise on the Sepik River to admire this diversity and meet the ethnic groups living on its banks. One of its tributaries, the Karawari, and the Arambak villages in the surrounding area, can be discovered by canoe.

• If you wish to discover the flora of the country without having to mount an expedition, you can visit the National Botanical Garden of Port Moresby, the Variata National Park of Sogeri nearby, the Moitaka Wildlife Sanctuary or the Botanical Garden of the city of Lae. You should note however that cities in Papua New Guinea are rarely very welcoming and are modern concret affairs with no architectural interest.

* The Highlands are the most populated and fertile land in the country. To discover this region, take the road from Lae to Kainantu via the Kassim Pass and visit the cultural center of the Eastern Highlands. You will then cross the mountains to Goroka and the village of Asaro, follow the Wahgi valley up to Mount Hagen and continue to Mendi, Poroma Valley, Tari and Koroba. In this area, don't miss the villages of the Huli and Duna tribes, famous for their decorations and body paintings, and the sumptuous landscapes along the Kutubu Lake.

* The hiking possibilities are impressive. For example, you can go from the north coast to the south coast by taking the Kokoda Trail or discover the panoramas and traditional villages of Mount Wilhelm. For beginner walkers, the Wedau - Alotau Coastal Walk offers swimming and jungle trails.

* The beaches of the Gulf of Papua, in the south, are the most popular, but those around Madang, a pretty coastal town, are also pleasant and offer their coral reef to divers.

* Five active and sixteen extinct or dormant volcanoes make New Britain a very mountainous island. It offers diving sites on its northern coast where barracudas, dolphins and sometimes sharks evolve in a decor of gigantic sponges. Near Rabaul, former capital of the island destroyed by a volcanic eruption in 1994, lie wrecks of Japanese ships dating from the Second World War and today are home to an impressive marine fauna.

* New Ireland is very little frequented by tourists even though it offers beautiful beaches and very pleasant places to relax like Kavieng, where you can rent a bicycle, go diving, canoeing, surfing and many other activities.

* The Trobriand Islands are worth a visit for their traditional culture which is still alive. The beauty of the handicrafts of the inhabitants and the yam festival at the beginning of July will mark the spirits.

Pitcairn

The Pitcairn Islands, the last British colony in the Pacific Ocean, is a set of five islands, only one of which is inhabited by nine families, making it the least populated political entity in the world.

* The vast majority of the inhabitants are descended from the mutineers of the HMS Bounty and their Tahitian wives. The remains of this ship can be found in Bounty Bay.

* Apart from the volcanic island of Pitcairn, the four others are coral atolls : Sandy Island (disappeared underwater), Oeno Island, Henderson Island and Ducie Island.

Samoa

Samoa is an independent state of Polynesia, comprising four inhabited islands (Savai'i, Upolu, Apolima and Manono) and five uninhabited islets in the southern Pacific Ocean, close to the international date line. Despite centuries of European influence, Samoa maintains its historical customs, social systems and language. Legend has it that Samoa is even the cradle of settlement for the other islands of Oceania. In this true tropical paradise, the beauty of the seabed competes with lava fields and idyllic beaches.

* The south coast of Upolu offers superb beaches sheltered by a coral reef, ideal for swimming and diving. Robert Louis Stevenson, the author of the famous novel Treasure Island, lived here until the end of his life. He is buried at the top of Mount Vaea which dominates his property that can be visited. On the east coast, the Falefa and Fuipisia Falls, as well as the Mafa Pass, are considered the prettiest places on the island. Don't miss also the Papasee'a Sliding Rock waterfall

where you will slide down the wet rocks like a toboggan before plunging into a natural pool.

• On Savai'i, the lunar landscape of the lava plateaus of the Matavanu crater is really worth the detour. The island is also home to heavenly beaches and lagoons.

American Samoa

American Samoa is an archipelago dependent on the United States composed of the islands of Tutuila, Manu'a, Ofu, Olosega, Ta'u and the island of Swains, located further north. Much smaller than their western neighbors, people come here mainly to dive or rest on deserted beaches. Although it is an overseas territory of the USA, the islands still retain a strong exotic character. Only a few incongruous signs, such as a McDonald's, really remind us of Uncle Sam's country.

• The main island, Tutuila, of volcanic origin, is home to a superb tropical rainforest now protected by a national park where hiking and bat watching are the preferred activities.

• In the north of the island, the site of Forbidden Bay is reputed to be one of the most beautiful in the South Pacific, you can walk there from the village of Fagasa. Ta'u Island, in the Manua archipelago, shelters the tombs of the former chiefs of the islands.

Solomon Islands

The Solomon Islands straddle two archipelagos: the Solomon Islands shared with Papua New Guinea to the northwest and the Santa Cruz Islands to the southeast. The main islands are Choiseul, New Georgia, Santa Isabel, Russel Islands, Florida, Malaita, Guadalcanal, Sikaiana, Maramasike, Ulawa, Uki, San Cristobal, Santa Ana, Rennell, Bellona and Santa Cruz Islands. Still a very confidential destination, the Solomon Islands offer many adventures between tropical forest and breathtaking seabed to travellers who have reached it.

• The Marovo Lagoon in the west of the archipelago is a coastal ecosystem of 700 square kilometers of incredible beauty, bordered by high reef barriers and backed by high volcanic islands with rainforests, it is in the heart of it that you will find the most beautiful beaches.

• The Solomon archipelago is world famous for its dive sites, which combine the vision of magnificent coral reefs and several hundred wrecks of warships, sunk during the Second World War. Guadalcanal, the "Slot", the island of Savo, all these names remind our memories of famous naval or air battles that saw hundreds of ships and planes destroyed and sunk. Ghavutu Pier, White Beach, Wreck of the Ann, Matimbako are among the most appreciated sites.

• Most of the islands are of volcanic origin and have a mountainous and rugged relief, covered with abundant tropical vegetation. There are many possibilities for hiking: From Honiara, the capital, you can for example go and see the Mataniko Falls, a two-hour walk in the mountains, which also contains huge caves. On the island of Malaita, the surroundings of the town of Auki are rich in discoveries. Rennell is almost entirely bordered by cliffs of 120 to 150 m and you will find to the east a brackish lake, the lake Te Nggano.

• Skull Island is a small earthly paradise sheltered from the crowds of about ten square kilometers of coconut plantations, on the edge of the Vona Vona lagoon. White coral beach and reef bordered by virgin waves a short distance away, it is above all a surfers' paradise. There are many other spots in the nearby islands (Bikiki, Rendova...).

Tonga

Tonga is a state of Polynesia, comprising more than 170 islands and islets, divided into three main archipelagos. A postcard where adventure is at the rendezvous with many hikes in the humid forests, strolls around the lakes located in the craters of volcanoes and discovery of the underwater world... - The east coast of Tongatapu offers the visitor an impressive number of archaeological sites, the most famous of which is that of Mu'a where monumental stone pyramids contain the ancient burials of the kings. On the west coast, you can visit the numerous vanilla plantations and admire the red parrots in the wild bird observation park.

• Eua, the second island of the archipelago, offers a mountainous and rugged relief, and vast humid forests, ideal for hiking.

• Tofua Island is very famous for its diving spots around the beaches of Tufuvai and Ha'aluma on the south coast. Theater of the Bounty revolt in 1789, it shelters a large lake where it is good to refresh oneself after a walk in the virgin forest.

• The group of Vava'u islands forms the emerged summit of a volcano, whose frequent eruptions cause underwater lava flows. They offer diving sites of rare beauty.

Tuvalu

The Archipelago of Tuvalu, in the heart of the Pacific Ocean, is made up of nine coral atolls, eight of which are inhabited even though it remains one of the least populated independent states in the world. According to experts, the Tuvalu Islands will disappear under the sea by 2050 due to global warming.

Today, due to their isolation and the scarcity of tourism infrastructure, the islands of Tuvalu are still protected from mass tourism. The main attraction of the kingdom remains the beaches and the seabed which will delight those who come to take a breath of fresh air and a large dose of rest, as well as those who come to try water sports.

Vanuatu

Welcome to the home of the world champions of happiness! According to an English sociological study, the Vanuatuans are the happiest people in the world... No need to expect a world of opulence because life in Vanuatu is very simple and the population is poor. A Franco-British consortium until 1980, this isolated archipelago of Melanesia is located at the end of the Pacific Ring of Fire, one of the most active volcanic areas on the planet, some 1500 km east of Australia. Out of 83 islands, you will be able to explore a dozen or so that will satisfy your appetite for adventure, discovery and encounters. The virgin forest is dense and hospitable, the protected seabed is of exceptional quality, the volcanoes are extremely active and the numerous tribal cultures are very rich (120 languages and dialects have been recorded). See you at the other end of the Earth, in the world of the happy!

• Efate is the main island where Port-Vila, the cosmopolitan capital, is located, recognized as the gastronomic capital of the South Pacific. The island has a rugged coastline, fast rivers, waterfalls, lagoons and secluded beaches. The interior is made up of tropical forests cut only by roads. On Hideway Island, post your letter in the only underwater post office in the world! You will be able to practice all kinds of nautical activities: deep-sea fishing, glass-bottomed boat, and of course diving. Mini-cruises are also proposed to visit turtle farms or simply snorkeling.

* Espiritu Santo, the largest of the islands, is best known for its dive sites, especially the underwater exploration of the wreck of "President Coolidge", the largest accessible wreck in the world, and that of three other vessels. Dive in the fresh water caves where passages connect the different caverns. Laze on the fine white sand of Champagne Beach, reputed to be the most beautiful beach in the entire South Pacific. Don't hesitate to visit the paradise islands located only a few hundred meters from the coconut tree lined beaches. Canoe, kayak, horseback riding or walking will also be on the program.

* Malekula is the wildest and most preserved island of Vanuatu. It is known for the cannibalism of the Nambas tribes which is still practiced. The island is famous for its masks and tribal cultures. If you feel like authenticity, discover the island of Vao by dugout canoe at 10 min from the mainland, where the welcome of the people is extraordinary or visit the Maskelynes islands, which have the reputation of being unforgettable.

* Ambrym, "Earth Before Time", is one of the last places in the world where you can see lava lakes in the heart of twin volcanoes. The island is in fact a gigantic volcano whose summit has collapsed giving way to the caldera, the ash plain and the Benbow and Maroum Mountains where you can admire the molten lava and abseil down into the active crater. Due to such underwater volcanism, the waters are particularly warm for swimming.

* Tanna is also famous for its active volcano, the Yasur, which you can explore at night to see the fireworks with incandescent sheaves that emanate from it. A unique experience! In addition to the volcano, Tanna offers a wide variety of attractions such as the dance of the Toka, the cult of the Cargo, the wild horses of the White Grass plain, the hot waterfalls of Port Resolution, the large waterfalls scattered over the island and accessible by foot and the almost daily events celebrated by the many tribes.

* The island of Pentecost is known to be the scene of a special and spectacular ceremony, the N'gol, the ancestor of bungee jumping. Originally, it is the illustration of an ancient legend where a man died while chasing his unfaithful wife who jumped from the top of a tree by roping herself into it. The N'gol is thus a ritual allowing men to signal that they will no longer be fooled while being a ceremony in honor of fertility. In April, the tribes build towers of about twenty meters from which the men, hung by lianas at knee level, throw themselves into the void after a small ceremony.

* The island of Maewo is an ideal place for bird watching. Both coasts are covered with black sand beaches. It has some of the most impressive waterfalls in the archipelago. Apart from that, the island is known for its traditional secret societies where men and women lead dances that can only be performed and observed by people of the same sex. Note that visitors will face the same restrictions.

* Banks and Torres Islands are famous for the huge coconut crabs that run on the white sandy beaches and the megapods that come here to bury their eggs. The Yeyenwu Caves on Hiu Island are home to a unique species of butterfly.

Wallis and Futuna

Here is a destination that is not common, that's for sure. The Wallis and Futuna islands (far away from each other) are the most secret corners of the French territory. Here it is the Pacific and especially Polynesia in all its splendor, both natural and cultural. How about France, of which the islands are an overseas territory ? A distant mirage, at most. It's very exotic and it's better to be adventurous (and have time) to leave for this destination, and you shouldn't expect an apotheosis once you get there, because they are small islands. A destination for explorers, or the very curious, with complicated and long access from anywhere.

• Wallis Island and Horn Islands (Futuna and Alofi) are separated from each other by about 230 kilometers. Wallis being the only one to have an international airport, access to the islands making up this destination remains difficult. Because of this and because of the poor hotel infrastructure, tourism is still very marginal.

• The cultural heritage of the inhabitants of Wallis and Futuna alone is worth the detour, you will admire the richness of the Polynesian way of life, their kindness and their traditions.

• Islets, turquoise lagoon, crater lakes... Although little known, the natural sites are also magnificent and the walks to do are numerous (Talietumu, Mount Puké, Loka cave, Lalolalo lake, Tamana). The cultural heritage is relatively rich, do not miss the Tongan forts and burials in Wallis and the site of Father Chanel, canonized in 1954, in Poï on Futuna. Of course, sunbathing on the white sandy beaches is a must, as the sites are so heavenly.

• Other activities are offered to tourists, such as trips in light planes to discover from the sky this little piece of France in the middle of the Pacific, very little known and very isolated.